VALUE JUDGEMENT AND INCOME DISTRIBUTION

VALUE JUDGEMENT AND INCOME DISTRIBUTION

edited by

Robert A. Solo
Charles W. Anderson

foreword by

Janos Horvath

Praeger Studies in Grants Economics

General Editors:
Kenneth E. Boulding
Janos Horvath

PRAEGER

PRAEGER SPECIAL STUDIES • PRAEGER SCIENTIFIC

Library of Congress Cataloging in Publication Data
Main entry under title:

Value judgement and income distribution.

(Praeger studies in grants economics)
1. Income distribution--Addresses, essays, lectures.
2. Distributive justice--Addresses, essays, lectures.
3. Policy sciences--Addresses, essays, lectures. I. Solo, Robert A. II. Anderson, Charles W. III. Series
HB523.V34 339.2 81-10553
ISBN 0-03-057587-7 AACR2

Published in 1981 by Praeger Publishers
CBS Educational and Professional Publishing
A Division of CBS, Inc.
521 Fifth Avenue, New York, New York 10175 U.S.A.

123456789 145 987654321

Printed in the United States of America

About the Editors and Contributors

CHARLES W. ANDERSON is professor of political science at the University of Wisconsin-Madison. His primary research and teaching interests are in the fields of normative and comparative policy analysis and political economy. His works include *Statecraft*, *The Political Economy of Modern Spain*, *Politics and Economic Change in Latin America*, *Issues of Political Development*, *The Political Economy of Mexico*, and, forthcoming, *A Discipline of Political Judgment*.

ROBERT SOLO received his undergraduate degree at Harvard and his doctorate at Cornell, and is now professor of economics at Michigan State University. He has taught in a number of American, French, and Canadian universities, has lectured extensively, and has published a dozen books and eighty journal articles and book chapters. Ideas developed in, "The Rules of Discourse," in this volume were first born in 1948 in an abortive effort to produce a dissertation at the London School of Economics. These ideas were developed in the essay, "Economics as Social Philosophy, Moral Philosophy and Technology," in *Economics and the Public Interest* (Rutgers, 1955), and later in, "New Maths and Old Sterilities," *Saturday Review* January 22, 1972; and finally and more fully in the present essay.

BRIAN BARRY is distinguished service professor in the departments of political science and philosophy at the University of Chicago. He is the author of *Political Argument* (1965), *Sociologists, Economists and Democracy* (1970), and *The Liberal Theory of Justice* (1973), and since 1979 has been the editor of *Ethics*.

BENJAMIN BEIT-HALLAHMI is currently senior lecturer in psychology at the University of Haifa. Previously, he has been affiliated with the University of Michigan, Michigan State University, Central Michigan University, University of Pennsylvania, Tel-Aviv University, The Hebrew University, and the Israel Institute of Technology. He has edited Research in Religious Behavior (1973) and Psychoanalysis and Religion: A Bibliography (1978), and has co-authored The Social Psychology of Religion (with M. Argyle, 1975) and Twenty Years Later: Kibbutz Children Grown Up (with A. I. Rabin, 1981). His research interests include the psychology of religion and the history of psychology in relation to its social functions.

KENNETH E. BOULDING is distinguished professor of economics emeritus at the University of Colorado, and a program director in the University's Institute of Behavioral Science. He was born in Liverpool, England, in 1910 and has taught at several universities in the United States since 1937. He is the past president of five scientific associations, author of many books, and a prolific writer and lecturer.

CAROL M. FESSLER is a third year graduate student in the department of political science at Yale University.

MICHAEL D. INTRILIGATOR has major research interests in the theory and applications of quantitative economics, including mathematical economic theory and econometrics and their applications to health economics and strategy and arms control. Among his several books in these areas are Mathematical Optimization and Economic Theory (Prentice-Hall, 1971; also translated into Spanish and Russian), Econometric Models, Techniques, and Applications (Prentice-Hall and North-Holland, 1978), and Strategy in a Missile War (UCLA Security Studies Project, 1967).

Intriligator received his Ph.D. in economics at MIT in 1963 and joined the faculty of the department of economics at UCLA, where he is now a professor of economics. He teaches upper division and graduate level courses in economic theory, mathematical economics, and econometrics, and he has won distinguished teaching awards for both graduate teaching (1966) and undergraduate teaching (1976, 1979).

AARON KATSENELINBOIGEN is professor of social systems sciences department, University of Pennsylvania. Former head of the department of complex systems at the Institute of Mathematical Economics of the Academy of Sciences of the USSR and professor of economics at Moscow State University, he immigrated to the USA in 1973. He has published eight books (two of them in the USA) and many articles.

THEODORE R. MARMOR received his A.B. and Ph.D. degrees from Harvard, held research fellowships at Wadham and Nuffield Colleges, Oxford, and taught at the Universities of Minnesota, Wisconsin, Essex (England), and Chicago before joining Yale's faculty as professor of political science and public health and chairman of the center for health studies. He has authored The Politics of Medicare and numerous articles on the politics and policies of the welfare state, particularly emphasizing social security, national health insurance, and health planning. A member of the Council on Foreign Relations, Mr. Marmor served as special assistant to HEW's undersecretary in 1966, was on the staff of the President's Commission on Income Maintenance Programs (1968-70), and was a member of the Presidential Commission on a National Agenda for the 80s.

PAUL L. MENCHIK received his Ph.D. in economics from the University of Pennsylvania in 1976 and was research associate from 1976 to 1979 at the Institute for Research on Poverty at the University of Wisconsin-Madison. In 1979 he became a member of the economics department at Michigan State University and is currently an associate professor. He has published a number of articles in the areas of the distribution of income and wealth, saving over the lifecycle, and intergenerational wealth transfers.

GUNNAR MYRDAL, Nobel Laureate in Economics, is currently affiliated with the Institute for International Economic Studies, Stockholm, Sweden. Among his works are: The Political Element in the Development of Economic Theory, An American Dilemma, Beyond the Welfare State, Objectivity in Social Research and Asian Drama. He has served as Professor of International Economics at the University of Stockholm, Minister of Trade and Commerce in the Swedish government during the formative years of the welfare state, and as Executive Secretary of the United Nations Economic Commission for Europe.

BENJAMIN I. PAGE received his Ph.D. in political science from Stanford and a law degree from Harvard. He has done postdoctoral work in economics at MIT and Harvard. Dr. Page is currently an associate professor of political science at the University of Chicago, a senior study director at the National Opinion Research Center, and a member of the Committee on Public Policy Studies. He previously taught at Dartmouth College and at the University of Wisconsin-Madison, where he was on the staff of the Institute for Research on Poverty. Page has published a number of books and articles concerning voting and elections, including *Choices and Echoes in Presidential Elections* (Chicago: University of Chicago Press, 1978), and is presently completing a book on the income distributional effects of government programs.

DOUGLAS W. RAE, Ph.D., is professor of political science at Yale University, director of graduate studies, and a member of the Institution for Social and Policy Studies. He is author of *The Political Consequences of Electoral Laws*, co-author of *The Analysis of Political Cleavages*, co-author of *Equality: Equalities* (forthcoming), and has contributed to the *American Political Science Review*, *Daedalus*, *The New Republic*, *Handbook of Political Science*, *Polity*, the *British Journal of Political Science*, and other journals. A former Associate Editor of the *American Political Science Review*, and board member of *Comparative Political Studies*, he now serves on the editorial board for *Ethics*. His principal interest in teaching and research is contemporary political theory.

WARREN J. SAMUELS is professor of economics, Michigan State University. He has been editor of the Journal of Economic Issues since 1971 and a member of the editorial board of History of Political Economy. He is a specialist in law and economics, history of economic thought, and methodology, including the problem of values and ideology in economics.

LESTER C. THUROW is a professor of economics and management at the Massachusetts Institute of Technology. He is the author of *The Zero-Sum Society* (1980) and writes an economics column for both the *New York Times* and the *Los Angeles Times*.

JOHN F. WITTE is assistant professor in the department of political science and the Center for Public Policy and Administration, University of Wisconsin-Madison. He received his Ph.D. from Yale University. He is the author of *Democracy, Authority, and Alienation in Work: Workers' Participation in an American Corporation*. His current research deals with the politics of federal income taxes.

Foreword

Throughout recorded history, income distribution has continued to be a main issue for human groups organizing themselves into society. Both the recurrence of golden ages and the approach of disintegrating crises have routinely had a great deal to do with excesses of income distribution. Nowadays the unfolding 1980s portend a period of veritable soulsearch, the re-thinking of premises and targets on one hand and re-ordering of values and priorities on the other. The outcome of these forthcoming processes should be predicted only with cautious restraint even if policy sciences basked in an aura of confidence and credibility. Alas, that is not the case. Yet, the gloomy realities and cynical inertia of yesteryear need not predestine tomorrow. This book is a trusty map of that watershed.

Prominent authorities and meticulous researchers scrutinize ideals and facts, as these things are mirrored through alternative perceptions of philosophy, expedience and legitimacy. The authors and editors have masterfully employed the state of the art and imaginatively enhanced the edifice of knowledge. There are some controversies which have been resolved; there remain controversies about substance as well as methods. Yet, an accomplishment of this book is that it mellows the rigidities of conventional scholarship which have long harped on the claim that the very diversity of issues makes appraisals conjectural. Conventional disclaimers matter-of-factly parrot that value judgments further compound the predicament of policy sciences.

The ritual is familiar. If one of the affected parties turns out to be disappointed with the results of an analysis, it may resort to a disparagement of the analysis itself. "You cannot compare apples and oranges"--a saying so often invoked with a ring of veto power. But it should be quite appropriate to conduct such comparisons if one adheres to the rules of consistency. First, apples and oranges are fruit. They are certainly not something imponderable out there within the vastly diverse multitude of produce, elements, and artifacts. Second, apples and oranges do provide nutrition, distinctly measurable in terms of vitamins, minerals, protein, sugar--while they substantially differ in texture from meat, cereals, dairy products, and so on. Additional methods may be used to compare apples and oranges. Then, after having done an objective examination, there could still remain unexplained those subjective differences that are in the rather narrow range of individual taste. The process of such contrasting and comparing can be likened to warming sunlight that dispels the fog, left behind after the dark and chilling night. The vision gained will facilitate the drawing of maps, the adaptation of pertinent nomenclature, or the designing of classification systems.

In this synergistic reassessment of components pertaining to value judgement and income distribution, grants economics offers a uniquely befitting conceptual framework. This book is one of the Grants Economics Series preceded and succeeded by a dozen other volumes that deal with the financial system, higher education, health care, regulatory impacts, etc. Since grants economics is the organizing motion of these endeavors, a sketch of it is offered hereon as orientation to the unfolding material.

Grants economics, defined simply, identifies the size and traces the leverage of grants elements as they interface with exchange elements in all kinds of economic processes. Grant describes the unmatched transaction where the net worth of one party--the grantor--diminishes, while the net worth of the other party--the grantee--increases. Deviating from the norm of exchanging equal values, such transactions contain certain grant elements. Beyond the clearly visible explicit grant--gift, aid, and unilateral transfer--there exists a vast network of implicit grants in the private as well as public sector of the economy. The visible explicit grants are only the tip of the iceberg while the much larger amorphic bulk of implicit grants remains hidden and therefore often escapes attention.

Grants economics provides a compass to rectify some delusions. The conventional view is that goods, services, and factors of production move from one party to another at a matching price (<u>quid pro quo</u>). Although it is recognized that there exists a broad assortment of subventions (subsidies, bounties, favoritism) on the one side, and also a broad assortment of tributes (underpayments, extortions, dispossessions) on the other side, but because these cases do not fit the neat abstractions of dominant theories, they are usually relegated to grey areas (assumed away) and the analysis continues *ceteris paribus*. Unfortunately, by ignoring or downgrading production and distribution processes which do not fit the Procrustian bed of neoclassical paradigm, the scope of economic policy analysis is unnecessarily narrowed.

The history of "grant" as economic-social-political organizer is perhaps older than recorded history itself. It is not unlikely that various unmatched transfers had preceded exchange transactions as communities practiced reciprocal granting. In due course, as exchange became common, the terms of trade favored the stronger party, thereby transferring tribute to priests and kings and artists. Such remained the dominant social characteristic through the feudal age. In modern times institutionalized transfers have provided a "big push" toward economic development. Nowadays, when traditional welfare roles--care for the poor, disabled, and elderly--shifts from the family to the public sector, furthermore, as government undertakes to deliver an increasing bundle of public goods--education, health, recreation, transportation, research--the share of the grants economy grows.

Much of the initial work in grants economics has dealt with the issues of the urbanized economy, income distribution and redistribution as these affect efficiency and equity, the tax-expenditure structure, externalities in the environment, intra-family and inter-generational granting. The international economy is a major field of inquiry. The inflation-unemployment dilemma is explained through institutional rigidities which generate implicit grants to those who restrain potential supply. A recurrent theme is that grants economics is a major instrument by which people hope to change the world for the better. In the macroeconomy a grant dollar spent tends to generate more production and income than an exchange dollar because the granting is often conditioned on complementary exchange transactions. As a network of policy instruments, the grants economy represents the heart of political economy, because routinely it is by pulling the levers of positive and negative subventions that the political system intervenes smoothly into the economic system.

On philosophical grounds, grants economics extends beyond neoclassical "exchange economics," "public choice," and "radical economics" in important respects, such as perceiving the motivation of economic actors and assessing the significance of distribution norms. To explain individual behavior, institutional dynamics, and normative policies, it is no longer necessary to regard unselfishness as an aberration from rationality. Grants economics provides a theory of transfers by affirming the interdependence of utility functions among individuals that integrates into economic science such agents as love, altruism, hate, and fear. Thus, utility interdependence considers (1) the utility derived from the contemplation of another person's welfare and (2) the utility derived from giving because it conforms to the individual's norms. Hence the benevolent behavior: the individual's increased utility due to more consumption is outweighed by his decreased utility due to the perception of the other's miserable state. This leads from the Pareto Optimum to the Boulding Optimum, bringing within the scope of economic analysis a humanly flair assumed away routinely in the name of value-free science. Now economics can tackle the axiom that whether life on earth is hell or heaven depends largely on the attitude of one human being toward others.

Grants economics might be accused of charting vague boundaries. But its boundaries are vague precisely because it is a link among all the disciplines of the social sciences. Providing a theory of reciprocity, it links economics, psychology, sociology, anthropology, and political science. Stretching over several disciplines, it points to the enormous economic importance of the family, an institution neglected in exchange economics. It is an important part of economics itself, where the grants structure profoundly affects the dynamics of the price system. Notwithstanding its versatility, the grants economy is subject to perverse effects. Just as the theory of market failures acknowledges that exchange economy cannot achieve certain types of economic ends, the pathologies of the grants economy call for diagnosis. Far from remedying all distortions brought about by the market process, it is a political irony that regulations and subventions have often exacerbated the problem. Indeed, grants economics could make a unique contribution to the regulatory reform through sorting out good grants and bad grants, i.e., those which achieve socially desirable goals from those with perverse effects.

The way this book assembles and integrates diverse ideas has had its genesis in programs of the Association for the Study of the Grants Economy at the annual meetings of the American Economic Association. The seminal thought for reappraising value judgement and income distribution through the notions of grants economics came from Kenneth E. Boulding. Then history repeated itself, as so frequently happens in so many scholarly ventures; his fertile mind and stimulating personality have mobilized vintages of contributors.

The evolving material provided a core which in the hands of Robert A. Solo, the economists' philosopher, has burgeoned into what this volume is. To observe Boulding and Solo contemplate the stages of this book's makings has amounted to a priceless reward to this witness.

JANOS HORVATH
The John W. Arbuckle Professor of Economics
Butler University

Contents

VALUE JUDGEMENT AND INCOME DISTRIBUTION

Introduction

Taken together, "value judgement" and "income distribution" bring into focus a central dilemma of contemporary policy science. We would deal simultaneously with a problem in the epistemology of the social sciences and a practical issue of public concern, hoping that a consideration of each can illuminate the other. The question of value judgement raises the theoretical issue, "How can disciplines committed to the ideals of value neutrality and scientific objectivity incorporate the process of evaluation that is inherent in any exercise of policy analysis, recommendation, or public choice?" The issue of income distribution poses the practical, substantive concern. Any public action will have distributive implications. It will reflect some conception of equity and social justice. What can the analyst say about this that is not a mere assertion of personal proclivity, commitment, or interest?

Policy science is social science applied to the formation of goals and priorities for public action and the analysis of problems of public choice. Historically, the methodology of the social sciences has rested on a rigorous distinction between questions of fact and questions of value. Science is presumed to be concerned with statements whose truth or falsity can be confirmed or denied by empirical, experimental procedures. Value judgements, lying beyond that purview, are dismissed as no more than personal preferences, products of cultural conditioning, and instinctual responses without scientific standing. In Arnold Brecht's words, "Anyone who claims scientific authority for a system of values is scientifically in error."

Today there are many who would regard the commitment to this imperative of scientific neutrality as both untenable and undesirable; untenable in that social science inquiry inevitably entails normative implications and presuppositions, undesirable in that it forestalls a deliberate and self-conscious approach by social science to crucial questions of public concern.

To assess public questions at all, value judgements have to be made. We have to decide, on some basis, that policies have succeeded or failed, that options for action are either desirable or undesirable, whether statements of proposed public purpose are good or bad. So the questions arise of how shall the policy sciences properly deal with the necessary and inevitable problem of value judgement, how they should go about the process of stipulating the standards in the light of which alternatives for public action will be evaluated and the results of public programs assessed and criticized.

The question goes to the heart of the enterprise of policy science. It is central to the organization of systematic discourse and inquiry in the policy sciences, in the consideration of the norms and canons by which professionals assess the significance and validity of the work of colleagues in the field. It is crucial to the practice of policy analysis, to the work of those who would act as professionals in the policy-making process. And it is critical to the role of the policy sciences as teaching professions, as disciplines entrusted with the responsibility for the formation of citizens and the preparation of those who will engage in the conduct of public affairs.

In focusing on the problems of income distribution, inequality, equity, and social justice, we take up the evaluative question in its most difficult and provocative dimensions. To some extent, the policy sciences have tried to avoid the more perplexing normative quandaries of public life by endorsing an ideal of instrumental rationality, or efficiency in the pursuit of postulated values. From this point of view, a policy is good if it was correctly designed to bring about an optimum realization of the goals of an authoritative decision maker, or to serve socially consensual values derived through legitimate procedures, or to satisfy an alleged aggregation of individual, self-regarding preferences. However, as we shall see, this method leads to peculiar implications and disturbing enigmas. We find that we can no longer evade the essential question. How should the equity or inequity of social arrangements be judged? How can social science analysis help us to clarify and, perhaps, to decide this question?

The purpose of this volume is to provide an opportunity for self-conscious reflection on the evaluative element in policy analysis, focusing on the specific issue of income distribution, in the hope that discussion of this critical and controversial problem will illuminate larger issues of theory and method in the policy sciences generally.

We have invited the collaboration of individuals who represent diverse perspectives and approaches so that the issue can be understood from various angles and at different levels of analysis. Thus the contributors include both distinguished political and economic theorists concerned with the epistemological foundations of their fields, as well as practitioners noted for their concrete contributions to the debate on concrete issues of social welfare and income distribution. Both "hard" and "soft" approaches to policy science inquiry are represented. Some essays emphasize logical rigor and quantitative methods, while others express a more humanistic and philosophic approach. The essays cover a spectrum of normative views, from a bold and uncompromising egalitarianism to skepticism that any credible justification for the redistributional function of the state can be found.

The volume is an interdisciplinary undertaking. Contributors have been drawn about equally from the fields of economics and political science, and psychology is represented as well.

In spite of the diversity of viewpoints and perspectives, a coherent, consistent line of thought emerges. Policy science and value judgement are not antithetical. Empirical research is prerequisite to rational and effective evaluation, and philosophical sophistication is required in approaching the deep dilemmas and paradoxes that attend issues of distributive equity. Strict value neutrality is no doctrinal imperative for the policy sciences and, in fact, evaluative research is alive and thriving.

Our book opens, in Part 1, with analyses of the norms of communication and of the rules of discourse that serve in the policy sciences to determine the significance, pertinence, and warrantability of statement. Both Robert Solo and Gunnar Myrdal challenge the positivist imperative of absolute "value neutrality" and attempt to provide foundations for a conception of policy science more open to explicit evaluation and normative choice.

In Part 2 Warren Samuels, Benjamin Beit-Hallahmi, and Brian Barry, from the diverse perspectives of an historian of economic ideas, a psychologist, and a political philosopher, consider how the ideologies of the social and behavioral sciences have treated the problems of inequality and distributive justice. They examine the normative presuppositions concerning these questions that are embedded in the method, theory, and historical development of these disciplines.

Part 3 is concerned with distributional theory. Within what framework of ideas should we understand these problems? Kenneth Boulding, Aaron Katsenelinboigen, and Michael Intriligator provide distinctive examples of the kinds of conceptual apparatus that can be brought to bear and the implications for a normatively informed policy analysis that follow from each.

Part 4 exemplifies the precision and rigor required to deal adequately with the conceptualization and measurement of income inequality. As Douglas Rae and Carol Fessler suggest, the principle of equality is hardly self-explanatory. There are, logically, many dimensions of inequality, and each has particular implications as a test or measure of public performance. Paul Menchik points up the many practical problems that arise when we try to create measures of income incquality as an essential empirical element in any effort to evaluate the distributive performance of a government or system.

In Part 5 the policy problem itself is confronted. What can be done? What should be done? A spectrum of alternative approaches, themes, and methods is provided. Lester Thurow relies on the comparative analysis of national economic performance to challenge the popular notion that the United States can purchase the acceleration of economic growth by accepting an even greater degree of income inequality, and he formulates a gloomy prognosis for the coming decade. Ben Page, accepting egalitarianism as a paradigmatic ideal and a normative vantage point, asks why government <u>doesn't</u> promote equality. Theodore Marmor's comparative policy analysis considers the plethora of criteria introduced in public debate to evaluate the success of a welfare state and of welfare policies. John Witte looks to tax theories for standards of policy equity and finds them wanting as guidelines for concrete public action in this realm. How then shall the practical policy analyst proceed? Robert Solo's note recommends a specific reform in the system of taxation.

In the concluding section, Charles Anderson considers the educational function of the policy sciences. Given what has been said about the rules of discourse in the policy sciences, the problems of rigorous conceptualizaton, method, and measurement, the various forms that policy argument and recommendation can take, how are we to teach the art of practical judgement and policy analysis to citizens, practitioners, and potential decision makers?

Aside from its substantive contribution, this volume should serve to display the broad range of possibilities that exist for normatively informed policy analysis and argument, while making apparent the perplexing puzzles and problems that remain to be unraveled in this field.

Humility is a recent advance in the policy sciences. A generation ago, these disciplines were marked by a certain aura of technocratic hubris. We were on the verge of assuming that the economy could be fine-tuned to create frictionless, lasting prosperity through the wonders of applied political economy, and that, through technical analysis, we could solve the problems of the ghetto as we had those of space flight and landing a man on the moon. Today all the policy sciences are going through something of an epistemological crisis. Basic constructs and models are relentlessly questioned, fundamental experimental findings systematically controverted; even the tenability of the enterprise itself has come under critical scrutiny. In a sense, what the policy sciences have to teach today is doubt, not doctrine. But these are also fields that are entering a new stage of theoretical ferment. The outcome is still uncertain, but there are straws in the wind that point to a more humane, skeptical, and creative understanding of their purposes. We hope this book suggests a few of these intimations and possibilities.

Robert A. Solo
Charles W. Anderson

Part I

RULES OF DISCOURSE

Solo deduces, compares and critiques the rules operating in the organization of the discourse in the social and physical sciences in the light of fundamental differences in the phenomena to which these sciences relate.

Myrdal's is a reasoned and impassioned plea that the social (and policy) sciences be opened to explicit evaluation of moral choice.

1. Values and Judgements in the Discourse of the Sciences

Robert A. Solo

In my time there have been just three significant changes in the character of Western economics. One was substantive, brought about as the agonized response to the absolute incapacity of neoclassical theory to comprehend the phenomenon of modern depression, producing Keynesian macroeconomics as an appendage to the neoclassicial core. The other two significant changes had to do with neither the explanation of phenomena nor the interpretation of event. Both were epistemological.

One was in formalizing--mathematizing--expression without changing the substance of what was expressed. The other was allegedly a purge of value judgement, splitting the old link between economics and the utilitarian ethic, negating by fiat certain propositions, but adding nothing to the substantive content of the discipline. Both were justified in the name of Science, following the doctrines of the positivist philosophers.

DISCOURSE AND STATEMENT: STATEMENT AND SIGN

Whatever else it may be, every science is and must be an organized system of discourse. Such systems of discourse are social contrivances, operating under sets of rules for the most part evolved organically and followed unconsciously.

The element of all discourse is the statement. The argument, the proposition, the hypothesis, the theory, the datum, the prediction is stated; and in response comes the statement as challenge, as question, as rebuttal, as correction, as elaboration, as datum, as prediction. Statement upon statement weave the endless web of discourse.

Taking off from Ferdinand Saussure, founder of

structuralist linguistics, any statement can be understood as a sign. For every sign there are two constituents, the "signifier" and the "signified." The signifier, that is, the formal, conventional, symbolic element--word, sentence, proposition, theory--is that which points. And the signified is that which is pointed to and/or pointed from; in other words, it is object or image. This relationship between the indicator on the one side and on the other the indicated/indicating is represented by the formula:

$$\frac{s(\text{signified})}{S(\text{signifier})} =$$  TREE

1. The signified may thus have a dual existence. It always has a subjective existence as a mental construct or image embedded in the psyche of the one who makes or who attempts to understand the statement (called the signified mental construct, s). The signified can also be an object, event, or condition to be observed or otherwise experienced (called the signified object, s'). Thus the signifier "cat" signals both the gray object resting in the crook of my arm (s') and the image of an animal in the realm of your thought or mine (s). A space for analysis resides in the relationships between s and s', between S and s', between s and S.

2. The viability and limitations of S depend on the capacity of this, the signifier, to express and convey s,s' which, in turn determines the effectiveness of discourse. Hence a primary objective of social learning, and more particularly, in the education of the scientist, is to develop clear and universal relationships between S and s. Those relationships, firmly imprinted through acculturation and training and vitally important for effective discourse, introduce into science, as will later be shown, a profound resistance to adaptation and change, hence to fundamental scientific advance.

3. The appropriate rules of discourse depend on the character of statement. Our interest is in three categories of statement differentiable in the relationships of signifier and signified. These categories will be called here the tautological, the empirical, and the expressive.

4. Tautological statements are those without an objective reference (s'), where the signifier is itself the signified, hence where s/S = s. The tautological statement is a sign enclosed within itself. It would include mathematical equations (1 + 1 = 2); definitions (pure competition is a condition of the market wherein the number of rational, informed, self-seeking individuals is so great, and the share of each in the

total transaction is so small, that none can, through sale or purchase, deliberately effect the price of what is bought or sold); and logical statements (given pure competition in a market that transacts the sale of X and Y, a relative increase in the demand for X will, other things remaining the same, increase the price of X relative to the price of Y). The aforementioned examples of the definitional and the logical taken together constitute a model about which more will be said later.

Tautological statements are ubiquitous and are an essential element in all discourse. In its elements, its parameters so to speak, the tautology does not escape from external linkage and objective reference, except in the case of the mathematical statement. In the aforementioned model for example, such terms as "individuals," "self-seeking," or "market" all derive from and refer to experienced phenomena and events. The point is that the statements themselves cannot be reached and challenged on grounds that "It's not like that" or "That's not the way it happens out there." Such statements can of course be repudiated as incoherent, inconsistent, incomplete. And they may be put down as irrelevant, but to consider their relevance is to demand that they be something other than tautological.

5. Empirical statements are about "it, out there." They have a referential, representational relationship to object, event, or condition to be observed or otherwise made subject to a shared experience, where the signifying psychic image $\underline{s}$ and the signifier $\underline{S}$ point to and are about $\underline{s'}$ in the domain of share experience, hence where $\underline{s}/\underline{S}/ = \underline{s'}$.

6. Expressive statements refer to a psychic condition, to a state of being, feeling, volition, or conviction that cannot be observed in common or otherwise made subject to a shared experience, but that is inherently particular to the one who feels, wills, states--for example, laughter, "ha ha," signaling, "I feel joy," or "That's funny" or "You're ridiculous." "I love you" is an expressive statement, and so is "I prefer brunets." Here the signifier $\underline{S}$ both expresses and refers to the psychic state of the one who does the signifying, hence $\underline{s}/ = \underline{s'}/\underline{S}$.

The expressive statement is no tautology. It refers to the experienced and observable, but in a domain to which the one who signifies has privileged entry. It is the expressive statement that raises the problem to be discussed later: interpersonal comparisons. While what is expressed by such a statement is uniquely the property of the individual, nevertheless another can speak empirically of that which has been expressed, as about any phenomenon. Laughter is expressive, but for me to say "He is laughing" is an empirical statement, and so, too, is my deduction that "He must think something is funny."

Our particular concern will be with those statements of this category that enter into the discourse not to express a psychic condition, but as imperatives; not simply "I love you," but "You should love your neighbor" or "It is better to love than to hate." These we term "value judgements."

Discourse in science cannot do without value judgements. For one thing, an organized discourse operates and must operate by rules, and the rule always expresses a value judgement.

There will be rules of communicability, clarity, and coherence as the a priori of all systematic discourse. And, particular to a given system of discourse, there will be rules of choice, rules of method, and rules of verification, which, along with a substantive body of explanations, images, conceptual categorizations, organized bodies of data, and search and experimental models, mark out its paths of inquiry. It will be our purpose in what follows to examine, to challenge, even to propose changes in some of those rules, or at least to bring them to the surface of consciousness as properly subject to challenge and change. Our interest will be with two sets of rules: those that relate to the admissibility of statement into a given system of discourse, and those that relate to the credibility and/or acceptability of statement.

In the first instance, let me propose a particular rule as one that will underlie my arguments, and also because it will demonstrate problems implicit in any value-based rule making. As a fundamental criterion for the economics discourse, I propose what might be called "the rule of social purpose," that:

> The purpose of economics should be to produce more benificent solutions to the economic problems of actual societies.

This states my felt convictions as a value imperative and asks of others that they accept that statement as a value judgement. Others need not accept the proposed rule. In practice, few economists do. Their acceptance or rejection (again a value-based rule) should occur through the process of a discourse that raises the issue to the level of choice, confronting such questions as these: Should the discipline be purposeless? If not this, then what should be its purpose or purposes?

These questions are not trivial. The criterion of purpose, of no-purpose, or of multipurpose will affect the direction and the character of inquiry, the choice of an appropriate methodology, and the boundaries of discourse. And though differences that arise between this or any other primary rule cannot be resolved through logical demonstration or objective testing, we may judge it valuable nevertheless in clarifying the basis, character, and extent of such differences.

In any case this rule of social purpose, which can be taken at least as a possible norm for the economic discourse, will be implicit in the arguments that I will make.

THE RULE OF ADMISSIBILITY AND THE BOUNDARIES OF DISCOURSE

Economics, psychology, physics, sociology, microbiology, astronomy--each, as an interchange of statements extending through time, is open-ended, but not open-sided. All are about something, but not about anything. Every science is bounded, with only certain statements admissible into its discourse. Among the most critical rules of all are those that impose or lift the barriers to the admissibility of statement. I mean simply the rules according to which the line is drawn between "This is economics" and "That is not economics" and hence that fix the boundaries of discourse.

Given the established rules, explanations, conceptualizations, analytic techniques and model experiments passed on from one generation of scientists to another, called by Thomas Kuhn a "paradigm" (the autonomous movement of price conceptualized as the equilibrating principle in a universe of free exchange, the assumption of price competition, techniques of marginal and regression analysis, a focus on the process of rational choice, a particular reference universe of statistical information are alike constituents of the paradigm of modern economics), the paradigm itself determines the permanent boundaries of discourse. Only that which is of, derived from, or commensurable with it may enter. Other assumptions, hypotheses, and problems are excluded, not because they are necessarily wrong or uninteresting, but because, by the rule of the paradigm, they do not belong; they are not physics, not medicine, not economics.

How can a given social science reorient itself? How can it reconceptualize its universe of inquiry? How can it incorporate an alternative frame of reference or another order of assumptions in seeking the solution or resolution to problems, hitherto intractable, that have been and are considered as being within its domain? Given the rule of the paradigm, it cannot. In the

Kuhnsian view, the "normal" operation of discourse in the sciences excludes the possibility of all fundamental change. Fundamental change and advance comes about only as a cataclysmic disruption of the discourse, as an event inexplicable on rational grounds. Certainly it has been so in economics, where the rule of the paradigm has allowed no avenue along which an alternative frame of reference, a new order of assumptions, or a reconceptualized universe of inquiry can enter into the discourse. Granted that in historical fact this has been the case, need it be so? Must the rule of the paradigm prevail as a matter of functional necessity? Could it be replaced by a different rule?

The rule of the paradigm, though it prevails, need not express a value commitment of the scientists who operate within its frame. It cannot be considered as a legislated ideal rationally applied, but must be differently explained. Though the cohorts of a science more or less value and believe in the substantive and methodological components of their paradigm, they are unlikely to be aware of, let alone committed to, its exclusionary role. Rather, the exclusionary power of the paradigm is rooted in the inertial attachment to acculturated, deeply imprinted habits of thought and practice, and in the self-interested protection of that corpus of thought which constitutes the intellectual-cum-professional stock-in-trade and the basis of status, income, and authority of the practicing scientist.

But again, that it is not a legislated ideal rationally applied. That it finds its force in habit, inertia, or vested interest rather than in a value commitment, is not to say that the exclusionary role of the paradigm does not have an intrinsic value, or if it were raised to the level of conscious choice, that it would not be consciously chosen. It has an intrinsic value. In imposing its boundaries upon the admissibility of statement, it assures the continuity of a discourse, serves to integrate the activity of a vast number of dispersed individuals into a coherent enterprise, facilitates the acquisition of the shared referential knowledge-base and of the stable system of signs that are essential for effective communications. Conversely, the changing of terms, the introduction of basic novelty--whether in premises, problems, foci of interest, analytic techniques, or whatever is outside of and incompatible with the established paradigm--will destabilize discourse, will enhance uncertainty and confusion, will fracture the integrity of the discipline and the coherence of the enterprise, and will bring well-oiled and spontaneous ease of communication to an end.

Though it does serve certain essential functional requisites of discourse, the rule of the paradigm nevertheless is a blind barrier to the admissibility of statement. What it excludes may be essential to the fundamental and necessary development of science. The question surely then is "What rule could replace this one that might better balance the functional requisites of continuity against the values of adaptability and openness to fundamental change?"

What rule for the admissibility of statement and the definition of boundaries in economics, for example, might satisfy the criterion of social purpose and yet provide reasonable boundaries to discourse, balancing the value of continuity with that of systemic change? Such a rule, value-based and consciously held, is especially important in social science since, as will be shown, in the social sciences there are great and particular difficulties in verification and falsification. Hence archaisms are harder to remove and the walls of the paradigm are more difficult to bring down. In the light of all this, we propose the following as the rule to control the admissibility of statement into the discourse of economics.

Economics should move continuously to the solution of social problems in the organization of production and distribution. What are those problems? They are exogenously determined and there has never been any mystery concerning them. They change as the circumstances and the values that prevail in society change, but always with a degree of continuity. That continuity would be an element of the discourse. Let economics be judged and judge itself by its capacity to offer benificent solutions to those problems. And let any statement (assumption, hypothesis, theory, technique) have entry into the discourse if it casts light on or helps explain the phenomena underlying, or otherwise clarifies or contributes to the solution of those problems. Statements that do not do so would have no right of entry. Relevance, in that sense, should be the only criterion of admissibility, defining the boundaries of the discipline. To understand the meaning and the need for such a rule, consider the following.

None would deny that economic growth--finding the means of producing more and having more to consume with given resources--is a critical problem in the organization of production and distribution in our time. Few fail to see that the key to thus increasing productivity is the system of technological advance. And yet, under the iron rule of its paradigm, Establishment Economics cannot take and has not taken any account of the systems of technological advance operating through public organization and state planning and diversely made manifest in the different sectors of the economy. Under the rule here proposed the consideration of these systems would not, for these many decades, have been excluded a priori from the discourse. An analogous rule for the admissibility of statement could apply for the discourse of any of the social sciences.

RULES OF DISCOURSE

Discourse in the social sciences requires and operates under distinct categories of rules and criteria, depending on the character of statement.

For the logical/tautological elements of any statement, there are rules for and of clarity, consistency, and coherence.

For the expressive statement that enters into discourse as an imperative, putting itself forward for value judgement, there are rules for and criteria of acceptability. Just so, as exemplified in this essay, for the rules themselves, the relevant criterion is of acceptability.

For the empirical statement referring to an object, event, or condition that can be observed or otherwise made subject to a shared experience, there are rules for the establishment of credibility. Modern philosophy of science has above all been concerned to determine the acceptable rule for establishing the credibility of empirical statements. Such will be our concern also in the sections which immediately follow, emphasizing the difference between what is required to establish the credibility of statement in the social sciences in contrast to the physical and biological sciences.

Finally, integrating the logical, expressive and empirical in the synthetic policy statement that would formulate options for choice and action, the appropriate rules and criteria would be of workability.

THE POSITIVIST RULE

We will confine our discussion to hypothesis (to be understood as a statement) and theory (to be understood as a set of related statements) with multiple implications in the explanation of phenomena, where the criterion of credibility has generally been a capacity to match experienced event with inferential predictions logically deduced from hypothesis or theory. Following the prevailing positivist norm, the test of credibility is thus: If what you say is true, then by logical inference, X, Y, and Z should follow. If they do, that supports the credibility of the statement. But, no matter how many of such tests have been successful, the failure of any one inferential prediction can definitively refute the hypothesis or theory (establishing that something is wrong, something is false about it).

For a positivist philosopher like Karl Popper, who takes physics as his model, statements that cannot conceivably be falsified through the inferential prediction of a specific event are not admissible into the discourse of science. And for Popper the very task of such discourse is continuously to expose statement to the test of new inferential prediction. This positivist rule follows: The statements of science are credible inasmuch as they have been exposed to numerous tests of inferential prediction and have never yet failed that test. We will call statements to which such a rule can conceivably be applied "positivist statements."

Even though the established paradigms of science in historical fact do withstand the force of numerous failures of inferential prediction, that is, they are not abandoned in the face of anomaly, the positivist rule retains its force as a criterion of the ideal. Certainly the physical sciences do engage in and rely upon the serious, systematic testing of statement through the inferential prediction of specific event. Indeed, given that there normally is no possibility of observing the postulated relationships in the universe of physical phenomena directly and in their totality, there is no other way than through such inferential prediction to explore hence test the implications of theory and hypothesis.

It is axiomatic that if a theory in the physical sciences were true and complete, and if experiment were errorless and observations accurate, there could be no failures in the inferential prediction of specific event. In these sciences moreover, once a specific relationship has been established experimentally, for example, in the qualities of a compound produced through a chemical synthesis, the statement of relationships remains absolute. The same synthesis will produce the same compound, and that same compound will always exhibit the same qualities.

All of this follows from and requires that the signified belong to a universe where the character of relationships does not change, where what is properly identified, for example, the hydrogen atom, retains these qualities by which it has been identified, and where if A cojoined with B produces C, then, parameters given, As cojoined with Bs will produce Cs throughout. Nor does it matter that C might be stated as a probability, so long as the universe of probabilities remains the same; nor that, given the limits of our capacity to measure and observe, relationships are stated as approximations.

The presumption of constant, continuous, consistent relationships remains here the basis of statement. By reference to that universe of relationships, the signifier is formed. A statement is positivist because it signifies a universe of continuous, consistent, constant relationships. Only then can any inferential prediction of specific event conceivably have a general or universal value in the falsification of statement. Whether as an ideal or a norm, or a practical or ultimate basis for establishing the credibility of statement, the positivist rule is credible only when it refers to a universe of constant, consistent, continuous relationships. When the results of every inferential prediction reflects, if it does not wholly reveal, such a body of relationships, inferential prediction can have great value in establishing the credibility of statement or, at least, in resolving conflicting claims and contradictions between statements.

The universe of physical phenomena, the domain of physics, the domain of chemistry, meet the preconditions of a viable positivist rule. What of statements that do not refer to such a universe? For there are empirical statements, statements about a discernible universe of experienced phenomena where those essential regularities are absent; for social phenomena specifically, these critical preconditions for the positivist rule do not obtain. The positivist rule has been applied nevertheless, but always only nominally, as a pretention, in a mismatch of signifier and signified. For that reason, in spite of the most strenuous efforts and the total professional commitment of economics and the other social sciences, there has not emerged a single significant statement (theory, law) where its credibility has been, is, or could be based on the inferential prediction of specific event.

EMPIRICO-JUDGEMENTAL STATEMENT AND ITS VERIFICATION

Many years ago I studied as a graduate student at the London School of Economics with Karl Popper. I recall posing this example to him. It expresses in a nutshell the dilemma of prediction in the social sciences. Indeed, it expresses the reason why--for social phenomena--the prediction of specific event cannot conceivably serve, even under ideal conditions, to establish the credibility or definitively to falsify hypothesis and theory.

Mr. Jones comes down to breakfast every morning, and every morning he orders orange juice, toast, and soft boiled eggs. But this day, all parameters as given, he comes down to breakfast and he thinks he will have grapefruit and a poached egg instead.

The key is that "he thinks," for individual behavior and (hence) the policies, choices, and institutions of society are functions of ideas, imageries, and ideologies, and are as transitory and discontinuous as these, born afresh and vanishing without residual. The most formidable of social institutions, the fearsome patterns of mass behavior, the rules, codes, and laws, the constitutions and commandments--though they are engraved in stone--are no more than reflections of ideas and images (a stuff without weight or dimension) proliferating in the mind. Social phenomena, the character of social relationships, the great artifacts of societies are creations of the darkness and light projected from the mind's domain. Social phenomena are operated and controlled by the imageries of the psyche and the ideologies of the group. Behavior and policy are the shadow of these shadows--and none can belong to the world of positivist statement.

The positivist rule is inherently incompatible with the universe of social phenomena because neither entities nor relationships in that universe are constant and continuing. In any specific instance, the given sign s/S may be, or may as well not be equated to s'. In the physical sciences, anomalies, failures of prediction, contradictions, and discontinuities of theory can be attributed only to the fallibilities of the theorist and to the limitations of the observer. Positivist statement in physics fails to meet the test of inferential prediction because the statement is at fault, and not as a consequence of the nature of the universe about which the statement is made. Prediction doesn't work, the theory doesn't explain, not because physical phenomena are what they are, but because of an incapacity to measure, to observe, and to comprehend the infinitely complex and ultimately unreachable phenomena of the physical world. In contrast, the social scientist enjoys the great advantages of a proximity to his universe of observation and of an ability to observe relationships and processes directly and in their fullness, and, through introspection, to enter into the realities of phenomena in a way that the physical scientist can never approach. The ultimate and pervasive limitation on prediction in the social sciences resides not in the sign-maker or in the sign making, but in the character of the phenomena the sign points to.

One is told that all market relationships perpetually tend to a point of long-run equilibrium; or that the rich have a higher propensity to save; or that population increases as a function of higher-than-subsistence wages and that man-hour productivity declines as a function of population increase; or that history is the story of class struggle; or that power corrupts and absolute power corrupts absolutely. In no instance is an experiment conceivable that would, through failure in the prediction of specific event or of any specific set of events, definitely refute such statements as these.

We know that in some specific instances the aforementioned statements of relationship (or any general statement about social phenomena) will not hold. Any generalization about social phenomena is sometimes so and sometimes no, true here, false there, overwhelming us today, vanished tomorrow. Empirical they are, referring to the observed and experienced--but not positivist; nor can the positivist rule of verification conceivably be applied. A positivist statement implying ineluctable regularities cannot be spoken about the universe of social phenomena when that order of regularity does not exist.

No matter what its pretensions, the valuable, viable, significant, useful statement in the social sciences is of a verity akin to what the ancient Greeks called an "essence," understood as an Idea of which encountered experience was but the varied, partial, corrupted expression. For us the Idea, as the wellspring of encountered phenomena, is not in the mind of God, as Plato would have had it. Our search for it leads us back to the psyche of the individual and to the ideologies that bind and define the group and are expressed institutions, in policies, in choices, in behavior.

How do we know when we have found that verity? How do we decide upon the credibility of statements that claim to express a truth that is not true in every instance, not even true in any particular instance, but credible in summing up a general (if transitory) configuration of particulars?

Given that there is no inherent constancy either in the specific relationship or in the field of probability, given that for any nontrivial theory or hypothesis there will be evidence, both pro and con, <u>the first rule is to judge,</u> and, for this empirical category of statement, the judgement is not of value but of credibility, not a value judgement, but a judgement of empirical truth. The only thing to do is to judge, to weigh the evidence and to render judgement, independently, fully conscious of the gap that forever separates judging and knowing, aware that all judgement is tentative, and that the judgements made upon the credibility of statement concerning the fleeting realities of social phenomena should be taken as transitory and made again and again, year by year, and by every generation.

The only alternative to judging independently is to accept the judgement of others, of "the experts," of "the authorities" safeguarded and trapped within their fortress paradigm, deferring to the word inscribed in monograph and text certified by the imprimatur of famous names. And if most of us choose to rely on the authority of experts rather than judging for ourselves, let us be aware at least of the fragile and transitory understructure of the statements we accept as true. Nor even is this wholly to escape from judging. Whose authority will be accepted? To which experts, to what text shall we defer? These also are questions to be answered by weighing the evidence pro and con.

This category of empirical statement, in which credibility must rest upon the act of judgement, will be termed here "empirico-judgmental."

MODEL BUILDING AS A FLIGHT FROM JUDGEMENT

Those statements that stand at the core of Western economics were made about the configuration of social phenomena as it was observed and experienced a century, even two centuries ago. Things have changed since then, rapidly and radically. The distance between that corpus of thought and encountered experience has widened, correspondingly the statements of the paradigm have ceased to be credible when exposed to open judgement.

In response to increasing vulnerability, as an escape from judgement, shielding the established paradigm and all mental constructs within its walls from any possibility of test or challenge, a new apologia has developed. In its terms, the statements at the core of the paradigm, the "pure theory," are not about any delimited, discernable universe of phenomena, but are "models" simply, and economists developing the logical implications of these statements are model builders. These models "composed of nothing but mental constructs,"(1) are not empirical but definitional and logical, hence tautological, to be kept safe and secure on the shelves of the discipline, to be taken down only if and when one can identify and isolate a circumstance that happens to correspond to all their functional assumptions. Then, it is to be presumed, the model can serve in the manner of a preprogrammed computer, to deduce the logical consequences of specified changes in its parameters. If it turns out that the deduced are not the same as the observed consequences, this is no refutation of the model or challenge to the paradigm. It indicates merely that the wrong subject was selected for study, that circumstances may not have corresponded to assumed relationships, or that extraneous variables were also at work. The statement never fails to correspond with phenomena; it is the phenomena that fail to correspond with the statement!

There is first the question of fact. Has economics ceased to be empirical; and have economists given up the pretention of saying something about experienced phenomena? There is second the question of value. Should economics preoccupy itself with "nothing but mental constructs," removing its statement from the measure of correspondence to become self-contained and tautological, with only an incidental relevance (if any) to the explanation of experienced event, to social problem solving and to the formations of policy?

Economists have never ceased to suppose that their theory explains encountered phenomena. Certainly their patrons and clients, those who foot the bill and ask for guidance, are being defrauded if they are paying for sets of mental constructs merely. Nor was this ever the intention of the greats of the discipline. The statements of the classical economists like Adam Smith, Ricardo, and Malthus, or neoclassicists like J. S. Mill or Alfred Marshall, of J. M. Keynes, of Joseph Schumpeter, of Karl Marx, were about a discernable, specifiable corpus of experienced phenomena. As for the question of value, a model-building enterprise is totally at odds with the rule of social purpose.

For all these reasons we will assume that the credibility of empirical statement remains at issue, and moreover, as we have demonstrated, that there is no rational basis for supposing that the statements of social science can be falsified (hence established) through the inferential prediction of specific event, not even with perfect measurement and a total ingathering of information. The positivist rule must be rejected for the social sciences, not on account of the limitations that inhere in the statement-maker, but rather on account of the universe of phenomena to which the statement refers. Judgement must be the rule, and given the rule of judgement, the question is this: What is the appropriate language of discourse, when the objective of discourse is to facilitate judgement?

WHAT LANGUAGE FOR SOCIAL SCIENCE?

What we are <u>not</u> talking about is the way in which one might choose to organize observation, thought, or experiment; nor are we discussing methods for testing the tautological. Our concern is with discourse, with language for the communication of empirico-judgemental statements, to enable the credibility of such statements to be tested by judging their correspondence with phenomena. Should such statement be mathematical or verbal; should the sign take the form of symbol or word?

Consider these two systems of signs: the symbolic, and the verbal--mathematics and the word. The critical attribute of mathematics in discourse is that it operates abstracted from sensual experience. It is without residue of the observed and the felt, nor does it convey any idea deriving from and referring to an observed, an observable, or a fancied reality. While the language of mathematics can be hooked into anything, it is about nothing. Our 2 + 2 = 4, could refer to Bill and Jane, Jim and Mary, or to apples, or to nations, or to corporations, or to galaxies, but qua language it does not convey the idea or image of any of these. It is image-free, image-less.

That attribute gives it its particular strength and value. Because it is purged of the essentially equivocal and only partially communicable character of the mind's imageries, mathematics and mathematics alone can convey exactly the same meaning to all. Because it is free of the inherent imprecision of the sensed and observed, mathematics alone can express itself precisely. Because it is detached from sensual experience and does not operate through a shadow replication in the mind of events as they might be observed and grasped through the senses, mathematics can express the simultaneity of complex operations that earthbound words cannot replicate in proxy of experience.

Certainly mathematics is unmatched as a means of exploring the inferential implications of theories, vectoring a matrix of simultaneous relations into the precise prediction of specific event. No other system of signs can so well chart distant inferences of statement over the horizons of possible consequence, thereby both explaining phenomena and (through inferential prediction) testing the credibility or establishing the limitations of what is said. Wherein as in physics,it is not necessary to convey an image of signified relationships to establish credibility, indeed, when there is no image to convey since the hidden processes signified are made manifest only at the pinpoint of experienced event, then mathematics is surely the appropriate language of discourse. Mathematics is the appropriate instrument for positivist statement when credibility is based on specific inferential prediction.

If mathematics is imageless, purged of the imprint of the senses, the word in natural language is imageful, and sense-related. Natural language operates through replicating, recalling, conjuring up images of the mind in proxy of direct experience, following the earthbound sequence of sensual impression. Word follows word, image follows image, just as observation must follow observaton, sluggard and unidimensional compared to the simultaneities in the free flight of logic open to mathematical construction. The word is equivocal because the images it summons, in your mind and in mine, are never identical. The word is imprecise because the imprint of experience, vague and fleeting or rich and deep, blurs at the margins and disintegrates in the microview.

The word nevertheless can do what mathematics can never do. It alone creates in the minds of communicants, speaker and spoken to, writer and written for, an idea of what is spoken about. As a reflection and replication of experience, the verbal statement alone produces an image in the mind to be compared with the evidence of experience, so that thought can be juxtaposed to observation, so that statement can be compared directly to experience, so that the stated and the observed--what is claimed and what is experienced--can be balanced on the same scale of judgement.

Only through verbal statement is it possible to create, bit by bit, in the minds of those to whom the word is spoken or written, a complex image of that which is spoken or written about, so that it can be recognized, questioned, and challenged as an image of experienced reality. Only verbal statement conveys a meaning capable of being judged against the mixed evidence of experiene. A statement made in the image-less symbolism of mathematics cannot of itself convey an idea of what is to be looked for in the world as a measure of credibility against evidence, gathered experimentally or directly encountered.

For the positivist statement all that matters for verification or refutation is that inferential prediction is on target. The form of statement is immaterial so long as it can extend deduction to an exact and certain end point. When judgement, not the targeting of inferential prediction is at issue, with the whole meaning of statement to be weighed in the balance, asking "Does it capture the essence of an activity and event in a universe forever in flux and transformation, where relationships are inherently transitory and uncertain, where contradiction abides, and where there is a pro for every con?"--then the statement must be image-full, in a language that reveals a whole meaning in terms that mirror and can be reflected back upon the universe of experience.

If mathematics is the language of inferential prediction, the verb is the instrument of individual judgement; and in the social sciences it is on judgement that the rational assessment of credibility must rely. The only rational way to establish the credibility of general statement in the social sciences is through judgement. To judge requires the image of what is to be judged, and that image can be conveyed only through verbal discourse. Nor do the theories and hypotheses of the social sciences refer to processes or phenomena outside the scope of common observation. On the contrary, they are about our thoughts, our behavior, our experience. They would explain the world we inhabit, the processes we operate, and the events we daily encounter. And, moreover, the discourse of the social sciences merges into and becomes an element of a larger discourse, that of public choice. And at that point the acceptance or rejection of the statements of social science become inseparable from the formation of social policy, which in the ethic of democracy is, or should be, accomplished through the judgement and choice of everyman. And the objective of discourse should be to inform and to facilitate that judgement.

This is not to say that the gathering of evidence as the basis for judgement does not require skilled and systematic analysis. It is not to say that evolved conceptualizations are not required for the organization of observation, as a basis for sound judgement. It is not to say that a verbal discourse will in any way assure a sensitive, a continuous, an informed process of judgement. It is to say that without verbal discourse and the image it conveys, judgement is impossible. It is to say that inasmuch as and to the degree that the image of the signified is hidden in the abracadabra of an image-less mathematics, judgement of statement becomes impossible. In that sense the mathematizational discourse is a barrier to judgement, hence to the only rational way of establishing or challenging the credibility of general statement in the social sciences.

SAY'S LAW, KEYNES AND THE KEYNESIAN DEMISE

No hypothesis, no theory in the social sciences should be examined, tested, and judged to be credible once and for all. The reason is simple: The universe of phenomena--the corpus and the character of the relationships to which that statement refers--changes, and changes fundamentally and continuously so that what is true was not true, need not be true, will not be true. The proof is never in. The issue is never closed. The evidence needs to be seen afresh, weighed again, year after year and by every generation.

So the discourse should be designed to permit and to promote an open and continuous process of judgement concerning that which we experience directly, intimately, in the world of commonplace observation. Our discourse, alas, has not been so designed. The novice instead is led to believe that though statement is out of kilter with encounter, incongruous in the light of experience, it must be accepted nevertheless because it works. Works where? In some esoteric realm of computer printouts and blackboard-filled equations to which only the properly indoctrinated expert is privy. What nonsense!

In comparing economics to the physical sciences, this very strange fact emerges. The statements of the physical sciences are about a universe of perpetual and universal relationships; and yet in the past two centuries periodically there have been radical alternations, fundamental changes, revolutionary transformations in the body of statements about relationships that have not changed. In contrast, the statements of economics are about a universe of transitory relationships in continuous and fundamental transformation; but the statements at the core of economics have in their essentials remained fixed and unchanging. Derived out of the experience of the seventeenth and eighteenth centuries, culminating in the organon of the nineteenth century, the character of economics remains fixed and impervious to the revolutionary transformations of the social universe to which it supposedly refers. In essentials the thought of Batiste, Say, Turgot, Hayek, and Friedman are indistinguishable. And this despite the most monstrous evidence of failure.

Say's Law, a logically irrefutable deduction from the core of economic theory, denied (and denies) the possibility of massive unemployment and sustained industrial depression. Given the verity of that theory, industrial depression could not exist, and yet it existed, visiting and revisiting the capitalist world with increasing severity from the late nineteenth century onward. It required no mathematical intervention, no sets of equations vectoring on the prediction of specific event to demonstrate that failure. Failure was writ large in the suffering and despair of millions. Yet the walls of the paradigm did not tumble. Policy floundered, benumbed by the impotence of the experts and the futility of an established, believed-in doctrine, certified as "scientific," until the unmeasured and immeasurable catastrophe of the great depression that began in the late 1920s. Then government after government, society after society as the price of survival (and not all of them did survive), was obliged to inflate (adding to) the stream of aggregate spending.

The economic sages of Western Europe and the United States cried woe and doom against these policies and acts of inflation. Horrendous tales were told and retold about Germany in the early 1920s when workmen brought home their wages in wheelbarrows. (The Germans had then in fact been using "printing press" money not to re-employ but to disemploy workers, not to increase but to stop production in a government supported general strike against the French occupation of the Ruhr.) Even as these seers were pointing to the dreadful German example, there were Hitler and the uninhibited Nazis, spending printing press money with a vengeance to make Germany into a bastion of industrial strength and military power. Other nations had to follow suit. It was inflate or collapse--in Great Britain through devaluation of the pound, in the United States through unprecedented levels of deficit spending.

The economists were isolated. Economics was trapped by the logic of Say's Law. Keynes and his followers did not invent a new policy, nor did they develop new instrumentalities for implementing an established one. Their achievement and their contribution were in extracting economics from that trap, by seeming to reconcile economic doctrine with the realities and necessities of the time, so that economists could rationalize and could play the going policy game without abandoning, or challenging, or changing their paradigm.

Instead of starting with individual-to-individual exchanges and building from there as the paradigm does, Keynes started from and worked only with aggregates, within which individual transactions were somewhere buried. He conveyed to his fellows an image of the economy as a kind of sphere (call it the "econosphere") floating in an ether of aggregated expenditures. When the pressure of total spending was too low, the econosphere dropped into the mire of depression and mass unemployment. When the pressure was too high, the econosphere shot up into the breathless stratosphere of inflation. The task of economic policy, then, was simply to maintain aggregate expenditure at that pressure--no more, no less--at which resources would be fully employed and prices would remain stable. All this could be done from outside the econosphere. Within the econosphere, that universe of individual-to-individual transaction was just as economists had always described it. Hence there was no need, no call for the state to intervene in the relationships within the econosphere. There all was in order; all the symmetries, all the autonomies, all the optimalities of the free market were operative. Within its new protective cover, the paradigm was firm and true as ever.

In our time the Keynesian dispensation has reached the end of its line. Its fatal flaw was precisely that which made it acceptable to the economists--namely, its pretention that the level of price and of employment are determined by forces exogenous to the econosphere, and hence can be dealt with without intervening in the relationships of exchange which prevail within the econosphere.

In fact the reconciliation offered by Keynesian theory was only apparent. Between the old economics and those of Keynes there was a hidden but fundamental contradiction. Established economic thought turned on the axis and absolutely required the assumption of free-moving autonomous price as the equilibrating element and the orchestrating force of all economic behavior. Keynesian theory, on the contrary, turns on the axis and absolutely requires the assumption of price/wage fixity so that an increase in aggregate spending--that is, greater demand--would not raise price, but would re-employ labor and increase output at given prices.

These assumptions of rigidity fitted the facts of trade union and corporate behavior in the 1920s and 1930s, but such behavior rests upon and requires a more fundamental base. If wages are rigid, that must mean that trade unions have the power to hold them at a given level regardless of the decline of demand; that the trade union does so, is a matter of policy. If corporate prices are rigid, that must mean that the corporation has the power to hold prices at a given level regardless of the decline of demand; that the corporation does so, is a matter of policy.

Thus necessarily we are led to conclude that within the econosphere, prices and wages do not move autonomously, automatically, as the spontaneous, equilibrating element and the force that orchestrates the flow of resources and total behavior of the economy, as Establishment Economics presupposes. Rather, for that organizational sector which dominates the modern economy, prices are a function of corporate policy, and wages are a function of trade union policy.

Certainly during the depression of the 1930s, then policy was to hold the wage-price line. But corporations can learn, trade unions can learn--and in the passage through historical time and vastly altered circumstances they did learn, and their policies changed. Corporate price policies and trade union wage policies have changed, from holding the wage-price line in the storm and stress of depression, periodically, systematically raising prices and raising wages in response to each group's expectations of betterment. This is what produces the phenomenon of stagflation, wherein rising prices and rising wages go hand-in-hand with declining demand, lower production, higher unemployment, and excess production capacity. Under these circumstances managing aggregate expenditures in the Keynesian mode simply cannot, and does not work. Hence the Keynesian demise.

Given the failure of Keynesianism, what way is open to economic policy? Either it must follow the inherent logic of the Keynesian position and act upon or control corporation price policy and trade union wage policy, entering into the sacred zone of free market relationships; or it must cut itself off from Keynesianism and seek a return to the golden age of laissez-faire, preserving the old paradigm intact. Economists seem to have chosen the latter course.

THE POSITIVIST BARRIER TO PARIDIGMATIC CHANGE

How can we explain the extraordinary resistance of economics--certainly the most evolved and (in its relation to policy) by far the most important of the social sciences--to any fundamental transformation, in contrast to the biological and physical sciences?

In part its persistence in the face of all manner of failure and catastrophe can be explained by its ideological character. It was born as, and it remains an antistate polemic, an apologia for property as the bastion of liberty in the free market. Hence its preservation is linked to the preservation of the structure of property power. It is kept intact as an instrument for keeping intact vested interests and an ongoing form of social organization. But there is more to it than that.

The extraordinary and strange incapacity of economics to adapt and change even in the face of the most basic reconfiguration of the social reality, of fundamental transformation in the matrix of relationships to which it refers, can also be seen as the consequence of a perverse commitment to positivist science. As a riposte to its failures, in each of its internal crises, its practitioners have sought to make economics more like physics. And they have succeeded in making it look more like physics and sound more like physics by using the language of physics with its practitioners acquiring the technical virtuosity of the physicist. But all this effort to follow to the positivist rule cannot be more than a pretense, a cover-up, an institutionalized deceit. The ideological character of the paradigm cannot be changed: It is made covert. The need for evaluation and judgement of values cannot be eliminated; it is hidden. Each step toward the positivist ideal reduces the possibility of substantive transformation, for each such step carries the statements of the discourse farther from the realm of informed and open judgement without ever reaching a domain where the credibility of statement can conceivably be falsified, hence possibly established through the inferential prediction of specific event. Where statement is empirico-judgmental, that domain is inherently unreachable.

In the late 1930s, in his Foundation of Economics, Paul Samuelson undertook to translate the verbal form of economic thought and theory into the mathematical sign. His purpose in so doing, he wrote, was to open the statements of economics to test and hence to definitive falsification through inferential prediction, following the positivist rule. Economists throughout the world followed his path. The language of economics was transformed, and economists acquired a mathematical virtuosity that might be the envy of the physicists. Testing through inferential prediction never came. Not a single hypothesis or theory in the established corpus of thought was subjected to such a test, falsified, eliminated. No other basis than judgement, for the establishment or disestablishment of credibility, has been found.

Yet the view of judgement is obscured. The proliferation of esoteric signs removes statement from its reach. To cloak the statement in the image-less sign is to shield its claims from the commonplace contrast and comparison with experienced realities. Thus while the post-World War II decades have been years of unprecedented power and affluence for economists, with more papers published displaying greater technical virtuosity than was imagined before, they have also been decades devoid of any significant advance in economic thought. The gap between statement and experience continues to widen, justifying Heilbronner's *mot* "greater rigor, correspondingly mortus."

THE PROBLEMS OF JUDGEMENT

One can understand why the philosophers glory in a positivist system of statement in which credibility could always be established and conflict always resolved through definitive test. If one could choose, that form of discourse might always be the chosen one. But for social science there is no choice. Its discourse must be empirico-judgmental because social phenomena are what they are. There is no option but to make credibility a matter of judgement, and judgement has its problems. It must take the evidence into account, of course, but when all the evidence is in, and judgements still differ over the weight to be given to the pros and to the cons, there is no objective test that can resolve that difference.

For the empirico-judgmental statement, what is

perpetually at issue is the weight of the evidence. Is there (or is there no) tendency to equilibrium, a force that holds the elements of the economy to their predestined course like some cosmic glue? Is it conflict, class against class, that is the decisive element in the capitalist economy, forming its path in history? Or does the market system turn on the axis of mutual advantage, with interdependence and harmony of interests as its essential quality?

These are empirical statements, statements about a world open to common observation. Are they true or untrue? Credible or not credible? There is evidence pro. There is evidence con. Our judgement will depend on the weight we give to a diversity of evidence. Discourse concerning such statements should be designed to facilitate the ingathering and the objective examination of evidence, disciplined to minimize the intrusion of covert values. The irresolvable and unresolved will nevertheless remain. We will hardly escape ambiguities and conflicts. Experience holds the trump card. One hopes that, and one can hope for no more than that an openness to encounter, with the process of judgement continuing and the evidence of experience accumulating, will produce less fallible images of reality.

THE VALUE JUDGEMENT

There remains to be considered the expressive statement of private preference, of a sense of what is right or wrong, better or worse, desirable, undesirable, good, bad, just, unjust, put forward as an imperative, as a statement of what ought and ought not to be, of ethic, of priority: the value judgement.

Aside from the rules of discourse, in which a set of value judgements are prerequisite to the ordered discourse in all the sciences, value judgement has a particular place in social science if and inasmuch as social science gears into the formulation of social policy and relates itself to the resolution of social problems.

Social scientists, certainly economists, have never ceased to recommend solutions and to devise policies for social choice. And in so doing they have done no more than meet the expectations and demands of those upon whose support their activity depends.

ANATHEMA ON VALUE JUDGEMENTS

Yet in the mid-1930s the high priests and authorities of economics pronounced Anathema, in the sacred name of Science, on value judgements. The rank and file of the discipline, well-disciplined, fell docily into line. What happened is instructive. Economics did not free itself from value judgements. It simply severed its connection with a long-standing commitment to a more equal distribution of income.

This commitment was deduced from two categories of statement, one explicit, the other implicit. Explicit was the law of diminishing marginal utility, which holds that in general each increment of real income yields to the individual progressively smaller increments of utility.(2) The textbook example was of the great pleasure in consuming the first apple, becoming a bellyful with the fifth, and a bellyache with the tenth. Coupled to this was the proposition, also explicit, that in general, the average utility derived by an individual of a given level of income and wealth from the receipt of an additional dollar is comparable to the utility that is derived from the reciept of an additional dollar by another average individual having the same level of income and wealth.

From these two propositions it follows that the general equalization of income will of itself increase the sum total of utilities enjoyed by all the individuals constituting society. Implicit is the statement that economics and economists _ought_ to be concerned with increasing the happiness of their fellows and the well-being of society. The two explicit propositions are empirico-judgmental statements. The implicit proposition, and it alone, is a value judgement.

The two empirico-judgemental statements were drummed out of the discipline. It was henceforth forbidden to assert as credible the statement that in general an impoverished and starving man receiving a dollar would derive a greater satisfaction from the use of that dollar than an average billionaire would, on the grounds that such a statement requires an interpersonal comparison and that interpersonal comparisons are incommensurable, since we are unable to enter into the mind of an individual and register its imageries or to measure the qualitative character of the psychic responses that occur there. Thus, for example, though the two of us call the rose we see "red," we cannot enter each other's minds to know that the redness of the rose is the same for the two of us. We simply judge that it is, and that your pain is like my pain, and that your joy and mine can be compared. Such judgements are the commonplace of communication and the essentials of community.

Be that as it may, said Sir John Hicks, whether or not such interpersonal comparisons are commonplace and necessary, they are not scientific! And economics must be, above all, scientific! Whereupon Sir John replaced the forbidden interpersonal comparisons with another set of interpersonal comparisons equally beyond the reach of instrumental verification and measurement and far less amenable to a reasoned judgement based on introspection and inferential observation--namely, that all individual behavior reflects and is controlled by an infinitely encompassing set of preordained, pre-existing indifference curves precisely engraved on every psyche by some invisible hand. All that can be claimed for this replacement of one set of empirico-judgemental propositions for another is that a paradigmatic commitment to greater income equality was thereby rendered void. For this grand achievement, Sir John Hicks would receive the Nobel Prize.

But note that this had nought to do with value judgements. Nor was the relevant value judgement that economics qua discipline should be concerned with human happiness and social well-being brought into question. In fact Sir John and his associates quickly proposed a formula, the Rule of Pareto Optimality, that would permit the economist to gear into social choice and to recommend policies just as before, except that no consideration must ever be given to the positive values of income redistribution.

So in the end all this esoteric argumentation and intellectual convolution came down to no more than the insertion of another value-based imperative, negative in this instance, a taboo against taking income redistribution into account in recommending public policy.

Economics is replete with built-in values. It values efficiency. By its mode of evaluating efficiency, it values individualized choice and, correspondingly, disvalues (or, which is to say the same thing, excludes from consideration the values of) collective choice. In relation to individualized choice, it values property as a form of power. It values consumer preferences and disvalues the preferences of producers and the public goals of citizens and the intrinsic character of social relationships. How, then, can we explain the singling out for ritual excommunication in the sacred name of Science, this particular paradigmatic commitment to income equalization?

Perhaps because during the long generations when intervention by the state was effectively proscribed under the prevailing ideology of laissez-faire liberalism, and when political power was fully and firmly in the hands of the propertied, the economist's commitment to greater income equality could be accepted as a harmless piety. But after World War I, with (in Britain at least) a radical shift in the locus of political power and the gradual emergence of a positive state capable of decisive economic control, a policy of income equalization becomes a threat to the affluent; and the defense of status shifts back into the institutions (like academia) of policy-legitimization and value formation. Hence the paradigmatic commitment to (or justification of) greater income equality becomes sharply and critically controversial in the Great Britain of the 1920s and 1930s--a controversy that could threaten the integrity of a discipline like economics whose partisans, participants, and patrons had from the outset been the defenders of property power and market autonomy. In detaching itself from the commitment to income equalization, economics was reaching not for the scientific but for the noncontroversial.

Sir John Hicks and those who followed him cannot be faulted for an effort to sever the commitment of economics to a more equal distribution of income, not at least on epistemological grounds. It was in their rationalization of that severance that they erred. The Anathema on value judgement was obscurantist. The obeisance to the positivist rules of science was epistemologically incongruous and self-deceiving. The economic discourse could not and did not dispense with value judgement. That is not to say that every value judgement is acceptable.

Suppose Sir John had argued as follows: Acceptability, not credibility, is the criterion of value judgement. The commitment to income equality has become highly controversial. It cannot anymore be regarded as a moral axiom acceptable to all, or even as generally acceptable as a basis for common endeavor. Therefore it behooves us to seek outside the zone of controversy for some other value base that will provide the discipline qua discipline with a common posture, a single voice. Thus we will be strengthened in our common endeavor. To that end I propose Pareto Optimality as such a value criterion.

Were that his statement, Sir John would have been arguing the arguable, and discourse might have ensued in terms proper to the acceptance or rejection of a value judgement.

VALUE AS FACT

The statement that expresses as an imperative the values of the speaker is a value judgement, but a specification of the speaker's values or a statement about evaluation as a social process is not. Neoclassical economics conceives market exchange to be a process of evaluation, wherein consumer values are expressed in the patterns of demand and priorities are registered in market price. Institutionalists in the Common's tradition emphasize the political system qua process of evaluation, in setting the legal parameters of market transactions. Marxists explain the formation of values as the expressions of class interest, with the values thus formed giving direction to the class struggle. Such statement refers to--and is to be accepted or rejected by--reference to psychological facts in explaining phenomena and event.

Values-as-fact are on a par with any other observable, analyzable phenomena and, as such, present no particular epistemological problem. Something might be said, nevertheless, concerning the approach of economics to the value-as-fact. Values-as-fact are no mere surface phenomena. Values are created, disseminated, perpetuated, transformed, replaced. And we have, alas, failed to conceptualize or to seek to understand the immensely complex and variable social processes of value formation, and the cognitive and cultural systems that overlap and interlink the psyche and society. Only in that region can one hope to discover how policy blueprints emerge, how institutions are created, how individual choice is formed, and where groups find their cohesion and character. And only there will we uncover the loci and dynamic of fundamental social change.

EVALUATIONAL DISCOURSE

Recognizing that in any discourse vectored to the recognition and resolution of social problems, the expressive, the empirical, and the tautological are intermingled, we will concern ourselves in the rest of this essay with the value element of discourse alone. Our questions are these: What are the prerequisites? The purposes? The possible value of a discourse understood itself as an evaluational process?

There is this first prerequisite for a value discourse: that value statements be overt, not covert, and that the peculiar character of such statements be recognized. It must be recognized, that is to say, that contradictions in statements of value need not be resolvable by reference to observation and the data of experience or by any objective test; and hence that a viable discourse requires a tolerance for such contradictions or differences, which limit but do not preclude the development of the value base needed to form coherent social policy.

For some, that alone would suffice: to be fully aware of one's values and to be ready to state them clearly so that others can agree or disagree as they will. Nor is this a small thing, or easy to do. There is a profound lack of self-awareness or awareness in the community of the social disciplines, of the value element of their discourse. The Hicksian anathema illustrates that confusion and self-deception. It is illustrated as well by the Byzantine artifices employed of late to find a certifiably scientific value-free return to the commitment to income equality, most recently manifest in the enthusiasm for John Rawls' Theory of Justice.

We have made our values explicit. We have shown our value-based proposals to be workable. What more is to be said? What can be gained through any further value-related discourse? What would be its purpose?

Two purposes. The first perhaps on a lower but more universal level would be to achieve consensus, for example, not to discover what is right and just but simply to mobilize a commitment to some shared idea of rightness and justice, whatever it might be, as a sufficient basis for communal choice and action. The second purpose of such a discourse would in this instance be to discover what is more nearly right and just, raising the guiding values of the community and its policies toward a closer approximation of some ultimate good.

TO ACHIEVE CONSENSUS

Social choice requires shared value commitments, and discourse in the policy sciences can aim toward the achievement of such consensus--not once and for all, but continuously. As social choice is a dynamic process, so also is the formation of its prerequisite value basis. Evaluation and value formation are functions also of the assessment of changing realities, of experience-rooted understanding of consequences, of notions of social receptivity, of the pressing social discomforts and the foci of social concern.

Consider rights. For the founding fathers, rights were entirely libertarian, designed to protect the privacy, the autonomy, the space for individualized choice in the simple arrangements of an economy in which the essential arrangement was in the order of individual to individual exchange. The drift of time, the processes of industrialization, produced a matrix of interdependencies beyond the scope of individual control, swept by forces beyond the individual ken. After the lesson of interdependence and systemic fragility had been hammered home by the great depression of the 1930s, came the idea of rights as a charter of social protections and guarantees against the arbitrary and overwhelming insecurities and inequities to which an industrialized economy is heir:

welfare rights. And in the postmodern universe of organizations, another species of rights, organizational rights that protect participation in the formation of policy, that affirm obligations and prerogatives of role, that determine access to niches in complex systems, become increasingly important.

Or consider the demise of Keynesianism in the thickets of stagflation. The lesson of stagflation is simply this: Prices and wages in the organizational sector are functions of corporation wage and of trade union wage policy. That policy cannot be reached through the management of aggregate spending or through monetary squeeze. There is simply no way of insuring price stability, and especially under conditions of full employment, except through public participation in the formation of corporate price and trade union wage policy, that is, through some form of wage-price control.

The accumulating failure of the conventional alternatives pushes each successive administration close to, or over the threshold of, the first primitive stage of price-wage control, namely the price-wage freeze. But (and here is the critical new area for evaluation and value formation) a system of wage-price control transforms income distribution from the sphere of market randomness and autonomy, accepted as an act of nature beyond question or justification, into a matter of social choice and public policy administered by bureaucracy under the aegis of the political authority. The "who gets what" must be justified and justifiable by reference to accepted value criteria. And the formation and acceptance of such value criteria for the distribution of income become the crux and absolute prerequisite for the distribution of income, become the crux and absolute prerequisite for any viable, continuing system of wage-price control, hence of high employment and stable prices in the postmodern economy.

We do not begin with a clean slate. We are born into a cultural system with its interlinked and overlapping processes of evaluation, imprinting values upon the psyche of succeeding generations. Through discourse, an already existing corpus of value commitments are interpreted and expressed as judgmental criteria and policy options in the light of an ever-changing configuration of circumstances and problems.

Through discourse also, the dialectic of commitment--say, to equality--finds one dimension of expression. Belief hurls itself against the inertial force of established institutions, against the resistance of endangered interests, in a point by point transformation of society. Such a value commitment can derive from a variety of grand philosphies or from no philosophy at all. It can be justified by and derived from biblical commandment (Love thy neighbor who is a man like unto thyself), from the Benthamite utility calculus, from the Schweitzerian reverence for life, or simply in contemplating the probable effects on the matrix of social relationships, or out of felt compassion for the impoverished and exploited. From whatever source it came, that commitment, once embedded in belief, takes on its own dynamic, shaping, transforming our institutions, imperceptibly sometimes, sometimes rapidly when eroded walls suddenly collapse.

In their revolution Americans fought for equality against the privileged rule of English king and Parliament. That equality embraced the notion, even demanded that among ourselves it be honored also. We delivered to it the inequalities of inherited political privilege and power. Omnivorous, it demanded equality of economic privilege and economic power, of wealth, of opportunity, of security, of income. Given equality among the whites, it demands equality for the blacks, for men, then for women, and for other peoples, other nations. Value commitment becomes the problem-maker, creates the problem, is source and reason for change, produces its reaction, carries its dangers.

A new value appears, an old one fades--but the stage on which our values play is never empty. On that stage are the same named actors, though speaking different lines, with one stepping into the foreground while others drift into the wings, deathless players acting roles we are forever creating for them. They have been masked in our day, under the censure of positivist science, entering the discourse of the social-cum-policy disciplines stealthily, covertly, by indirection.

In mobilizing value commitments as a basis for choice, the need for choice--the need to act as an alternative to inaction, to nonchoice, to drifting--becomes itself a value against which others must be balanced. Thus preferring the smaller reform to no reform, some strength to impotence, we compromise, re-evaluate, lower our sights to find some common moral ground for workable consensus.

The transformations of commitment into policies, of policies into practice, with practice institutionalized and the experienced consequences of all this in the experience of life as it is lived; such is the stuff of moral learning.

DISCOURSE AND THE FORMATION OF VALUES

Can we go further? Can we, in value-oriented discourse, go beyond the logical, analytic, and empirical, building upon exogenously determined, already established sets of value commitment? Could such discourse be organized for the positive formation of values? And would values thus formed be higher, better? In that sense, if we consider culture as the value-generating, value-perpetuating, evaluating system, can such a discourse raise the level of culture?

Beyond empirical science, there is another dimension of learning. To know who I am and what I am, and to become what I can be, belongs to the domain of moral development and of value formation. Through experience we discover pain and pleasure, sorrow and joy, anguish and serenity, hate and love, friendship and enmity as states of self-being, and through experience we can come to know the interior and exterior causes and consequences of these. In our striving as a species, we seek to have more, to know more, and also to become more, in the sense of realizing potentials that experience discovers. Does this take us from lower to higher, in closer approximation of an ultimate good? That too is a matter of judgement to be made only by the individual with reference to an interior stream of events. We make and articulate that judgement, in the hope that it will strike a common chord.

I judge that through experience we can move from lower to higher states of being. True for the individual, can it be true also for society? If we are enough alike that I can learn about myself from you, follow your path of self-becoming, use your queries to question what I am, benefit from the failure for which you have paid the price, and conversely you from me, it follows that through discourse we can, qua group and as a society, learn together and form values in a process that leads to a higher common basis for collective action.

The question, "Who am I, and what is my identity," becomes in part, "With whom do I identify? My child? My friends? This group or that? Nation? Society? Humankind? Posterity? Life?" If I identify with you, then my self-knowledge is to know you as well, and my self-realization is also in the realization of your potential. Through discourse can we transcend the encapsulation of self, reaching out to identify with and to know that with which we identify? Through discourse can we discover, develop, and in the design of collective conditions realize the potentials of a larger or more encompassing identity? Given the interdependencies of a world teetering on the edge of catastrophes, there is the need, surely, to widen and to extend the base of self-identification.

Alas, the capacity for value discourse has been lost. It has been difficult to confess a need for it. A modern babel, fashioned out of the proliferating niches of specialization, has made that discourse more difficult still. There are on the other hand centripetal forces drawing us into more encompassing spheres of association, not the least of these being the extraordinary power of the new technologies of communication, the phenomenon of mass travel, the homogenization of social and economic conditions, and that very interdependence that gives the localized event a universal significance.

It may be, moreover, that the Freudian revolution, for all its fadism and self-indulgences, will add a new dimension to the value discourse by introducing uniquely disciplined, serious, and systematic efforts to obtain self-knowledge, self-realization, and a knowledge of the other.

What of conventional philosophy? Let the philosopher answer the question "What is the Good?" It is not the same as, nor has it been helpful in answering our questions, which are of the order of "What is a good tax system?" A mode of philosophizing that would postulate a single set of moral principles as axiomatic, and through logical inference try to build these into a perfect and all-encompassing system, which turns out always to be unacceptable in its absolutes, with discourse caught and going around and around in the small gullies of paradox, is not what the policy sciences need.

We in the policy sciences are concerned with social arrangements in relation to life as lived: a man's life, a woman's life, and not values in a series, or values laid side-by-side somehow with conflicts compromised and incompatibilities resolved; but with a life that is integral, unsegmented, burning single as a flame.

What captures us, sends us, mobilizes our commitment and draws upon our deep experience, is an idea of how things might be, an image of a way of life and a pattern of social organization that seems to us workable, possible, and good, or, in the context of our time, better than what we have. Our value discourse in the policy sciences needs to begin not with first principles but with envisaged blueprints, images of life as lived, into which we can project ourselves, and upon which we can build our world. This is a time for utopian thinking. The subject of our value discourse should be utopias, small ones and large.

NOTES

1. Fritz Machlup, Methodology of Economics and Other Social Sciences. Academic Press, 1978, p. 179. See also pp. 137-188.
2. "Utility" has been variously equated to happiness, satisfaction, well-being.

2. What is Political Economy?

Gunnar Myrdal

We all know that the academic discipline now commonly referred to as economics was equally commonly called political economy only a couple of generations ago. The first chair I held at the University of Stockholm after 1933, as successor to Gustav Cassel, was named "Political Economy and Financial Science."

What did economists in earlier times mean by inserting the adjective "political"? And why was it dropped? Was the change only meant to be a rationalizing abridgment without logical significance? Or can we find a deeper significance motivating the change?

When the idiomatic alteration from political economy to economics gradually occurred, it was seldom if ever discussed as a problem or even noted as signifying an important change in the emphasis or direction of our work. However, looking backward it seems to me to have been important as a sign of a change in the pursuit of our work. It pertained to a fundamental difference in approach when studying the economy.

II

As early as the beginning of the eighteenth and into the early nineteenth centuries, economists unhesitatingly saw themselves as political economists. They firmly believed it was part of their duty to draw policy conclusions. And they held that they were entitled to do this on rational grounds, that is, as logical inferences from their knowledge about the facts.

It is true that in the classical line, at least from the early part of the nineteenth century, the more sophisticated economists often emphasized that their "theory" did not permit them to draw policy conclusions.

What they claimed was impossible to serve as basis

for policy conclusions was, however, their "theory" in a restricted sense. From Ricardo on, that theory had become a very simplified deductive analysis built upon a few abstract assumptions; Senior reckoned four. Even though the attempt was to make the assumptions as realistic as possible, the more thoughtful writers were in principle aware of the need to encompass much detailed data on how various other social conditions actually were in order to formulate valid policy conclusions. In that sense they were in principle institutionalists. To this I will return.

But they also needed a valuational basis for these policy conclusions. In the meaning clarified by John Stuart Mill in his earliest works, the study of the economy is a "moral science," as in his view are all social sciences. Crucial to this view, which from then on expressively established economic science as political economy, was the concept that there were objective values that could be known as facts, could be observed and analyzed, and so laid as a basis both for the study of all other facts and for rational policy conclusions.

This value basis for economic study was provided by the moral philosophy of that time, initially by the natural law philosophy and later by the utilitarian philosophy which, as I have shown, was only a variation and reformulation of the old natural law philosophy.

The neoclassical authors then refined this moral philosophy and, in particular, its foundation in the hedonistic associational psychology. As a matter of fact, the marginal theory of value from the 1870s stands out as giving the finishing touch to the moral philosophy of utilitarianism. Many of the prominent economists of that era, for instance Sidgwick, also figure prominently in the pantheon of philosophers in that line of thought.

The welfare theory developed by the first generation of neoclassical authors thus had its logical foundation in the utilitarian moral philosophy, which, in turn, rested on the hedonistic associational psychology. This development happened at about the time when both the utilitarian moral philosophy and, in particular, the basic hedonistic associational psychology lost their characteristic self-evidence, if they were not abandoned entirely by the professional philosophers and psychologists. The very apparent isolation of economic science from the other social sciences, and from philosophy as these disciplines developed, dates from that time.

III

Modern establishment economists have retained the welfare theory but have done their best to conceal and forget its foundation in a particular and now obsolete moral philosophy and an equally obsolete psychology. They have then succeeded in pursuing what appears to be an amoral economic theory, and they are proud of stressing this. They are not programmatically political economists, as were our forebears.

By demonstrating the superficiality and logical inconsistency of this modern welfare theory almost 50 years ago--in a book published in Swedish in 1931 but translated into English first in 1953, The Political Element in the Development of Economic Theory--I thought I had finally disposed of it. But it grows like a malignant tumor. Hundreds of books and articles are produced every year on welfare economics, reasoning in terms of individual or social "utility" or some substitute for that term. But if the approach is not entirely meaningless, it has a meaning only in terms of a forlorn hedonistic psychology, and a utilitarian moral philosophy built upon that psychology. I have always wondered why the psychologists and philosophers have left the economists alone and undisturbed in their futile exercise.

The trend toward narrow professionalism in contemporary establishment economics in regard to training, reading, and indeed awareness of everything outside the narrow field they have staked out for their work, protects them from being disturbed by much knowledge about modern psychology and philosophy. And the relative neglect we can now find in the curricula at most universities of the study of the history of economic science helps them have an exaggerated belief in the newness of their own contributions to welfare economics. In particular, it protects them from grasping that what they are attempting is normative economic theory, but in disguise since they are not prepared to call themselves political economists.

Those great economists who a century ago originally developed the hedonistic and utilitarian welfare theory--among them Jevons, Sidgwick, and Edgeworth--could work with conviction and in clear terms, since they were aware of what they were doing. They were not apt to skip over the basic psychological and philosophical assumptions implied in welfare theory. The contemporary welfare theorists mostly miss the historical perspective they would gain by intensive study of their predecessors and, at the same time, the awareness they could get from such studies of where the basic difficulties are buried.

Few attempts have been made by contemporary establishment economists to study--empirically and in terms of modern psychology and sociology--people's behavior as income earners, consumers, savers, investors, and as members of interest organizations and political parties. What attempts have been made outside our fraternity to carry out realistic psychological and sociological research about economic behavior, free from the assumptions of the old and new welfare theory, have been disregarded in establishment economics. The deeper reason for this neglect is, of course, that the results of such research cannot possibly be integrated into the conceptual framework of a welfare theory of the inherited and still dominant type.

IV

In one fundamental sense a student who is prepared, as I am, to call himself a political economist and thus recognizes that economics is a moral science, works in the great tradition that became established in the eighteenth century and more definitely formalized in the nineteenth. When, at the same time, he discards the moral philosophy of utilitarianism and its implied hedonistic psychology, which traditionally was laid as a basis for political economy--and is a hidden and repressed assumption even for welfare theory in modern economics--he then has to account for what other valuational basis he has for his work.

Valuations are always with us. Disinterested research there has never been and can never be. Before we can have answers there must be questions. There can be no view except from a viewpoint. In the questions raised and the viewpoint chosen, valuations are implied.

Our valuations determine our approach to a problem, the definition of concepts, the choice of models, the selection of observations and, at the end, the presentation of research results--in fact, the whole pursuit of a study from the beginning to the end. When we remain unaware of the valuations basic to our research, it implies that we succeed to reason with one main premise missing. And the result is an indeterminateness that opens the door for systematic biases.

The old book of mine that I mentioned was devoted to finding out by immanent analysis, the hidden common biases in different epochs by different main authors. As a logical critique of economic science, as it developed within the classical and neoclassical line, I hold it sill valid. However, the book did not enlarge upon the psychological and sociological problems of how the space of indeterminateness--by avoiding spelling out more specifically the underlying valuations--has actually come to be utilized for reaching the specific biased views.

While we are studying intensely all sorts of groups in society and their behavior, we have preserved a taboo about our own behavior as researchers. But we are certainly not automatons like some of our modern research facilities. What we actually come to do in our research depends not only on our inherited personality traits, but also on the strong traditions in our craft and the influence from the surrounding society. The forces working on all economists of a time (except for a few dissenters), are apparently strong enough to result in substantial conformity in shaping the dominant views in an epoch.

When I have urged the development of a psychology and sociology of social science and scientists, it is also for the practical reason that it would be important in helping avoid biases by sharpening our awareness of the problem and heightening our efforts to avoid biases. The term bias and the reality behind it is shunned by economists in the establishment line.

V

Valuations are always implied in research, as I said, but they should not be brushed under the carpet. Instead they should be made conscious. They represent a volitional element in research, which for the sake of honesty and clarity should be explicitly stated. They are needed for establishing relevant facts, not only for drawing policy conclusions.

Only in this way can we aspire to "objectivity in research," in the only sense this term can be given any meaning. The prevalent endeavor to be like the natural scientists, to whom valuations do not play the same role for research, and to believe that what we are doing is simply observing and establishing the facts and factual relationships, is an illusion.

The use of explicit value premises serves three purposes. It determines in a rational way the statement of problems, the approach and the definition of concepts used in a study. It further lays a tenable, logical basis for reaching policy conclusions through rational reasoning. And it helps to purge, as far as possible, the scientific investigation of distorting biases.

By working with specific and explicit value premises, we are not simply expressing our own biases, as is often suggested. For biases are ordinarily not conscious to the researcher and are thus not under his control, and this opens the door to arbitrariness. Loose declarations of personal biases are no substitute for a rational procedure.

The value premises cannot be chosen arbitrarily. They have to be relevant and significant for the society studied, logically consistent, and feasible. The difficulties of thus realistically basing our value premises on prevalent valuations in the society we are studying should not be concealed, although I shall not elaborate on that point here.

I do insist, however, that when a researcher disciplines himself to spell out, in as definite terms as he can, a set of instrumental value premises--however they have been reached and whichever they are--and if he allows them to determine his approach, the definition of concepts, and his formulation of models and theories, he has enhanced the effectiveness of research, particularly in defending himself against biases.

By so spelling out the role certain valuations have played in his research, he has also aided his critics. Anyone willing to challenge his choice of value premises is relieved of the cumbersome task of discovering, through immanent criticism, the otherwise only implicit valuations and the way they have steered research.

VI

When in many fields of study I have tried to apply this insight, and felt compelled to state my value premises explicitly and justify their selection, I feel in one sense that I am working in the great tradition that began in the eighteenth century. Since it implies that economic policy conclusions can rationally be inferred from these value premises and from the facts ascertained from the viewpoint of the same value premises, economic science has been restored to a moral science in the meaning of John Stuart Mill--though deprived of the reliance the old political economists had on the existence of an objective system of values.

Even in another respect I feel aligned to the old tradition. When the writers in the classical and neoclassical line observed that their abstract theory could not permit them to draw policy conclusions, this was, as I pointed out, a recognition of the need for a much fuller knowledge of the society they were studying. Only by widening the horizon could they pretend to be political economists.

But, as I have shown, while the value theory always remained central and was finally worked out with considerable thoroughness by the first generation of neoclassical economists a hundred years ago--in their welfare theory--the other props under their pretension of being political economists (namely, the inclusion in their study of all relevant conditions besides the economic factors in their theory) has never systematically worked out as a principle of research.

It is true that without such a methodological

clarification many of the writers in the classical and neoclassical line, from Adam Smith to Alfred Marshall, did stretch their analysis far outside the realm of economic factors. This was, of course, still more true in regard to authors outside that main line as, for instance, the German Historical School and individual writers like Karl Marx and, one generation earlier, Friedrich List.

It was only after World War II that conventional economists narrowed and hardened their isolation from the other social sciences. This isolation has, for instance, almost made it possible for a group of economists in the 1950s to aspire to have made a discovery by stressing the importance of education in development. But they retreated immediately to deal with it as an "investment in man" together with physical investment in the capital/output ratio, an approach that Marshall, who of course also made space for education in his writings, had expressly warned against.

VII

If, with the indulgence of my friendly audience, I be permitted a brief autobiographical note on this point, I should confess that it was not simply the logic, as I am presenting it today, but my actual research experiences in the type of problems I came to work on that brought me to clarity in regard to the two methodological issues I deal with here.

The previously mentioned book contained a critical review of the development of economic theory from its early beginning, where by immanent logical criticism I demonstrated how in every earlier epoch, and also at the time when I wrote my book, the economists in the classical and neoclassical line had fallen into the fault of biased views. As a critical and historical analysis I believe it stands valid today.

But throughout the presentation lurks the idea that if only biases were purged there would remain a solid and objective economic theory from which, by adding value premises, rational political conclusions could be inferred. It was not yet clear to me that valuations enter already in the ascertaining of the facts, making necessary explicit value premises as early as at that stage of a study.

At the end of the 1930s I became committed to making a comprehensive and objective study of the Negro problem in America. As I faced this task, that problem was not only immensely complicated, involving practically all phases of American civilization, but it was charged with violent emotions, manifesting themselves also in opportunistically distorted views about reality. In this situation even the scholarly literature was heavily influenced and was very apparently biased in different directions. That this was so was part of the reality I was studying. I found myself quoting books, not simply to try to establish how race relations actually were, but to demonstrate other facts--how writers in different categories were perceiving and thinking about this reality.

In this situation I felt compelled to explain from what valuational angle I was ascertaining and analyzing what I could observe and substantiate of actual race relations. I chose as instrumental value premises what I called the American Creed, the set of ideals and moral commitments, which in America during the Revolution--and later in the efforts to make a nation of immigrants from so many and different countries and cultures--had been spread and given consciousness unmatched in any other country.

I had to specify my chosen value premises for the several categories of problems, and in methodological appendices to develop the general reasons why value premises were needed in such research and how they should be selected. After this experience I have in all my work been careful to spell out my value premises and how I have arrived at them. Particularly in my work on underdeveloped countries' planning problems, which has taken up the major part of my years since then, I have felt the need for explicit value premises as logically pressing as in my work on An American Dilemma.

The second influence of my work on An American Dilemma was to make me a full-fledged institutional economist. That there was a close interrelation between the economic situation of Negroes in America and all other conditions of their life, and that of all others, was only too apparent. Nothing of scientific importance could be ascertained except by transgressing the boundaries between our inherited disciplines. Even in this respect I have in my later work adhered to this principle.

I came to see that in reality there are no economic, or sociological, or psychological problems, but just problems, and they are all mixed and composite. In research the only permissible demarcation is between relevant and irrelevant conditions. The problems also have to be seen regularly in historical perspective.

VIII

I proceed now to attempt to give a more systematic account of what I mean by institutional economics. The borderline is somewhat blurred as some economists of the conventional school sometimes venture to take a broader approach to practical problems. The conscious and systematic institutionalists are, however, in a tiny minority. The reasons for the broader approach I will now formulate in logical terms.

The most fundamental thought that holds institutional economists together, despite how different they otherwise are, is our recognition that even if we focus attention on specific economic problems, our study must take account of the entire social system, including everything else of importance to what happens in the economic field: Foremost, among other things, is distribution of power in society and, generally, economic, social, and political stratification and indeed all institutions and attitudes. To this we have to add, as an exogenous set of factors, induced policy measures, applied with the purpose of changing one or several of these endogenous factors.

The dynamics of this social system are determined by the fact that among all the endogenous conditions there is "circular causation," implying that, if there is change in one condition, others will change in response. Those secondary changes in their turn will cause new changes all around, even reaching back to the condition whose change we assumed initiated the process, and so on in further rounds.

So the whole system will be moving in one direction or another, and it may even be turning around its axis. There is no one basic factor, but everything causes everything else. This implies interdependence within the whole social process. And there is generally no equilibrium in sight.

One important aspect of this process is that most often, though not always, changes that are reactions to a more primary change tend to go in the same direction. To give an abstract example: Improved nutrition among poverty-stricken masses in an underdeveloped country will raise the productivity of labor and, in turn, that will increase the opportunity to improve production and nutrition further. This is why circular causation normally will have cumulative effects. Through feedbacks regularly causing more primary changes to have repercussions in the same direction, the results, for good or ill, may after some time be quite out of proportion to an initial impulse of change of one or several conditions.

Those initial changes, which in this model are defined as exogenous, that is, the policy interventions, are under a wider perspective also dependent on the endogenous conditions and their changes, to which they are reactions, and which also in many ways constrict and influence their scope and direction. When kept separate in this model of circular causation with cumulative effects, this is done to preserve a room of freedom for an analysis in terms of planning, that is, policy deliberations and decisions conceived of as not entirely restricted and determined by the existing conditions and ongoing changes.

As the system is moving, partly under the influence of policy measures, the coefficients of interrelations among the various conditions in circular causation are ordinarily not known with quantitative precision. Elements of inertia, time lags, and in extreme cases the total nonresponsiveness of one or several conditions to changes in some set of other conditions, raise problems about which precise knowledge is seldom available. This is largely true even in developed countries with their more complete accounting for all social conditions and their more perfected statistical services. But it is particularly true in underdeveloped countries.

Consequently, our analysis of development problems must often end in tentative generalizations and mere plausible hypotheses, built upon limited observations, discernment, and conjectural judgements. Even in developed countries the widening of the perspective implied in this institutional approach will regularly destroy the neat simplicity of both analysis and conclusions in conventional economics.

Our endeavor, of course, must be to develop concepts that more adequately grasp real conditions and their interrelations, and to direct empirical study to ascertain the quantitative coefficients of those interrelations. But we should be aware of the huge area of less reliable, complete, and precise knowledge.

These remarks are offered as hints toward the master model of institutional economics, which must be holistic, even when focused on particular economic problems. I believe it is common for institutional economists to have in the back of their minds the master model of the movement of the whole social system within which there is causal interdependence. While studying an economic problem they will therefore come to include in their economic analysis noneconomic factors, selected by the criterion of relevance for what happens.

IX

In calling the holistic approach the fundamental principle of institutional economics, I imply that our main criticism of ordinary economists is that they work with narrowly closed models, limiting the analysis to too few conditions. These are traditionally chosen from conditions called economic factors, which regularly are more susceptible to quantification, although even this quality is often opportunistically exaggerated, and so not only in regard to underdeveloped countries.

Holding down the variables to only a few that can be quantified makes it possible to use impressive mathematical models. They regularly presuppose a sharp restriction of vision. Almost the entire social system is kept out of sight. This should at least have required a clear statement of assumptions about conditions and determinants not considered. Such an account of implied assumptions about what is left out is regularly not given. Most of the time it is not even consciously perceived.

I should add that when in recent decades some economists (but more often sociologists) actually attempt to account for, besides the economic factors, the importance of one or another condition which they can measure, for instance a vital index, it is most often done in a similarly restricted way in regard to all other conditions in the social system. And again it is done without spelling out in clear terms of assumptions all that is not considered, and still less attempting to integrate their findings into a broader framework. In our journals, we are getting a crop of ever more minute studies, which lack even attempts toward what the institutionalists demand: integration into a view of the whole social system. I find them therefore irrelevant and therefore uninteresting.

The institutional economists will so regularly stretch out their analyses into fields where, for reasons already hinted at, quantitative precision is not yet possible. This easily leads to a facile characterization of much of our research as qualitative instead of quantitative. But we are equally or more intent upon reaching quantitative knowledge as soon and as widely as possible. We are in fundamental agreement with Jeveon's old dictum, that more perfect knowledge is attainable only when we can measure conditions and changes of conditions.

The seemingly greater precision in conventional economic analysis is attained only by leaving out a whole world of relevant things. But as we institutionalists became accustomed and trained to treat matters that, though relevant, cannot easily be represented by figures, we have generally developed a more critical scrutiny of statistics. Particularly when conventional economists turn to discuss practical and political problems, but also in their abstract models, they too often with--with great carelessness--aggregate figures for gross national product or unemployment or other economic matters within their view. In their dealing with figures ordinary economists don't show the same urge for clear concepts and the same concern for estimating uncertainty of measurements, as, for instance, has always been standard in demographic research.

I should add that when institutional economists have to be critical of the closed models of their conventional colleagues, this does not, of course, imply that we are hostile to models and theories. But we want the models and theories--by us regularly conceived as logically integrated systems of questions to the empirical reality around us--to be more adequate to this reality.

X

I should at last point out that institutional economists generally are, at the same time, political economists. For all of us, as far as I know, economics is a moral science in Mill's meaning of the term. While ordinary economists, like most other social scientists, are what is known in the history of philosophy as "naive empiricists," having convinced themselves that they are simply dealing with observable facts, we institutionalists have been involved in the problem of how to account for the role of human valuations in research.

We are all utterly sceptical toward the welfare theory of ordinary economists. Since we cannot accept as a valuational basis for our research the outmoded moral philosophy and hedonistic psychology of our classical and neoclassical predecessors, we have to account for what other valuational basis we have for our research.

We have thus generally had our eyes open for prevailing biases in research when valuational assumptions are concealed, while the very idea of that type of opportunistic distortion is an almost forbidden thought in conventional economics. Studies of how influences from the surrounding society have conditioned economic research are almost missing in the writings of ordinary economists. Looking back, these influences are more apparent. I suspect the unwillingness to be aware of the problem of prevalent and systematic biases in economic research may be one of the explanations for the disinterest in the history of economics, about which I complained.

One common bias among most ordinary economists is the more or less explicit assumption of market rationality and optimality, while actual markets are becoming less and less perfect and in some areas disappearing altogether.

XI

I have so far been attempting to argue the case for political and institutional economics in terms of logic. When, however, I believe that soon it is destined to gain ground at the expense of conventional economics, it is not primarily because of the strength of its logic, but because it will be needed for dealing in an effective way with the practical and political problems that are now towering and threatening to overwhelm us. Much of present establishment economics, and in particular those very abstract theoretical constructs which up till now have enjoyed highest prestige among economists will, I believe, be left by the wayside as irrelevant and uninteresting.

Part II

IDEOLOGIES IN THE SOCIAL AND BEHAVIORAL SCIENCES, INEQUALITY AND DISTRIBUTIVE JUSTICE

Samuels develops the historical relations of ideology to the practice of economists and other social scientists in dealing with the problems of income distribution and with the phenomenon of inequality.

Beit-Hallahmi traces the ideological roots of the psychological explanations of income inequalities, distinguishing between conservative, liberal and radical interpretations of the same body of facts.

Barry subjects the methodological assumptions and ideological implications of the policy sciences to critical philosophical scrutiny, and goes on to suggest how the empirical research of the social sciences might help clarify the philosopher's conceptions in dealing with the problem of distributive justice.

3. The Historical Treatment of the Problem of Value Judgements: An Interpretation

Warren J. Samuels

This chapter will venture to explain the ways in which economists and other social scientists have dealt with the problems of values, or valuation, particularly in relation to income distribution.

Ideology as well as the (narrower) problem of values must be taken into account.(1) By "ideology" I mean systems of belief concerning the definition of reality and values, or the combination of "is" and "ought" with regard to some field of action. By the "problem of values" I mean determination of what ought to be, the choice of goals or objectives, the formation of priorities, particularly at the level of public policy.(2)

Ideas of (1) reality and (2) values are not mutuallly exclusive: Values may be defined in "is" terms (although it is strictly impossible to derive an "ought" from an "is" alone; however, "oughts" often masquerade as "is" statements); and, too, values may be and frequently are used to define reality.(3) The differentiation of "is" and "ought" is quite difficult to accomplish in practice.

The first part of the chapter presents conclusions regarding the ultimate subject matter of the value problem; the second, more substantive conclusions regarding the handling of and/or responses to the value problem.

THE DOMAIN OF THE VALUE PROBLEM

The overriding questions on which the value problem and all valuation touches are, Whose interests are to count, and conversely, Whose interests are to be sacrificed? What is the mode or modes by which interests are perceived and acted upon? What is the mode or modes by which interests are weighted and some chosen over others?

Economics, qua scientific, professional discipline, evolved as both an explanation and a justificaton of the existing economic order. Both explanation and justification are fundamental social processes, and in practice the two have been deeply and perhaps inextricably intertwined. Accordingly, economics has been impregnated with valuation, both in relation to the system itself and with regard to specific values (interests).

From a somewhat different and broader perspective (but to the same effect), economics has had three roles and therefore three facets of meaning: in the extension of knowledge, in the exercise of social control, and as a psychic balm. Though economists may consider themselves to be principally engaged in the pursuit of knowledge, the discipline has served, and not merely through deliberate attempts to influence policy, as both social control and psychic balm. It has helped to define our perception of socioeconomic reality, values, the possible, the likely, and the desirable, and has served to set minds at rest by providing a sense of order, coherence, oneness, permanence, and certitude.(4) Thus, as with art and religion, in certain of its aspects economics partakes in the provision of myths, symbols, and what Pareto called "derivations" (rationalizations),(5) as one facet of the social comprehension and construction of reality.(6) In all these respects, values have permeated economic thought.

An inescapable, value-based issue for economics and the other social sciences is the problem of order--namely, the continuing reconciliation of freedom (or autonomy) with control, continuity with change, and hierarchy with equality. These antinomies, often perceived as the conflict of the individual with society, refer ultimately to the structure of power. Here also arise questions of the relation of order to choice, the specifics of order and of choice, the relative reliance upon deliberative and nondeliberative decision making and between different modes of rationality, and the static versus the dynamic perspective upon reality. Valuations in the social sciences ultimately deal with the problem of order and its ramifications.

Valuations in economics, often only implicit, ultimately deal with the normative structure of society. They may treat that structure as a whole. More typically, they selectively reinforce or weaken certain of its components.

The question of distribution--of income, wealth, and power--is central, not peripheral, to the domain of the value problem in economics. The biting edge of the problem of order, whether specified in terms of freedom versus control, continuity versus change, or hierarchy versus equality--but most conspicuously, of course, the last--is ultimately the distribution of opportunity, power, autonomy, and exposure to the opportunity, freedom, and power of others, with the distributions of income and wealth as cause and consequence of these.

Ours is a world of radical indeterminacy in which socioeconomic order is created in part through both our efforts to apprehend it and our choices and normative valuations concerning it. Determinate solutions are evolved from an array of contingent possibilities. In this valuational process, economics is a force and economists are actors, not solely observers.

THE TREATMENT OF VALUE JUDGEMENTS

Certain tensions mark the treatment of value judgements in economics. There is tension between a desire for, even a commitment to, value-free analysis, and a sense that evaluation is unavoidable. And, related to this, there is a tension between a desire to be policy-relevant and the intention of being scientific, safely beyond those conflictual issues of distribution and order and the transient problems of policy choice. Tension arises from a felt need to differentiate between economists in their capacities as economists and as citizens. However difficult it may be to distinguish in practice between these two roles, a belief in the possibility and desirability of doing so has been one important response to the value problem. Economists would like to have something important if not definitive and dispositive to say on policy, while remaining perceived (and self-perceived) as objective scientists. While for some economists, all this is seriously disturbing, most of them blithely ignore the problem of values, identifying themselves with an ideology of positive science that rules values out of scientific bounds and provides a confidence (possibly misplaced) that diligent attention to technique and certain other rules will avoid the intrusion of values.

The tensions are most manifest in the so-called applied fields--in public finance, for example--between those who believe that through the tools of theory, policy problems are amenable to a purely technical resolution and those who see that tax and expenditure policy is pervaded with values and that technical solutions inevitably are secondary to normative judgements. Price analysis also reflects this dichotomy of outlook, juxtaposing the technical and the normative. For some, market prices are objectively given and therefore nonnormative. For others, prices are coefficients of choice which give effect to the underlying power structure (including income and wealth distribution). This structure governs whose interests will or will not be registered in the market and count as a cost to others; hence it can be questioned by reference to a structure of power that is, in turn, a function of policy and a subject for choice. The intrusion of values is nowhere more evident than in this controversy over the positive versus the normative character of market prices and the relevance of the distribution-specific character of prices and optimal solutions in resource allocation.(7)

Glenn Johnson and Lewis Zerby(8) have identified the following value-related practices of economists (and, by extension, all social scientists). They may engage in outright normativism, asserting specific answers to questions about goodness and badness per se independent of "is" considerations. Sometimes they engage in pragmatism, presupposing that the values of means and ends are interdependent and that workability is a valid criterion for determining the acceptability of means and ends.

Many economists, committed to positivism, deny that values enter into their analysis, but in fact practice a conditional normativism, taking as given certain ends that define the problem, and/or normative concepts, from which the desirable and the undesirable can be deduced. In those terms the economist seeks his optimizing solutions. Differentiating between (1) what is the case, (2) what ought to be the case, and (3) what is necessary or instrumentally useful given what ought to be the case, it is an approach seen by some as an exercise in social engineering and not normative at all.(9)

It is no doubt the general sharing of a common belief system under the aegis of middle-class society that has permitted the relatively easy coexistence among these diverse value-related practices. Positivism itself, as the ideology of value-free science, may be seen at least in part as a response to the problem of values. Certainly those who see in positivist economics essentially bourgeois apologetics have this view, but so also do those who believe that there is a symbiotic relationship between what is and the study of what is, each casting luster upon the other. However, the determinants of ideology, including values, are complex and go beyond (although they do not exclude) considerations of class and the specific conditions of a particular period. The principal points, however, following Johnson and Zerby, are that economists exhibit a diversity of practices in response to the problem of valuation, and that the principal practice is conditional normativism or instrumentalism.

Historically the outlook on values has been

ambivalent. Whatever lip service has been given to their importance, they have generally been left out of serious discussion, overshadowed by the drive (sometimes but not always under the aegis of science) to discover transcendent principles and general laws. During the last two centuries the discipline has been formed under the imperative of natural science with the assertion of natural economic laws, and eventually, with Alfred Marshall, of laws conceived only as statements of behavioral tendency. Nor in the nineteenth century were economists any longer confident of discovering and following a moral order which was pre-existent and pre-eminent to man.

The eighteenth century belief in an inner, innate order of moral intelligence was, by the late nineteenth century, replaced by a faith in an evolutionism wherein market survival selected the fittest institutions. The evolutionist mechanism provided a critique or defense of established institutions, necessarily value-laden.

All this, moreover, was but one facet of a regnant utilitarianism which takes the market as its value-reference, and which has dominated the profession of economics to the present day: Cost-effectiveness, however technically specified, has meant at once an agnostic attitude toward institutions and the selective valuations of particular institutions.

The quest for a value-neutral science was perhaps less a response to the threat of Marx and socialism and more to a desire to give to professional work the patina of science. Mechanistic theorizing comports with utilitarian calculations in the effort to avoid value dilemmas. The ideology of science nurtured by Nassau Senior, John Neville Keynes, Lionel Robbins, and most mainstream economists has provided comfort and guidance to its practitioners. Others, however, have stressed that economics nonetheless has been a means of formulating and expressing an ideological-valuational system (indeed, as will be seen below, such has been accepted by some as a professional obligation).

Therefore some have argued that the profession does (but should not) tend to accept uncritically valuations and ideologies that are system-specific, and furthermore that both the oversimplification of the entitlement system of society and the selective specificaton of rights concerning whose interests are to count, have served to introduce into problem construction and theory design important but implicit normative premises. Thus, for example, economics (and not solely the modern neoclassical theory of property rights) exhibits and gives (selective) effect to the systemic myth of the possibility of the Lockean view of inalienable property rights.

It remains true that most work in economics is

undertaken without sustained, direct attention to valuational elements. Technique (quantitative formalism) and "objective" data are seen as a guarantee of scientific success, without having to give attention to the normative premises entering into discourse. Values are not avoided but made invisible. It is awareness of the value problem, and not the introduction of values, that is shunned. The treatment of values, such as it is, is largely covert and tertiary, not central, open, and fundamental.

Economists have tended to take general systemic values as given, their working procedures expressing deep structural and valuational elements in the societal (and professional) belief system. But that general system of values has been used only selectively, especially in the case of rights. The nominal exclusion of the normative structure of society (its power structure and institutions) from the domain of conscious economic thought has removed certain problems from the scope of policy analysis, while at the same time selective assumptions about the normative structure of society inhere in analyses of theory and policy.

"Value free" is a principal theme in the ideology of science. But the social sciences clearly are only partly scientific in that sense. Their quest for determinate solutions to intellectual puzzles constitutes an avoidance of the necessity of choice given by radical indeterminacy. Social science gives a privileged position to its perception of the status quo: Social science explains what is and both reinforces and is reinforced by it. All this is complicated by the kaleidoscopic character and selective perception of the status quo. That selective perception is, ipso facto, valuational. Social science thus reifies its own presuppositions.

No wonder that empiricism has been criticized as making "a fetish of science as the correct description of those frozen structures that confront the individual as 'social reality'" and mistaking "the reified structures of immediate experience for permanent constituents of reality."(10) It would seem that for all the ideology of falsificationist verification in modern positive science, "The pretended privilege of the real world over the world of ideas" may be "nothing more than the privilege of one [value-laden] discursive order over another."(11)

Thus inevitably such science has political significance, and within its sociocultural situation, a functional significance with regard to the problem of order, the normative structure of society, social control, psychic balm, and so on. This certainly was the case with the economic theory of free trade in relation to free trade as a central tenet of nineteenth century liberalism; but such political significance exists even when the theorems are not identified with specific political programs.

For this and other reasons, the development of economics as a science is marked far more by Kuhnian sociological factors than Popperian canons of epistemological propriety. Valuational attractiveness, collegial acceptability, and paradigmatic consonance have been important conditions of cognitive acceptability and all are laden with valuation.

The tension between the canons of scientific objectivity and the desire to participate in the formation of policy should not be allowed to obscure the inherently normative character of the subject matter of economics and the other social sciences. Nor should it be allowed to obscure the fact that it is exceedingly difficult, if not impossible, seriously to discuss normative subjects in a strictly positive (that is, value-free) way.

Criticism of extant arrangements and policies (for example, protectionism) is often forthcoming from within the domain of economic orthodoxy. Such criticism derives from a singular set of inculcated normative premises and in no way signals a discourse open to the critical and free examination and demystification of established institutions and their underlying values. Heterodox (Marxist and institutionalist) economics exists in Western society largely only at the margins of the discipline. This phenomenon reflects as well the response to those questions regarding the problem of order, of methodology, and of distribution raised by the heterodox, and made invisible, explained away, or otherwise rationalized under the rule of _ceteris paribus_ by the orthodox.

It has been the role of economists, assumed since the early nineteenth century, to rationalize or justify the reigning economic order. Mainstream economics has been both an expression and the most sophisticated formulation of the systemic ideology and its value system. Deeply impregnated with values that perform a legitimizing and even obscurantist role, economics has served as an instrument of fundamental social control. Deliberately or not, economists have become the high priests of ideological liberalism in a search for and an articulation of an effective propaganda for economic freedom (in Frank Knight's felicitous phrase), simultaneously explaining and rationalizing the system.

The secularization of society and the disembedded character of the economy (in Karl Polanyi's sense) seem to have left some economists with a felt need to provide a secular substitute for the old religion in a world dominated by the economic, especially with regard to perceived threats to the system and its distributive processes. Accordingly, for example, whereas in the early nineteenth century, the defense of the established system was conducted largely (though not solely) in terms of class, by the late nineteenth century rationalization had turned largely from hierarchic to individualist forms, the very concept of class being considered passé if not heretical. Rationalization by virtue of power structure turned into rationalization denying and ignoring (and thereby rendering invisible) the power structure. Affirmation of control by class turned into affirmation of reliance on the market, wherein, presumably, no real control prevailed. This is amply evident in the history of nineteenth century value theory, but nowhere is this more marked than in the theory of distribution.

The discipline's prevailing rationalization has involved the wholesale omission of conflict. The discipline has adopted harmony models, and indeed a harmony paradigm, as its principal world view: The notion of a continual reconciliation of divergent interests through the market, the idea of a perpetual reaching toward equilibrium, the presumption of Pareto Optimality--all project the value-laden nuances of harmony as opposed to conflict. Again, nowhere is this more marked than in the theory of distribution.

Distribution is a key topic wherein values are inherently functional. Beliefs about income, wealth, poverty, entitlement, productivity, and so on, are critical in defining problems and suggesting solutions--and in channeling the uses to which government is put. The history of distribution theory is in no small part a history of efforts to establish and defend lines of reasoning that would both explain and rationalize market-based distribution (profit, interest, and rent) in the face of criticism.

There have been three principal approaches to distribution in the history of economics. The neoclassical approach assumes a given initial set of entitlements and explores income distribution as a matter of the disaggregation of productivity through factor pricing. It further supposes that the initial set of entitlements, taken to include the distribution of wealth in all forms, reflects the accumulation of past contributions to production.

The Marxian approach also begins with a given initial set of entitlements but explores income distribution as a matter of exploitation based on class (as it were) ownership versus nonownership of the means of production. The distribution of property, that is, the initial set of entitlements, is understood as the consequence of prior expropriations and exploitation. The conclusions of analysis and their implications for policy derive logically for both systems from their respective premises of individual productivity cum market harmony in the one instance, and property-based exploitation cum class conflict in the other.

A third approach may be called the Weberian or institutionalist. Whereas the neoclassical and Marxist are heavily normative and value-laden (and derive their sharp thrust therefrom), the institutionalist approach is relatively agnostic (and therefore much less ideologically bound). It begins with a given set of initial entitlements, however acquired, and then explores income distribution as arising from a generalized contest over income and output. Its emphasis is on appropriation and therefore a general analysis of power: Each economic actor or subgroup is portrayed as attempting to appropriate, however it can, as much of the income stream for itself as it can, without any necessary attribution of justification (as by productivity) or condemnation (as with exploitation).

Although it has been said that orthodox, neoclassical economics neglects distribution and the resulting value problem (which it does with respect to considerations raised by the other two approaches), the situation is less one of neglect than of confining the analysis of distribution, and thereby the value problem, within the limits of productivity analysis. For neoclassical thought the issue of income distribution is secondary to the increase in the magnitude of what is to be distributed, that is, secondary to economic growth. On that account its emphasis on economic efficiency puts the question of distribution into the shade.

Furthermore, analysis within the neoclassical rubric always is coupled with selective, implicit, antecedent premises regarding whose interests are to count and thereby govern, however indirectly and implicitly, the distributional results. This is done in two general ways: first, through the selective identification of entitlements; and second, by (often selectively) using the existing distribution of wealth as the basis for resource allocation, price, efficiency, and distribution analysis. There is, however, no unique Pareto optimal (or efficient) solution. There are as many different Pareto optimal resource allocations as there are different distributions of entitlements. If there is any change in that set of rights and the relationships of prices, then the allocation of resources, the distribution of income, and the outputs themselves will all be changed as well.

Several considerations, largely implicit in the foregoing, deserve mention. First, the emphasis on technique serves, intentionally or inadvertently, to evade the value question while in no sense avoiding value-based analysis. Second, the preoccupation with mathematically determinate outcomes obscures the real process of choice, notwithstanding an acceptance of the economy as a decision-making process. Technical relationships are allowed to eclipse the underlying choice processes at work. Third, the focus on the value of efficiency (Pareto Optimality) excludes all other values (with the exception of economic growth) from consideration, to the point that an effort to take other values into account tends to discredit one's status as an economist. Moreover, Pareto Optimality is not so minimally normative as has been alleged; it masks a number of important and deep values.(12) Efficiency is postulated as the guiding criterion (especially in applied work but also in welfare economics, and in public choice, regulatory, and property rights theory) with selective premises of whose interests count implicitly in problem solving that leads to determinate answers that are thenceforth arrogantly asserted to be <u>the</u> economic, <u>the</u> efficient solution, to the exclusion of any other. Furthermore, the paradigm takes into account consumer utility and systematically eliminates other social values from analytical and policy consideration. For example, it eliminates satisfaction in being a group member and worker preferences, and thus it aborts considerations of power or questions concerning the restructuring of power.

Nineteenth century utilitarianism has been rendered safe (and "scientific") by exorcising its egalitarian implications. To analyze maximizing behavior from within given opportunity sets, under a rule that excludes the factors and forces that largely govern the composition and structure of opportunity sets, is surely to follow a value imperative, and one that is most strongly evident to those few economists, such as myself, who are concerned with the question of power in economic affairs.

Let me again stress the importance of selectiveness in the practice of economics. Without any value bias on the part of the model builders, and without a consciousness that in what is selected and, hence, what is excluded, there is of necessity a value-related choice; parameters are built into formalist models concerning for example, (1) the constituent elements of the problem of order (freedom, control, continuity, change, hierarchy, equality), (2) the circumstances of voluntary exchange, (3) legal rights and redefined legal rights (so as to permit optimal solutions), (4) individualism (specifically, which individuals, the relation of the individual to the legal system, de facto versus de jure opportunity, and the role of legal change), (5) injury and evidence of injury (one of the sources of problem identification and theory application), (6) competition, (7) market, and so on. And on these factors will depend the solutions that the model is capable of producing and, in turn, the policy recommendations derived from them: problem solutions and policy recommendations with predetermined answers to the critical value-related questions of whose interests are to count, who gets what, and which institutions will be protected and promoted, and which will not.

Values concerning power enter economic analysis not so much through ignoring power but by acting upon selective assumptions about the determinants of power. Although neoclassicism tends to define power solely in terms of control over price, power also involves the organization and control of the institutional structure of the economy, the interrelations between economic and political-legal processes, and the instrumental use of government by the agents of economic choice. Position itself in the socioeconomic complex and in the network of information flow is a significant element in the distribution of power. Specifically, the emphasis of economics on mechanistic models obscures to the point of invisibility not only the essential nature of choice but also power as an element in economic relationships and choice. Moreover, the assumptions built into the theory generally have the effect of supporting establishmentarian values, for example, in treating the megacorporation as merely another individual economic actor subordinated to the sanctifying sanctions of competition, while bridling at the dangerous powers of the trade union.

It is, of course, with regard to government that extensive and fundamental values are inevitably injected into economic analysis. Libertarian clamoring should not obscure the fact that the issue is never government versus no government, but always what role government is to have, and whose interests government is going to protect. Any specification of rights, any system for determining entitlements, implies and indeed requires that government protect certain interests and not others. To ignore the potential variability of rights and to take a system of entitlements as given, must build a value-bias into analysis. The pretense of the separability of economics and politics, however useful for making analysis manageable, permits the selective introduction of values, especially those values determining whose interests are to count through legal protection taken for granted in how the economy is defined.

In sum, legal institutions and arrangements, which again are almost always selectively specified, may be treated as given, objective facts or as normative, evolutionary, and power- and conflict-laden phenomena. The former approach converts a set of normative phenomena into an apparently positive set, and both make valuational issues of power invisible and permit the introduction of selective value-laden assumptions regarding power structure.

IN CONCLUSION

It is not the purpose of this chapter to pass judgement on the practice of economics and the other social sciences. I have tried rather to show the ways in which values have been dealt with, how they have in fact infiltrated allegedly value-free analysis, and the approaches to or the evasions of the inescapable problem of values. I have not ventured to suggest how the social disciplines and policy sciences ought to deal with values and evaluation.

It should be clear that for economics, distribution is, if not the bottom line, at least critical to the value problem. Howsoever we choose to deal with values, that choice will have distributional results. Therefore it is understandable that the treatment of the value problem has been profoundly influenced by economists' anxieties and aims concerning distribution as a central problem of political economy.

NOTES

1. See Warren J. Samuels, "Ideology in Economics," in Sidney Weintraub, ed., Modern Economic Thought (Philadelphia: University of Pennsylvania Press, 1977), pp. 467-484. Much of the discussion in this chapter is an extension of analysis presented therein, as well as in "The Nature and Scope of Economic Policy," in The Classical Theory of Economic Policy (Cleveland: World Publishing Co., 1966), pp. 237-309; "The History of Economic Thought as Intellectual History," History of Political Economy, Vol. 6 (Fall 1974), pp. 305-323; "Normative Premises in Regulatory Theory," Journal of Post Keynesian Economics, Vol. 1 (Fall 1978), pp. 100-114; "Interrelations Between Legal and Economic Processes," Journal of Law and Economics, Vol. 14 (October 1971), pp. 435-450; "Welfare Economics, Power and Property," in G. Wunderlich and W. L. Gibson, Jr., eds., Perspectives of Property (University Park: Institute for Research on Land and Water Resources, Pennsylvania State University, 1972), pp. 61-148; "An Economic Perspective on the Compensation Problem," Wayne Law

Review, Vol. 21 (November 1974), pp. 113-134; (with A. Allan Schmid) "Polluters: Profit and Political Response: The Dynamics of Rights Creation," *Public Choice*, Vol. 28 (Winter 1976), pp. 99-105; (with Nicholas Mercuro) "The Role and Resolution of the Compensation Principle in Society: Part One--The Role," *Research in Law and Economics*, Vol. 1 (1979), pp. 157-194; and "On the Nature of Economics as a Science and its Relation to Policy: The Example of Free Trade" (mimeographed).

2. The problem also arises--in a less clearly recognized but no less important way--in deliberative policy making by other large, powerful institutions, for example, the large corporation.

3. Karl Brunner, "Knowledge, Values and the Choice of Economic Organization," *Kyklos*, Vol. 23 (1970), pp. 558, 569 and passim.

4. *Ibid*, p. 558; G. L. S. Shackle, *The Years of High Theory* (New York: Cambridge University Press, 1967), p. 286 and passim; John Kenneth Galbraith, *The Affluent Society* (Boston: Houghton Mifflin, 2nd ed., Revised 1969); and George Lichtheim, *The Concept of Ideology and Other Essays* (New York: Vintage Books, 1967), p. 40.

5. Warren J. Samuels, *Pareto on Policy* (New York: Elsevier, 1974); see also "Legal Realism and the Burden of Symbolism: The Correspondence of Thurman Arnold," *Law and Society Review*, forthcoming.

6. Peter L. Berger and Thomas Luckmann, *The Social Construction of Reality* (Garden City, N.Y.: Anchor Books, 1966).

7. See Samuels, "On the Nature of Economics as a Science and its Relation to Policy," *op. cit.*

8. Glenn L. Johnson and Lewis K. Zerby, *What Economists Do About Values* (East Lansing: Center for Rural Manpower and Public Affairs, Michigan State University, 1973).

9. Yew-Kwang Ng, "Value Judgments and Economists' Role in Policy Recommendation," *Economic Journal*, Vol. 82 (September 1972), p. 1017.

10. Lichtheim, *op. cit.*, pp. 37, 45.

11. Keith Tribe, *Land, Labour and Economic Discourse* (Boston: Routledge & Kegan Paul, 1978), pp. 8-9.

12. See Samuels, "Normative Premises in Regulatory Theory," *op. cit.*

4. Ideology in Psychology: How Psychologists Explain Inequality

Benjamin Beit-Hallahmi

Economic inequality is a part of social structure, and contemporary psychology, with its individualistic orientation, tends to ignore the social, concentrating instead on internal, individual processes that are presumed to be universal for the species. But whenever psychologists move from the realm of the abstract and the universal to that which is particular to the individual, they are confronted with the effects of inequality. Aside from their interest in psychological inequalities, that is, individual differences on psychological measures, they are likely to encounter the issue of income inequality whenever they research social behavior in the real world. How then do they deal with psychological findings related to income inequality, and how are psychological concepts used to understand and explain its causes and consequences?

Income differences are not a psychological variable, but psychological variables may be related to income differences as causes, correlates, or consequences. What follows deals with the literature using psychological concepts (such as personality attributes, motivation, psychopathology, or "mental ability") whether produced by psychologists, psychiatrists, economists, or sociologists in relation to income inequality.

The interpretations of psychological findings to be surveyed in this chapter have clear policy implications. They can be categorized as conservative (opposed to social change), as liberal (favoring reform of the social order), or as radical (seeking a complete restructuring of the social system).

Research studies made with reference to social classes, socioeconomic status (SES), disadvantaged groups, deprived groups, underprivileged groups, and culturally deprived groups or individuals have found a significant correlation between personality development, scholastic ability, and other psychological traits, and income inequality. Controversy arises not over the facts (as long as the facts are simply defined as numbers, scores, or "data"), but in the interpretation of these facts in accordance with an idea of what social reality is and what it should be.

FINDINGS

Before we turn to purely psychological measures, there is a relevant body of evidence correlating physical health and social status with mortality rates for different social classes (Matras, 1973, 1975). Mortality rates are higher not only for men employed in lower income jobs, but also for their wives. Mortality rates are also inversely related to education (Kitagawa & Hauser, 1973). Higher mortality rates in low SES groups reflect a combination of higher levels of exposure to illness and disability, and lower levels of access to medical care (Matras, 1975). Berelson and Steiner (1964) summarize class differences in health as follows: "The higher the class, the lower the morbidity rate (including severe mental illness and suicide) and the lower the life expectancy--mainly due to the nutritive, hygienic, and medical advantages that money can buy" (p. 477).

The most consistent finding in all epidemiological studies of psychological disorders in relation to social background variables has been the inverse relationship between socioeconomic status and mental disorder (Hollingshead & Redlich, 1958; Coleman, Butcher, & Carson, 1980; Dohrenwend & Dohrenwend, 1969; Dohrenwend, 1975). The best summary of studies on social class and psychopathology, by Dohrenwend and Dohrenwend (1969), states that "20 out of 25 studies that presented data on the relationship with social class yielded the highest rate of judged psychopathology in the lowest economic stratum" (p. 16), and that "low socioeconomic status within a community is consistently found to be associated with relatively high overall rates of disorder and with high rates of both schizophrenia and personality disorder" (p. 31).

Langner (1963b) states that "persons of low SES . . . are suspicious, and have a fatalistic outlook on life. They do not plan ahead, a characteristic associated with their fatalism. They are prone to depression, have feelings of futility, lack of belongingness, friendlessness, and lack of trust in others. They are more authoritarian in their attitudes, stressing obedience, power, and hierarchical relations"

(p. 436). Differences between lower-class and middle-class individuals were also found in future orientation and time perspective (Schmidt, Lamm, & Trommsdorff, 1978). Middle-class individuals manifested a more extended future orientation, viewed the future more optimistically, and believed that the realization of their fears or hopes depended on their own actions.

The nondeferred gratification pattern has been often mentioned as a characteristic typical of the lower classes. Schneider and Lysgaard (1953) suggested that lower-class life is characterized by an inability to delay gratification, and by "impulse following" rather than "impulse renunciation." Miller, Riessman, & Seagull (1968) correctly pointed out that the findings regarding delay of gratification and social class are not clear, and that other factors seem to be at work to produce the reported differences. Nevertheless, the common generalization in the literature is that the nondeferred gratification pattern is typical of the lower class (cf Beilin, 1956; Straus, 1962). Thus, Phillips (1968) describes middle-class values as including "the postponement of immediate satisfactions in the service of long-range goals, acceptance of responsibility, and constructive use of one's time" (p. 46), while lower-class individuals opt for more immediate gratifications. This is interpreted in psychoanalytic terms as related to a deficient development of both ego and superego. Hollingshead and Redlich (1958) describe a "defective superego" as characteristic of lower-class children, and according to Coleman, Butcher, and Carson (1980), the "antisocial personality" pattern is more common in the lower class.

IQ TESTS, "MENTAL ABILITY," MENTAL RETARDATION, AND INCOME INEQUALITY

We will use the term "IQ test" because there is really no agreement in the literature on what the tests measure, but many authorities agree that it does not measure intelligence in the normal sense of the term (cf Hudson, 1972). IQ tests, nevertheless, have become the most popular psychological instrument, and they have been used extensively. IQ scores are positively correlated with achievement in formal schooling. Findings on IQ differences, when social classes are compared, have been reported many times, by many sources (Johnson, 1948; Conway, 1959; Stewart, 1947; Harrell & Harrell, 1945; Ball, 1938). IQ differences related to social class were reported as early as 1916, by Terman. There are also well-known studies by Burt (1959, 1961) but these are regarded today as total fabrications. When findings of differences in IQ levels are presented, the socioeconomic measure used is normally occupational level (Eysenck, 1971). The division into occupational levels fits rather well with prestige ratings (Duncan, 1961).

In all of these studies, IQ measured by standard psychological tests correlated positively with social status, which was measured usually by occupational groupings. Members of professional and managerial occupational groups averaged more than one standard deviation above the mean (100), while members of the skilled and unskilled labor groups scored just below and above the mean.

Social class becomes a crucial variable in child development, starting at birth: "The data from . . . logitudinal studies of prenatal and perinatal complications have yet to produce a single predictive variable more potent than the familial and socioeconomic characteristics of the caretaking environment" (Sameroff, 1979, p. 128). How early these developmental differences appear is shown by Sameroff, Bakow, and McComb (1978), who report a higher heart rate in the newborn babies of lower-income groups. Lower income is positively correlated with a higher incidence of prematurity, physical and neural defects in infants, and infant mortality (Birch & Gussow, 1970). These early difficulties are likely to continue later on during infancy and childhood (Sameroff & Chandler, 1975).

Differences in the behavior of children are related to the way their parents socialize them, so that we can assume differences in parenting styles related to income levels. The evidence from several studies indicates that lower-class parents are more likely to emphasize obedience, while middle-class parents tend to be more permissive and encourage self-control in their children (Kohn, 1977; Pearlin & Kohn, 1966; Rapp, 1961).

Gecas (1979) provided the most comprehensive survey of literature on social class and socialization. We will report his generalizations, based on the research of the past 50 years. SES has been found to be positively related to egalitarian relationships between parents and children, and to emphasis on independence and achievement. SES is negatively related to the use of commands and imperatives by parents, and is positively related to the use of personal appeals on the part of parents. Another aspect of parenting is the extreme mistreatment of children by their parents. Here we find income level differences as well.

Child abuse in families is negatively correlated with income. It tends to occur more often in poorer families (Gil, 1970; Pelton, 1980). Phillips (1968) summarizes the findings on psychological development as follows: "The social class level of parents appears to influence developmental rate, with those born into middle-class (and presumably also upper class) levels appearing relatively more advanced and those of lower-class levels relatively less advanced in psychological development" (p. 48).

THE PROTESTANT ETHIC, ACHIEVEMENT MOTIVATION, AND INCOME INEQUALITY

Achievement motivation, defined as the internal disposition to compete against a standard of excellence (not necessarily against somebody else), is sometimes seen as a psychological elaboration of the Protestant ethic (Weber, 1904). McClelland (1961) suggested that the Protestant ethic ideal produces a certain way of child rearing, which leads to higher levels of achievement motivation. This particular way of child rearing emphasizes early independence, and is more prevalent in certain social groups. McClelland (1961) claimed quite explicitly that higher levels of achievement are related to both collective and individual economic progress, that is, to economic growth on the collective level, and to social mobility on the individual level. He found achievement level differences between social classes, with the middle class higher on the average.

A different version of the same idea was presented by Strodtbeck (1958), who contends that there is an American achievement ethic whose values are learned by children in their families--values that include a "belief that the world is orderly and amenable to rational mastery . . . A willingness to leave home to make one's way in life . . . A preference for individual rather than collective credit for work done" (pp. 186-187). Such values are more likely to be learned in middle-class families, and middle-class children are correspondingly more liable to acquire the achievement ethic. Rosen (1956), who divided his respondents into five classes, found a perfect correlation between class level and achievement motivation, and numerous later studies have found that need for achievement is positively correlated with socioeconomic status (Jessor & Richardson, 1968).

RELIGIOSITY AND INCOME INEQUALITY

The relationship between religiosity and income levels varies depending on the nature of the behavior observed (Argyle & Beit-Hallahmi, 1975). The correlation between income and formal participation in religious activities is positive, that is, higher income is tied to greater participation. When it comes to religious beliefs, the opposite is true. As Lynd and Lynd (1929) observed, "Members of the working class show a disposition to believe their religion more ardently and to accumulate more emotionally charged values around their beliefs" (p. 329). Johnson (1962) showed that members of the working class held more fundmentalist religious beliefs, which in turn were related to conservative political attitudes. Many other studies show a clear relationship between lower income and fundamentalist religiosity. Lower-income groups also provide the membership for the majority of religious sects and cults, and report more "religious experiences" (Argyle & Beit-Hallahmi, 1975).

PERSONAL LOCUS OF CONTROL AND INCOME INEQUALITY

The sense of personal or internal control of the environment, measured by a well-known psychological instrument (Rotter, Seeman, & Liverant, 1962), has been found to be lacking in lower-class children and adults (Jessor & Richardson, 1968). Members of lower income groups express a belief in the externality of control, that is, a belief that their lives are directed from the outside, and they have little control over their fate (Battle & Rotter, 1963; Campbell et al, 1977; Ramey & Campbell, 1976).

A related research finding has to do with the concept of field dependence. Lower-class membership has been associated with low levels of field independence, that is, "self consistent patterns of thought and behavior that individuals use when interacting with their environment. . . . The independent pattern requires the imposing of structure on unstructured fields or the restructuring of previously structured fields. The dependent pattern reflects an undifferentiated or global response to both structured and unstructured fields" (MacEacheron & Gruenfeld, 1978, pp. 49-50).

SELF-ESTEEM AND INCOME INEQUALITY

Rosenberg and Pearlin (1978) found that the relationship between social class and self-esteem depended on the age of the individuals involved. For children, there was no relationship at all, for adolescents a modest relationship, and for adults a moderate relationship. When found, the relationship was inverse: Lower class related to lower self-esteem. The authors explain the findings on the basis of the fact that the child is less aware of social class differences and status comparisons. In addition, "by the adult, social class is interpreted as an outcome of one's own behavior, by the child, it is not" (p. 72). We may conclude that with the passage of time, the individual is socialized into learning the psychological meaning of economic inferiority. Phillips (1968) described "strong feelings of inferiority and inadequacy and low self esteem" (p. 44) as characterizing members of the lower class. Bakke (1940) reported that unemployed workers during the depression felt personally responsible for their economic failure. Other findings indicate that the lower-class individual has a variety of negative feelings about himself, and about his self. These feelings include a sense of inadequacy, inferiority feelings, shame, self-doubt, and self-accusation for presumed failure (Sennet & Cobb, 1972).

REPORTED HAPPINESS AND INCOME INEQUALITY

Easterlin (1974) reported that a positive association between income and happiness was found in every one of 19 countries studied. Bradburn (1969), Gurin, Veroff, & Feld (1960), and Wilson (1967) reported similar findings. Inkeles (1960), summarizing such findings, stated:

> Those who are economically well off, those with more education or whose jobs require more training and skill, more often report themselves happy, joyous, laughing, free of sorrow, satisfied with life's progress. Even though the pattern is weak or ambiguous in some cases, there has not been a single case of a *reversal* of the pattern, that is, a case where measures of happiness are inversely related to measures of status, in studies involving fifteen different countries. . . . There is, then, good reason to challenge the image of the "carefree but happy poor" (p. 17, italics in original).

Andrews and Withey (1976) studied the life satisfaction of the American population and reported that

> A feeling of deprivation is also apparent in the responses of low SES people to questions on their physical needs, their health, their jobs, and to some extent, in the amount of fun and enjoyment they experience. A picture of sharp discouragement also appears in their evaluations of their chances

of getting a good job, if they tried, and the degree to which they were achieving success and getting ahead (p. 294).

Though the picture is not totally bleak, and low SES people reported some satisfactions in interpersonal relationships, the authors state that "They appear preoccupied and overwhelmed with the clear problems of being poor" (p. 295). In terms of self-reports on happiness and progress, similar differences were found: "As SES increased, feelings of general well being--from both absolute and relative perspectives--increased, as did reports of satisfaction and happiness" (p. 335). Campbell and associates (1976) reported a clear positive correlation between income and degree of happiness, as indicated by the percentage of respondents describing themselves as "very happy" in a nationwide survey.

SUMMARY OF RESEARCH FINDINGS

Our survey of the research literature on psychological variables and income inequality is by no means comprehensive. We did not attempt to cover all areas where findings have been reported. To mention two examples, we did not cover how sexual behavior and aspirations and ambitions are related to income levels. Nevertheless, our survey deals with the best known, and most meaningful patterns of differences among individuals coming from different income levels. Our survey shows that most studies that have looked for social class differences have found them in the form of deficiencies (lower scores) in the lower class. Some studies have found no differences, but almost no studies show the lower class to be superior. These findings can lead one to establish clear psychological deficits in the lower classes.

One way of summarizing the findings is by pointing to obvious connections between economic inequality and psychological inequality. There is a clear correlation between income and level of psychological development and actualization in both children and adults. Poverty, the existence of significant numbers of individuals at the lower end of the income distribution who live far below the average living standards of the population, has been defined as a problem in the social science literature. The problem of poverty has often been defined in psychological terms as a form of social deviance, or the result of psychological deviance. To paraphrase F. Scott Fitzgerald, the poor are different from you and me--they're just not like the rest of us.

Knupfer (1947) proposed an early description of

the "culture of poverty" in a sympathetic and compassionate discussion of the underdog: "The economic and educational limitations accompanying low status produce a lack of interest in and a lack of self-confidence in dealing with certain important areas of our culture; as a result, there is reduced participation . . . in these areas" (p. 104). Knupfer summarized the experience of lower-income groups in stating that "closely linked with economic underprivilege is psychological underprivilege" (p. 114).

The findings of all social science and medical science research on the effects of poverty can be simply summarized by the familiar warning label, "Poverty is hazardous to your physical and mental health." In a positive way, we can summarize the findings by saying that, from a psychological point of view, high income is not only advisable, but highly recommended.

Keniston (1979) stated that "virtually every index of harm to children, from death at birth to poor school performance, from malnutrition to low self-esteem, is firmly associated with poverty" (p. ix). And "Almost every index of physical, human, and spiritual harm to children is strongly associated with inequalities of income" (p. xi). We could extend these generalizations to include not only children, but adults as well, adults who are naturally the parents of those children. As stated above, we will not discuss specifically any findings regarding blacks as an ethnic group in the United States. Not all lower-class members are black, but most blacks are by any measure in the low SES stratum; hence all findings with regard to lower-class or low-SES individuals apply to the black majority. When differences between blacks and white lower-class members occur in the literature, most often the blacks show even greater differences (or psychological deficits), compared to the middle class.

Most of the findings reported so far are beyond dispute. It is the interpretation of the data that becomes controversial. The internal psychological deficit is clearly related to an external economic deficit. The question is in the direction of causation. Do the psychological deficits displayed by the members of the lower classes precede or follow income differences? Are they causal or caused? For example, the findings show clearly that the more prosperous members of society have higher IQ scores. The question is whether this finding reflects a causal relationship (from IQ to success), a correlate (going both ways) or a consequence (from success to IQ). These classifications themselves imply a hierarchy that reflects the values of the classifier. Indeed Sherwood and Nataupsky (1968) have shown that there is a social psychology of innate versus environmental interpretations in psychological research. They found that those favoring hereditarian interpretations tend to come from higher socioeconomic backgrounds.

In the discussions that follow and constitute the rest of this chapter, we will classify interpretations, roughly and tentatively, into three schools of thought: the conservative, the liberal, and the radical. The essence of the difference between these three can be found in their attitude toward the existing social order. The conservatives would explain and justify social reality in its present form. The liberals analyze existing realities, recognize deficiencies, and are ready to weigh the costs and benefits of piecemeal change. The radicals are committed a priori to an overall structural transformation. In the particular instance these distinctions will be blurred; and though, as a matter of didactic convenience, we will differentiate viewpoints and schools of thought categorically, one might more appropriately think in terms of a conservative-liberal, and a liberal-radical continuum.

There is even a difference in the use of labels among the different schools. Conservatives are likely to refer to the lower class, liberals to the disadvantaged, radicals to the workers. There are differences also in the sorts of inquiries undertaken. Conservatives study the differences in IQ, liberals are interested in childhood development, radicals focus on the psychological effects of economic crisis.

THE CONSERVATIVE INTERPRETATION

Hogan and Emler (1978) listed as the two first assumptions of psychological conservatism, a belief in an innate human nature, where "differences in native endowments lead to differential status" (p. 483), hence where economic inequality is the result of psychological inequality. Because it has its source in an inherent inequality of talent, economic inequality is inevitable and inescapable. Innate psychological characteristics leading to differential achievement explain the observed economic inequalities. Psychological differences cause (and explain) income differences. Economic status is a function of the individual's contribution to society, and that contribution depends on innate psychological qualities.

As we will see later, liberals also emphasize the importance of psychological variables as determinants of income variance but look upon these traits as acquired rather than inherited. In the conservative-liberal continuum there is a common stress on the importance of psychological characteristics in the causation of income differences, but disagreement over the origins of these psychological factors. The liberal-radical continuum stresses the environmental sources of psychological differences, with disagreement over the primacy of economic and social structure as the essential determinant of income differences.

"Can it be that the class structure of modern society is essentially a function of the innately differing intellectual and other qualities of people making up these classes?" (Eysenck, 1973, p. 19). Those who pose this question are usually those who answer it, and with a resounding affirmative. Such is the essence of the conservative view. The conservative doctrine of reward and punishment is expressed here in material rewards not for actions, but for innate qualities, over which the individual has no choice and no control. Choose the right parents, and you'll be rewarded.

Conservatives often refer to the functional theory of stratification, that is, the necessity of differential rewards in society, and then explain differential rewards as the result of innate potentials. Thus, in a classical exposition of the conservative position, Hollingworth (1926) states: "A competitive social-economic system . . . secures the full services of the intelligent, for the common use. These services could probably not be secured in any other way, human nature being what it is. Not even intellect is likely to work hard and long for nothing" (p. 358). But later on Hollingworth switches to a purely hereditary explanation of the stratification system:

> One who comprehends at first hand the facts which we have endeavored to discuss in this volume, has insight in the failure of realization [sic], which has been the common lot of various schemes proposed for economic Utopia. These schemes do not found themselves on the existing distribution of biological endowment. Their authors do not always remember that men have for their sustenance only that which they are able to obtain from the earth by mental and physical labor, and apparently they do not know that only a few men have, or ever can develop, sufficient power of thinking to secure large surplus returns for their labor. The immemorial division of mankind into "lower," "middle," and "upper" classes, economically speaking, rests on a biological foundation which guarantees the stubborn permanence with which it persists in spite of all efforts to abolish it by artifice (p. 360).

Pastore (1949) succinctly summarizes Hollingworth's view by stating: "She was convinced that the justness of the present economic system was assured because it was rooted in psychological and biological law" (p. 105).

The contemporary conservative viewpoint has been clearly expressed in the writings of Burt (1969), Eysenck (1971, 1973), Jensen (1969), and Herrnstein (1973). Herrnstein (1973) offers the most detailed conservative explanation of social class differences in IQ: "For my purposes, inherited individual differences said something interesting about the membership of social classes. . . . Or to put it more simply, social position tends to run in families for genetic, as well as for social reasons" (p. 13). And "the main premises of my argument are that there are inherited differences in IQ and that IQ contributes, in some measure, and by some means, to what our society (at least) considers success" (p. 48).

Herrnstein summarizes the conservative view of inequality as caused by inherited psychological abilities in his famous syllogism:

> For if mental capacity is to any degree inherited social standing must be a mirror, albeit an imperfect one, of inherited ability. Moreover, as society equalizes the opportunities for advancement, which is to say as society becomes fairer, by the ordinary standards of fairness, it will tend more and more to base its social distinctions on genetic grounds. In other words, if parents no longer can pass social and economic advantages on to their children--let us say, because of taxes and welfare and public housing and uniformly excellent public schools--they will instead contribute to their children's success and failure only by their generic legacy . . . Equalizing educational opportunity may have the unwelcome effect of emphasizing the inborn intellectual differences between people (1973, pp. 9-10).

Here Herrnstein predicts that the effects of liberal reforms will not be to reduce inequality, but to increase it.

Conservative interpretations of social class differences have mostly dealt with the findings on IQ. Another finding that has been the subject of conservative interpretation is the finding of the inverse relationship between class level and psychopathology, and especially psychosis. The conservative theory of social selection, or downward-drift, suggests that more mentally disordered people are found among lower-income groups because such people's psychological problems make them drift downward in the social structure; the result is an accumulated buildup of social residue at the bottom of the social hierarchy.

The "drift" hypothesis has received little support in research studies, and all the major studies (Hollingshead & Redlich, 1958; Srole, Langner, Michael, Opler, & Rennie, 1962; Dunham, 1955) showed no support for it (cf Schwab & Schwab, 1978). Kohn (1973) stated that "the weight of evidence lies against the drift hypothesis providing a sufficient explanation of the class-schizophrenia relationship" (p. 64). Rejecting the conservative ideology behind the "drift" hypothesis, Dunham (1955) stated, "we shall see the 'drift' hypothesis for what it really is, namely, an attempt to annihilate the significance of the ecological findings in much the same fashion that certain persons during the thirties tried to dismiss the depression by explaining the loss of a job on the basis of a person's neurotic makeup or emotional stability" (pp. 174-175).

There are conservative psychiatrists, such as Lamb and Zusman (1979), who simply do not believe that difficult life circumstances lead to psychological difficulties. They claim that mental illness is determined genetically, and hence is not preventable. A conservative "interactionist" explanation for the higher prevalence of psychiatric disorder in the lower class is offered by Brill (1978), who believes that the lower class represents a depository of genetic predisposition to mental illness, which together with a "distorted perception of reality," and real life difficulties, produce mental disorders and prevent upward mobility.

There are few conservative interpretations of specific findings in areas other than IQ scores and psychopathology. As has been noted, in the works of the leading conservatives one finds an assumption of an "invisible hand" in the form of genetic selection, which leads to a variety of behavioral differences (Burt, 1969). Banfield (1970, 1974) seems to believe in the existence of class subcultures, which may be transmitted through learning but are just as effective in keeping people in their class as genetic selection.

If all individuals have the freedom to compete in the marketplace for their economic rewards, under the conditions of free enterprise, then differences in their success in the marketplace and the resulting class structure must be the result of differences in native ability. Hence, given an equal opportunity to compete in a free and fair marketplace, the psychologist can do no more than report the results of a "natural selection" that makes innate psychological differences manifest as income differentials. The conservatives (together with the liberals, as we will see later on) believe in success as a reward, which, in their case, is often a reward for innate qualities. "You get what you deserve" and you succeed if "You've got what it takes."

Not much attention is paid to the losers. The question is what makes the winners win. The established connection between superior scores on psychological tests and high income seems to be a clear justification of the existing distribution. The effect of this outlook is to legitimize the existing social order. The conservative interpretation assumes a good, or even perfect, correlation between the unequal distribution of individual talents and abilities and the unequal distribution of economic rewards in society. The justification for the existing inequality is explicit. Unlike the writer of the Book of Ecclesiastes (9:11), the conservatives believe that the race is to the swift, the battle to the strong, the bread to the wise, the favor to men of skill, and the riches to men of understanding. It is not a matter of time and chance, but a matter of getting what you deserve, and deserving what you get.

THE LIBERAL INTERPRETATION

John Stuart Mill--whom Burt (1969) called a "philosophical radical"--articulated the basic social critique of the liberals and the radicals more than a century ago, thus:

> I have long felt that the prevailing tendency to regard all the marked distinctions of human character as innate, and in the main indelible, and to ignore the irresistible proofs that by far the greater part of those differences, whether between individuals, races, or sexes, are such as not only might but naturally would be produced by differences in circumstances, is one of the chief hindrances to the rational treatment of great social questions, and one of the greatest stumbling blocks to human improvement (1969, p. 162).

Hogan and Emler (1978) describe individualism as the dominant idea in contemporary social psychology, together with a liberalism that tends to deny the existence of innate differences among people. What Hogan and Emler (1978) write about the ideology of social psychology can be extended to cover academic psychology and applied psychology as a whole (Beit-Hallahmi, 1974, 1977a, 1977b). The liberals, like the conservatives, emphasize internal-psychological causation of income differences, adopting and promoting the ideology of success.

The ideology of success and individual achievement asserts that individuals attain social positions and social rewards on the basis of their merits: mental abilities, motives and ambitions, and hard work. Liberals accept the elemental conservative metaphor of the race for economic success, which regards the individual as competing against others and against himself in a race, with success marking the finish line. The expression "most likely to succeed" in the judgement of high school classmates is an expression of the ideology that sees success as the result of a configuration of individual qualities.

A purely psychological liberal explanation of income differences would go something like this: Differences in abilities and performance lead to differences in success, with compensation awarded accordingly. The end result is an unequal distribution of income and the existence of social classes. This is really a translation of the functionalist sociological explanation of stratification, presented by Davis (1949) as follows: "Social inequality is thus an unconsciously evolved device by which societies ensure that the most important positions are conscientiously filled by the most qualified individuals" (p. 367). The psychological qualities involved in economic success are not necessarily innate, according to the liberal view. The need for achievement (McClelland, 1961) can be learned and can be increased, but it is still an internalized, psychological factor.

The liberal view of individual success as dependent on acquired personal characteristics is expressed in a cynical, exploitive way in a title of a book by Hawes, Weiss, and Weiss (1980): <u>How To Raise Your Child To Be A Winner</u>. The book purports to be "a proven program that shows how to guide your child--from infancy on--to ultimate self-fulfillment," because "what Dr. Spock's book was to the physical growth and health of your child, this book is to your child's educational and social development." These ideas seem to reflect the genuine apprehension and real anxieties of middle-class parents, who are concerned about transmitting their (relative) privileges in society to their children, and are not ready to rely on genetic transmission alone.

Much of the findings on achievement motivation and "success" can be interpreted as supporting the well-known claim that the poor are lacking in ambition, and that this is a major cause of their poverty. This viewpoint is nevertheless more "liberal" than that of the conservative, who sees the poor as doomed by their genes. Both liberals and conservatives see the origin and cause of inequality within the individual. Whether these causes are defined in new psychological terms or through the old concepts of sloth, shiftlessness, and sinfulness, the causes are always internal and individual. Political liberalism emphasizes the equality of opportunity, that is, equality at the starting point of the race for success, rather than equality of outcome. "Let's give everybody a fair chance, and may the best man win!" Such is the liberal slogan, more concerned with unfairness than with income inequality. When the best man wins, he can win big, and the losers deserve the leavings of failure. Schlesinger (1980), in his defense of contemporary liberalism, denies the conservative accusation that liberals believe in the "perfectability of Man." The liberal doctrine of equal opportunity is similar to the doctrine of equal chances, advocated by Sumner (1883), among the best-known American Social Darwinists: "We each owe it to the other to guarantee rights. Rights do not pertain to *results*, but only to *chance*. They pertain to the *conditions* of the struggle for existence, not to any of the results of it; to the *pursuit* of happiness, not to the possession of happiness" (p. 163, italics in the original). It seems that what was considered Social Darwinism a hundred years ago has become the liberalism of today.

INTERPRETING RESEARCH FINDINGS

When it comes to the topics chosen for research, it might be said that conservatives concentrate on early or genetic differences, while liberals and radicals focus on differences that appear later in life and have their origin in postinfantile and adult experience. In explaining the psychological differences related to income distribution, the liberals attribute the larger part of the revealed variance to social factors.

Liberals regard economic insecurity as the cause of personality traits typical of the lower class: "The lower class people look upon life as a recurrent series of depressions and peaks with regard to gratification of their basic needs. In their lives it is all or nothing. . . . The learned fears of deprivation drive lower class people to get all they can of other physical gratification, 'while the getting is good'" (Davis, 1949, p. 27). Schneider and Lysgaard (1953) actually suggested that the alleged lack of ability (or desire) to delay gratification among the lower classes may have its advantages, namely immediate pleasures instead of long-term gains or security.

Centers (1949) explained class differences in values as follows: "The interpretation offered is that security is a basic need of all, but since middle class people have typically already achieved a substantial measure of it they are emancipated from great concern with it and, unlike most working class people, can be dominated by other, and in a sense higher, values" (p. 216). This interpretation can be easily translated into the language of the hierarchy of needs, proposed by Maslow (1970).

In explaining the phenomenon of "working class authoritarianism," Lipset (1960) suggests that "the lower class individual is likely to have been exposed to punishment, lack of love, and a general atmosphere of tension and aggression since early childhood--all experiences which tend to produce deep-seated hostilities expressed by ethnic prejudice, political authoritarianism, and chiliastic transvaluational religion" (p. 120).

A capsule summary of many liberal views of the lower class is contained in the concept of lower-class subculture, or "the culture of poverty." Lower-class people are different, because they are members of another subculture. They are outside the mainstream of so-called middle-class values. If only they acquired these values, their position in society would change. That is why liberals emphasize education (De Lone, 1979) as the main cure to the problem of poverty. Yando, Seitz, and Sigler (1979) "believe that it is time for behavioral scientists to reject the deficit model and to adopt in its place a different approach in which no group is considered to be inferior or superior to any other and in which differences among groups are viewed instead as important empirical phenomena to be investigated" (p. 2).

The liberal school, in our view, overpsychologizes economic inequality, ignoring its structural aspects. The liberals support early intervention in the education of children, but do not support change in the social structure that constrains, stratifies, and gives a functional focus to the character of learning. The liberals would compensate for the disadvantages that inhere in the environment of poverty rather than attacking the elements of the system that produce that environment.

Liberal, humanitarian, environmentalist in their beliefs about the causation of psychological attributes, Ramey and Campbell (1976) are conceiving of poverty in psychological rather than in institutional terms, when they write that "The mechanisms by which poverty is perpetuated are not fully understood. One assumption has been that lower class parents differ in critical ways from parents in other levels of society in their attitudes toward life and toward their children" (p. 3).

The psychologistic approach to the explanation of economic inequality and the class structure was delineated by Davis (1937) in his discussion of the "mental hygiene" movement:

> By the psychologistic approach is meant the explanation of human conduct in terms of traits originating within the individual, as over against traits originating within society. Any explanation is psychologistic, for example, which builds its analysis upon motives, drives, instincts, urges, prepotent reflexes, or what not, ignoring the social genesis of what is called by these names. In mental hygiene these elements are taken as given in the individual, existing prior to social forces and determining concrete actions. Since they are prior to the social, the only other alternative in accounting for them is that they are biologically given. The psychologistic interpretation is individualistic, then, in the sense that it bases its explanation upon that which is purely individual, i.e., the biologically inherited constitution (the purely non-social part) of the person (p. 60).

And this psychologism can readily be used to justify the system as it is:

> The philosophy of private initiative, personal responsibility, and individual achievement falls easily into an interpretation of human nature in individualistic terms. Furthermore, for those who are naive in the analysis of social relations and generally unaware of the sociological premises of their own thinking, it is extremely easy to read into the individual, as given in his nature, the characteristics that are really given in his society (p. 60).

THE RADICAL INTERPRETATION

A radical approach, as defined by Flacks and Turkel (1978) "rests on the assumption that the significant constraints on human action are man-made and/or subject to change through conscious human effort" and "rejects any strategy of explanation that posits any agency or cause or constraint that is universal, inherent, or otherwise incapable of eventual transformation through human agency" (p. 194). It also starts with the notion of the infinite perfectability of humanity. What animates the radical critique (and the radical critics) is first and foremost a commitment to an ideal of equality, and a total opposition to every rationalization of inequality. That is why the radical reacts so strongly to any purportedly objective investigation that may be used to justify existing inequality. The main aim of the radical critique is to block any rational justification of inequality, and to show inequality as a social arrangement, relative and historical, and not a fact based on a historical biological or psychological law.

The ultimate radical position asserts the economic as the primary cause of inequality, dismissing the psychological correlates of inequality and all the presumed connections with heredity (other than social status heredity) as irrelevant. Its critical theory consists of, first a critique and refutation of the established conservative and liberal views, and second, an exposition of the social and political realities that gave rise to those views. The radical viewpoint has been expressed most clearly and most eloquently by Ryan (1976) and Chorover (1979).

The differences between liberals and radicals are in the language of their discourse and in their recommendations for action. Liberals use the language of psychology and psychological processes in explaining social class differences. Radicals use the language of the social system, with less attention paid to psychological process. Accordingly, liberals recommend reforms in education and in the extension of opportunities, while for radicals nothing short of a complete social overhaul will produce the requisite psychological change. The difference can be expressed in the answer to these questions: How far should we go in the prevention of psychological problems? Should we strive for equal opportunity? Should our focus be on outcomes, rather than opportunities?

Liberals accept the conservative language of discourse, at least vis-à-vis the psychological enterprise. The radicals reject both, attacking the value of psychological instruments and the meaning of their social use. Liberals agree with conservatives that psychological differences, such as achievement motivation (McClelland, 1961), are important in creating economic inequality, but in opposition to the conservatives, liberals claim these are acquired rather than genetic in origin.

What the liberal lacks is any theory that explains (or any positive attitude vis-à-vis) those social structures that he maintains have imprinted upon the psyche of the poor those configurations that perpetuate their poverty. But for the radical, that social structure and its consequence are the overwhelming issues. The radical searches for the root of inequality and claims to find it in the social and economic structure. While liberal theorists focus on the psychology of the individual, with emphasis on early childhood determinism, the radical theorist emphasizes the social context of individual behavior and explains patterns of behavior as adaptations to social and historical circumstances (De Lone, 1979). The radical refuses to accept that the individual psyche can be isolabled from its context, and the radical vision seeks to encompass the whole social system while selecting particular social networks as crucial in determining behavior.

Critiques of the conservative establishment can be divided into two kinds: the technical critique and the social critique. Technical critiques deal with the logic and meaning of psychological findings. Social-structural critiques deal with aspects of society, which are only reflected in psychological technology.

The data on IQ come mostly from the conservatives, since they have conducted most of the studies on that subject. Hence they have been the targets of the criticism leveled against those studies on methodological grounds, discrediting data as fraudulent, or reasoning as faulty. Less interested in undertaking IQ research themselves, radicals have been content to challenge the data or the interpretations offered (Blum, 1978; Lawler, 1978). Because IQ scores have been a conservative mainstay in explaining social divisions, it is understandable that the radical critics have taken this line of attack.

Blum (1978) combines a technical and methodological criticism of the concept of IQ with a critique of its social uses. Without going into technical detail, the elements of this critique can be summarized as follows:

1. IQ tests are not intelligence tests. Herrnstein (1971) states that "The measurement of intelligence is psychology's most telling accomplishment to date" (p. 45). If there has been such an accomplishment, only Herrnstein, whose whole professional career has been spent teaching pigeons to respond to stimuli, and who has never given an IQ test himself, has noticed it. Those engaged in IQ testing know that nobody has been able to define intelligence in any measurable way. The favorite definition of intelligence, used in every introductory psychology class, is that intelligence is what IQ tests measure. No better definition has been found.

2. There is no single standard IQ test. References to IQ scores are made on the basis of the use of many tests differing in content, length, and mode of administration. The classical intelligence

tests, such as the Wechsler test, or the Stanford-Binet, are administered individually and take much time and specialized work to score. These are not the tests used in most studies. Quite often the tests used to measure ability are recognized to measure achievement instead, and yet they continue to be used as measures of ability.

How many scholars, familiar with the IQ literature, are aware that many times in actual practice children's IQ scores are determined by one drawing of one human figure in the child's hand (Harris, 1963)? Children's performance on the Draw-A-Person IQ test is as culture-dependent as children's performance on a verbal IQ test. Many presumed experts, including psychologists, simply do not have a direct knowledge of IQ tests and the problems involved in obtaining IQ scores. The attraction of a single number score is enough to blind many cautious scholars to the dangers involved in using this doubtful abstraction as something similar to physical measurements.

3. Most of the IQ tests used in research are heavily, or solely, based on verbal ability, essentially the command of vocabulary. Most short group IQ tests are based on vocabulary. It is well known, for example, that on the Wechsler test, which has 11 subtests, the one subtest that correlates best with the whole test is the vocabulary subtest. Clinical psychologists under time pressure will legitimately and reasonably use the vocabulary subtest to estimate an individual's IQ and will lose very little information in so doing.

4. Most IQ tests are good predictors of scholastic performance, almost as good as past scholastic performance in predicting future performance. In other words, if we want to predict a first-grader's success in second grade, we can use either the first-grade performance or an IQ test. Both IQ tests and scholastic performance are best at predicting over the short run. It is easy to predict second-grade but not sixth-grade performance from first-grade performance. Primary school grades are not good predictors of college performance, but high school grades are. While IQ scores at age 16 will be a good predictor of college performance, IQ scores at age 6 will not. On the whole, however, there is undoubtedly a strong relationship between IQ and scholastic performance, which is in no way to say that IQ is a measure of innate intelligence.

5. There are problems of bias in administering and scoring both group tests and individual ones. There is evidence of a social bias against lower-income subjects in research or clinical work (cf Hendren & Routh, 1979). Again, as those who have given IQ tests

know, scoring on many IQ test items is not objective, but is left to the discretion of the examiner.

The technical criticism of the conservative position often extends from disagreement over the meaning of the IQ concept to the meaning of heredity and heritability (Block & Dworkin, 1976). The conservative presentation of genetic data, and their use of genetic concepts, has been severely criticized by authorities in the field of genetics (Topoff, 1974). Technical criticisms by geneticists of the hereditarian viewpoint have been extensive, especially in regard to use of the concept heritability, which is characteristic of populations (Layzer, 1974; Feldman & Lewontin, 1975). As Medawar (1977) pointed out, most leading geneticists, who should be biased to the side of heredity by their professional experiences and their professional self-interest, totally reject such new allies as Jensen and Eysenck and the argument favoring heritability of IQ. Medawar (1975) also observed that the most important form of inheritance in mankind's biological experience is exogenetic or exosomatic heredity. This is the way in which information is transmitted from one generation to the next through learning and culture. Heredity then can encompass human experience and adaptation at every level. The exogenetic is different from biological heredity in being Lamarckian: The experience of one generation becomes part of the inheritance of the next.

The basic model of heritability presented by the conservatives (Jensen, 1969; Herrnstein, 1973; Eysenck, 1971, 1973) is identical to the one developed by Cyril Burt (1969). Cyril Burt was the great mind of the conservative school. His research on the correlations in the IQ scores of identical twins, and his research on the IQ score differences between the social classes provided the conservatives' basic research cornerstone (Eysenck, 1971, 1973; Herrnstein, 1973; Jensen, 1969). Much of the evidence used by psychologists who support the hereditarian view on human intelligence, such as Jensen (1972), is based on studies by Burt (1957, 1959, 1961, 1966, 1971). Eysenck (1973) proudly states his reliance on Burt's studies: "The long-continued studies of Burt have been particularly valuable in throwing light on the relation between IQ and social class. I shall draw rather heavily on his work--partly because few others have given much attention to this problem, partly of course because of the outstanding quality of the design and the statistical treatment in his studies" (p. 137).

In a scandal that compares to the Piltown affair and the infamous experiments of Michurin and Lysenko, it was discovered that Burt's findings were pure invention and his research totally fraudulent. This exposure was a hard blow to the conservative school and their hereditarian position. Still, that Burt (for some hereditary reason, no doubt) was a fraud, a forger, and a liar does not in itself disprove his theory.

If radicals refer to IQ findings, their explanations emphasize those environmental factors that would depress the scores of the deprived. Hurley (1969) makes an amply documented case for the environmental causation of mental retardation among the poor by dint of deficiencies in health care, poor nutrition during the early years, and lack of intellectual stimulation. Deficiencies in early development, both physiological and psychological, have been tied to deficiencies in nutrition (Brazelton et al, 1977; Brozek, 1979).

Radicals do not debate conservatives on their own grounds by offering technical critiques or measurement of differing interpretations of the same findings, for they cannot accept that the questions asked are viable or that the answers sought can be meaningful, given the social context. In the instance of the celebrated World War I data on IQ scores expressed in mental age, (Brigham, 1930), the scores are real and reflect a correct technical use of the test. The numbers reported are all correct. The data have not been altered in any way, and they are truthfully reported. Nevertheless, the findings with these American soldiers are today the subject only of ridicule and derision because the character of the inquiry ignored critical social variables. One might say that the psychology of individual variance offers a method of classification that exactly parallels differences in wealth and status. The social hierarchy is reflected in a psychological hierarchy.

The radical explanation of social class differences in the socialization of children has to do with the direct life experiences of parents in different classes. Kohn (1977) reported that middle-class parents emphasize self-direction in their children, while working-class parents emphasize conformity and discipline. Pearlin and Kohn (1966) suggested that

> . . . parents of both social classes value for their children the characteristics that seem most appropriate to the conditions of parents' lives. In particular, class differences in parental values appear to parallel, and may very well be a result of, the characteristically different occupational experiences of middle and working class parents. Self-direction seems more possible and more necessary in middle class occupations; working class occupations allow much less room for, and in fact may penalize, anything other than obedience to rules and directives set down by others. (p. 466)

Socialization, in the family and in schools, means preparing the child for eventual work roles in the economy. Since these roles are different for middle-class and lower-class individuals, the preparation in childhood is different (Kohn, 1977; Bowles & Gintis, 1976). The nature of work experience for different social groups becomes a crucial determinant of psychological qualities and experiences (Kohn & Schooler, 1973; Kohn, 1976). Gecas (1979) accepts Kohn's (1977) ideas about self-direction at work as the causal variable, leading to social class differences in socializing children. Parents enjoying more occupational self-direction (and usually higher income) will raise their children to be more self-directed, or at least will attempt that. Parents being subject to conformity at work will transmit that experience to their children, and will prepare them for a life of conformity. Class differences in socializing for achievement motivation may be a similar reflection of the differences in parents' experiences at work.

Psychological differences in relation to income levels, and especially psychological deficits, are explained by the radicals as reflecting the reality of class society:

> The essence of higher class position is the expectation that one's decisions and actions can be consequential; the essence of lower class position is the belief that one is at the mercy of forces and people beyond one's control, often beyond one's understanding. Self-direction--acting on the basis of one's own judgment, attending to internal dynamics as well as external consequences, being openminded, being trustful of others, holding personally responsible moral standards--this is possible only if the actual conditions of life allow some freedom of action, some reason to feel in control of fate. Conformity--following the dictates of authority, focusing on external consequences to the exclusion of internal processes, being intolerant of nonconformity and dissent, being distrustful of others, having moral standards that strongly emphasize obedience to the letter of the law--this is the inevitable result of conditions of life that allow little freedom of action, little reason to feel in control of fate (Kohn, 1977, p. 189).

The real life conditions of adult members of different status groups determine their psychological experiences. Their self-perceptions are rooted in reality; people feel that they have no control over their fate when they really have no control.

Kohn and Schooler (1973) have shown how objective working conditions lead to psychological differences. It is the direct experience at work, and the nature of the work process, that have the critical psychological effects on the personality of the workers, and the kind of work is directly related to social class and position (Kohn & Schooler, 1973; Kohn, 1980). Pearlin and Kohn (1966) suggested that parents "value for their children the characteristics that seem most appropriate to the conditions of the parents' lives" (p. 466). Kohn (1976) started with the relations of production and the nature of work roles. The work experience is the individual's starting point in defining other social roles and their psychological content. Alienation at work leads to alienation in other areas of life.

The radical view is that psychological deficits among low-income individuals reflect the nature of social structure and its demands and pressures. Members of the lower class feel inferior because they carry the stigma of failure. Adult members feel that they have failed in moving ahead. Children learn early that their parents are social also-rans. "The sense of being identified with low status parents who are recognized by the child as disapproved or rejected by the community, and the constant reminders in the mass media of the stigma attached to low status contribute to an emerging sense of being 'nobody' in the 'low-SES child'" (Phillips, 1968, p. 44).

How does the working class accept its position in society? What kinds of mechanism does society use to insure that members of the working class accept the authority above them? According to Sennett and Cobb (1972), the answer lies in the feelings of inadequacy generated by the ideology of success, which states that those with lower incomes are failures in the race to succeed. If income is a matter of individual success, then low income will lead to self-blame, inferiority, and self-hatred. Most of the psychological characteristics typical of lower-income individuals can be viewed as manifestations of false consciousness, which serves to "keep the workers in their place" (Szymanski & Goertzel, 1979). "Manual workers are taught in school, brainwashed . . . and constantly told on the job . . . that they themselves are in their lowly positions because they are lazy, didn't have the proper schooling, aren't bright or ambitious enough, etc. Without these feelings of inadequacy, so carefully built up in working people . . . the system could not function" (p. 138).

The systematic causes of low self-esteem among lower-income individuals are most eloquently described by Kurt Vonnegut in Slaughterhouse Five (1969). Vonnegut puts these words into the mouth of Howard W. Campbell, an American Nazi:

> America is the wealthiest nation on earth, but its people are mainly poor, and poor Americans are

> urged to hate themselves. . . . Americans, like human beings everywhere, believe many things that are obviously untrue. . . . The most destructive untruth is that it is very easy for any American to make money . . . those who have no money blame and blame and blame themselves. This inward blame has been a treasure for the rich and the powerful, who have had to do less for their poor, publicly and privately, than any other ruling class since, say Napoleonic times. Many novelties have come from America. The most startling of these, a thing without precedent, is a mass of undignified poor. They do not love one another because they do not love themselves. (pp. 129-130)

The difference between class awareness, which exists in the United States, and class consciousness, which does not, is that class consciousness leads to solidarity and pride. In Europe there is class consciousness and class pride; in the United States there is neither (Sennett & Cobb, 1972).

The basic conservative world view in politics relies on two claims regarding the way things should be: what had been in the past, and what is natural. Learning from the past is a conservative virtue that can hardly be faulted. The question is only whether the past is a good guide to the present and future. Usually, the past view and the natural view are combined: What has been in the past must be natural. The conservative idea boils down to the ancient claim of the identity between the natural order and the social order, while the radical view emphasizes the relativity of society and history. The idea that the social and the natural order are identical, or that the social order is natural, has been discredited as many times as it has been proposed. As Condorcet has said, these are attempts to "make nature herself an accomplice in the crime of political inequality."

In the feudal system the social order was regarded (and described by great scholars) not only as natural, but as divinely determined. Today, the conservatives claim that the social order is not only natural, but scientifically (objectively) determined. The conservative argument of reliance on biological forces is both the classical argument of defending the social order as a part of the natural order, and the claim that attempts to change it are hopeless rebellions against victorious elements of nature. "You can't fool mother nature!" This seems to be the modern version of the divine right theory. When you can no longer rely on divine right, because the force of religion has declined in the face of rising science, you can try to use science as the new source of authority, and this has been done since the early days of scientific racism to these days of sophisticated scientific psychology. The conservatives are attempting to prove that today's capitalism is natural and eternal in the same fashion in which wise men in earlier times sought to prove that feudalism was divinely inspired, natural, and eternal.

SUMMARY

Our survey of the contemporary research literature dealing with psychological concepts in relation to economic inequality shows that this issue is handled in three typical ways. The first is the conservative-genetic, the second is the liberal-subjective, and the third is the radical-structural.

The conservative-genetic approach does have historical priority, and it quite simply sees income differences as a consequence of innate differences in ability. By far the most common psychological concept used to explain inequality is IQ. It has been used as an explanatory concept and as a model for general explanations of inequality. This explanatory model concentrates on the innate inequality of individuals. And this basic innate inequality of psychological and physiological characteristics leads to social and economic inequalities, which are only the natural consequences of inherent basic individual differences. The formation of stable income differences among social groups is also the reflection of such innate differences, which are genetically transmitted from one generation to the next. This approach is clearly and explicitly conservative; it puts the weight of biological causation behind existing social arrangements. Because of its historical priority and its political commitment to the established order, it is the object of much criticism, and the starting point for the formation of the other two approaches.

The liberal subjective approach, which also conceives of inequality as a consequence of psychological differences, uses the concepts of individual economic success or achievement as they are related to the psychological factors of intelligence, ability, and motivation. Inequality is then measured in terms of an individual's success, and then success, or the lack of it, is related to psychological qualities. In a more ambitious extension of the same concept, nations are treated as individuals, and differences in the economic development of nations are related to national motivational levels. If inequality is indeed the result of unequal psychological abilities, then attention must be paid to individual differences in these abilities. Individuals differ also in their aspirations to economic success, which then leads to inequality. These aspirations are not innate but are formed early in life and have an effect on individual careers.

The findings are acknowledged to be part of social reality, and are accepted as such. They may be discussed in relation to other psychological data. The ideology of inequality may then be served by the acceptance of this piece of social reality, without an attempt at explanation. This is the most common approach, with liberal psychologists usually limiting themselves to what they regard as their proper professional field of competence, which does not include the explanation of inequality. Even when liberal psychologists report only psychological findings related to economic inequality, they may differ in the attention they give to this background factor.

The third approach to the question of psychological factors and economic inequality differs from the other two in taking an explicit or implicit ideological stand against the alleged psychological preconditions of economic inequality. Rather than looking at the psychological causes, it looks for the psychological consequences of inequality, with individual maladjustment portrayed as the result of poverty, unemployment, and discrimination, hence as the psychological human cost of inequality. The well-being of individuals depends then on changes in social arrangements rather than on changes in individual motivation or abilities. Advocates of this viewpoint are interested in the primary prevention of psychological problems through changes in institutional structures and especially in the economic system.

The three approaches can be summarized in the following table:

Approach	Place of inequality as a variable	Ideological stand	Inequality as related to psychological factors
Establishment liberal	correlate	"neutral"	correlate
Establishment conservative	dependent	supporting status quo	consequence
Reformist-radical	independent	against status quo	cause

It should be clear from the presentation so far that using psychology to explain income inequality involves a question of values, and really boils down to one simple issue: "What kind of society do you want? How much equality do you really want?" In the conclusion of his classical study of the question of "nature and nurture," Pastore (1949) stated that "the sociopolitical allegiances of the scientists were a significant determinant of their position on nature-nurture questions . . . these allegiances had a marked effect upon the formulation of a hypothesis and the method of its verification, the conclusions drawn from an investigation, and the statement of implications of these conclusions for society" (p. 181). In other words psychologists have their ideologies and their value commitments, which are the prior determinants of findings and opinions. There are conservative psychologists, liberal psychologists, and radical psychologists, just as there are conservative economists, liberal economists, or radical economists.

On the basis of our literature survey, what conclusions, or generalizations, can we offer? First and foremost, economic inequality is an economic fact. Income differences are regarded by economists as necessary components of an economic system in which labor is regulated by market dynamics, where unemployment and income inequality are not only expected, but also predicted and predictable (Figueira-McDonough, 1978). Psychological factors may explain some differences between individuals, but they do not explain large-scale differences in income.

The following proposition is put forward as self-evident, or at least as supported by all the available evidence: Economic insecurity and deprivation have a negative physical and psychological impact on individuals who are subject to them. Economic insecurity leads to psychological insecurity. Those twin insecurities and the problems attendant upon them remain as a curse upon most of the human race today.

Using Maslow's (1970) concept of the need hierarchy, we may postulate that as long as people are preoccupied with basic needs they cannot move on to higher levels of psychological development. Abraham Maslow, in a film interview, said something like this: "People ask: What kind of society does human nature allow? What we should ask is what kind of human nature does society allow!" The kind of society we have will determine the kind of human nature that we have and the kind of psychological traits that will be found there.

REFERENCES

Andrews, F. M., & Withey, S. B. Social indicators of well being: Americans' perceptions of life quality. New York: Plenum Press, 1976.

Argyle, M., & Beit-Hallahmi, B. The social psychology of religion. London & Boston: Routledge & Kegan Paul, 1975.

Bakke, E. W. The unemployed worker. New Haven: Yale University Press, 1940.

Ball, R. S. The predictability of occupational level from intelligence. Journal of Consulting Psychology, 1938, 2, 184-186.

Banfield, E. C. The unheavenly city. Boston: Little, Brown, 1970.

Banfield, E. C. The unheavenly city revisited. Boston: LIttle, Brown, 1974.

Battle, E. S., & Rotter, J. B. Children's feelings of personal control as related to social class and ethnic group. Journal of Personality, 1963, 31, 482-490.

Beilin, H. The pattern of postponability and its relation to social class and mobility. Journal of Social Psychology, 1956, 44, 33-48.

Beit-Hallahmi, B. Salvation and its vicissitudes: Clinical psychology and political values. American Psychologist, 1974, 29, 124-129.

Beit-Hallahmi, B. Humanistic psychology--progressive or reactionary? Self and Society, 1977a, 12, 57-69.

Beit-Hallahmi, B. Overcoming the "objective" language of violence. Aggressive Behavior, 1977b, 3, 251-259.

Beit-Hallahmi, B. Personal and social components of the protestant ethic. Journal of Social Psychology, 1979, 109, 263-267.

Berelson, B., & Steiner, G. A. Human behavior: An inventory of scientific findings. New York: Harcourt, Brace & World, 1964.

Birch, H. G., & Gussow, J. D. Disadvantaged children: Health, nutrition and school failure. New York: Grune & Stratton, 1970.

Block, N. J., & Dworkin, G. IQ, heritability, and inequality. In N. J. Block, & G. Dworkin (Eds.), The IQ controversy. New York: Pantheon Books, 1976.

Blum, J. M. Pseudoscience and mental ability. New York: Monthly Review Press, 1978.

Bowles, S., & Gintis, H. Schooling in capitalist America. New York: Basic Books, 1976.

Bradburn, N. M. The structure of psychological well-being. Chicago: Aldine, 1969.

Brazelton, T. B., et al. The behavior of nutritionally deprived Guatemalan infants. Developmental Medicine and Child Neurology, 1977, 19, 364-372.

Brigham, C. C. Intelligence test of immigrant groups. The Psychological Review, 1930.

Brill, N. Q. Poverty and mental illness in the United States. Journal of Continuing Education in Psychiatry, 1978, 39, 23-34.

Brozek, J. (Ed.). Behavioral effects of energy and protein deficits. NIH Publication No. 79-1906. Washington, DC: National Institutes of Health, 1979.

Burt, C. The distribution of intelligence. British Journal of Psychology, 1957, 48, 161-175.

Burt, C. Class differences in general intelligence. III. British Journal of Statistical Psychology, 1959, 12, 15-33.

Burt, C. Intelligence and social mobility. British Journal of Statistical Psychology, 1961, 14, 3-24.

Burt, C. The genetic determination of differences in intelligence: A study of monozygotic twins reared together and apart. British Journal of Psychology, 1966, 57, 147-153.

Burt, C. The inheritance of mental ability. In D. Wolfle (Ed.), The Discovery of Talent. Cambridge: Harvard University Press, 1969.

Burt, C. Quantitative genetics in psychology. British Journal of Mathematical and Statistical Psychology, 1971, 24, 1-21.

Campbell, A., et al. The quality of American life. New York: Russell Sage Foundation, 1976.

Campbell, F., et al. A comparison of the factor structure of Rotter's internality-externality scale in advantaged and disadvantaged young mothers. Journal of Genetic Psychology, 1977, 130, 201-209.

Centers, R. The psychology of social classes. Princeton: Princeton University Press, 1949.

Chorover, S. From genesis to genocide. Cambridge: MIT Press, 1979.

Coleman, J. C., Butcher, J. N., & Carson, R. C. Abnormal psychology and modern life. Glenview, IL: Scott, Foresman, 1980.

Conway, J. Class differences in general intelligence. III. British Journal of Statistical Psychology, 1959, 12, 5-14.

Davis, A. Social class influences upon learning. Cambridge: Harvard University Press, 1949.

Davis, K. Mental hygiene and the class structure. Psychiatry, 1937, 1, 55-65.

Davis, K. Human society. New York: Macmillan, 1949.

De Lone, R. H. Small futures: Children, inequality, and the limits of liberal reform. New York: Harcourt Brace Jovanovich, 1979.

Dohrenwend, B. P. Sociocultural and social psychological factors in the genesis of mental disorders. Journal of Health and Social Behavior, 1975, 16, 365-392.

Dohrenwend, B. P., & Dohrenwend, B. S. Social status and psychological disorder: A causal inquiry. New York: John Wiley and Sons, 1969.

Duncan, O. D. A socioeconomic index for all occupations. In A. J. Reiss, Jr., et al., Occupations and social status. New York: Free Press, 1961.

Dunham, H. W. Current status of ecological research in mental disorder. In A. M. Rose (Ed.), Mental health and mental disorder: A sociological approach. New York: Norton, 1955.

Easterlin, R. A. Does economic growth improve the human lot? Some empirical evidence. In P. A. David & M. W. Reder, Nations and households in economic growth. New York: Academic Press, 1974.

Eysenck, H. J. The IQ argument: Race, intelligence and education. New York: The Library Press, 1971.

Eysenck, H. J. The inequality of man. London: Temple Smith, 1973.

Feldman, M. W., & Lewontin, R. C. The heritability hang-up. Science, 1975, 190, 1163-1168.

Figuera-McDonough, J. Mental health among unemployed Detroiters. Social Science Review, 1978, 52, 383-399.

Flacks, R., & Turkel, G. Radical sociology: The emergence of neo-Marxian perspectives in US sociology. Annual Review of Sociology, 1978, 4, 193-238.

Gecas, V. The influence of social class on socialization. In W. R. Burr, R. Hill, F. I. Nye, & I. L. Reiss (Eds.), Contemporary theories about the family, Vol. I., New York: Free Press, 1979.

Gil, D. Violence against children. Cambridge: Harvard University Press, 1970.

Gurin, G., Veroff, J., & Feld, S. Americans view their mental health. New York: Basic Books, 1960.

Harrell, T. W., & Harrell, M. S. Army general classification test scores for civilian occupations. Educational and Psychological Measurement, 1945, 5, 220-239.

Harris, D. B. Children's drawings as measures of intellectual maturity: A revision and extension of the Goodenough draw-a-man test. New York: Harcourt, Brace and World, 1963.

Hawes, G. R., Weiss, H. G., & Weiss, M. S. How to raise your child to be a winner. New York: Rawson Wade, 1980.

Hendren, T. E., & Routh, D. K. Social class bias in psychologists' evaluation of children. Journal of Pediatric Psychology, 1979, 4, 353-362.

Herrnstein, R. J. I.Q. The Atlantic Monthly, September 1971, 43-64.

Herrnstein, R. J. I.Q. in the meritocracy. Boston: Little, Brown, 1973.

Hogan, R. T., & Emler, N. P. The biases in contemporary social psychology. Social Research, 1978, 45, 478-534.

Hollingshead, A. B., & Redlich, F. C. Social class and mental illness. New York: John Wiley and Sons, 1958.

Hollingworth, L. S. Gifted children: Their nature and nurture. New York: Macmillan, 1926.

Hudson, L. The cult of the fact. London: Cape, 1972.

Hurley, R. Poverty and mental retardation: A causal relationship. New York: Random House, 1969.

Inkeles, A. Industrial man: The relation of status to experience, perception and value. American Journal of Sociology, 1960, 66, 1-31.

Jensen, A. R. How much can we boost IQ and scholastic achievement? Harvard Educational Review, 1969, 39, 1-123.

Jessor, R., & Richardson, S. Psychosocial deprivation and personality development. In Perspectives on human deprivation: Biological, psychological, and sociological. Washington, DC: National Institute of Child Health and Human Development, 1968.

Johnson, B. Ascetic protestantism and political preference. Public Opinion Quarterly, 1962, 26, 35-46.

Johnson, D. M. Applications of the standard score IQ to social statistics. Journal of Social Psychology, 1948, 27, 217-227.

Kawin, L. J. The science and politics of I.Q. Potomac, MD: Lawrence Erlbaum Associates, 1974.

Keniston, K. Introduction. In R. De Lone, Small futures: Children, inequality, and the limits of liberal reform. New York: Harcourt Brace Jovanovich, 1979.

Kitagawa, E. M., & Hauser, P. M. Differential mortality in the United States. Cambridge: Harvard University Press, 1973.

Knupfer, G. Portrait of the underdog. Public Opinion Quarterly, 1947, 11, 103-114.

Kohn, M. L. Social class and schizophrenia: A critical review and a reformulation. Schizophrenia Bulletin, 1973, 7, 60-69.

Kohn, M. L. Looking back--a 25-year review and appraisal of social problems research. Social Problems, 1976, 24, 94-112.

Kohn, M. L. Class and conformity: A study in values, 2nd Ed. Chicago: University of Chicago Press, 1977.

Kohn, M. L. Job complexity and adult personality. In N. J. Smelser, & E. H. Erikson (Eds.), Themes of work and love in adulthood. Cambridge: Harvard University Press, 1980.

Kohn, M. L., & Schooler, C. Occupational experience and psychological functioning: An assessment of reciprocal effects. American Sociological Review, 1973, 38, 97-118.

Lamb, H. R., & Zusman, J. Primary prevention in perspective. American Journal of Psychiatry, 1979, 136, 12-17.

Langner, T. S. Social mobility, socioeconomic status, and types of mental disturbance. In T. S. Langner, & S.

T. Michael, Life stress and mental health. Glencoe, IL: Free Press of Glencoe, 1963.

Lawler, J. M. IQ, heritability and racism. New York: International Publishers, 1978.

Layzer, D. Heritability analyses of IQ scores: Science or numerology? Science, 1974, 183, 1259-1266.

Lipset, S. M. Political man. Garden City, N.Y.: Doubleday, 1960.

Lynd, R., & Lynd, H. Middletown. New York: Harcourt, Brace, 1929.

MacEacheron, A. E., & Gruenfeld, L. W. The effects of family authority structure and socioeconomic status on field independence. Journal of Social Psychology, 1978, 104, 49-56.

Maslow, A. H. Motivation and personality, 2nd Ed. New York: Harper & Row, 1970.

Matras, J. Populations and societies. Englewood Cliffs, NJ: Prentice-Hall, 1973.

Matras, J. Social inequality, stratification, and mobility. Englewood Cliffs, NJ: Prentice-Hall, 1975.

McClelland, D. C. The achieving society. Princeton, NJ: Van Nostrand, 1961.

Medawar, P. B. The frontiers of knowledge. Garden City, NY: Doubleday, 1975.

Medawar, P. B. Unnatural science. The New York Review of Books, February 3, 1977.

Miller, S. M., Riessman, F., & Seagull, A. A. Poverty and self-indulgence: A critique of the non-deferred gratification pattern. In L. A. Ferman, J. L. Kornbluh, & M. Haber (Eds.), Poverty in America, Rev. Ed. Ann Arbor, University of Michigan Press, 1968.

Pastore, N. The nature-nurture controversy. New York: King's Crown Press, 1949.

Pearlin, L. I., & Kohn, M. L. Social class, occupation, and parental values. American Sociological Review, 1966, 31, 466-479.

Pelton, L. H. (Ed.), The social context of child abuse and neglect. New York: Human Sciences Press, 1980.

Phillips, L. Human adaptation and its failures. New York: Academic Press, 1968.

Ramey, C. T., & Campbell, F. A. Parental attitudes and poverty. Journal of Genetic Psychology, 1976, 128, 3-6.

Rapp, D. W. Childrearing attitudes of mothers in Germany and the United States. Child Development, 1961, 32, 669-678.

Rosen, B. C. The achievement syndrome: A psychocultural dimension of social stratification. American Sociological Review, 1956, 21, 203-211.

Rosenberg, M., & Pearlin, L. I. Social class and self-esteem among children and adults. American Journal of Sociology, 1978, 84, 53-77.

Rotter, J. B., Seeman, M., & Liverant, S. Internal vs. external control of reinforcement: A major variable in behavior theory. In N. F. Washburne (Ed.), Decisions, values and groups. London: Pergamon Press, 1962.

Ryan, W. Blaming the victim, Rev. Ed. New York: Random House, 1976.

Sameroff, A. J. The etiology of cognitive competence: A systems perspective. In R. B. Kearsley, & I. E. Sigel (Eds.), Infants at risk: Assessment of cognitive functioning. Hillsdale, NJ: Lawrence Erlbaum Associates, 1979.

Sameroff, A. J., Bakow, H. A., & McComb, N. Racial and social class differences in newborn heart rate. Infant Behavior and Development, 1978, 1, 199-204.

Sameroff, A. J., & Chandler, M. J. Perinatal risk and the continuum of caretaking casualty. In F. D. Horowitz, M. Heatherington, S. Scarr-Salapatek, & G. Siegel (Eds.), Review of child development research, Vol. 4. Chicago: University of Chicago Press, 1975.

Schlesinger, A., Jr. Is liberalism dead? The New York Times, March 30, 1980.

Schmidt, R. W., Lamm, H., & Trommsdorff, G. Social class and sex as determinants of future orientation. European Journal of Social Psychology, 1978, 8, 71-90.

Schneider, L., & Lysgaard, S. The deferred gratification pattern: A preliminary study. American Sociological Review, 1953, 18, 142-149.

Schwab, J. J., & Schwab, M. E. Sociocultural roots of mental illness. New York: Plenum, 1978.

Sennett, R., & Cobb, J. The hidden injuries of class. New York: Knopf, 1972.

Sherwood, J. J., & Nataupsky, M. Predicting the conclusions of Negro-white intelligence research from biographical characteristics of the investigator. Journal of Personality and Social Psychology, 1968, 8, 53-58.

Srole, L., Langner, T. S., Michael, S. T., Opler, M. K., & Rennie, T. A. C. Mental health in the metropolis: The midtown Manhattan study. New York: McGraw-Hill, 1962.

Stewart, N. A. G. C. T. scores of army personnel grouped by occupation. Occupations, 1947, 26, 5-41.

Straus, M. Deferred gratification, social class, and the achievement syndrome. American Sociological Review, 1962, 27, 326-335.

Strodtbeck, F. L. Family interaction, values, and achievement. In D. C. McClelland, A. L. Baldwin, U. Bronfenbrenner, & F. L. Strodtbeck, Talent and Society. Princeton, NJ: Van Nostrand, 1958.

Sumner, W. G. What social classes owe to each other. New York: Harper, 1883.

Szymanski, A. J., & Goertzel, T. G. Sociology: Class, consciousness, and contradictions. New York: Van Nostrand, 1979.

Terman, L. M. The measurement of intelligence. Boston: Houghton Mifflin, 1916.

Topoff, H. R. Genes, intelligence, and race. In E. Toback, et al (Eds.), The four horsemen: Racism, sexism, militarism and social Darwinism. New York: Behavioral Publications, 1974.

Vonnegut, Kurt, Jr. Slaughterhouse Five. New York: Dell, 1969.

Weber, M. The protestant ethic and the spirit of capitalism. London: Allen & Unwin, 1930 (Original, 1904).

Wilson, W. Correlates of avowed happiness. Psychological Bulletin, 1967, 67, 294-306.

Yando, R., Seitz, V., & Zigler, E. Intellectual and personality characteristics of children: Social class and ethnic group differences. Hillsdale, NJ: Lawrence Erlbaum Associates, 1979.

5. Social Science and Distributive Justice

Brian Barry

INTRODUCTION: CULTURAL LAG IN ACADEMIA

Anyone with an interest in both social science and philosophy must, I think, be distressed by the present relations between them--though also, perhaps, encouraged by making a comparison with the situation 10 years ago or more. A familiar phenomenon pervades all branches of knowledge, that of the practitioners in one discipline taking over the theories from other disciplines only when they are thoroughly discredited in the original discipline. In the present context we can see instances on all sides, as philosophers base their work on outmoded social science and social scientists return the compliment.

The most blatant examples are to be found in the trade between philosophers and economists. Thus, Robert Nozick's (1974) presentation of the case for capitalism would have brought a blush to the cheeks of a mid-Victorian hack like Harriet Martineau, author of improving tracts for the workers devoted to explaining how all was for the best in the best of all economic systems. Conversely, one still finds highly respected economists talking about value judgements as "preferences" in a way that would have been regarded as a bit crude in philosophical circles (even the Vienna circle) circa 1936.

Perhaps even more remarkable is the survival of the idea that interpersonal comparisons of utility are by their nature impossible, and that what purports to be such a comparison in fact expresses not a judgement of fact but another value judgement. Taken literally, this seems absurd: Surely, we can be in little doubt

---

I am indebted to James D. Andrews for preparing a draft of section III.

that being burned is more painful than being pricked with a pin, whether we are comparing the effects on the same person or different people. How then did the idea that interpersonal comparisons are meaningless come about?

The answer seems to be that Lionel Robbins studied with the Vienna circle and contracted a severe case of naive verificationism, which subsequently infected the rest of the profession (see Robbins, 1932). Thus it was held that we can in principle give an operational definition of preference, because we can observe people choosing between alternatives, and from this we can construct their "revealed preference" schedule. But we cannot observe pain or pleasure, and any imputation of pain or pleasure to people is subjective. We can, indeed, develop a measure of strength of preference between alternatives for a single individual by presenting him with a series of lotteries. But these "cardinal utilities" do not give us a basis on which to compare the utilities of different people.

There are two lines of objection to this kind of view. The first is that the program of constructed revealed preference schedules cannot in fact be carried out in a coherent fashion (see especially Sen, 1973a). The other is that we need not cry about this, because there is nothing much to be said for the verificationist criterion of meaning, construed so that interpersonal comparisons of utility are meaningless. In fact, human behavior could not even be described in an intelligible way as a series of physical movements, noises, and so on. Our vocabulary is designed for describing what people do, and describing what they do entails our having some ideas about what they intend, what they believe, and so on. But once we allow that, we are already well outside the sphere of naive verificationism and there is no reason why we should hesitate to say, for example, that A enjoyed the concert a lot more than did B. In many cases, the evidence for saying such a thing will be very strong.

At another level, the argument about "interpersonal comparisons of utility" may be seen as a piece of ideological skirmishing. As we shall see, the classical utilitarians (a line which we may for this purpose regard as running up through Pigou) concluded from the rough similarity of human beings in their capacity to turn income into utility that an equal distribution of income would approximately maximize the aggregate utility derived from a given income stream. The extreme skepticism introduced into economics by Robbins undercut this egalitarian argument. Utilitarianism could no longer be defined in terms of maximizing the sum of individual utilities but had to be redefined to make use only of ordinal utilities (that is, individual preference orderings) as against interpersonally comparable cardinal utilities.

The utilitarian criterion expressed in ordinal utilities, however, reduces to the Pareto criterion, which reads that situation X is better than situation Y if and only if nobody prefers Y to X and at least one person prefers X to Y. As it stands, the Pareto principle is mute about almost any large-scale change that ever occurs or is ever proposed, since it is just about inconceivable that there would not be at least one person who loses from the change and at least one who gains from it. (Bear in mind that losses and gains are to be understood as defined in terms of preferences.)

One way of getting results out of the Pareto criterion has been to admit that in practice it is not feasible to arrange that in any change from one situation to another nobody will lose; but then we would argue that as a second-best approximation we may say that a change is desirable if the gainers could more than compensate the losers, even if they never in fact do so. This was the leading idea of the so-called new welfare economics of the 1940s and 50s.

It seems to me that this modification of the Pareto principle has all the faults of classical utilitarianism without any of its virtues. It is completely indifferent to any questions of equity in distribution, like classical utilitarianism; but, unlike classical utilitarianism, it provides us with no reason for supposing that aggregate utility will be increased if its prescriptions are followed. A Pareto-superior situation may not maximize aggregate utility, and, if we go outside the utilitarian framework for a moment, we can add that it will tend to preserve any existing inequities in the status quo. But we can at least be assured that, if some gain and none lose, aggregate utility must have increased. We no longer have any reason for such assurance if some actually lose, even if we believe that the gainers could have compensated the losers fully and still come out ahead. Indeed, on the assumption of the decreasing marginal utility of money, we have good reason to anticipate a loss of aggregate utility when the gainers are richer than the losers.

The other route is the one taken by James Buchanan and what we may call the Virginia school of political economy, who have in effect reinvented the social contract. This is a school which illustrates how welfare economics, having started out in the eighteenth century and proceeded through the nineteenth and early twentieth centuries, has now regressed to the seventeenth. It discards the painfully won understanding of the past three centuries and substitutes an a priori therory of politics founded on the presumed interests of presocial individuals in a state of nature. There is no evidence that the members of this school have examined with care the reasons why this mode of proceeding has fallen into such universal contempt in the last couple of centuries and have, on mature reflection, found them wanting. Rather, they seem to me to display a kind of willful, arrogant ignorance about the entire history of historical and social thought.

The basic idea is as follows. It may be recalled that the Pareto principle, interpreted as saying only that a change from which everyone gains is an improvement, was forced to be agnostic about most changes. The Virginia school avoided this problem of indeterminacy by saying that Pareto superiority is not only a sufficient condition of a change's being an improvement, but also a necessary condition.

The obvious problem that this raises--quite apart from the question of whether there is any reason for accepting the criterion in this form--is that we have to have some baseline from which to reckon Pareto superiority. And this, it seems, is going to have to come out of some quite different sort of moral theory.

At this point Buchanan (1975) invokes the notion of the social contract in the hopes that it will provide the foundation he needs. The idea is that we start from a Hobbesian state of nature and somehow derive Lockean conclusions. Buchanan's state of nature is super-Hobbesian in that there are no moral constraints operating within it. But, unlike Hobbes, Buchanan apparently does not believe in the approximate natural equality of all men, so he allows for the possibility that some will be able to dominate or (de facto) enslave others.

The unappetizing scenario constitutes Buchanan's baseline. He argues, again on Hobbesian lines, that the people in his state of nature would find it mutually advantageous (that is, Pareto superior) to replace it with settled laws, enforced by a sovereign. But a shift to Locke occurs at this point. For, whereas Hobbes argues that everyone gains by setting up an absolute sovereign, who can make all the subsequent arrangements (including, for example, creating property rights by fiat), Buchanan insists that people should keep the specific advantages they had in the state of nature. The Pareto superiority consists in everybody keeping what they had but being secured in the possession of it. Thus, civil society, far from operating to compensate for natural inequalities in physical and mental capacity, puts the force of law behind the perpetuation of the material inequalities that would arise from them in the state of nature. We might think of this as an artificial analogue of the process whereby, in the Gombe Stream reserve, the dominance hierarchy is maintained without continuous fighting.

I shall not spend time criticizing this as an ethical theory--the criticisms are obvious--because in any case Buchanan doesn't really use it. He never really asks what things would be like in a state of nature and then tries to see what allocations of rights and benefits would be Pareto superior to it. No doubt it is a sign of good sense that he does not, since the inquiry would be an absurd one. But it does, of course, mean that he is back with a criterion--Pareto superiority--that lacks a foundation.

At this point, Buchanan makes a prodigious leap and says that as a second best to going back to the state of nature and starting from there, we should start from the status quo and freeze the distribution of rights and benefits we have now, or whatever modification of it would be generally agreed to, out of altruism or fear among those who would give things up. "We start from here," as Buchanan says. But this clearly raises equally serious ethical problems. Unless there is some independent basis for saying that the status quo is just, it is hard to see what the ethical attraction is of arranging things so that nobody can be adversely affected in relation to it.

Writing in 1885, Henry Sidgwick was able to remark complacently that, although there had once been people who declared "the 'inalienable right of every man freely to exchange the result of his labour for the productions of other people,'" to be "'one of the principles of eternal justice,'" English political economy had shaken off all connection with these "antiquated metaphysics" under the "more philosophic guidance of J. S. Mill" (Sidgwick, 1904, pp. 173-174). Sidgwick spoke a good deal too soon. Almost a century after he addressed the Economics and Statistics section of the British Association for the Advancement of Science in those words, we are in the midst of an extraordinary revival of Lockean fundamentalism.

As we have seen, James Buchanan's use of the criterion of Pareto superiority rests, at any rate in theory, upon the foundation of a curious kind of contract theory in which property rights are carried into civil society from a state of nature in which there are no rights but only de facto possessions. And, in political philosophy, we have, as I noted, Nozick's _Anarchy, State and Utopia_ (1974), which is more Lockean than Locke himself, inasfar as it would render illegitimate the role that Locke left for majoritarian decision making in matters of property and taxation. It has to be said at once that Nozick does not appear to have made many converts among the ranks of

Anglo-American philosophers, but the large amount of interest and the volume of response generated by this piece of archaism must itself be regarded as a significant cultural phenomenon.

The problem, as I see it, is to find a way of remedying the defects of utilitarianism without retreating into the kind of primitive natural rights theory that I have just mentioned. In this chapter I shall first trace the development of utilitarian thinking about income distribution. I shall then take up what seem to me reasonable objections to utilitarianism that have been advanced by philosophers in recent decades. After that I shall turn the discussion round and ask what contributions social science could make to the normative analysis of income distribution.

THE DEVELOPMENT OF A UTILITARIAN THEORY OF INCOME DISTRIBUTION

The logical place to start is with Jeremy Bentham. Bentham assumed that each person both must (as a matter of psychological necessity) and should pursue his own happiness, but that the standard for a society was the maxmization of the aggregate happiness of its members. The two could be reconciled in two ways: by the natural harmony of interests and by the artificial harmony of interests. The idea of the natural harmony of interests is that if people understand their own individual interests correctly they will see that they are not incompatible with those of others. The idea of the artificial harmony of interests is that, when this fails, public institutions should provide sanctions to insure that the pursuit of individual self-interest will in fact be led to conduce to the general happiness. (We can see in both ideas Adam Smith's omnipresent "hidden hand," though stripped of its deistic underpinnings.)

Bentham in practice reached much the same economic prescriptions as Smith had--that within the sphere of divisible and excludable goods, the only need for state sanctions is to protect property and enforce contracts. (Thus, since the interest rate is the cost of borrowing money, the Defence of Usury is simply the application of Smith's strictures on attempts to regulate prices to the special case of interest rates.) However, although the conclusions are the same as those of Smith, the method--the appeal to the single criterion of aggregate happiness--is different, and over the course of the nineteenth century this gained decisive importance.

Doctor Johnson once said of David Hume that he was "a Tory by chance," meaning that there was nothing in

Hume's principles that led him inexorably toward Toryism, but that it was only because he attached great importance to political stability that he happened to end up as a Tory. (It had earlier been said of Hobbes, equally correctly, that he was a monarchist only by chance, in the same sense, and indeed Johnson acutely described Hume's principles as "Hobbist.") Now, in exactly the same sense, Bentham was an upholder of the untrammeled operation of the market only by chance. Given his assumptions about the basic compatibility of individual interest and general interest, it followed that the best plan was *laissez-faire.* But, whereas Smith talked about "the system of natural liberty," Bentham had no time for liberty as such: Liberty was important to the extent that it was a means of happiness and only to that extent.

Thus, although he thought slavery should be abolished, he thought it would be because of its inefficiency--because "a free man produces more than a slave" and because slavery is, as a matter of fact, disliked by slaves. But if that dislike were overbalanced by the additional happiness of the owner, then slavery would be justifiable. And indeed Bentham said that if things could be arranged so that "there would be only one slave to one master," the sum of good would just about balance the sum of evil (Parekh, 1970, p. 489; Bowring, 1843, I, p. 344).

And in defending his projected Panopticon, a prison for "grinding rogues into honest men and idle ones into industrious" by supervision and regimentation 24 hours a day, Bentham wrote: "Call them soldiers, call them monks, call them machines, so they were but happy ones, I should not care" (Parekh, 1970, p. 495; Bowring, 1843, IV, p. 64).

Bentham's psychology, which he took over from the associationist psychologist David Hartley, was a forerunner of Skinnerian behaviorism. Extreme environmentalism of this kind seems to have as its inevitable concomitant the devaluation of freedom as an end in itself. For if everything is externally determined, the concept of autonomy has no meaning. If Bentham's Panopticon bears a certain resemblance to Skinner's *Walden Two,* this is not accidental. Both were, in Skinner's words, *Beyond Freedom and Dignity.*

Utilitarianism provides a standard for judging economic systems that is, at any rate in principle, definite: The best system is the one that maximizes the aggregate amount of happiness. As the earlier discussion of slavery indicated, there is nothing in the utilitarian principle that sets any constraints on the way in which happiness should be distributed. The right distribution simply is the one that maximizes aggregate happiness. Thus there is no room for any notion that the prices and incomes that arise in a competitive market have a sort of ethically preferred status by virtue of being natural. If it will increase happiness, prices and incomes can be manipulated in whatever way is required.

Suppose that we have a fixed amount of stuff--call it cake--to distribute. If we knew everybody's utility schedule (that is to say, the amount of pleasure each person derives from eating various amounts of cake), the utilitarian rule for dividing it up would be to give each person whatever share of the cake makes the marginal utility of cake the same for everybody. In other words the maximizing condition is that the amount of pleasure or satisfaction each person gets from the last crumb of cake should be equal.

Now this is not in general going to result in an equal distribution of cake, since there is no reason for expecting utility schedules to be identical. And the departure from equality will be in a direction that might naturally be regarded as perverse. For the implication of the rule for distribution that we deduced from the utilitarian principle is as follows: Suppose that there are two people, one of whom gets a higher marginal utility than the other for any given amount of cake consumption. Then the rule says that the one with the higher level of marginal utility should get more cake. Thus the natural advantage of this person in getting more enjoyment out of any given amount of cake is compounded by the working of the utilitarian criterion. In addition to getting more pleasure per unit of cake he or she gets more cake!

This conclusion was embraced by one distinguished utilitarian economist, F. Y. Edgeworth (1967, 1977), but most have been uncomfortable with it. The usual escape route has been to argue that, although the conclusion follows in theory, in practice the information required to give effect to it is not available. Clearly, if this line is pushed too far it is liable to lead to skeptical thoughts about the utilitarian principle itself. (Does it make much sense to set up as a criterion the maximization of something we can't recognize?) But it is possible to make a claim that falls short of that. It may be said that we do indeed have some rough idea of the differences between people, but that these differences are too subjective and the appearances are too open to manipulation by people to form a sound basis for social policy. And the discretionary power that would have to be entrusted to the officials charged with making the estimates would be something that, on utilitarian grounds, we would wish to avoid.

If, then, for purposes of social policy we are going to decide to take no account of individual differences in utility schedules, what should be done about distribution? If we claimed total agnosticism, we would be able to say nothing about it. But if we make one quite weak assumption, that cake has diminishing marginal utility, then we can derive the conclusion that an equal distribution is more likely to maximize the total sum of happiness than any other. In other words, although we don't know that it will maximize it, and indeed have every reason to believe that some other would be better, we don't know what the other is. Thus the situation is like that of the accounts manager who once said that he was sure that half of his advertising budget was wasted but had no idea which half. The point is that any arbitrary deviation from equality has a greater probability of decreasing aggregate satisfaction than increasing it. So, in the absence of individualized information, the best we can do is divide the cake up equally.

Both premises seem strong. It surely would be unpleasant to live in a society in which material things were allocated according to an individualized utilitarian calculus. And the idea of diminishing marginal utility is surely plausible. It does seem reasonable to suppose that the less you have of something, the more pleasure you get from a bit more. However, it is worth noticing that the whole line of argument here could alternatively be seen as a backhanded way of transcending utilitarianism. We could thus regard it as an attempt to use the utilitarian framework to generate conclusions whose basic ethical underpinnings are nonutilitarian.

Let me explain what I have in mind here. One way of arguing against allocations of things--cake, income, or whatever--based on direct utility calculations is, as we have seen, that they would involve intrusive information gathering, arbitrary discretion, and so on. But alternatively we might say that, even if this were not so, it would still be morally objectionable to make allocations depend on what people get out of the stuff they receive. The issue is still one of freedom, but in a more subtle way. The point of this alternative view is that people should have a chance to control certain resources irrespective of the use they make of them. Even if they don't make productive, felicific use of them, that shouldn't be a reason, even in principle, for taking them away and giving them to someone else.

We can interpret along the same lines the argument that derives equal distribution from skepticism about individual differences plus knowledge of the general fact of diminishing marginal utility. What we will now say is that this is an obscure and convoluted way of putting forward a claim that is in essence nonutilitarian. The claim is that each person has his or her hierarchy of priorities in life, and should have an equal chance to get as far as possible down the list of them. And an equal chance here should be understood as an equal claim on resources. Thus the underlying idea is not so much that we can't reduce the different ends that people have to a common measure, but rather that the result of our doing so is not ethically significant.

This idea, which I have barely sketched, is manifestly another liberal, individualist one, but it comes out of the tradition of rights doctrines rather than from the utilitarian traditions. It underlies Rawls's (1971) conception of primary goods as the subjects of justice, and has recently been identified with liberalism by Ronald Dworkin (1978) under the name of "neutrality." And more recently still, Bruce Ackerman (1980) made this same concept of neutrality the centerpiece of his book, Social Justice in the Liberal State.

So far I have been talking about the distribution of some quantity of material stuff that is assumed somehow already to be in existence. Even Bentham maintained that, in the absence of specific individualized information about utility schedules, the mode of distribution in that case should be an equal one, though his reasoning did not involve explicit reference to diminishing marginal utility.

His reasoning was in fact bogus. He argued that if you have two people with equal amounts, and take half away from one and give it to the other, you have reduced one person by half but increased the other by only a third. Therefore there must be a net loss of utility. This is clearly incorrect: If utility were linear with income (or whatever), it would be unchanged by the transfer. The only way of making sense of Bentham here seems to me to be to assume that he is in a confused way arguing for diminishing marginal utility.

In any case Bentham regarded this egalitarian conclusion as having very little in the way of practical implications because he was so impressed with the importance of supporting the market and therefore accepting whatever distribution of income came out of its workings. It was in this respect that the later utilitarians diverged from him. The tendency in later economists was to give the market its due as an efficient mechanism, but to suggest that it would be possible to increase the aggregate utility by redistributing income. We can see this move in utilitarian economics in John Stuart Mill's Principles of Political Economy in the mid-nineteenth century and, more systematically, in Pigou's The Economics of Welfare ([1920] 1932).

Although Mill, in his Autobiography, looked

forward to a time in which people would work for the common good without requiring material incentives, utilitarian analyses always actually continued with the assumption of individual self-interest. The problem for a utilitarian policy on economic distribution thus became to find the optimal level of redistribution, allowing for the need for incentives.

The considerations that arise here for a utilitarian (or indeed for others) are familiar enough. Taxes of the usual kind, whether on income or on consumption, have the effect at some point of discouraging effort. (At 100% they obviously discourage it completely, if people dislike work and are motivated by self-interest. So by an assumption of continuity we must suppose that lesser rates do so too.) But these taxes provide the wherewithal for paying those who would otherwise have little or nothing, so that the money so disposed has high marginal utility, much higher than it would have left in the hands of highly productive people. Maximum utility thus requires some redistribution--but not too much--from the highly productive to the nonproductive (and also perhaps to the able-bodied but relatively incompetent).

As Pigou said, "The correct formal answer to our question is that economic welfare is best promoted by a minimum standard raised to such a level that the direct good resulting from the transference of the marginal pound transferred to the poor just balances the indirect evil brought about by the consequent reduction of the dividend" (Pigou, [1920] 1932, p. 761). But, as Pigou himself admitted, this is entirely formal--indeed, a simple tautology--and does not in itself give us any guidance on what to do. To get a complete answer we clearly would need to know about each individual's consumption utility schedules and each ablebodied person's production disutility schedules, plus information on the way in which their actual production varied with the post-tax incentives they faced. We should then have to work out, on different tax rates, how much would be produced and how it would finish up by being distributed. We could then pick the tax rates that maximized aggregate utility.

In practice, none of this information is available. However, it is possible to work out the implications of alternative assumptions, and it has been found that a utilitarian income tax would not have very high marginal rates of tax, on any vaguely plausible assumptions. Although there is not much loss to aggregate utility by taking away high incomes, because the utility of a marginal dollar is low, by the same token the incentive provided to effort by a marginal dollar is also low. So the more one believes in declining marginal utility of money, the more good the transfer from the rich does, but the more serious the incentive problem becomes.

This of course presupposes that the efforts of high-income earners are sensitive to variations in post-tax income. As far as directors of large companies are concerned, it seems doubtful that paying them a half a million rather than a quarter of a million dollars per year would have any effect on their efforts, so tax rates approaching 100% at this income level are probably almost pure gain for the aggregate utility.

ALTERNATIVES TO THE UTILITARIAN CRITERION

Interest in the topics of distribution in general, and of social justice in particular, has increased dramatically in recent years, concurrently with an increasing skepticism about the claims of utilitarianism to provide an adequate single principle of evaluation (see Barry, 1978). Classical utilitarianism holds that any act or rule is good, if and only if it increases the total (or average) amount of satisfaction (utility) in a society. (Sidgwick [1907] still gives the best systematic exposition of utilitarian ethics. Miller [1976, pp. 31-40] provides a useful discussion of utilitarianism that includes a list of variations on the principle.) We may say that utilitarianism is therefore a nondistributive or aggregative moral principle (Barry, 1965, Ch. 3). This means, among other things, that distribution per se is not a central issue for the utilitarian, and that distributions are evaluatively relevant only on the basis of their effect on total or average social utility.

Using a common argument, let us imagine a situation in which keeping a portion of a society in bondage increases its GNP more than any other alternative. If this is so, then--assuming that GNP is a proper surrogate for social utility, that nobody outside the society is affected, and that all other indicators remain constant--it would follow that keeping slaves is a good thing in this society. Utilitarians would of course tend to deny that slavery would ever really be mandated by the principle. But they could not dispute the main point: that <u>how</u> things are actually distributed is germane only insofar as the distribution affects the aggregate (or average) level of satisfaction in a society.

It should hardly come as a surprise, then, that contemporary advocates of distributive principles focus on precisely this point when comparing their doctrines to utilitarian ones. Rawls, for example, sees <u>A Theory</u>

of Justice (1971) as a real alternative to utilitarianism--an attempt to preclude the possibility of a morally repugnant distribution, such as a slave economy, from ever arising. Indeed, if we are to take Rawls at his word, this is a major reason for his emphasis on the "priority of liberty" and the condition of the worst-off segment of society: He believes that, given a utilitarian moral view, there is a serious possibility of a society trading away the political liberty and economic well-being of some of its members in order to make some overall economic gain. (See Rawls [1971] especially pp. 150-192. The relation between Rawls's theory and utilitarianism is discussed in Taylor [1972], Arrow [1973], Braybrooke [1973], Coleman [1974], Harsanyi [1975], Rae [1975], Sen [1975], and Wolff [1977].)

Of course, Rawls's own position is not without its problems. Speaking from the utilitarian camp, David Lyons (1975) notes that for Rawls political liberty has priority (that is, it cannot be traded away) only in societies with high levels of civilization (Rawls, 1971, pp. 151-152). He then points out that if a society with a high level of civilization were to distribute according to utilitarian criteria instead of Rawlsian ones, the net result, at least in terms of the distribution of political liberty, would be the same. This is so because in relatively affluent societies the gains in efficiency achieved from an unequal distribution of liberty would be outweighed by losses in other areas. Thus a tradeoff would not be chosen. Indeed, if one looks at the situation closely, affluent societies might experience a real loss of efficiency if liberty were traded away (Barry, 1973, Ch. 7). Above all this, Lyons argues that in societies with low levels of civilization Rawls's principles would do no more to assure the equal distribution of political liberty than utilitarianism, since the priority of liberty is abandoned anyway. The only difference would be in how the distribution was justified; there would be no difference in fact. (For more on the priority of liberty in Rawls, see Nielsen [1977], Hart [1975], and Daniels [1975].)

The rejection of utilitarianism as a unique criterion for the evaluation of states of affairs sets the stage for an analysis of a variety of criteria of distributive justice. Although many such criteria have been identified in the recent literature, it will be convenient to follow David Miller's (1976) classification of criteria into three kinds: those that base the distribution on rights, those that base it on deserts, and those that base it on needs. The rights principle, put formally, states that "A is due x because A has a right to it." The deserts principle states that "A is due x because A deserves it." And the needs principle states that "A is due x because A needs it."

Recent work in contemporary political theory on social justice has had to face up to the critical problem of how all these competing principles relate to each other. If, say, a distribution according to the criteria of social justice ends up causing a drastic decline in productivity, thus assuring that all men will justly starve together, then it seems plain enough that we have to consider whether or not the requirements of social justice ought to be the sole criteria of distribution. It would clearly be irrational, not to say absurd, for a society to distribute on the basis of any principle if it produces outcomes that would be considered pernicious on almost any other ground.

But this is no simple matter. H. J. McCloskey (1963) once argued that if a sheriff of a small town could prevent severe rioting--in which hundreds of people would be killed--only by framing and killing an innocent man, the utilitarian would have no choice but to say that the sheriff ought to ready the gallows. Now, on the grounds of social justice--especially on the basis of the rights principle in societies with established legal rights and/or moral rights to live--this outcome would hardly be judged acceptable. (Miller [1976, pp. 52-82] distinguished the different kinds of rights.) But, as J. J. C. Smart points out, "the anti-utilitarian conclusion is a very unpalatable one too, namely that in some circumstances one must choose the greater misery, perhaps the very much greater misery, such as that of hundreds of people suffering painful deaths" (Smart & Williams, 1973, p. 72). One need not subscribe to a utilitarian view to see that Smart's statement is not without merit. There are many such hard cases in the application of principles: Indeed, the same tables that always seem to favor the house where utilitarianism is concerned can be turned on the principles of social justice.

Consider the complex case of distribution according to the needs principle. Following A. K. Sen (1973b, Ch. 4), let us suppose that in some hypothetical society people have two choices, to work hard or not to work hard. Let us further suppose that social resources (in this case, money) are distributed according to need, and that all persons in our society are primarily interested in their own welfare. Representing the two choices for any individual as I-1 (work hard) and I-0 (not work hard), and everyone else's choices as R-1 (work hard) and R-0 (not work hard), we can say that for any individual (I), the ordering of social situations, from most preferred to least preferred, is: (I-0)(R-1), (I-1)(R-1), (I-0)(R-0), (I-1)(R-0). This follows directly from the premises.

An individual primarily concerned with his own welfare, when faced with a situation in which the amount of labor time he puts into the production of the social dividend has almost no effect on the amount he actually receives, would obviously prefer to do nothing while everyone else is working (especially since he knows that his own lack of contribution will not seriously affect the total amount produced), and would least prefer to be working while everyone else is sitting around. The problem with this is, of course, that if every individual chooses his first preference (not an unreasonable assumption), absolutely nothing would get produced. (For a good technical discussion of the general form of this problem, the "prisoners' dilemma," see Luce and Raiffa [1957, pp. 94-102]. See also Olson [1965] for some applications of the problem to political situations.)

Over 100 years ago Marx recognized this as a real problem. Believing, with justification, that a distribution based on need would run into insurmountable difficulties in a society with an unreconstructed mentality, Marx recommended that societies in the early states of socialism should distribute on the basis of desert. Of course, Marx's concept of desert focused entirely on contribution (Marx, 1972), which is only one possible way of viewing the matter. And, it should be noted, the distributive result of the desert-as-contribution criterion varies, depending on who is applying it. A Marxist, using as his basis the labor theory of value, and a marginalist, using as his basis the relative contributions of factors of production, would come up with entirely different distributions, even though they agreed on the contribution principle.

Marxists and marginalists would probably also agree that the outcome of a needs-based distributive scheme in a society of self-interested persons is simply unacceptable. The way out appears to be either to pick another principle on which distribution can be based or somehow to change individual preferences. Clearly, if one chose to circumvent the incentive problem by distributing according to contributions, one would not face the prospect of an economic calamity arising from a lack of production. But one would have to figure out what to do about people who, for one reason or another, cannot contribute to the social product. Here, desert becomes problematic. Starvation is, after all, still starvation, and it is not pleasant to contemplate whether everybody starving together because nobody is willing to be the first to push a plough is really better or worse than certain groups starving separately because they are too old or too ill to do anything of substance. (See Miller [1976, pp. 83-121], Feinberg [1970, pp. 55-94], and Kleinig [1971] for discussions of desert.)

On the other hand, if the problem of incentive is to be solved by manipulating individual preference orderings in such a way that incentive really ceases to be a problem at all, that immediately raises some very tricky questions about the nature and origins of preferences and attitudes--and their relation to the social structure. It can surely be said that the social change required to make the needs principle work would be very great, and that the social cost for present generations in material and other terms would also be very great. What nobody seems to know is what sort of changes would be required, and precisely how high the social costs involved would be. It is clear that in this case we still face a tough choice if we want to stick to the needs principle: We can distribute on the basis of need now, with the obvious consequences; or we can begin a process of drastic social change, which is likely to be very costly.

Problems such as this one arise in connection with every principle. It is plain that certain types of political, social, and economic arrangements are better suited than others to the advancement of certain principles. But precisely which principles fit with which arrangements? It is as hard to imagine a desert-based distribution in a society of serfs and vassals as it is to imagine a need-based distribution in a society of personal welfare maximizers. But in other cases there is much disagreement on the relation of principles and social arrangements. For example, rights theorists, such as Nozick (1974) and Hayek (1976), argue that established property rights are most compatible with market arrangements, whereas Miller (1976, pp. 286-299), following Herbert Spencer and others, tends to argue that desert fits best with a market system. (See Miller [1976, Part 3] for an attempt to spell out connections between the three principles of justice and the types of society with which they are most compatible.)

The addition of rights to the discussion tends to confuse the issue of the relation between principles even more. This is so because in the rights language it is possible to argue that a person or group has a right to be treated under some <u>other</u> principle. For instance, it is possible to say that "A has a right to what he deserves" or "A has a right to an equal share of the social dividend." But it is not clear in these cases whether or not the rights principle has any independent justificatory force. What it seems we are really saying here is "Apply the desert principle" or "Apply the equality principle." If this is correct, then many apparently conflicting rights claims may in fact be claims based on principles other than rights. The right to free health care versus the right of the medical profession to charge high rates for its services may be a real rights conflict: There may be an established right to free health care (although it would have to have been fairly recently established) and an established right of independent professionals to set their own prices. On the other hand, the conflict may turn out to be between needs and deserts, both couched in rights language.

Even once a particular set of rights has been settled on, we still need to consider how they relate to other principles. The case of the sheriff, for example, seemed to show how rights and utility conflict: Rights-based distributions are immune to considerations of general social consequences. But there is a strain in utilitarianism spanning two centuries, from Hume (1888, Bk. III, Pt. II) to Mill (1957, Sec. V) to Lyons (1977), that tries to make a case for distribution according to a system of rights. The general argument is that although a single violation of the rights principle, considered independently of everything else, may increase the level of satisfaction in a society, many violations of established rights, considered together, will produce an outcome less optimal in terms of utility than that produced when no rights violations occur. The problem here is that since rights and utility do conflict when both are applied simultaneously, what this position apparently calls for is the abandonment of the utility principle for the sake of utility. And if this is so, one has to wonder whether it makes sense in this case to talk about utility at all (Smart & Williams, 1973, pp. 118-135).

That the utilitarian may be forced either to accept a morally offensive distribution outcome or to abandon his utilitarianism altogether is a central reason why political theorists have turned away from aggregate utility as a sole criterion and toward distributive considerations. But clearly, just because utilitarianism does not seem to be able to stand up on its own, does this necessarily mean that we should forgo utilitarian considerations entirely? Would it, after all, really be justifiable for a society to distribute on the basis of social justice alone, if the cost in terms of aggregate utility is enormous? Is it sensible to set up a need-based distribution even when faced with the prospect of mass starvation?

Distributive principles do not appear to be any more immune to criticism on the ground of producing repugnant outcomes than utilitarianism. Perhaps the most important effect of the vigorous debate about the implications of distributive principles has been the fairly conclusive demonstration that no single principle is entirely free of difficulties when applied without qualification.

But do we need to distribute according to any one principle? Obviously not. Should we be blindly committed, say, to the principle of desert, even if it entails a monstrous Spencerian world in which the less well-endowed are allowed to die off like giraffes with short necks? Or should we stick with a theory of property rights à la Nozick (1974), having the implications drawn by Malthus (1803)? "A man who is born into a world already possessed, if he cannot get substance from his parents on whom he has a just demand, and if the society does not want his labour, has no claim of right to the smallest portion of food, and, in fact, has no business to be where he is. At Nature's mighty feast there is no vacant cover for him. She tells him to be gone, and will quickly execute her own orders" (p. 531). But the obvious corrective, a principle of justice as the satisfaction of need, runs into the difficulties already touched on if applied without regard to any other considerations.

SOCIAL JUSTICE: ITS SUBJECT MATTER AND SCOPE

I shall not be so foolhardy as to attempt, in what remains of this chapter, to resolve the problems I raised in the previous section. I hope that the references given will be of assistance to those who are unfamiliar with recent philosophical work and would like to find out more. What I should like to do in the space that is left is to suggest how empirical considerations underlie the practical applications of normative principles.

Let us ask a question that has so far been ducked: What is the subject matter of social justice? I think that the context in which the term normally occurs is this: We may wish to ask to what extent those things that are widely valued and of basic importance are distributed among the members of a society in accordance with the requirements of justice. We ask that question by asking whether social justice obtains. In particular, we refer to social injustice when the maldistribution takes on a systematic rather than a random quality.

I do not know when the use of the term "social injustice" originated, though my guess would be the second quarter of the nineteenth century (see Hayek, 1976, p. 63 and n. 8, p. 176). Of course people had criticized particular legal privileges or tax exemptions, or particular methods of allocating obligations (for example, the press gang as a means of recruitment) before that. But I think the idea that the distribution of all the advantages and disadvantages derived from living together in a society (including those that are not the direct result of political decisions) can be subject to an overall judgement in terms of justice or injustice was an invention as momentous as that of the steam engine.

I have just said that the expression "social justice" is used when we ask about the distribution of "those things that are widely valued and of basic importance." That something is widely valued and of basic importance is, however, not a sufficient condition of its falling within the ambit of social justice. There are two further conditions, scarcity and (with an apology for inelegance) distributability. Whether these obtain in a given case is in principle a matter of fact. But it is by no means a simple matter of fact. Indeed, the question of distributability involves some of the hoariest problems in social and political theory.

Let's start with scarcity. The traditional example of a widely valued and important good that is not scarce is air. This is not in fact an entirely simple case in that the maintenance of air that is healthy to breathe may require the imposition of controls on air pollution. But it is of course true that in any given area the amount of air that one person breathes does not leave measurably less for others. Air consumption does not therefore pose a problem of social justice.

As a result of population growth or technical change, something may move into the sphere of social justice in the course of time. Thus when Locke (1965) wrote the Second Treatise of Government he could describe the ocean as "that great and still remaining Common of Mankind" (p. 331), and the technology of the seventeenth century probably did leave "enough, and as good" (p. 333) for others in the sea. As the Conference on the Law of the Sea shows clearly enough, this is certainly not true now, and the question of how access to the resources of the sea is to be allocated is a pressing and controversial one.

The other condition is the one that I called distributability. Something is distributable if the amount of it received by different people can be affected by human actions. The outer limits of social justice are the limits of distributability. As the Bible remarks, it raineth alike on the just and the unjust, and that is indeed the paradigm of a distribution that is not subject to criticism on the basis of social justice (or at least was so until cloud seeding). If nobody knows how to produce a certain outcome, then it cannot be a demand of social justice that the outcome be produced, even if it looks as if somebody ought to know.

Thus Christopher Jencks has argued that American schools do an equally bad job of teaching poor black and poor white children with low test scores on entry into the school system, and there are simply proportionally far more black children in that position: "The primary problem is not racism or malice but simple ignorance. Most educators just don't know how to teach these children much. Nor do I. Until we learn, no amount of pressure or money will help" (Jencks, 1973, p. 152). If one accepts this, then some aspects of the way scholastic attainment is distributed cannot be criticized on the basis of social justice, though one may of course wish to go on to say that it is a requirement of social justice that substantial efforts should be made to find out how to teach disadvantaged children more effectively.

If the outer perimeter of the scope of social justice is those things whose distribution can be affected by human action, an important boundary within that perimeter divides those things whose distribution can be affected by political decision making from those things whose distribution is affected by human actions but impervious to political manipulation. Consider the Indian caste system. A child born into an untouchable subcaste is condemned to a narrow range of occupational choice, little or no access to the main institutions of the society, and a lifetime of stigmatization. Yet in spite of the official abolition of untouchability and special measures designed to help untouchables, many millions of Indians are still in much the same condition as before Independence.

This problem is surely within the outer perimeter of social justice since it is the product of a multitude of human actions, yet if the political system is powerless to change it we cannot as a matter of strict logic say that it is failing to promote social justice. This of course immediately raises the question of whether the Indian government has done everything possible to correct the problem. More might be done by a government that was prepared to mount an all-out attack on the entire varna system, like the Maoist assault on Confucianism, backed up by a network of informers and thought police.

The commonsense reaction to this is that there are two questions here. First there is the question of fact: How much social justice is obtainable by political means? And second, there is the question of value: How much is worth obtaining by political means? The first is indeed a matter of fact so long as we acknowledge that there can be matters of fact for which conclusive evidence is not obtainable. (After all, the existence or nonexistence of God is a matter of fact.) But to say that the question "How much social justice is worth obtaining by political means?" is a question of value oversimplifying things.

To make the discussion more definite and more manageable, let us suppose that the only value in competition with social justice is liberty. Then there are really two components involved in any view of the amount of social justice worth pursuing: How much liberty in fact has to be given up for a certain gain in social justice? And what is the relative value of liberty as against social justice? The first is an empirical question--though again of the slippery kind that involves basic ideas about human nature--while the second is indeed properly thought of as a value judgement. (I should, however, emphasize that I do not believe that saying something is a value judgement puts it beyond rational discussion.)

This is, I realize, terribly abstract and more than a little artificial. But I do want to maintain that the ideas of trade-off and limits are necessary, and I think they can be illustrated by looking at the things whose distribution is the subject matter of social justice. What are these? In the most general terms, there is, I suggest, the familiar trilogy of money, status, and power. They are widely, even if not universally, valued and they are important in that the possession or lack of possession of them makes a fundamental difference in the range of possibilities open in one's life, so they meet the first two conditions.

They are also scarce--status most obviously because status is inherently invidious: There can be no top dogs without bottom dogs. That status is invidious--that high rank entails low rank--does not mean that status is strictly zero sum. If we are prepared to ascribe absolute levels of status, we may find that in some society the position of groups with high and low status remains the same while, within certain limits, the ratio of the sizes of the groups changes. In that case average status would have gone up if the superior group had increased proportionally, and down if it were the subordinate group that had shown the increase. But because differential status is invidious, the supply cannot be indefinitely expanded.

Whether or not power should be conceived of as zero sum, so that the total amount of power in a social system is always a fixed amount, is a question that has generated more heat than light among social scientists. If we think of a person's power as the ability to impose some kind of sanction on others unless they do what he wants, or the ability to offer some kind of reward if they do what he wants, the total amount of power increases with the complexity and interdependence of the society. More power is held by the members of a modern industrial society than by the members of a society of largely self-sufficient settlers, for example. But if we think of an individual's net power as his power over others minus others' power over him, then it is clear that the net power of all the individuals in a society (positive and negative) must sum to zero.

Money is also scarce. Of course the nominal currency can be multiplied indefinitely, but the total of real claims of goods and services that can be made good is limited at any given time and can be expanded over time only by a few percent each year. It might be said that whereas the scarcity of status and power is imposed by logic, the scarcity of money is an empirical matter. It is certainly an important distinction between money on the one side and status and power on the other that the amount of money can be increased over time, since this means that it is possible to improve the position of some without making anyone else worse off. This is politically significant because where there is economic growth and its benefits are widely diffused, it does in fact seem to be very rare for economic grievances to be acute enough to focus into a violent protest movement unless the poor also form a group distinguished by low collective status or by collective exclusion from power. But although one can imagine without too much difficulty a society whose members were satiated with mass-produced consumer goods, it becomes more and more apparent as societies approach that point that the limiting factor is the supply of personal services.

So much for scarcity. What about distributability? Let us again take up our trilogy of status, power, and wealth. Status systems are interesting because they are pure human artifacts: The forms of status differential that exist in a society and the way in which the superior and inferior positions are allocated are entirely constituted by human actions. The whole status hierarchy therefore falls within what I called the outer perimeter of the sphere of social justice. On the other hand, the extent to which the status system can be manipulated by political decisions is limited.

It is difficult to generalize because of the vast range of phenomena included under the term "status system." At one end are legally created group statuses, defined by a complex of privileges and disabilities. This would include the three or four estates into which most European populations were divided until the nineteenth century, and any society with a legal distinction between free men and slaves or serfs. It would also include any society that subjects part of the population to a complex of legal disabilities--restrictions on residence, movement, political rights, ownership of property, occupation, and so on. Examples would be all the European settler regimes in relation to the indigenous population from the seventeenth century on (including the protestant settlement in Ireland), contemporary South Africa, and the American South after the abolition of slavery. All these have the characteristic that, having been created by law they can be abolished by law, and most of those I mentioned have been. We can give a definite date for the abolition of an estate system, slavery, serfdom, and so on.

At the other extreme is the system of occupational prestige in modern industrial societies. This does not rest on a legal basis and is very difficult to manipulate by state action. Indeed, surely one of the most striking uniformities in social science is the close correlation between the prestige ranking of occupations in different modern industrial societies in spite of differences in culture, economic system, or official political ideology. The explanation may be that occupational prestige is a fairly realistic reflection of the responsibility, autonomy, and skill called for by various jobs, and that there is some sort of natural tendency for these features of occupations to be a source of prestige.

Power is like status in that its distribution is entirely constituted of human decisions. This puts the distribution of power entirely within what I called the outer perimeter of social justice. If we turn to the inner perimeter of social justice--that which is susceptible to change by political means--we find that power differs from status in two opposite ways. On the one hand the identity of those occupying positions with more or less power is obviously subject to political determination. That is to say, within a certain structure of roles defining positions in the hierarchy of power, one individual can be replaced by another and the new individual has (allowing for the personal equation) the same power as his predecessor. In this sense power can be directly distributed by political fiat in a way that status cannot: The distribution of status can be causally affected by political decisions, but it cannot actually be allocated.

On the other hand the hierarchical structure itself is ultimately more plastic in the case of status than in that of power. The observed variations in the height of the status hierarchy are immense--from slavery or the earlier Indian caste system to the relative equality of some small contemporary countries like New Zealand and Denmark. And at any rate it makes sense--even if it is utopian to expect it to be fully realized--that there might be a society in which people are respected for their personal achievements, scientific, literary, athletic, or whatever, but in which there are no gradations of overall status. The observed variations in the power hierarchy are also very great, of course. But the spread from the powerful to the least powerful person in even the most equal modern societies is still enormous. And it is impossible to imagine any way in which a sharp hierarchy of power could be dispensed with.

The implication of this is that power, considered as an attribute of individuals, cannot be distributed with more than a very low degree of equality. It cannot therefore be an intelligible demand in the name of social justice that it should be more equal than that. However, I think it is questionable whether power is correctly conceived of as an object of general desire, in the sense that most people would always prefer to have more than less (see Mansbridge, 1977). Personal power is a taste which, once acquired, is very strong--so strong that few political leaders retire while they are still in good health and face no immediate prospect of defeat. (When one does, as Sir Harold Wilson did, it is so unusual that scarcely anyone is at first inclined to believe that the public explanation is also the real one.) But perhaps personal power should be construed on the model of an addiction--once you have the craving life seems empty without it, but that doesn't mean that you're better off with the craving than without it.

I would suggest that for most people what is important is not power over others but security--that is to say, protection against power wielded by others. And this can be provided by suitable institutions. The citizen requires a civilian review board to handle complaints against the police, some kind of procedure for appealing against the actions of civil servants, and the right to a fair trial. The employee requires an enforceable grievance procedure and protection against arbitrary dismissal. The tenant requires legal protection against eviction and harassment. The patient in a hospital requires the right to complain about neglect or maltreatment to an impartial body without having to fear retaliation. And so on. All measures of this kind reduce the dependence of anyone on the arbitrary will of another--the worst feature in the eyes of many of the _ancien régime_ in France, American slavery, the Nazi concentration camps, and secret police like Duvalier's _tontons macoutes,_ and Stalin's NKVD.

What is, however, equally important as a means of

distributing defensive power is a well-founded belief that the interests one shares with others are capable of being defended against attack. The means of producing this kind of group security are more various and more problematic than those of producing security against the arbitrary exercise of power against individuals. The most reliable source of security is an organization controlled by the members of the group with a common interest and capable of mobilizing most or all of its members to give rewards or apply sanctions in accordance with strategic requirements. A good example would be trade unions, which in every Western country have succeeded in cutting into so-called management prerogatives and improving working conditions. (For illustrations of unfettered management prerogatives, see Bendix [1963].) Another would be the Indian caste associations, which bargain with politicians, civil servants, and other relevant actors on behalf of the members of a jati, using offers of votes, threats of civil disturbances, and so on (see Rudolph and Rudolph, 1967, pp. 29-36).

A second way in which the members of a group may feel a certain degree of well-founded security is simply in knowing that among those individuals who have most power in the society, those with the interests of one's group at heart, are well represented. This means, obviously, representation on the central decision making authority (cabinet, council of ministers, or whatever), but it may well also mean representation in the civil service, the judiciary, the police force, and the armed services (at all levels). Indeed, such representation is valuable, even if the government itself is not representative, because it would make it difficult for the government to implement plans for the oppression of one group.

We may in a loose way say that a social group is powerful if it has a powerful organization to defend its interests. Similarly, we can loosely say that a social group is powerful if its members are well represented in positions of power and can be counted on to pursue the interests of the social group.

The implication of this analysis is that inequality in the distribution of power among individuals is not significant, subject to the proviso that there is protection against its arbitrary use. What is much more significant from the standpoint of social justice is the way the distribution of power among individuals either concentrates power in the hands of representatives of certain social groups rather than others, or diffuses it. A sharp pyramid of power in which all social groups are represented at the top is more equal, if we focus our attention on the prospects for social groups, than a flatter pyramid in which most or all the higher positions are filled by representatives of a single social group.

The third member of the triad is money. Unlike status and power, money, in the sense of command over economic resources, is not simply constituted of human actions. The outer perimeter of social justice therefore consists of all quantities and distributions of goods and services that could be brought about by the members of a society if they chose to do so. The inner perimeter is set by those quantities and distributions that could be brought about by political arrangements (where "political arrangements" is understood to include creating the legal framework for a market and accepting whatever comes out of it).

If economic goods fell from heaven like manna (or cargo, for those who prefer a more up-to-date religion), the only problem would be how they should be distributed, and in principle any distribution could be maintained indefinitely by political fiat (see Nozick, 1974). In the real world it is true that at any given time the goods in the shops and warehouses could be distributed according to any plan thought fit by those with the political power to implement it. But then the problem arises of replenishing the shelves. Taking the long view, we may say that people have to be motivated somehow to produce the goods before they can be distributed.

One obvious way to motivate people, which almost all societies make <u>some</u> use of, though its relative importance varies, is to make the quantity of economic goods received by a person depend in some way on the contribution he makes to producing economic goods. Once a society is committed to using this method of motivating people to produce (even if not exclusively), distributions that would otherwise be feasible--in the sense that the total quantity of goods to bring them about could be produced if everybody chose to work hard enough--would cease to be feasible because they are incompatible with providing an adequate economic incentive.

A good example of the distance one may be carried by such considerations is offered by Johns Rawls's treatment of income inequalities in <u>A Theory of Justice</u> (1971, pp. 258-284, 303-325). The principle that Rawls proposes is that inequalities should be arranged so as to make the worst-off as well off as possible. In a manna economy this would entail an equal distribution, because any inequality would make the worst-off worse off than they might be. But given the need for incentives to get people to work (and also to acquire skills and other qualifications), Rawls allows for whatever inequalities are necessary to stimulate effort, as long as the net result is at all beneficial to the worst-off compared to a situation with less equality. In practice the kind of economic system that Rawls endorses as just is one in which economic rewards are allocated by a market mechanism, and equalization is then carried out by some kind of personal income tax, but only to the point where the net (post-transfer) income of the worst-off reaches a maximum.

Rawls himself apparently believes that with equality of educational opportunity and the absence of restrictions on occupational entry the inequalities in earned income would be relatively small--a view that is strikingly reminiscent of the lyrical final stage ("The Future Progress of the Human Mind") of Condorcet's (1955) Sketch for a Historical Picture of the Progress of the Human Mind:

> It is easy to prove that wealth has a natural tendency to equality, and that any excessive disproportion could not exist or at least would rapidly disappear if civil laws did not provide artificial ways of perpetuating and uniting fortunes; if free trade and industry were allowed to remove the advantages that accrued wealth derives from any restrictive law or fiscal privilege; . . . if the administration of the country did not afford some men ways of making their fortune that were closed to other citizens. (p. 180)

It may perhaps be questioned whether the optimism of the 1790s, when a market society was still a twinkle in the eye of Adam Smith, can reasonably be retained in the 1980s when market societies have had a good chance to show their potential. That need not be decided here. What is to the point is that the use of economic incentives must set limits to the range of feasible distributions.

Rawls does not discuss alternatives to economic incentives, but it is clear that in principle any incentive may be utilized. To the extent that people are prepared to work because they enjoy it or feel a sense of social responsibility to work, economic incentives are not needed. Alternatively, economic incentives may be replaced by direction of labor into jobs and threats of punishment for not working hard enough. It need hardly be said that there would be objections to such methods on grounds of individual liberty, even if it were conceded that they made possible a more just distribution of economic goods than that arising from the reliance on economic incentives. But we are at present asking not what is desirable but what is feasible. (See Rawls [1977], Barry [1973, pp. 154-165], and Nozick [1974, pp.

149-275] for some different views on the incentive question.)

CONCLUSION

I have tried in this chapter to indicate what social scientists might be able to get from philosophers, and what philosophers might be able to get from social scientists. I cannot pretend to have demonstrated that the disciplines will be mutually enriched by greater attention in each to what is going on in the other. At the most I hope to have made it sufficiently plausible to encourage people on both sides to invest the time and effort in learning more. If I have succeeded in that, then I shall be satisfied.

REFERENCES

Ackerman, B. *Social justice in the liberal state.* New Haven: Yale University Press, 1980.

Arrow, K. J. Some ordinalist-utilitarian notes on Rawls' theory of justice. *Journal of Philosophy,* 1973, *70,* 254.

Barry, B. *Political argument.* London: Routledge and Kegan Paul, 1965.

Barry, B. *The liberal theory of justice: A critical examination of the principal doctrines in a theory of justice by John Rawls.* Oxford: Clarendon Press, 1973.

Barry, B. And who is my neighbor? Review of *right and wrong* by Charles Fried. *Yale Law Journal,* 1978, *88,* 629-658.

Bendix R. *Work and authority in industry.* New York: Harper & Row, 1963.

Bentham, J. *Defense of usury.* London: Payne & Foss, 1818.

Bowring, J. *The works of J. Bentham.* Edinburgh: W. Tait, 1843.

Braybrooke, D. Utilitarianism with a difference: Rawls' position in ethics. *Canadian Journal of Philosophy,* 1973, *3,* 303-331.

Buchanan, J. *The limits of liberty.* Chicago: University of Chicago Press, 1975.

Coleman, J. S. Inequality, sociology, and moral philosophy. American Journal of Sociology, 1974, 80, 739-764.

Condorcet, M.-J.-A.-N.C. Sketch for a historical picture of the progress of the human mind (June Barraclough, trans). London: Weidenfeld and Nicolson, 1955.

Daniels, N. Equal liberty and unequal worth of liberty. In N. Daniels (Ed.), Reading Rawls. New York: Basic Books, 1975.

Dworkin, R. Liberalism. In S. Hampshire (Ed.), Public and private morality. Cambridge: Cambridge University Press, 1978.

Edgeworth, F. Y. Mathematical psychics. New York: A. M. Kelley, 1967.

Edgeworth, F. Y. New and old methods of ethics. Oxford: J. Parker, 1877.

Feinberg, J. Doing and deserving. Princeton: Princeton University Press, 1970.

Harsanyi, J. C. Can the maximin principle serve as a basis for morality? American Political Science Review, 1975, 69, 594-606.

Hart, H. L. A. Are there any natural rights? Philosophy Review, 1955, 64, 175-191.

Hayek, F. A. Law, legislation and liberty, Vol. 2: The mirage of social justice. Chicago: University of Chicago Press, 1976.

Hume, D. A treatise of human nature. L. A. Selby-Bigage (Ed.). Oxford: Clarendon Press, 1888.

Jencks, C. Inequality in retrospect. Harvard Education Review, 1973, 43, 138-164.

Kleinig, J. The concept of desert. American Philosophy Quarterly, 1971, 8, 71-78.

Locke, J. Two treatises of government, P. Laslett (Ed.). New York: New American Library, 1965.

Luce, R. D., & Raiffa, H. Games and decisions. New York: John Wiley and Sons, 1957.

Lyons, D. The nature and soundness of the contract and coherence arguments. See Daniels, 1975, pp. 141-167.

Lyons, D. Human rights and the general welfare. *Philosophy and Public Affairs,* 1977, *6,* 113-129.

Malthus, T. *An essay on the principle of population* (2nd Ed.). *London: J. Johnson, 1803.*

Mansbridge, J. J. Acceptable inequalities. *British Journal of Political Science,* 1977, *7,* 321-326.

Marx, K. *Critique of the Gotha program.* In R. C. Tucker (Ed.), *The Marx-Engels reader.* New York: W. W. Norton, 1972.

McCloskey, H. J. A note on utilitarian punishment. *Mind,* 1963, *72,* 599.

Mill, J. S. *Utilitarianism,* O. Piest (Ed.) New York: Bobbs-Merrill, 1957.

Mill, J. S. *Autobiography.* New York: Columbia University Press, 1960.

Mill, J. S. *Principles of political economy.* Totonto: University of Toronto Press, 1965.

Miller, D. *Social justice.* Oxford: Clarendon Press, 1976.

Nielsen, K. The priority of liberty examined. *Indian Political Science Review,* 1977, *11,* 49-59.

Nozick, R. *Anarchy, state, and utopia.* New York: Basic Books, 1974.

Olson, M., Jr. *The logic of collective action.* Cambridge, MA: Harvard University Press, 1965.

Parekh, B. Bentham's theory of equality. *Polit. Studies* 1970, *18,* 478-495.

Pigou, C. *The economics of welfare.* London: Macmillan, [1920] 1932.

Rae, D. W. Maximin justice and an alternative principle of general advantage. *American Political Science Review,* 1975, *69,* 630-647.

Rawls, J. *A theory of justice.* Cambridge, MA: Belknap Press of Harvard University Press, 1971.

Rawls, J. The basic structure as subject. *American Philosophy Quarterly,* 1977, *14,* 159-165.

Robbins, L. The nature and significance of economic science. London: Macmillan, 1932.

Rudolph, L., & Rudolph, S. H. The modernity of tradition. Chicago: The University of Chicago Press, 1967.

Sen, A. K. Behaviour and the concept of preference. Inaugural lecture, the London school of economics and political science, 1973a.

Sen, A. K. On economic inequality. Oxford: Clarendon Press, 1973b.

Sen, A. K. Rawls versus Bentham: An axiomatic examination of the pure distribution problem. See Daniels, 1975, pp. 283-292.

Sidgwick, H. Bentham and Benthamism in politics and ethics (1877). Miscellaneous essays and addresses. London and New York: Macmillan, 1904.

Sidgwick, H. The methods of ethics. London: Macmillan, 1907.

Smart, J. J. C., & Williams, B. Utilitarianism: For and against. Cambridge: Cambridge University Press, 1973.

Taylor, P. Utility and justice. Canadian Journal of Philosophy, 1972, 1, 327-350.

Wolff, R. P. Understanding Rawls. Princeton: Princeton University Press, 1977.

Part III

THE THEORY OF INCOME DISTRIBUTION

Boulding explores that puzzling characteristic of the market economy wherein an integral movement at once affects the allocation of resources, to be evaluated by reference to the criterion of efficiency, and distribution of income to be judged by reference to the standard of justice and equity.

Katsenelinboigen abstracts the elements of a general system of values and exchange encompassing physical as well as social and economic phenomena.

Intriligator confronts the elusive task of conceptualizing the construction of an aggregate social preference function in relation to the choice of a system of income redistribution.

6. Allocation and Distribution: The Quarrelsome Twins

Kenneth E. Boulding

Between them, allocation and distribution cover a very large part of economics. Allocation covers the question of what is produced and how, distribution covers the question of who gets what and how. It would be hard to point to any decision or even any external change in the economic system that did not have an impact on both allocation and on distribution. Almost anything that happens in the economic system changes the input and the output processes of production and is also likely to redistribute net worth, income, or both, among the persons of the economy. Nevertheless, the concepts of allocation and distribution are distinct and each represents an aspect or dimension of the total system, even if we cannot change one without changing the other.

Both dimensions are also significant in the overall evaluation of changes in the system and are often in conflict. A change that is favorable from the point of view of allocation, resulting in a more efficient use of resources and an increase in output per unit of input, however these are identified, may be adverse from the point of view of distribution, either rewarding or punishing the undeserving or moving the system away from what is regarded as an optimum degree of equality.

There are three different aspects of both allocation and distribution, interrelated but again distinct. The first might be called the occupational aspect. On the allocational side it involves the distribution of the resources of society among various occupations and industries. This again involves at least three further problems. First is the distribution of assets in the wider sense of the word (economically significant stocks) among different occupations. This would include the labor force as human capital, land area, natural resources, and physical capital, defined as economically significant material artifacts of all kinds. Second, there is a problem of allocation of assets or resources over time among different occupations, which makes things even more complicated. A third problem is the allocation of the use of these assets in various occupations, for instance, whether they are fully used or partly or wholly unemployed.

The distributional element in the occupational aspect consists of the distribution of the economic welfare of individuals according to the extent to which their personal resources are devoted to one occupation or another. This also involves both an asset and an income element: first the rates of return on investment in human capital to people with different skills and trades, and also to different occupations of personally owned land or capital, and then the incomes that result from these investments.

A second aspect of both allocation and distribution is what is frequently called functional. This is most obvious on the side of distribution, where it emerges as the problem of what determines the proportional distribution of national income--or some suitable aggregate--among the functional shares: wages, profit, interest, rent, and so on. A simpler but very meaningful taxonomy is between labor income and nonlabor income. Another important aspect of functional distribution involves the valuation of assets and the rate of return on capital, which again is related to distribution over time.

Functional distribution also involves certain allocational problems, for instance, between investment and consumption, or between investment in human capital and investment in material capital. The rate of return on capital is important in this connection also, as is the distribution of income from assets between interest and profit. In many cases it is not easy to separate out the allocational from the distributional aspects of the problem.

A problem that somewhat defies the above taxonomy is unemployment. In some regards this can be put under occupational allocation, simply as an industry with no products. However, it has important relationships with the functional aspect of the demand for labor, and depends in part on processes of functional distribution--how much goes to wages, how much to interest, how much to profits, and so on.

A third aspect is distribution among persons and groups, of both assets and income; who, for instance, is rich and who is poor? There are allocational problems here as well. How persons, households or groups allocate their income, for instance, among different consumer goods and forms of personal saving and investment, affects allocation by occupation and also affects functional distribution between labor and nonlabor income. We have here an immense interconnecting web of actions, reactions, and feedbacks that we cannot claim to have untangled it completely. Indeed, its disentanglement comprises a very large part of the discipline of economics.

OCCUPATIONAL ALLOCATION AND DISTRIBUTION

At the level of occupations and industries, the rough but intimate connection between allocation and distribution can be illustrated by consideration of the classical theory of relative prices. This was formulated in every essential respect by Adam Smith in *The Wealth of Nations*, especially in Book I, Chapter 7. All subsequent elaborations by Marshall,(1) Walras,(2) Pareto,(3) E. H. Chamberlain,(4) Joan Robinson,(5) and so on, have been relatively minor reformulations and modifications of Adam Smith's basic theory.

The theory begins with the proposition that market prices, that is, the actual prices in current exchanges, will change if they do not clear the market, that is, if they leave unsatisfied buyers or unsatisfied sellers who would like to exchange at the existing price but cannot find a trading partner. If there are unsatisfied buyers, they will try to improve their own economic welfare by raising the price at which they are offering to buy in the hope of attracting new sellers, perhaps by transforming some buyers into sellers. In a competitive market, this will cause the price to rise on all transactions. If there are unsatisfied sellers, they will lower the price at which they are offering to sell in the hope of unloading the commodity onto new buyers.

In all this there is no production or consumption; the allocational aspects of the problem consist of the constant shift of fixed stocks of assets of different kinds--money, commodities, securities, and so on--from one set of owners to others. The distributional aspect of the problem is that a rise in the price of a commodity shifts the distribution of net worth in the market toward those who hold the larger stocks of it and away from those who hold larger stocks of money, and a fall in the price shifts net worth toward those who hold money and away from those who hold a commodity. It is nearly impossible for a price to change without having substantial impact on the distribution of net worth among the marketers.

Even in a market with a constant set of different assets, there may be speculative cycles in prices resulting from the fact that the aggregate preferences for, shall we say, a commodity or money, depend on some aggregate or average of the expectations of the future. If prices are generally expected to rise, this will encourage buyers and discourage sellers. Prices will then rise, and if the rise confirms the expectations they will rise still further. Prices cannot rise, however, without eventually becoming "high," at which point they will begin to fall and will continue to fall until they become "low," after which they will rise again.

All of this fluctuation is without regard to production or consumption, but it results in constant distributional shifts between the successful speculators who anticipate price changes correctly and the unsuccessful ones who anticipate price changes incorrectly. The unsuccessful speculators tend to be eliminated from the market as their net worth falls below what makes it possible for them to operate, and new marketers may constantly come in from outside to take their place. There may be some equilibrium pattern of distribution of net worth as a result of continued operation of a market of this kind. What determines this pattern is a question that, so far as I know, has never been answered; I suspect it is capable of an answer if the parameters of the problem could be defined.

From Adam Smith on, economists have always gone beyond the immediate and perhaps cyclical equilibrium of market price to something that Smith called the "natural" price(6) and Marshall the "normal" price.(7) This is a set of relative prices which would persist indefinitely if there are no changes in underlying production or consumption functions, resulting in a distribution of income or, more broadly, economic welfare among the individuals of a society such that there would be no net movement of resources and production from any one commodity to any other.

This assumes that there is a set function relating the relative price structure in the market to the distribution of incomes or economic welfare by industries or productive occupations. If the price of, say, wheat on the market is perceived to be high, that is, above its normal price, and the price of wool is low, that is, below its natural price, the distribution of economic welfare by occupations will be such that individuals and groups whose income is derived primarily from the production of wheat will be relatively well off while those whose income is derived from the production of wool will be relatively worse off.

This goes back to a further proposition that individual economic welfare is closely related to the individual's terms of trade, that is, to how much he can buy per unit of what he sells. If a bushel of wheat buy an increased quantity of other goods, the wheat producer becomes better off in consequence. The next proposition is that the structure of terms of trade of all individuals is a function of the total relative price structure. A rise in the relative price of any one commodity, such as wheat, redistributes income or economic welfare toward the wheat producer and away from the producers of all of the things that the wheat producer buys with his wheat.

A further proposition is that the distribution of economic welfare among groups or producers of different commodities changes the allocation of resources among these occupational groups. If the price of wheat is perceived as being high, and wheat producers correspondingly as unusually well off, more people will go into wheat production. If the price of wool is low, with wool producers perceived as relatively worse off, people will go out of wool production. As people come into wheat production, however, the output of wheat will increase, the stocks of wheat will increase, the price of wheat will fall. As people leave the wool industry, wool production will decline, and this will make the price of wool rise in the market.

Such is the notion of general equilibrium; which, except for aesthetic reasons need not be expressed as a system of simultaneous equations. If the set of market prices does not correspond to the set of natural prices, those that are high will fall, those that are low will rise. There is a constant tendency for the set of market prices to move toward the set of normal prices. The mechanism is precisely the interaction between allocation and distribution. The mathematician can, at least formally, resolve the question of whether and when these dynamic movements would move the system toward an equilibrium or when lags in reaction and the momentum of change would create overshoots in cycles producing perhaps even permanent cyclical fluctuations. But the cycles are always around some equilibrium position or trend.

The introduction of monopoly and imperfect competition into this picture modifies it but does not fundamentally change it. Monopoly power consists in the ability of a group of producers or a single producer of a particular commodity to maintain a level of output at which the market price is above the natural price, by preventing others (through law, force, or fraud) from entering this occupation from less favored occupations. It is this artificial restriction of entry that is the essence of monopoly power. It simply means, however, that monopoly power is one of the parameters of the system, and that there is a natural equilibrium of the price system relative to whatever degree of monopoly power exists in it.

Monopoly power is never unlimited. If production is too severely curtailed, the net returns to the monopolist will decline. Monopoly power, moreover, is often restrained by the fear that the high prices will attract new competitors whom the monopolist will not be able to control or police. The easiest way to sustain monopoly power is to exercise it very sparingly.

Imperfection in competition is a somewhat different matter. It can take many forms. One is ignorance, which may become a form of monopoly power, perhaps rather randomly distributed from time to time. Another is differentiation of the product, which may lead, as Chamberlain has shown,(8) to misallocation rather than to maldistribution. There may be no monopoly profits or incomes, but there may be excessive movement of resources into those occupations in which the market is imperfect.

Imperfection of the market, however, may be inevitable simply as a result of the geographic distribution of buyers and sellers and the cost of transporting goods and information to them. However, this again does not disturb the fundamental principle that the relative price structure, the relative structure of outputs of different commodities (that is, allocation), and the relative distribution of income among occupations (which is at least one aspect of distribution) tend toward some equilibrium determined by the whole environment. This equilibrium itself is continually changing, but it is useful in defining a position toward which the system is moving at any one time. Oligopoly is a trickier case, which may involve irregular oscillations between price wars and formal or informal cartel agreements, but even these oscillations have a limited equilibrium range under given parameters.

Equilibrium distribution of income among occupations, as Adam Smith also saw very clearly, by no means implies equality of income among different occupations. Other things being equal, workers in unpleasant and disreputable occupations will have to be paid more than those in pleasant and reputable ones, and occupations involving investment in the acquisition of skill and certification will have to be paid more than those that do not--otherwise people will move out of the better paid to the worse paid occupations that have higher nonmonetary rewards.

Exceptionally rare and prized skills, for instance in the arts, literature, or in executive or political capacities, are a form of natural monopoly and sometimes may command very high incomes, simply because there is nobody who can offer to do the same thing for less. Occupations, however, with these glittering prizes may have a low average remuneration, because they attract too many people into them who hope, but fail, to win these lotteries of life.

Too much equality can therefore have an adverse effect on the efficiency of allocation, since highly productive occupations will be neglected because their relative rewards are not sufficient to attract resources into them, and resources will be underutilized and pushed toward less productive uses. Even socialist countries with strong egalitarian ideology have often been forced to move toward inequality in the interest of allocative efficiency. Equal division of the pie leads to a smaller pie.

FUNCTIONAL DISTRIBUTION AND ALLOCATION

The problem of functional distribution and allocation is perhaps the most difficult in all of economics. There is a certain consensus about it in the standard textbooks, but I must confess that I belong to a dissident minority, to which belong some distinguished names--John M. Keynes, Nicholas Kaldor, and Michael Kalecki--and there is not much agreement even among the dissidents themselves.(9) The controversy centers mainly around the question of what determines the overall distribution of, say, the national income or some other measure of aggregate product between aggregate labor income on the one hand and aggregate nonlabor income on the other.

In the United States today aggregate labor income may be estimated roughly at about 80% and nonlabor income at 20% of national income. In 1929 the proportion was more like 65% to labor and 35% to nonlabor income. The rise in the proportion of national income going to labor, incidentally, seems to characterize all the developed capitalist economies, and undermines both the classical and the Marxist view that labor income will be kept down, either by the tendency of laborers to increase their population at any wage above some subsistence level faster than the demand for labor grows, or by the ability of employers to force wages down to subsistence or below, in the presence of unemployment. This should imply that if a society got richer, most of the increase would go to nonlabor income, and the proportion going to labor income should therefore decline. This has very rarely happened in any society undergoing development, except for short periods, perhaps, in the early stages of socialist development. In classical economics the wages fund theory provided a short-run explanation of the demand for labor--that the total of real wages was what the employing class decided to pay the laborer out of its capital. If this left wages above subsistence, the labor force would grow until it was forced down to subsistence again in the long run.

The collapse both of the subsistence theory, or

perhaps its postponement to the very long run, and of the wages fund theory, left economics with a large hole in it. Conventional textbook wisdom is that the aggregate marginal productivity theory plugged the hole, assuming some sort of profit maximization as a basis for economic decisions. Any factor will be employed up to the point where the value of its marginal products is equal to the value of its marginal costs, which in turn depends largely on the price of the factor services. If we subtract from the gross marginal product those costs that are not directly related to the purchase of the factor to get a net marginal product, then the price of the factor's services should be equal to the net marginal product. If we assume that if any of the factors is unemployed the price of its services will come down until it is fully employed (a very dubious assumption), then when the factor is fully employed, the net marginal value product of the amount of the factor that is employed should be equal to the price of its services, for instance, the wage in the case of labor. Wicksteed(10) showed that if the production function relating the inputs of all factors to total output was homogeneous in the first degree (implying constant returns to scale), and if the total income distributed to each factor was equal to its net marginal value product multiplied by the amount purchased, then the sum of the incomes distributed to all the factors would be exactly equal to the value of the product, which is the amount to be distributed, leaving no surplus or deficit. This theory can be summarized with great mathematical elegance in the famous Cobb Douglas function, and there is a strong tendency to believe that because it is beautiful it must be true.(11)

To my mind this theory has some fatal weaknesses. In the first place it leaps from a microassumption about profit maximization in the firm to an assertion that the price of each factor equals its marginal value product in the macroeconomy according to some aggregate production function. This involves the fallacy of composition, among other things. As each firm attempts to expand the employment of each factor to the point where its marginal cost is equal to the value of its marginal product, even assuming perfect competition with rational profit maximization, this would change the market environments of all other firms. Even if the equations of general equilibrium yield a determinate solution, with equality of price of each factor and its marginal value product in each firm, this does not mean that these individual production functions can simply be aggregated into an aggregate production function.

A second fallacy of the marginal productivity approach is that it treats capital as if it were a homogeneous physical quantity. The wage of capital then is an income (something like a rent) per physical unit, but a unit consisting of a hopelessly hetrogeneous aggregate of buildings, land, machines, goods in process, inventories, and so on, which cannot be reduced to a common measure without valuation, and this depends in turn on the rent itself--a beautifully circular argument! This does not come to grips at all with the problem of rates of return on investment, nor does it come to grips with what may be the most significant parameter determining not only the volume of investment but also the demand for labor: the difference between prospective rates of interest and rates of profit.

An aggregate of the quantity of capital, of the Cobb Douglas formula, can only be made if we can weight the innumerably diverse items that comprise it, each by some kind of a value. This value must consist of costs minus depreciation, but plus some sort of allowance for compounding at some rate of return. Without a rate of return, therefore, even the quantity of capital itself cannot be calculated. But the crude marginal productivity of capital formula gives us no clue to what the rate of return might be. The rate of return is not a factor price: It is a rate of growth (percent per annum). It simply does not emerge out of the crude marginal analysis, though there are subtle arguments in capital theory (see especially Irving Fisher(12)) which imply some sort of general equilibrium determination of the rate of return.

A third objection to the macromarginal productivity theory is that its taxonomy of production and productive factors and its concept of production itself is wholly inadequate. It assumes what I call a cookbook theory in that we take land, labor, and capital and mix them up in a saucepan and out comes the product. In fact, production is a complex process over time which begins with some genetic factor of know-how, which is then able to direct energy and information toward the selection, transportation, and transformation of materials into the improbable shapes of the product. Production, in other words, is how we get from the genotype to the phenotype, whether this is the chicken from an egg or the automobile from a blueprint and design. The traditional factors of production, land, labor, and capital, are all heterogeneous aggregates of know-how, energy, and materials, to which one should probably add space and time. The genetic factor, know-how, is the positive factor; without it, nothing can happen. Energy, materials, space, and time are limiting factors. If they are not present in sufficient quantities and kinds, the potential of the know-how cannot be realized.

The traditional factors, land, labor, and capital, are significant, however, as aggregates that participate in exchange, though each in a very different way. That for which we pay a wage is the combination of know-how in the worker's body, the energy of muscles derived from the burning of material food input, and the materials of the body which decay and have to be replaced, again by food. The worker can also put out more energy and more know-how if the body is kept warm and if the surroundings are psychologically rewarding and cheerful. Employment, hiring someone for a wage, is a complicated human relationship involving certain degrees of trust and reciprocity. It is a much more complicated relationship than buying a bag of groceries. The employer is really buying a slice of human life, and it is not surprising that the transaction gets hedged around with all kinds of rules and regulations, both governmental and privately negotiated, as, for instance, when there is a union contract.

In a free society a labor bargain will be struck if both parties feel that they benefit and, furthermore, benefit more than they could by some alternative course of action. At a given wage offer from one employer the worker may have a prospective offer from another employer or might simply prefer to be idle for a while. The employer may have another worker in prospect, or may use the money that would be paid out in the wage for other things--purchasing materials, various goods, or securities, putting it out in interest, or simply holding it as liquid assets.

Therefore employment for a wage exchange will take place only if both the worker and the employer have no better alternatives. The worker's alternatives determine the supply of labor, the employer's alternatives the demand. This is usually overlooked, although it is implied in the simple marginal productivity theory of the demand for labor. In particular, the value of a product must be discounted back to the time of giving employment at a rate of return at least equal to and probably in excess of the rate of interest that the employer could earn on the money that would otherwise be spent on the wage. This gap between prospective interest and profit is a crucial variable in determining the demand for labor, which the crude marginal productivity theory tends to overlook.

The marginal physical product depends on what mix of genetic productive inputs--know-how, energy, and materials--the worker is offering, and this varies substantially from person to person. Here the know-how element is crucial. Energy and materials tend to be similar for all human bodies, though there are some people who are paid for having an abnormal energy capacity, both physically and psychologically. The difference between the wage of the movie star and the executive on the one hand, and the unskilled worker on the other, is almost wholly a factor of know-how. The market does not differentiate between know-how, energy, and materials, simply because in the individual person these are almost indissolubly packaged. We do not get a separate wage for each, but implicitly wage differentials reflect these tremendous differences in the genetic factors that the employer is actually paying to obtain.

Land is another interesting case. Essentially, the unit of purchase here is area. Whether this is outright purchase of land as capital, or purchase for use for a period of time (in which it appears as rent), the significance of any particular area depends again on the mix of genetic and limiting factors that it represents. Fertile land has the right mix of materials, a certain amount of potential know-how in the seeds and soil bacteria that produces differentials in the capacity for capturing solar energy and differentials in the yield of crops. Location, however, is also a critical factor in land values or rents, simply because of the energy and materials requirements in transportation in the course of production. Land that is close to some market is in a sense a ticket for cheaper transportation.

The geographical immobility of land is a very important element in determining its price or rent. The prices or rents of acres of land in different locations exhibit a much wider range than the wages of different hours of labor. The geography of allocation and distribution is indeed another fascinating aspect of the whole problem. If the price for an acre of land or an hour of labor is greater in one place than in another, there will be motivation to move from the less rewarding place to the more rewarding place. If this cannot be done, the differentials will be stable. In the case of land it cannot be done at all, which accounts for many of the peculiarities of land rent. Even in the case of labor, up to some point movement is impossible. Indeed, Adam Smith thought it was very difficult, though it has become easier with improved transportation. Some physical capital, like buildings, possess the properties of land and cannot be moved geographically, while others, like automobiles and house trailers, foodstuffs and small manufactured goods, are geographically mobile, and the geographical price differences are much less.

Of all the traditional factors of production, capital presents the greatest problem. Physical capital can be thought of as simply a population of valuable material objects, in which land would be included, and indeed human bodies and minds, often called human capital. The use of any such item can hypothetically be granted for a period on the payment of a rent or wage. Or such items can be bought and sold outright, with the one exception of human capital, when slavery, its outright purchase and sale, is prohibited. Rents might be called temporary transfer; outright purchase and sale, permanent transfer.

The rate of return on capital, which dimensionally is essentially a rate of growth, depends mainly on the relation between the price paid for permanent transfer and the expected prices of temporary transfer. This is determined by the interaction and outcomes of these two markets. A rate of return is a mathematical characteristic of what might be called the property history, which is a series of numbers representing the initial purchase of an item of property, the rent received in different periods, and the amount received for the final sale. The higher the initial price paid for a given set of expected payments in the future, the lower the rate of return.(13) The rate of interest is the name given to the rate of return when the property history involves a contract to pay definite sums in the future, as with loans and bonds. The rate of profit is the rate of return in a property history, which consists of uncertain payments in the future, whether this is a result of engaging in production or speculation.

Now we come to the critical questions. First, what really determines the distribution of the national income between labor income and nonlabor income; then within nonlabor income, between interest and profit? In the second place, what determines the overall rate of return, or rather the structure of rates of return, on different property histories? In regard to the first question, my own heretical view is very similar to the widow's curse theory of John Maynard Keynes,(14) which is that aggregate profit is determined mainly by the savings of the owners of capital, that is, the addition to their net worth in a standard time period, plus distributions of capital income to the owners in the form of dividends and interest. This view is in a sense a descendant of the wages fund theory, that real wages consist of what is left of the total product after investment is taken out of it in the form of cumulations of goods, and when the purchases of those who derive income from capital has been taken out of it. If decisions are made that increase investment, that is, the total stock of goods, and that also increase the consumption out of capital income, then (assuming full employment) there will be less left for real wages.(15)

The question of what determines the real rate of

return on capital is even more difficult. As we have seen it is not a price that is determined in its own market, but a mathematical by-product of two sets of markets--those for property itself and those for the income or rent on property. Just what conditions in these markets raise or lower the rate of return is by no means easy to say. Irving Fisher saw it as being raised by impatience, that is, the unwillingness to wait for benefits. This results in demand for benefits now rather than in the future, or a demand for present consumption rather than for savings. On the supply side Fisher and other capital theorists have seen the productivity of waiting, that is, the accumulation of capital goods now in the expectation of a greater product profit later. How these things are translated into the actual dynamics of current markets, however, is a problem that has really not been solved.

If the theory of distribution by factor shares is a morass, its allocational problems are hardly less treacherous. The main problem here, of course, is how the rewards of the different factors affect the proportions that are used in production. Any historical study of the relation between inputs and outputs always comes to the conclusion that land, labor, and capital cannot account for more than a moderate proportion in the increase in output, and the difference has to be categorized under some such item as technology or know-how. But no matter how we define the factors of production, a fairly simple principle emerges--that "expensive" factors will be economized, conserved, used sparingly, and that there will be a tendency to find substitutes for them, while "cheap" factors will be used lavishly, will not be conserved, and will be substituted for others. Thus if wages are high, we substitute capital for labor; if wages are low, labor will be substituted for capital; if land is cheap and plentiful, it will not be conserved; yields of crops per acre will be low, and cities will sprawl. If profit and interest rates are high capital will be accumulated more rapidly than if they are low, and people will be induced to save more, at least up to a point.

The same principles apply, though in a rather more complicated way, to the genetic factor of production, know-how, and the limiting factors, energy, materials, space, and time. Here the dynamics of the system dominate it, for there really is no equilibrium, and changes over time in scarcities and prices may have more effect than any absolute levels. Thus if energy becomes scarcer and its real price tends to rise, the knowledge enterprise will tend to be directed toward this problem and we may expect know-how to increase, concerning the economization of energy or the finding of new sources.

Thus, the increasing scarcity of wood in England

led to the development of the know-how of using coal to produce iron and steel and as a source of kinetic energy in the steam engine. It is hardly an accident either that the increasing scarcity of whale oil led to the development of the oil industry in the United States, which was used first of all to produce and use kerosene instead of whale oil for illumination. A scarcity in one material will direct the drive for knowledge into the finding of substitutes.

The overall relative price structure, particularly as it affects various forms of energy and materials, will therefore have a distinct effect on the rise of know-how in various fields. Similarly, increasing scarcity of space with a rising population leads to skyscrapers in the cities and to hybrid corn with increased yields in agriculture. Whether an increase in the rate of return on capital, which increases the cost of future payoffs and in that sense is an indication of the increasing scarcity of time, will lead to time-saving inventions and discoveries, such as speedier transportation, more rapid industrial transformations, and so on, is a problem that, as far as I know, has never been studied. It would be surprising, however, if there was no connection between time saving improvements and the relative cost of waiting.

PERSONAL AND GROUP DISTRIBUTION AND ALLOCATION

The third aspect of distribution and allocation involves that between individuals or groups. Usually this distribution issue is discussed in terms of income. For some purposes, however, the distribution of wealth in terms of net worth may be more significant. The basic concept of personal income is that of gross additions to personal net worth in the course of the appropriate time period, measured by the rate of addition per unit of time.

Total net worth is the sum of all items of property, including of course the person's mind and body, that have significant value to the person and to which a value, quantitiative or qualitative, can be attached. Within this large concept, there are these subsets: First, there are those values perceived only by the accountant in dollar terms. Then there is a large area of values that are perceived as greater or less, but are not measured in money--for example, love, friendship, respect, health, and their opposites. There is no great conceptual problem here, although there may be a semantic one in finding the appropriate words to describe the subsets.

Personal net worth is constantly being diminished by consumption, depreciation, aging, decay of status, loss of respect and friendship, and so on. Personal income adds to net worth by earnings, production, healing, learning, etc. If these additions are equal to the subtractions, personal net worth is stable. If the additions are greater than the subtractions, personal net worth rises. If they are less, personal net worth falls. If A's personal net worth rises and B's falls, there is a redistribution of personal net worth.

The most general concept is distribution of welfare or well-being. We can postulate a welfare function for each individual, $W = F_W(A, B, C, \ldots)$, where A might be personal net worth, B might be accounting net worth, C might be consumption, and so on. We do value throughput as well as stocks; for instance, we like eating as well as being well-fed. We value durables for their newness as well as for their services, and we value the variety that comes from throughput.

It is, however, at least a plausible hypothesis that all these throughput factors are relatively minor compared with the personal net worth factor. Conventional economic thought, by contrast, tends to measure riches or economic welfare by consumption, that is, by throughput rather than by stock. The best argument for the opposite position is that overall economies in consumption clearly make us richer. If by some additive we could get more miles to the gallon in the same car, and if the value of the gasoline saved were more than the cost of the additive, we would consume less (assuming an inelastic demand) but we would clearly be richer unless, of course, the consumption is regarded as good in itself; as it is, for instance, in Veblen's examples of conspicuous consumption. Even this usually involves conspicuous display rather than consumption, that is, conspicuous items of net worth--houses, fine clothes, and so on.

If the rate of throughput, that is, the ratio of a stable net worth to its rate of consumption or production (income), is fairly constant, distribution of income is a fairly good surrogate for distribution of net worth. The increase in net worth itself is frequently a value, since people like getting richer as well as being rich. Even then, however, the higher the income, the easier it is for income to exceed consumption--and so the easier it is to have a higher rate of accumulation or increase in net worth. Therefore the argument that the distribution of income is a reasonably good measure of the distribution of welfare is at least plausible. This may be one case in which we have to take an available measure as a surrogate for what we really want to know, and console ourselves for its inaccuracy.

A further difficulty which we will neglect for the moment is that personal net worths include a valuation of the net worths of others, either positive for those we love or negative for those we hate. Another difficulty is that distribution by groups may sometimes be more significant than distribution by individuals. We see this, for instance, in the pronounced tendency to regard the family as a single unit from the point of view of economic distribution. The assumption implied is that each member of a family regards the welfare of each of the other members equivalent to his or her own. Whether this is a realistic assumption is a nice point.

In statistical presentations there is a strong tendency to calculate distribution by nations, or at least nation-states, with a hidden assumption that poor people somehow derive satisfaction from the contemplation of rich people in their own country but not from the contemplation of rich people elsewhere. This again seems a bit unrealistic. Within a country we sometimes have groupings by race, culture, or class, which again suffer from the same difficulties. This does not deny, of course, that distribution by groups can be interesting, but we have to be very careful in interpreting the results. In any case, if we know the distribution by persons, we can aggregate them into groups.

The distribution of personal net worth by persons is a result of a complex historical process involving inheritance, saving, dissaving, migration, education, pursuit of new opportunities, investment, capital loss, and so on. It may or may not show tendencies toward some kind of distributional equilbrium. One possibility is that there is a dynamic process of increasing inequality which will proceed to some sort of catastrophe in war or in revolution, after which the process may simply begin again--a very depressing prospect. There may be some kind of organizational watershed over which a society must pass to achieve a large enough population and enough inheritance control in all sectors to prevent this dynamic of increasing poverty and inequality, checked by catastrophe.

Models can be constructed, however, in which these processes reach some sort of equilibrium distribution or pattern. We can show, for instance, that equality is likely to be unstable if two conditions that are highly plausible prevails. One is that the richer people are, the easier it is for them to get richer, for the greater their total personal net worth, the greater tends to be the gross additions to it (income), and also the easier it becomes to save, that is, to get consumption below income.

The second condition is that there should be random fluctuations away from equality, which would make some people richer, who could therefore get richer more easily, and some people poorer, who will therefore get poorer more easily. If it is also postulated, however, that this process is nonlinear, particularly that the advantages that riches give in getting richer diminishes as wealth increases, particularly over generations in the family or in groups, an equilibrium distribution may be possible. Thus, especially if those who have inherited tend to squander their inheritance, and if there is a minimum level of poverty tolerated by society, we might postulate some kind of ultimate equilibrium at which a degree of inequality insures that the rich do not get richer and the poor do not get poorer, at least not in sizable groups.

For the most part, the dynamic processes of the social system are so complex and so constantly subject to parametric change that stable distributional equilibria may not be common in human history. Nevertheless, it is striking that the distribution of income, and even of assets as far as data are available, often exhibits extraordinary stability over time. In the United States, for instance, it has hardly changed at all in the last 40 years, at least by fairly large income classes.

UNEMPLOYMENT AS AN ALLOCATIONAL AND DISTRIBUTIONAL PROBLEM

A problem that sprawls over all three of our previous headings is unemployment. It is certainly a problem in the allocation of resources. Unemployed labor, unemployed land, and unemployed physical capital represent an allocation of these resources to producing nothing. Unemployment can thus be thought of as a highly pathological "industry," which attracts resources into it if the overall economic and psychological returns are greater for doing nothing than they are for any practical alternative for doing something.

The distributional impacts of allocating resources to unemployment are very severe. The owners of unemployed resources, whether persons, land, or goods, suffer severe loss of income, and the overall loss to society is concentrated heavily in its unemployed section. The employed get a larger proportion of a diminished aggregate income and may even be better off when there is unemployment, though this is rather unlikely.

The sources of, and the solution to, the problem of involuntary unemployment are to be found mainly in the area of functional allocation and distribution. The phenomenon is a complex one, particularly when the labor force is highly heterogeneous. We can, however, distinguish two major sources of unemployment. The first is an insufficient gap between interest and the prospects of profit, such as was experienced in a very striking way from 1930 to 1933 in the United States, when real interest rates were on the order of 3 or 4%

and real profit rates were -3 or -4%. Under these circumstances, a potential employer would almost always do better by not hiring someone and putting the wage that he saved out to interest. Under these circumstances, it is astonishing that unemployment was only 25%. The only thing that prevented it from going to 75% was, I think, sheer habit and the desire of employers to hold their organizations together in the hope of better times to come.

The second source of unemployment, which might be described as Keynesian, is unwanted accumulations of goods, especially of finished goods in the hands of the producers because of a deficiency in the purchases of these goods by households, governments, or other firms. When a worker is hired, the immediate result is a diminution in cash in the balance sheet and an increase in inventory of some kind. If inventory is already perceived as too large, the prospective profit rate on hiring the worker will be perceived as low. If, in addition, the money stock in a time of deflation bears a positive real interest, and if short-term interest-bearing investments look very attractive, the worker will not be hired. The failure to hire the worker, however, diminishes his income, which diminishes his consumption, which may lead to further unwanted increases in inventories in other parts of the economy. Thus as unemployment rises, inventories continue to rise, so unemployment also continues to rise until some sort of bottoming out is reached, at which point the addition to inventories is so small that they begin to decline or at least stabilize. This is the Keynesian underemployment equilibrium.

The only answers to this condition seem to be a spontaneous recovery of consumption (that is, a rise in the amount that will be consumed at each income), a spontaneous rise in investment, such as happened after 1933, or a public grants economy through taxes and subsidies of various kinds, designed to increase the consumption at each level of income. This might be done, for instance, by redistributing income to the poor who consume most of their income, or by directly increasing government consumption or purchases, especially when financed by a budget deficit that does not reduce private consumption. In addition, there may be subsidies to investors to persuade them to increase their holdings of physical capital.

THE ROLE OF THE GRANTS ECONOMY

The role of the grants economy, as a large and complex matrix of one-way transfers of economic goods, is critical not only in understanding unemployment and the interactions of allocation and distribution, but also in solving the policy dilemma of the conflict between allocational and distributional objectives. As we have seen, it is almost impossible to do anything that will fail to change both the allocation of resources and the mix of outputs and the distribution of welfare in all its many components, whether in terms of net worth or in terms of income. All these various effects require separate evaluation if we are to have an overall evaluation of the impact of a decision, and still more the evaluation of a policy that guides decision, a policy being a decision about future decisions. A policy whose overall effects on allocation are regarded as good may also have effects on distributions that are regarded as bad, and vice versa. Policies may have quite unexpected effects on both allocation and distribution because of the complexities of the system, according to the famous principle of counterintuitive systems.

Grants (one-way) are of two kinds, explicit and implicit. In an explicit grant, an economic good of some kind, which may be either money, securities, or commodities, is transferred from a donor to a recipient, thus diminishing the net worth of the donor and increasing the net worth of the recipient, as well as changing the distribution of particular assets. Implicit grants are those redistributions of net worth in society that take place as a result of laws, regulations, quotas, quantitative restrictions, licensing, cartels and monopolies, and so on.

Both kinds of grants have both allocative and distributive effects. The immediate, though not the ultimate distributive effects are obvious. The allocative effects depend on the difference between what the donor would have done and what the recipient would have done with whatever it is that has been granted. If the donor has no real use for what is granted or is not skilled in its use, whereas the recipient is highly skilled in its use, then the allocative effects may be very favorable. If the reverse is true, they may be unfavorable. Thus the productivity the individuals, agencies or functions who are the recipients of grants is a very important factor in determining the value of grants and also to some extent the supply of them. People are much more willing to make grants that they think are going to be productive than those that will not benefit the recipient much.

Of course, the distributional impact of grants also plays some role in their evaluation. For example, what might be called the "Robin Hood principle," grants from the undeserving rich to the deserving poor, are apt to be regarded much more favorably than grants from the deserving poor to the undeserving rich, apart from any allocative effects.

Implicit grants are much more difficult to assess, simply because it is much more difficult to find out what they are, and their incidence is often extremely surprising once it is discovered. This is because of the great ecological complexity of the social system, with its vast and complex net of interactions. We do something to A, who as a result does something to B, who as a result does something to C, and so on all down the alphabet. The effects may be dissipative or cumulative, so that sometimes we do something to A and the main effect is on Z, a very remote part of the system. On the other hand, it is also possible that if we do something to A, the effects are not passed on at all. There is a very broad and not very reliable principle that implicit grants tend to end up somewhere in the system as economic rents, which tend to appear where demands and supplies are inelastic and behavior does not adjust very much to changes in circumstances. The principle here is that what adjusts is adjustable, and the adustable will continue adjusting all through the system until finally it hits something that doesn't adjust, and that is where the impact stops.

A good example of these principles would be the impact of the tobacco quota which the United States imposed in 1934. Virtually every farmer who was growing tobacco on a commercial scale was given a quota in proportion to how much he was producing in 1934. This probably would restrict his output a little in subsequent years and raise the price of tobacco a little. The demand was very inelastic and may not have had much impact on consumption, but smokers would have to spend a little more, which means that they could spend less on other things, and the effects of this would run all through the economy. The rise in the price of tobacco increased the income of those who were growing it, but only those farms that were growing it in 1934 could grow it now. Hence the market price of a farm with a quota might be six times as high as that of an identical neighboring farm without a quota. Therefore the distributional impact was to increase the net worth of those who happened to be growing tobacco in 1934 and their descendants. This seems a very odd principle of social justice. The allocational impacts were probably very small, though there may have been some improvement in methods of production as a result of diminished uncertainties.

We see these principles operating on a larger scale in the general American policy of price supports for agricultural products, a policy followed in many other countries as well. This was conceived primarily as a distributional policy, on the theory that farmers were undeservedly poorer than nonfarmers, and the way to make them richer was to improve their terms of trade. The similarity with the New International Economic

Order, incidentally, is very striking. The terms of trade were improved essentially by a grants system, immediately from government but of course ultimately from the rest of us, toward the farmers. This system, however, turned out to give grants to the rich farmers rather than to the poor, because the grant was proportional to how much farmers had to sell, and obviously rich farmers had more to sell than poor ones. The immediate distributional impact, therefore, was that the rich farmers were made richer. Poor farmers for the most part were not, and so they left agriculture in very large numbers, perhaps, who knows, to become better off as a result.

The allocational impacts of this policy, however, were unexpected and startling. The price supports helped diminish uncertainty for farmers and so increased enormously their willingness to invest and to innovate. The result was an extraordinary 40 years of productivity increase, averaging almost 6% per annum, which transformed American agriculture and indeed was a major source of the increased riches of the whole society, as the people displaced from agriculture expanded the production of manufactured goods and services. Increased productivity in other sectors also contributed to this prosperity, but to a rather smaller degree.

CONCLUDING HYPOTHESES CONCERNING THE GRANTS ECONOMY

It is clear from the above example that the way in which grants are given will have a very great effect on their consequences. That the allocational impact of grants feeds back on the distributional impact, as it did in the case of American agriculture, makes the problem even more complicated. One almost despairs of straightening out this tangle. Nevertheless, a few plausible hypotheses emerge:

1. The allocation of resources, whether of human time and activity, land, raw materials, fossil fuel deposits, or the stock of human artifacts, is profoundly affected by the relative price structure and by the structure of terms of trade which is largely determined by it. Allocation will expand toward uses where terms of trade are favorable, contract where they are unfavorable. Therefore, insofar as the grants economy affects the relative price structure and terms of trade, it will have a profound effect on allocation.

2. There is no reason to suppose that a purely laissez-faire price structure or terms of trade structure is necessarily optimum from the point of view of some prevailing policy criteria of public policy. It

is not surprising, therefore, that policies are directed toward the restructuring of price relationships. The objectives of such policies, however are often both obscure and confused by distributional considerations.

A plausible objective is to act in anticipation of future price structures. We see this, for instance, in current energy policies. It seems highly probable that not only energy in general, but fuel energy in particular, will be much more expensive in 50 years than it is now because of the exhaustion of cheap sources, especially oil and natural gas. Adjustments to these changes are slow and difficult, so there is much to be said for anticipating them, that is, for making energy more expensive now than the market alone would provide. Nobody will conserve anything that is cheap, and nobody will find substitutes for it. Therefore the anticipation of the kind of relative price changes that will make conservation and the search for substitutes attractive, seems a remarkably persuasive objective of policy. This can easily be done through the grants economy, especially through the tax system. What we have been doing, however, is precisely the opposite. We have been subsidizing energy to make it cheap, a policy that is a sure recipe for long-run disaster, and that we are only beginning to change.

3. A third proposition is that if we wish to use grants primarily for their distributional impacts, rather than for their allocative impacts, they should be directed as far as possible either toward diminishing or increasing economic rents, that is, incomes that do not much affect people's behavior because they do not change as behavior changes. This is why economists have frequently advocated lump sum taxes and subsidies, negative income taxes, and direct grants rather than indirect grants. There are other reasons for these measures related to political visibility and the avoidance of counterintuitive systems. Conversely, economists have been rather hostile to grants, taxes, and subsidies proportional to prices, when the object is essentially distributive.

Even if the "attack economic rent" principle is accepted, the identification of economic rents is quite difficult. This is indeed why Henry George produced such magnificent principles and so little practice. Nevertheless, the identification of economic rents is very much worth pursuing because the more we can identify them, the more capable we are of changing distribution without changing allocation; and if, as many people think, it is much easier to change allocation for the worse than for the better, this may at least be a desirable skill.

Evaluational problems here are difficult because there is no proposition which says that policies should be carefully separated out into those with distributional and those with allocative impacts. Indeed, this would be an almost impossible task. What we really have to do is evaluate both the distributional and the allocative impacts of any policy, and there is no reason why policy, if we can devise it, should not be directed toward favorable changes both in distribution and allocation. Given the present state of political confusion concerning distribution and allocation it is at least worthwhile calling attention to the distinction between the two.

Indeed, what one would like to see is a capability for developing both distributional impact statements and allocational impact statements, particularly in regard to public decisions. These may be valuable as well in the case of private decisions, in weighing the case for public intervention. Without some such attempt at clarification, the whole evaluational system of society gets bogged down in counterintuitive systems. This is not to say that such impact statements would be easy to make. Quite the contrary. Nor is this a need that can be met simply by passing laws that require them: They would probably be even more vacuous than many environmental impact statements. Still, the steady pursuit of this skill, the long-range development of this capability could have great benefits for the human race. It is a project on which it is highly desirable to embark.

NOTES

1. Alfred Marshall, Principles of Economics, 8th ed. (London: Macmillan, 1938).

2. Léon Walras, Elements of Pure Economics, trans. William Jaffé (Homewood, Il: Richard D. Irwin, 1954).

3. Vilfredo Pareto, Manual of Political Economy, ed. Alfred N. Page, trans. Ann Schweir (New York: Kelley, 1969).

4. E. H. Chamberlain, The Theory of Monopolistic Competition (Cambridge, Ma: Harvard University Press, 1933).

5. Joan Robinson, The Economics of Imperfect Competition (London: Macmillan, 1933).

6. Adam Smith, The Wealth of Nations, Book I, Chapter 7.

7. Alfred Marshall, Principles of Economics.

8. E. H. Chamberlain, The Theory of Monopolistic Competition.

9. An excellent discussion of this controversy

can be found in Martin Bronfenbrenner, Income Distribution Theory, Chapter 16 (Chicago: Aldine/Atherton, 1971).

10. Philip H. Wicksteed, Essay on the Coordination of the Laws of Distribution (London School of Economics Reprint, 1932).

11. The Cobb Douglas function is usually expressed in a form such as $x = x_0 a^{\alpha} b^{1-\alpha}$, where x is the total product, x_0 is a constant which represents roughly the state of knowledge and technology, a is the total amount of labor employed, b is the total amount of capital used, and α and $1-\alpha$ are constants which turn out to be equal to the proportion of the total product going to labor and capital respectively.

12. Irving Fisher, The Theory of Interest (New York: Macmillan, 1930).

13. Suppose a "property history" or a "single investment" consists of a sequence of net payments (which may be either positive or negative), P_0 in year 0, P_1 in year 1, P_t in year t. The rate of return, r, is then given by the equation
$P_0 + P_1(1+r)^{-1} + P_2(1+r)^{-2} + . . . +$
$P (1+r)^{-t} = 0$.

14. J. M. Keynes, A Treatise on Money (New York: Harcourt Brace and Company, 1930).

15. The following identities may clarify the problem:

Total real wages	= Net national product - investment - government purchases - consumption out of income from capital
∴ Total capital income	= Net national product - total real wages - government purchases
	= Investment + consumption out of income from capital.

7. Exchange and Values

Aaron Katsenelinboigen

Differentiation and integration are the two great principles at the heart of the development of any system.(1) The greater its level of differentiation, the more complex is the mechanism needed for its integration. That is why, for example, in social systems where one encounters relatively simple mechanisms of integration (for example, in a bureaucracy), there arises an opposite problem: to reduce the level of differentiation to its minimum, to try to establish complete uniformity.(2) The existence of differentation in the system creates the conditions for exchange, which in turn fulfills the role of an integrative mechanism.

The exchange problem is first of all concerned with analyzing a variety of exchange relations and values involved in them. In this regard Boulding has emphasized (1) exchange as a general systems category, and (2) a variety of different sorts of transaction (for example, the so-called grants economy) in the economic system that makes possible a corresponding variety of economic relations.(3)(4) In this paper I would like to concentrate on several aspects of the exchange problem in economics that have either been ignored, or in my view discussed inadequately. These problems include: (1) interpretation of exchange in terms of interaction of objects in a system that employs both horizontal and vertical mechanisms; (2) analysis of the role of local and global values in acts

---

Translated into English by Gregory Katsenelinboigen.
I am quite grateful to Professor Robert Solo for his comments which have enabled me to make significant improvements in the paper.

of exchange; (3) specification of the role of certain institutions (such as money) with a role in acts of exchange.

EXCHANGE RELATIONS AND VALUES AS GENERAL SYSTEMS CATEGORIES

The Exchange Matrix

One can interpret all interactions in the system in terms of exchange relations. Substituting the term "interaction" for "exchange" in a broad sense emphasizes the loss-gain (cost-benefit) aspect for objects in interaction. In general, every object involved loses something and gains something. However, different situations can also be seen. For instance, when one object loses and gains but the other object gains only without losing anything, it is a case of altruism. The other distinguishing characteristic of altruism lies in the fact that the sacrifice is made deliberately in the name of a higher purpose, devotion to God, or perhaps, helping one's neighbor without expecting reciprocity. What the person gets in return is the satisfaction to be derived from serving a higher end, which in turn constitutes an integrative element in the world.

If one takes the balance of gain and loss as a final characteristic of the activities of an object, a matrix of four elements could reflect the possible combinations of loss and gain of two interacting objects: both objects can lose, or one can lose and the other gain, or both can gain. With the additional assumption that the gain-loss balance involves a long period of time, normal exchange could be defined as an exchange in which both objects gain (or at least neither one loses). For example, it is the essence of voluntary, that is, market or economic exchange, that both expect gain, otherwise one or the other would not have entered into the transaction.

An extreme case of pathological exchange would be a situation in which all interacting objects lose. This is typical for the interactions between cancer and normal cells in the body, and such a situation would occur in global nuclear war. A case of pathological exchange in which one object gains and the other loses exists in the interaction between a host and its parasites.

Attractors

Since exchange is based on the operation of the mechanism of gains-losses, one faces the problem of revealing the formative structure of this mechanism. This, in turn, calls for two things: (1) explicit formulation of exchangeable ingredients that can be transferred from one object to the other; and (2) elucidation of the forces of attraction or repulsion. These forces indicate to the object being attracted-repulsed how far and in which direction it should move. For the sake of simplicity, rather than specifying these forces as attractors and repulsors we will use only one term, attractors.(5)

Attractors operate in different systems under different names. In physical systems they are called forces; in biological systems, biological drives in psychic systems, emotions; and in social systems, values.

It should be stressed that attractors are objects in contrast to shadows. What is characteristic of the shadow is that one cannot modify it without at the same time modifying the source-object that determines it. Attractors, however, can be modified regardless of the system in which they function. Modified attractors can in turn influence the motion of objects that they attract. The physical hypothesis concerning the existence of gravitons can be regarded as a materialization of this kind of attractor. Emotional centers discovered in animals and human beings also confirm the existence of special structures in their brains that shape their behavior. Values created by economic and social systems get fixed as bits of information and become independent objects that can later influence the development of these systems.

Vertical and Horizontal Mechanisms and Exchange

Exchange relations in different systems can be performed by two classes of mechanisms (severally or in combination). These classes of mechanisms can be named vertical and horizontal.

Let us define a vertical mechanism as a mechanism in which one object uses command as attractors, that is, forcibly compels (coerces) another object(s) to change its (their) position. Let us define a horizontal mechanism as a mechanism in which attractors in all interacting objects have the capacity to influence significantly the position of these objects.

Thus, for example, the solar system can be regarded as a combination of the vertical mechanisms, the effect of the sun, and horizontal ones, interactions between planets. In economic systems governmental rule is an example of vertical mechanisms, whereas the market exemplifies horizontal ones.(6) The linchpin in Boulding's definition of economics is the relationship of exchange as distinct from relations based on threat, with exchange understood as based on the principle: "You do what I want, and I will do what you want" (p. 9).(4)

Certainly this represents one kind of exchange, which one might call voluntary exchange, or trade. But if one understands exchange in the larger sense of interaction between objects, then exchange can also exist in situations in which the government directs the subordinate economic units and tells them what they should produce and consume. Although in that situation the subordinated economic units do as they are directed, they are engaged, nevertheless, in a network of exchange.

Thus threats also may serve to bring about relations of exchange.

The purpose of this short exercise in terminological precision is to enable us to generalize upon the essential character of developed economic systems of both market and centralized variety and to avoid the false simplification that would reduce or oversimplify one's understanding of centralized economic systems either by restricting them to the special, limiting case of the single, all-encompassing firm (represented by the government), or by portraying them according to the economics of Robinson Crusoe.

Indeed, as experience has shown, the developed centralized economic systems operate with a wide gamut of complex institutions which are characteristic of horizontal mechanisms--encompassing market-type economies involving prices, interest rates, money, and so on. These institutions underlie interactions in vertical mechanisms between the government and operating units, as well as interactions in horizontal mechanisms between operating units themselves.

To regard these institutions as invariants, characteristic of developed economic systems of different types, would enable a deeper understanding of those systems. In particular this involves a proper understanding of the roles of prices and money, the subject of the fourth part of this paper.

Languages of Exchange

Exchange relations and attractors that are involved in them constitute the subject matters of many different disciplines: physics, chemistry, economics, sociology, and so on. Each of these disciplines has developed its own language for the analysis of systems under study.

I think that the analytics of exchange relations has been best developed by economics, and economists continue to improve their analysis by borrowing ideas from the research of other disciplines. So too scientists in disciplines other than ours have found in economics, images useful for their own research. This form of mutual enrichment is related to the problem of translation from the language of one discipline into that of another one. This can be performed either through a universal, intermediary language, or directly. The first proceeds through the use of mathematics, the second through analogy.

The work of L. Rozenoer(7) examplifies the use of the first method, when mathematical models formulated in economics were used to analyze the exchange relations in physical thermodynamic systems. The second method is exemplified by the work of B. Heinrich(8) and F. Pryor,(9) which deals with ecological problems from the standpoint of economics in general and exchange processes in particular. A developing trend in sociology that looks upon social processes as those of exchange borrows directly from the vocabulary of economics.(10) Therefore this trend also constitutes the case of a direct translation from the language of one discipline into that of another one without an intermediary language.

LOCAL AND GLOBAL VALUES IN EXCHANGE

Definitions

Local attractors are those attractors that reflect the peculiarities of a given object; global attractors belong to the system as a whole. Thus subjective utilities (preferences) will constitute attractors of the first kind; prices will be an example of the second.

Local attractors, in turn, can either be external or internal. If they are external they determine the object's activity. Internal attractors function within the passive object.

Thus animals have both internal and external attractors; the former regulate organic life, the latter control interactions with its environment. Stones, by contrast, have only internal attractors; their interaction with the environment is triggered only by forces external to them.

The notions of local and global attractors are relative notions. If we deal with a multilevel structure, we can see that each level will have its own global and local attractors. The structuralization of mankind, from this standpoint, would seem rather complex. But even such three-level entities as religions (ideologies), countries, and regions enable us to perceive the diversity of local values and the unity of global values within the bounds of each structure.

Signs of Attractors

To begin with, local and global attractors that guide the motions of objects can be distinguished one from the other according to their sign. The choice of a sign will correspond to a system of coordinates selected. For instance, in economic systems, prices (as global attractors) can be either positive or negative.(11) From the individual standpoint prices signal both the attractiveness, desirability, and availability of objects, and also the scarcity, unpleasantness, harmfulness, and sacrifices connected with objects. In other words both positive and negative signals emanate from prices. And indeed what is a positive signal for A, the seller, is a negative (cost) signal for B the buyer. Sometimes, as with environmental pollutants, the established system of prices fails to give a true signal of cost and danger.

A similar phenomenon can be observed where the individual is taken as the object with positive and negative emotions operating as attractors. Positive emotions are related to those objects that enable the individual to integrate himself with his environment (tasty food, love, and so on); negative emotions reflect the presence of destructive objects (such as hunger, harmful substances in food, fear of annihilation).

Just as society does not possess an ideal pricing system, man does not possess an ideal emotional mechanism that can protect him against the threat of annihilation posed by various destructive objects. There are at least two reasons for this. The first has to do with organic changes within the emotional structure of the brain that can make negatively perceived objects take on the aspect of positive emotions, and vice versa. Usually the man who sustains an injury experiences acute pain, that is, a negative emotion. But when a masochist gets injured he may experience positive emotions.

The second reason for the inefficiency of the emotional mechanism is the possible lack of correspondence between the strengths of different emotions. In order for the existing positive emotions to play a constructive role, that is, to be able to help a man actually integrate himself with his environment, it is necessary to achieve a certain degree of coordination between different emotions.(12)

Otherwise (that is, if they act separately), they can sometimes perform a destructive role.

For example, positive emotions that come from sexual attraction can degenerate into lust if they are not correlated with other emotions that give rise to respect, devotion, and so on; finally, all these emotions culminate in such sentiments as love. Positive emotions derived from eating, if not constrained by such considerations as the fear of falling ill, can be conducive to overeating, with all the attendant negative consequences. Such, alas, is too often the case for those who live in the developed countries.

It seems to me that the question of devilish temptation has to do precisely with the failure to coordinate the separate (and first of all) positive emotions that guide human behavior. This lack of coordination between different emotions can result from two things: (1) organic disturbances in the emotional mechanism (overemphasis on one emotion compared with others); or (2) absence of correspondence between the biological basis of emotions and the need for altered emotions that stems from the artificial man-made environment.

Differentiation, Integration and Attractors

Local and global attractors can be represented as objects that express (in the system) the principles of differentiation and integration respectively. Local attractors express the principle of differentiation in the system, that is, the fact that each possesses its own individual characteristics. Therefore local attractors are diverse. Global attractors express the principle of integration in the system. They can be unitary, for they are common for the entire system.

The Diversity of Individual Values

Differences between people can be seen not only in their physical characteristics, but also in their value systems; and both physical characteristics and value systems are significantly determined by biological factors. It may be as difficult to change a man's value systems as his physical characteristics. Because the bundle of values will vary between individuals and in their distribution between social groups, and because the configuration of values is critical in determining the course of social events and the character of individual interaction, it would surely be useful to discover the actual topographies of values.

A first approximation of the distribution of human values might be achieved by borrowing from mathematics.* When a mathematician investigates a complex structure that does not lend itself to direct analysis, he first of all tries to find singular points in it. Investigating the structure of these points can enable a mathematician to discern many important phenomena that can then be applied to the overall structure.

It seems to me that the psychological disorders of people in a society represent precisely these singular points in the diverse field of human values. Cases of psychological disorder might provide us with a perspective from which to study human values in general, since in them these values are thrown into bold relief. Whereas in normal situations those values remain hidden.

The supposition that psychological disorders represent singular points stems from the fact that any kind of human value can in the extreme case reach a pathological state. That those points can be taken as representative of the universe of values requires a second assumption, one that would appear to be considerably less well-grounded. I would venture to propose it nevertheless; namely that the percentage of psychological deviations in every type of human value is approximately the same.

If this last proposition is accepted, then it can be further surmised that the proportions between different kinds of psychological disorders are approximately the same as those between different kinds of normal human values. Their realm is to a certain extent a cultural one. Thus if one looks, for example, at the ratios of such psychological disorders as megalomania, kleptomania, superaltruism,(13) and so on, one may perhaps have something to say about the general distribution of values in the cultural system. We might tentatively hypothesize that the pattern of human values along its intensity dimension follows that of the normal distribution.

Prices

Economists have investigated global parameters such as prices. The study of prices can be conducted from different viewpoints. Thus it follows that

---

*I am grateful to B. Moishenson for telling me about this method of mathematical investigation. No doubt, Professor Moishenson cannot be held responsible for any of my speculations on the possibilities of applying this method to social phenomena.

different definitions of prices can also be given. I think that, just as with any other nontrivial case, one cannot find a single exhaustive definition of prices. The existing set of definitions should be expanded as new aspects of the price phenomenon become apparent. (Of course, I do not mean new definitions that are logically identical to old ones.) Every scholar will then select from this set of definitions that one which he thinks is most helpful to him in his research.

Thus economists have elaborated a set of definitions for prices that reflect the following concerns: (1) discovering the optimal exchange ratios between commodities; (2) discovering the degree of scarcity of resources, that is, the degree of dependence on a given resource; and (3) establishing a network of guideposts for activities of economic units, that is, elaborating a set of parameters that can show which commodities should have priority in production and the consumption of which resources should be subject to more stringent economizing criteria.

This latter approach to prices holds special interest since it enables one to understand why both market and planned economies need the institution of prices so badly. The invariant nature of price relationships in both types of systems is underscored by the fact that they involve the interaction of economic units that have certain degrees of freedom (internal production possibilities of different commodities and different resources). At the same time these units are unaware (and cannot but be unaware) of each other's internal production possibilities. Prices as global parameters enable each economic unit to obtain condensed information about the entire system on the basis of which a given unit can then decide what it should produce and consume with due regard to the interests of other units (the Pareto optimum principle).

Economists have understood in good part the limitations of price as a global attractor, that is, they have elaborated that set of conditions required in order that price perform its role as a balancer in the economic system based on the actions of autonomous units. Much remains to be done in elaborating the conditions for the operation of other institutions that could augment price support, correct or compensate the pricing function in bringing the system more rapidly, more economically, ultimately, into a state of equilibrium, for example through the use of subsidies and fines.

Coordination of Local and Global Attractors

The greater the variety of local attractors, the more sophisticated should be the mechanism needed for coordinating them with global attractors. (Some of these mechanisms will be analyzed in the fourth part of this paper.) Simplified systems that lack a variety of local attractors and suffer from a corresponding low degree of differentiation can prove to be less effective than their more diversified counterparts.

For example, in social systems a variety of individual values makes it difficult to coordinate them through any value consensus. Sometimes the way to overcome that difficulty is perceived to lie in eliminating the variety of individual values, that is, in propagating an identical set of values. In all the individuals in the system, these individual values should correspond with the societal ones. The homogenization of individual values, as a policy characteristic of totalitarian bureaucratic regimes, proves inefficient in satisfying human needs.

Evolution and Attractors

It would be of great interest to study evolution in the formation and interaction of local and global attractors. I think it will be worthwhile to analyze different cosmological theories and theories of elementary particles, as well as the entire evolution of the inorganic world (in particular, the general field theory) from the standpoint of the formation of and interactions between local and global attractors.

Thus, for example, we can ask whether the early stages of the development of the universe are characterized by the presence of global attractors in the field along with passive objects, and whether the latter subsequently become active because of the integration of these objects and the transformation of their global attractors into external, local ones. One could also adopt another line of reasoning: Even at the early stages there is a variety of objects with a corresponding variety of external local attractors. In the course of the development of the universe there appeared global attractors that regularize interactions between objects.

With the transition from the inorganic to the organic world, objects acquire both internal attractors and external local attractors that generate their activities. Moreover, what is characteristic of biological and social systems is not only that their local attractors are of an external variety, but also that global attractors have their locus in the object. This enables purposeful behavior by the living organism. However, under dynamic conditions such global parameters change rather rapidly, and it is not easy to find them. In this case the responsibility for setting global attractors again passes to the special coordinating organ, which in one way or another embodies the functions of an integrator for the collectivity.

Furthermore, it would be interesting to study how local and global attractors have been and are now being implemented in artificial, man-made engineering systems. (In principle, the development of these systems can lead to the emergence of new more complex, species in the evolution of the universe.)

In most highly developed modern engineering systems an upper unit supplies the lower one only with global attractors. Thus, for example, oil refineries that are built (with the aid of computers) on the hierarchical principle of control have units that enjoy certain degrees of freedom in controlling their internal and external parameters. For one reason or another, computers on a higher level of control lack the necessary information concerning these parameters. To bring its structure into optimum accord with the requirements of the system as a whole, the computer of a given unit must receive the necessary information from the system. This information can be transmitted in the form of global attractors which are set by computers on a higher level.(14)

TYPES OF EXCHANGE

The following section will analyze two kinds of exchange in which the role of attractors will be made more evident:

1. Direct exchange or barter.
2. Exchange through an object-intermediary.

Barter

This, the simplest type of exchange, is characteristic of the early stages of economic development, and is known in economics by the name of "barter." Widely accepted in social relationships, it finds its expression in such sayings as "I'll scratch your back if you scratch mine."

The barter method can include the exchange of the most diverse kinds of goods--not only the exchange of material commodities for others, but also the exchange of material commodities for such goods as reminiscence. The memories of past events that we preserve can be regarded as some sort of durable good. And people often are quite willing to undertake considerable expenditures to obtain this sort of goods. Thus, for example, many poor people are known to organize grandiose wedding ceremonies on which they spend an enormous amount of resources. One reason that organizers of these weddings might have for undertaking such enormous expenditures is to be able to enjoy the sweet memories later on. Many people attend these festivities and spend a great deal of their time and resources on transportation, gifts, and so on. In return they get all sorts of pleasures; among them the memory of the occasion has a prominent place.

In spite of all its apparent simplicity, barter exchange can be differentially regularized. It can be spontaneous and sporadic, based on the local values of the individuals who take part in it, or it can make use of such global parameters as prices. There is a rather widespread belief that prices emerge only with appearance of money. However, price can exist even without money.

This can be explained as follows. A sufficient characteristic of prices is their ability to perform the role of global parameters, which enable each participant in the economic process to secure information about the optimal possible ratios of exchange in a given situation. (These ratios can be gradated in such a way that their sum would add up to unity.) What is characteristic of regularized exchange relations is that each party or the centralized agency makes a good estimate of the optimal possible ratios of exchange on the basis of encounters with other parties. The knowledge of these ratios makes it possible for each party to make its best decision in the event of small, unexpected fluctuations in the environment, for example, the unexpected appearance of new parties eager to participate in exchange. These ratios can be known, hence the pricing function fulfilled, with or without money.

Barter relations in social life can also be brought to a rather high degree of regularization, up to the introduction of a counterpart of prices into social relations. Such parameters are characteristic of the workings of the justice system. The system of unified kinds of punishment for similar crimes (which one can see in operation in many countries) represents precisely this sort of pricing. These judicial norms replaced those that were represented either by the unregularized horizontal mechanism that meted out punishment through an act of mob outrage, or those that relied on the vertical mechanism in which the supreme ruler (or his representatives) would carry out verdicts at his or their own discretion.

Naturally, the establishment of unified judicial norms has not been nearly as well regularized as norms in the economy. Nor has there been a consensus or much understanding of the initial principles for establishing such juridical norms. In other words, it's not clear from what standpoint we should approach their establishment: (1) reforming the criminal; (2) forcing the criminal to provide compensation for the damages that he caused; (3) by force or example, preventing new crimes by other members of society, (4) removing from society those who, by way of their proclivities are considered to be a danger to society, (5) exacting social vengeance.

I would also like to note that moral norms like the Ten Commandments, although they also represent global parameters, are not the equivalent of prices. The reason is this. It is characteristic of prices that they are determined by the existing situation, that is, by the entire combination of prevailing conditions.(15) Moral norms, however, are unconditional.

Exchange Through An Object-Intermediary

For understandable reasons, barter relations limit the possibilities of perfecting exchange relations since they require that each party should possess the objects sought for by the other party. The introduction of money as a universal medium of exchange brought about a substantial expansion in the domain of exchange.

Of course, the domain of operation of this universal medium is strictly limited. In any country not all commodities are for sale: Military airplanes and tanks, for example, cannot be sold to private persons. Monetary fines are not used in situations in which a given person must bear personal responsibility for his actions. Moreover, the boundaries within which money can operate in a system of exchange are flexible, and shifting. Thus in the Middle Ages the Catholic Church used to sell indulgences. These indulgences were of different sorts--from permits to pilgrims to use the Church's property on their way to the Holy Land, up to the total remission of all sins and the soul's salvation in purgatory.(16)

One may get an impression that planning systems in which the government directs the traffic of exchange do not need money. Prices may prove sufficient to enable self-acting economic units to function successfully. However, planning economies also use money. The presence of money is needed for the very process of planning, not only for carrying out the plan.

Planning is an iterative process. At each of its steps the government must provide economic units with condensed information pertaining to the requirements of the system as a whole, and must get back another set of condensed information pertaining to the possibilities of operating units. This kind of condensed information that the government sends to the units can be expressed not only in terms of prices but also in terms of the overall amount of money that the units can spend for acquiring any kind of goods that they may need. In this case money constitutes the universal constraint for the units. Due to its versatility, money represents a more flexible constraint than one that would limit the allowable consumption of certain goods. In the same way money can be used in the process of carrying out the plan.

In comparing the role that money plays in market and planning economies, one notices certain similarities. The major similarity of course is that money represents a universal constraint in acts of exchange. The difference between planning and market systems is in how this constraint is formed.

The institution of money (as described above) represents a somewhat idealized picture. The idealization has crept in with the assumption of the absolute universality of money, that is, that within that zone where a given form of currency (the dollar, the yen, the ruble) constitutes legal tender, it is possible to purchase any goods that can legally be purchased. However, it is possible to imagine contour or sectoral kinds of money, each of which can be used only for purchasing a limited category of goods. (It seems to me that the economic system that uses contour money can be likened to a vessel which, for reasons of security, has a number of isolated sectors.)

The extent of the use of sectoral money varies greatly from one economic system to the next. In market economies they are present in only a small part of the economy; for example, food stamps for the poor groups in the society can be regarded as sectoral money.

In rigidly centralized planning systems, sectoral money has acquired a rather widespread use. Thus, for example, in the USSR money used for foreign trade is strictly separated from that used inside the country, since the ruble is not a convertible currency. Domestically, wages and other kinds of incomes are paid out in types of money that can be used for purchasing only consumer goods and services. For the use of enterprises there is a wide variety of different types of money, each of which can be used for purchasing only a specified group of goods (equipment, materials, and so on).

Money as a mediator in exchange has its counterpart in prestige in social systems. There are both horizontal and vertical mechanisms for earning prestige. With the former, prestige may be the reward realized for the performance of good deeds, that is, a recognition that is accepted by many. Such recognition makes it possible for the one who possesses prestige to receive advantages of many sorts in her dealings with others. Prestige (like money) can sometimes be passed on from one generation to the next; in other words, it can be inherited.

Much as the introduction of money into the economy made it possible to expand significantly the scope of exchange relations and increase the efficiency of the economic system, people's desire to earn prestige for themselves makes it possible to increase the efficiency of the social system.

Here I note that acts of social exchange often contain the elements of both prestige earning and altruism. Superficially, the person who does some good thing for another person without engaging in barter is an altruist. With the simplified dichotomous classification of all people into good ones and bad ones, a good person must of necessity be an altruist. However, there exists a whole spectrum of human types and there are those who engage in beneficent behavior only because of the advantages of the prestige they seek to gain thereby. To castigate those who are engaged in doing good for the sake of earning prestige would slow the development of positive social relationships. The last statements should by no means be taken to imply that one shouldn't roundly praise altriusm as an ideal system of exchange relations.

Prestige can also be earned through vertical mechanisms, when the government, for example, praises a person for doing deeds that are deemed important for members of the collectivity. So also for those who act because they expect their reward in heaven, or by God on earth. Different kinds of social institutions have been designed to stretch out the period of time within which the person can expect his reward. Thus monuments erected in the memory of great people, celebration of the dates of their births and deaths, and similar institutions reinforce the man's prestige for a long time to come as a form of attractor that operates beyond the scope of immediate reward.

Religion plays a big role in shaping this sort of deferred reward. It is known that Judaism is closest to the earthly interests of people; its mystical elements primarily concern God and His actions, and to a considerably lesser extent do they touch on other mystical phenomena, such as the existence of an independent soul that can survive for long (or even forever) after the person's death. According to Judaism, God's rewards and punishments will affect future generations for a long time to come (Exodus, 34:7). In Christianity (Catholicism and Orthodoxy), Islam, and Buddhism, the survival, in one form or another, of the soul after the person's death depends on his actions in this world. Thus the latter religions relate deferred rewards to the dual mystical principle: the existence of both God and soul.

Possible Regularization of Different Types of Exchange Relations

Now I would like to ask whether it is possible to regularize the above-mentioned types of exchange relations, to place them along some scale depending on the magnitude of some given parameter. I think that such regularization is possible, and for an appropriate parameter I suggest the degree of dependence of people on each other.(17)

People can radically reduce their dependence on each other in three different ways. The first has to do with reducing their desire for goods without any kind of compensation. I am not familiar with any real-life, successful implementation of this kind of method; it has been portrayed only in utopias like Huxley's Brave New World, where people with predetermined values are produced in test tubes. If the person is willing to reduce his desire for one kind of good, he usually demands some compensation for himself. Most religious faiths, in urging man toward ascetism, have usually promised him in return the attainment of higher forms of satisfaction such as paradise or nirvana.

The other methods of radically solving the problem of independence stem from the proposition that man is full of all sorts of different desires. The first of them is based on the idea of autarchy. Usually the expansion of exchange favors a further development of the system in realizing advantages related to separation of functions and specialization. At the same time, the expansion of exchange increases the dependence of a given part of the system upon other parts. Under certain conditions this will be considered undesirable inasmuch as, for example, such dependence carries with it the implication of political subordination. This is not to suggest that autarchy represents the best way of guaranteeing a country's military security, for in such cases, the benefits of economic independence must be balanced against the economic losses consequent upon the constraint on trade. Therefore, in the name of security, one may seek rather to achieve a condition wherein no country participating in the system of trade can terminate the exchange without at the same time running the risk of drastically reducing its economic potential.

The barter exchange and exchange through an object-intermediary are predicated on the assumption that the strength of dependence of a given individual on others can be reduced only to a certain extent.(18) For example, in the practice of hiring people a shift toward the use of money (which can be accumulated) and away from payments in kind represents an important step in the achievement of independence for employees. It is not by accident that in bureaucratic systems of the Soviet type a major portion of the income of top officials consists of income in kind and perquisites. This enables the leaders of the country to hold these officials in strict obedience: Should they lose their position, the benefits to which they have become accustomed also become inaccessible to them.

Since there are material benefits on the one hand and some loss of independence on the other hand implicit in any system of exchange, societies reflecting different sets of values have established differing proportions in their use of various types of exchange. The analysis of these proportions in different societies is a subject for another paper.

REFERENCES AND NOTES

1. The usual view that differentiation is opposed to integration treats the problem as one-dimensional in nature. Professor J. Gharajedaghi from the University of Pennsylvania is conducting interesting research in which he studies the said processes as existing in a two-dimensional space. The reader can find a brief summary of conclusions that flow from this kind of approach in Gharajedaghi's works "Corporate Pathology" and "Obstructions to Development" (the working papers of the Social Systems Sciences Unit at the University of Pennsylvania).

2. Thus toward the end of the Stalinist period in the USSR more and more employees had to show up at work in uniforms. Miners, railroad people, diplomats, bank tellers, lawyers, military men, and others had their own uniforms. Differences between the uniforms of various professions were insignificant; they reduced themselves mainly to differences in the color of fabric used for making uniforms, types of cockades, and so on.

Of course, such a criterion as the introduction of uniforms is not, in and of itself, indicative of the bureaucratization of the system. If both students and professors at Eaton and Cambridge used to wear uniforms, it did not mean that their schools were more bureaucratized than shoddy grammer schools or working class universities where uniforms had not been introduced. The same goes for the Army as compared to governmental organizations where employees do not wear uniforms.

The fact is that the introduction of uniforms can

aim at different objectives. One of them is related to the attempt to shift the focus of attention away from the outward characteristics of the person and move it toward greater concentration on the process being carried out. Many professors knew how elegantly dressed female students are capable of distracting them during their lectures.

At the same time the uniform can sometimes brutalize the man or, at any rate, in many cases it can fail to accentuate his positive characteristics and succeed in masking his unpleasant ones. A variety of dress (which can also include uniforms) serves to bring out the person's unique characteristics and emphasize those that strengthen him while masking others that are unpleasant either to him personally or to people around him.

Thus there is a problem in comparing positive and negative aspects in the introduction of uniforms. One can see in the experiences of democratic countries that their development has been accompanied by the tendency toward expanding a variety of dress. Uniforms have been used only in those rare situations where the advantages of having them have been immediately apparent--first of all, in the Army.

The example of massive introduction of uniforms during the postwar period in the USSR that has been cited above can still be regarded as an indicator of growing uniformity within the society, which chose to suppress individual interests in a situation in which such sacrifices were not dictated by organizational conveniences.

3. K. Boulding, Beyond Economics, Ann Arbor, MI: University of Michigan Press, 1968.

4. K. Boulding, Economics as Science, New York: McGraw-Hill Book Company, 1970.

5. A. Katsenelinboigen, "General Systems Theory and Axiology," General Systems, Vol. XIX, 1974, pp. 19-26.

6. A. Katsenelinboigen, "Vertical and Horizontal Mechanisms in Complex Systems," Proceedings of the Twenty-Second Annual North Meeting of the Society of General Systems Research, Washington, DC, February 13-15, 1978, pp. 276-280.

7. L. Rozonoer, "A Generalized Thermodynamic Approach to Resource Exchange and Allocation," Automation and Remote Control, No. 5, 1973, pp. 781-795; No. 6, 1973, pp. 915-927; No. 8, 1973, pp. 1272-1289.

8. B. Heinrich, Bumblebee Economics, Cambridge, MA: Harvard University Press, 1979.

9. F. Pryor, "The Economic Systems of Wild Chimpanzees and Baboons," Journal of Economic Issues, Vol. 15, No. 1, March, 1981, pp. 33-59.

10. R. M. Hingers and D. Willer, "Prevailing Postulates of Social Exchange Theory," Theoretical

Perspectives in Sociology, Edited by S. McWall, New York: St. Martin's Press, 1979.

11. Negative prices can be related to costs either through fines or expenditures for disposal. Let me explain this statement as it applies to a situation of equilibrium in which marginal production costs equal marginal utility of the product produced. Usually production is characterized by the output of indivisible goods; such is the nature of technology. This principle can be seen not only in the production of chemical stuffs, but also in many other industrial operations that involve processing. For example, the mechanical treatment of metals results in the output of the needed item and shavings. Even mechanical assembly operations can be accompanied by wastes in the form of unneeded rubbing materials.

The utility of items produced in these indivisible bunches can vary; some of them can even be harmful to the living environment.

Thus the total utility of the output equals the sum of the output of useful items (which have the sign "+") and harmful ones (which have the sign "-"). Accordingly, costs equal the utility of the output. Fines for the production of harmful items express the sum by which the utility of produced goods is reduced.

In disposing of harmful products, the utility of disposed items equals the costs of disposal.

12. A similar problem occurs with the necessity of coordinating separate characteristics of human personality. Thus, persistence is a merit, a positive characteristic. But if unconstrained, it can become a shortcoming, a negative characteristic, and be given the name of stubbornness. Cleverness, apparently, is the device that keeps our strengths from turning into our weaknesses.

13. Heinrich Böll, in his novel Billiards at Half-Past Nine, gives us the portrait of a psychological disorder in a woman who finds the highest pleasure in giving away everything she has to other people. To do that, she would sometimes even strip herself naked in the street.

14. L. Pliskin, "Dekompozitionnaia Dinamicheskaia Optimizatsiia Proizvodstva S Ieararkhicheskoj Structuroi Upravleniia," Avtomatika i Telemekhanika, Nos. 3-4, 1969.

15. The Nobel Prize winner for Economics L. V. Kantorovich, in his work The Best Use of Economic Resources (Cambridge, MA: Harvard University Press, 1965), focused on just this fact that prices are determined by the whole combination of conditions in the system in which they function. It is not surprising that Kantorovich called prices "the objectively determined valuations."

16. "The Sale of Indulgences: Archbishop Albert's

Instructions to the Sub-Commissioners; A Sermon on Indulgences Given by Tetzel," Translations and Reprints from the Original Sources of European History, Vol. II, The Period of Early Reformation in Germany, No. 6, 1900, pp. 4-11.

17. I am grateful to Professor V. Sachs for our conversation concerning the dependence of people on each other and on their surroundings. This conversation stimulated my search for the generalizations presented here.

18. In this regard I would like to note the following paradoxical phenomenon. In Russia, both before and after 1917, the institution of friendship has been more developed than in the leading Western countries, for example, in the U.S.A. The concept of individualism has been considerably less developed in Russia, and it is not accidental that such terms as "privacy" do not have an equivalent in the Russian language. Dostoevsky thought of Russia as the country that would show the West a way to salvation by freeing it from individualism.

In my opinion, however, friendship in the USSR (as well as in Russia) has been largely a result of people's dependence on their environment and on the lack of a sense of security. Here I am not even talking about the dependence on the environment in situations marked by a low level of production which increases peoples' dependence on each other by necessitating mutual help. The rigid political system which oppressed man in Russia (and which oppresses him now in the USSR), and the necessity to operate outside the law in order to increase his income, engender a strong demand for friends; for only friends can help the man and his family in case he is arrested. The absence of credit cards and other forms of credit, along with a chronic shortage of needed goods, have all conspired to produce a situation in which--should the opportunity present itself for buying some needed goods--someone should be there to lend the money. And only friends can do that.

Difficult life conditions that necessitate the practice of mutual help also produce strong and deeply felt sentiments of friendship between people. These sentiments have also come to acquire an independent status; the value of means becomes independent from the value of ends that brought them about.

8. Probabilistic Mechanisms of Social Choice and Income Redistribution

Michael D. Intriligator

In probabilistic mechanisms of social choice, the problem of a choice for society of one of several alternatives is reoriented away from the traditional approach in which individual preferences are used to construct social preferences, which are then used to select a most preferred alternative. Rather the individual preferences, expressed as individual probabilities of choosing a particular social alternative, are used to construct social probabilities of choosing among the various alternatives. The selection of one alternative is then accomplished by a random mechanism, such as a table of random numbers, keyed with these probabilities. This probabilistic approach uses the impersonal mechanism of a random device to adjudicate differences in individual preferences, and it takes account of all of these preferences and their intensity. In this paper the probabilistic mechanism of social choice is described, contrasted to traditional approaches, and applied to problems of elections and taxation, the former exemplifying the social choice problem and the latter providing the major avenue of income redistribution, as one of the fundamental issues of social choice.

INTRODUCTION, PURPOSE, AND ORGANIZATION

Much of the social choice literature, as originally developed by Arrow, entails an impossibility theorem, a fundamentally negative result. Probabilistic mechanisms of social choice, by contrast, represent an alternative way of configuring the problem of social choice, which leads to positive and intuitively plausible results in such areas as elections and taxation. The purpose of this paper is to provide an overview of such probabilistic mechanisms of social choice. The paper presents a brief summary of the social choice problem and the impossibility theorem, a discussion of the probabilistic mechanism of social choice, an example of its application to elections, a discussion of its application to income redistribution and taxation, and a conclusion.

THE SOCIAL CHOICE PROBLEM AND THE IMPOSSIBILITY THEOREM

The classic problem of social choice postulates a society of individuals that must decide among a given set of alternatives. The society might range from a committee to an entire nation, and the alternatives might range from candidates in an election or rival policies to a complete specification of future societal actions.

The _locus classicus_ of this problem is Arrow's _Social Choice and Individual Values_, which has had a profound influence on a whole generation of economists and political scientists since its initial publication in 1951.(1) Arrow conceived of the problem as one in which the individuals each have well-behaved preferences over the social alternatives, and the problem facing society is somehow to aggregate these preferences into a well-behaved set of social preferences. Society would then presumably act as if it were a single individual with these preferences, choosing the highest ranked alternative within its opportunity set of available alternatives.

Arrow imposed four requirements, which he argued were reasonable, on the aggregation of individual preferences into social preferences. First, he required universal domain, meaning that all conceivable combinations of individual preferences could be treated, any conceivable combination of individual preferences yielding a unique, well-behaved, and, in particular, transitive set of social preferences. Second, he required the Pareto principle, meaning that if all individuals prefer one alternative to another, then so does society. Third, he required independence of irrelevant alternatives, meaning that social rankings depend only on the alternatives that are in fact available, and particularly that adding (or deleting) alternatives does not change the social ordering of the initial (or remaining) alternatives. Finally, fourth, he required nondictatorship, meaning that there is no individual (the dictator) whose individual preferences are automatically those of society, regardless of the preferences of the other individuals.

With these conditions on social preferences, Arrow was able to prove two important theorems on social choice. The first theorem, the possibility theorem, states that if there are only two alternatives for the society, such as in a two-party system of elections, then majority rule satisfies all four conditions. In particular, if everyone votes according to his or her individual preferences, then the social preference for which the alternative with the greater number of votes is preferred satisfies all four of the Arrow conditions. Aggregation of individual preferences into social preferences using such a system of majority rule gives definite and consistent social preferences and satisfies the Pareto principle, independence of irrelevant alternatives, and nondictatorship requirements.

The second Arrow theorem, which is deeper and more famous, is the impossibility theorem, which states that if there are three or more alternatives for society then no system of aggregation of individual preferences, whether majority rule or any other system, simultaneously satisfies all four conditions.(2) Equivalently, it is impossible to aggregate individual preferences into social preferences in such a way that all four conditions are met. Thus, for example, any system that satisfies universal domain, the Pareto principle, and independence of irrelevant alternatives must, of necessity, be a dictatorial one, in which one individual's preferences determine those of society.

The most famous example of the impossibility theorem is the Condorcet voting paradox showing the failure of majority rule when there are three alternatives. Consider a society of three individuals conducting an election among three candidates, A, B, and C. The first individual prefers A to B, B to C, and thus, by transitivity (which is part of the requirement that preferences be well-behaved), A to C. The second individual prefers B to C, C to A, and thus B to A. The third individual prefers C to A, A to B, and thus C to B. By majority rule the society prefers A to B since two of the three individuals (the first and third) prefer A to B. Similarly the society prefers B to C (since the first and second do so). Thus if the society's preferences were well-behaved it should, by transitivity, prefer A to C. But by majority rule the society prefers C to A (since that is the preference of the second and third individuals). Thus there is a paradox of voting.

One manifestation of this paradox is that the individual setting the agenda can control the outcome. If the first individual, who prefers A, were setting the agenda, he or she would call first for the pairwise choice of B and C, knocking out C, then for the pairwise choice of A and B, choosing A. If, however, the second individual, who prefers B, were setting the agenda, he or she would call first for the pairwise choice of C and A (knocking out A), then the pairwise choice of B and C (choosing B). Similarly, the third individual would start with A and B (knocking out B) and end with A and C (choosing C).

This influence of the person setting the agenda on the outcome is symptomatic of the impossibility theorem. While the Condorcet voting paradox discussed here is indicative of the impossibility theorem, the theorem in fact states that not only majority rule, as used in the Condorcet example, but in fact any system of aggregation would fail to satisfy the four conditions if there are three or more alternatives.

The impossibility theorem has led to a considerable literature seeking to explain it or to circumvent it. Some see it, together with the possibility theorem, as a justification for a two-party system. Others see it as requiring some societal consensus (violating universal domain), such that, without disparate individual preferences it is possible to aggregate such preferences in a meaningful way. Yet others have proposed schemes that entail dropping the independence of irrelevant alternatives requirement.

PROBABILISTIC MECHANISMS OF SOCIAL CHOICE

Probabilistic mechanisms of social choice involve a reorientation of the problem of social choice.(3) Rather than aggregating individual preferences into social preferences, as in the Arrow approach, the probabilistic mechanism of social choice aggregates individual preferences, expressed as individual probabilities of choosing among social alternatives, into social probabilities of choosing among these alternatives.(4) The final choice of a particular alternative is then accomplished by a random mechanism keyed with these probabilities. The random mechanism might, for example, be a toss of a coin or use of a table of random numbers. Such a probabilistic mechanism has the advantage of using the impersonal mechanism of a random device to adjudicate differences in individual probabilities, where all individual preferences and their intensity can be taken into account.(5)

Three axioms on probabilistic social choice imply a unique rule for aggregating individual probabilities into social probabilities.(6) First is the existence of social probabilities axiom, analogous to the universal domain postulate of Arrow, which requires that given any set of individual probabilities (which are nonnegative and sum to unity), there exists a corresponding and meaningful set of social probabilities (which are also nonnegative and sum to unity). Second is the unanimity preserving for a loser axiom, according to which society never chooses a certain alternative (that is, chooses it with zero probability) if no individual would ever choose this alternative (that is, all individuals choose it with zero probability). The third and last axiom is that of strict and equal sensitivity of social probabilities to individual probabilities, according to which an increase in any individual probability of choosing a particular alternative always increases the social probability of choosing that alternative, and the amount by which the social probability is increased is the same regardless of which individual probability has increased.

With these three axioms there is a unique rule for determining social probabilities from the individual probabilities, the average rule. This method of aggregating individual probabilities is consistent with all three axioms, and it is the only rule that satisfies all of these axioms. This rule says simply that social probabilities are simple averages of individual probabilities. Equivalently, the rule states that each of the individuals has an equal chance of choosing for society, in which case the social probabilities are the same as those of the individual so allowed to choose.

In addition to satisfying the three axioms that uniquely imply it, the average rule also satisfies other conditions that are reasonable ones for social choice. It satisfies collective rationality in that the implied social preferences form a complete ordering (exhibiting reflexivity, connectedness, and transitivity) where greater social probability means social preference; it satisfies citizens sovereignty in that no social probability vectors are excluded, independent of all individuals' preferences; it satisfies nondictatorship in that no single individual or coalition of individuals smaller than the whole society can determine social probabilities independently of the other individuals; it satisfies symmetry in that social probabilities are unchanged if the individuals are relabeled; it satisfies unanimous preference preserving in that if all individuals prefer one alternative to another then so does society; it satisfies Pareto optimality in that if all individuals are indifferent between two alternatives and one individual prefers one of these alternatives then so does society; it satisfies the certainty principle in that society chooses an alternative with certainty if and only if all individuals choose it with certainty; it satisfies unanimity preservation in that if all individuals choose an alternative with the same probability then society also chooses that alternative with that probability; and it satisfies independence in that the social probability of choosing one alternative depends only on the individual probabilities of choosing that particular alternative.(7)

The average rule for aggregating individual probabilities is generally different from the majority rule for aggregation and from other rules that have been suggested or used, as will be illustrated in the next section. Majority rule, in particular, does not satisfy the third axiom of strict and equal sensitivity of social probabilities to individual probabilities. Once a majority opts for a particular alternative, this alternative is chosen with certainty. At this point, then, if any individual changes his or her probabilities in favor of the chosen alternative, there is no way to increase the probability of choosing this alternative.

AN EXAMPLE OF PROBABILISTIC SOCIAL CHOICE: ELECTIONS

The nature of probabilistic social choice and the contrast between majority rule and other rules can be illustrated by an example. The example involves the application of social choice to elections, a principal motivation for social choice theory.

In this example there are three voters--1, 2, 3--and three candidates--A, B, C. The first and second voters have exactly the same preferences over the three candidates expressed by the individual probability vector (0.6, 0.4, 0). The meaning of this individual probability vector is that the first and second voters would choose the candidate A with probability 0.6, candidate B with probability 0.4, and candidate C with probability 0. The third voter has the probability vector (0, 0.4, 0.6), meaning that he or she would choose candidate A with zero probability, candidate B with probability 0.4, and candidate C with probability 0.6.

The average rule for this election would yield a social probability vector (0.4, 0.4, 0.2). Here the first 0.4, the social probability of choosing candidate A, is the simple average of 0.6, 0.6, and 0. The second 0.4, the social probability of choosing candidate B, is the simple average of 0.4, 0.4, and 0.4. Finally, 0.2, the social probability of choosing candidate C, is the simple average of 0, 0, and 0.6. This result is consistent with the axioms, being defined and meaningful as a (social) probability vector, satisfying unanimity preserving for a loser (vacuously here, since there is no loser), and satisfying strict and equal sensitivity of social probabilities to individual probabilities (for example, increasing the second voter's probability of choosing A to 0.9 would increase the social probability of choosing A to 0.5).

The average rule can be contrasted to other rules. Majority rule in this context means that all alternatives in the set of alternatives which a majority prefers to all others receive equal social probability. For example the majority rule yields (1, 0, 0), since a majority of two of the three voters prefer candidate A to the other two candidates.

Another rule, the Borda rule, in this context means that all alternatives tied for the maximum social probability using the average rule receive equal social probability. In this example the Borda rule yields (1/2, 1/2, 0), since candidates A and B are tied for the maximum social probability using the average rule.

A third rule, the Pareto rule, in this context means that all alternatives not dominated in the sense of Pareto by some other alternative receive equal social probability. The expression "not dominated in the sense of Pareto" means that there is no other alternative that all individuals prefer to the alternative or for which all individuals prefer the other alternative or are indifferent between the two while some strictly prefer the other alternative. In the example no alternative is dominated in the sense of Pareto, so the Pareto rule would yield (1/3, 1/3, 1/3).

A fourth rule, the intersection rule, is a formalization of the concept of a dark horse candidate. According to it, all alternatives in the lowest numbered nonempty social choice set receive equal probability, where the rth social choice set is the intersection of the top-ranked r choices of all individuals. In this example the first social choice set is the intersection of A, A, C, which is empty, while the second social choice set is AB, AB, BC, yielding the dark horse B as the intersection. Thus the intersection rule yields (0, 1, 0) in this case.

To summarize, for this example:

Average rule:	(0.4, 0.4, 0.2)
Majority rule:	(1, 0, 0)
Borda rule:	(1/2, 1/2, 0)
Pareto rule:	(1/3, 1/3, 1/3)
Intersection rule:	(0, 1, 0)

Thus in this case all five rules give different social probabilities. Only the average rule, however, considers the intensity of all individual preferences, responding strictly and equally to changes in individual probabilities.

APPLICATION OF PROBABILISTIC SOCIAL CHOICE TO INCOME REDISTRIBUTION

One of the most important issues of social choice is income redistribution, that is, the use of various policy instruments, including taxes, social security, public assistance, rationing, price controls, public provision of goods and services, expenditure policy, and so on, to influence the distribution of income. The problem is choosing a set of effective taxes, which can be positive or negative (in which case it represents a subsidy), changing initial levels of income to a final distribution of income. This problem can be addressed using the probabilistic social choice mechanism.(8)

There are four basic principles that any reasonable system of redistribution of income should satisfy. The first principle states that equally situated individuals, that is, individuals with the same initial level of income and the same base level of income should receive the same final income, formalizing the concept of economic equality. The second principle states that no individual should receive a level of income less than a certain given base level, which can be interpreted as the subsistence level of income, so that no one in the society becomes destitute. The third principle states that if initial income increases, then final income should also increase, ensuring that all individuals have an incentive to earn more (initial) income. The fourth principle states that each individual's income should increase as total income increases, holding the individual's own initial income and base income constant, so that all individuals share in general increases in the level of well-being of the society, even if their own initial income and base level of income do not change.

The probabilistic model of social choice can be applied to alternative final distributions of income to identify a general class of income redistributions that is consistent with the four principles. Consider as alternative final distributions those in which each individual receives his or her given base income but one person receives, in addition, all surplus income, that is, all income in excess of all base levels of income. Using the average rule, the probabilistic approach would imply that each individual should have an equal chance of receiving the surplus income, the probability being the reciprocal of the number of people in the society. With the remaining probability the individual would receive his or her base level of income. This gamble can, in fact, be replaced by its expectation, which would be preferred by risk-averse individuals. The resulting redistribution, called the equality income system, is one in which each individual receives his or her base level of income plus an equal share of the surplus. The implied effective tax is a linear income tax, with a constant marginal tax rate which is the same for all individuals, and with a negative intercept, yielding subsidies for all individuals below a certain cutoff level of income.(9)

The equality income system, which was obtained via the probabilistic model of social choice, satisfies the four principles of income distribution in the small-numbers case of a society with a few individuals, such as a family or a business partnership. It fails to satisfy the last two principles, however, in the large-numbers case. The equality income system, however, is a member of a whole class of income redistribution systems, some of which do satisfy all of the principles, even in the large-numbers case. This class is the linear income system, in which each individual receives his or her base level of income plus a certain share of the surplus income.(10) The equality income system is the special case of the linear income system in which the shares are all equal. A member of this class that satisfies all four principles of income redistribution, even in the large-numbers case, is the proportional income system, in which the shares are the proportion of total income contributed by the individual. This system or one like it might be a reasonable method of income redistribution when there is a large number of individuals among whom income is to be redistributed.

CONCLUSION

Probabilistic mechanisms of social choice and of income redistribution represent feasible and, in certain respects, desirable approaches to societal issues of elections and taxation. Such mechanisms have the advantage of taking account of relevant aspects of each individual's situation with regard to preferences and base income, treating all individuals equally and responding to changes in any individual's situation. These mechanisms, which can perhaps be applied to other societal issues as well, represent a new approach to reconciling individual differences that might provide a way of improving existing mechanisms of social choice and income redistribution.

NOTES

1. See Arrow (1963), originally published in 1951. For discussions of later developments see Sen

(1970, 1977, forthcoming), Fishburn (1973), and Phelps (1977).

2. The terminology used to describe the two Arrow theorems is somewhat confused, and some authors refer to the impossibility theorem as the possibility theorem.

3. See Intriligator (1973). See also Fishburn (1975) and Fishburn and Gehrlein (1976, 1977). The idea of probabilistic social choice is mentioned but not developed in May (1954), Luce and Raiffa (1957), and Coleman (1966).

4. It is assumed here that individual preferences can be summarized by the probabilities that individuals would use in choosing among the alternatives. These probabilities can be considered the relative frequencies of choosing each of the alternatives in a series of Gedanken experiments in which the individual acts as the dictator in the society. For discussions of the representation of individual preferences by probabilities see May (1954), Luce and Raiffa (1957), Debreu (1958, 1960), Luce (1958), Davidson and Marschak (1959), Chipman (1960), Suppes (1961), and Raiffa (1968). This literature, however, typically considers individual stochastic choice only for pairs of alternatives rather than for individual probability distributions over a larger set of alternatives.

5. The initial idea for using social probabilities stemmed, in part, from parallels between game theory and social choice theory. The problem of solving two-person zero-sum games that are not strictly determined was resolved by von Neumann by using mixed strategies, that is, probability mixtures over the pure strategies. Similarly it was felt that the problem of social choice might, in part, be resolved by resorting to a richer space of possibilities, that of probabilities (see Intriligator [1971] for a discussion of game theory). It should be emphasized, however, that the probabilistic approach to social choice is not a counterexample to the impossibility theorem since it violates the axiom of independence of irrelevant alternatives.

6. For related axioms--typically applying, however, to individual and social rankings rather than to individual and social probabilities--see May (1952, 1954), Harsanyi (1955), and Vickrey (1960).

7. The independence property here is not the same as independence of irrelevant alternatives, discussed in the second section of this paper.

8. See Intriligator (1979). For general discussions of the question of income distribution, see Champernowne (1973), Sen (1973), Atkinson (1975), and Phelps (1977).

9. For related discussions of a linear income tax with subsidies at low levels of income, see Mirrlees (1971), Phelps (1973), Sheshinski (1972, 1977), Sadka (1976), Hammond (1977), Aumann and Kurz (1977), and Brito and Oakland (1977).

10. The name "linear income system" was chosen to emphasize the similarities to the linear expenditure system. In the linear expenditure system discussed in Phlips (1974) and Intriligator (1978), an individual divides his or her income among expenditures on different goods by choosing base levels of expenditure for each good and marginal budget shares, which consist of the proportion of income in excess of total base expenditures that is spent on each good. Using parallel reasoning and terminology, in the linear income system society divides its income among individuals by choosing base levels of income for each individual and marginal income shares, which consist of the proportion of total income in excess of total base income that is allocated to each individual.

BIBLIOGRAPHY

Arrow, K. J. Social choice and individual values, 2nd Ed. New York: John Wiley & Sons, 1963.

Atkinson, A. B. The economics of inequality, Oxford: Clarendon Press, 1975.

Aumann, R. J., & Kurz, M. Power and Taxes. Econometrica, 1977, 45, 1137-1161.

Brito, D. L., & Oakland, W. H. Some properties of the optimal income tax. International Economic Review, 1977, 18, 407-423.

Champernowne, D. G. The distribution of income between persons. Cambridge: Cambridge University Press, 1973.

Chipman, J. Stochastic choice and subjective probability. In D. Willner (Ed.), Decisions, values, and groups. New York: Pergamon Press, 1960.

Coleman, J. S. The possibility of a social welfare function. American Economic Review, 1966, 56, 1105-1122.

Davidson, D., & Marschak, J. Experimental tests of stochastic decision theory. In C. W. Churchman & P. Ratoosh (Eds.), Measurement: Definitions and theories. New York: John Wiley & Sons, 1959.

Debreu, G. Stochastic choice and cardinal utility. Econometrica, 1958, 26, 440-444.

Debreu, G. Topological methods in cardinal utility theory. In K. J. Arrow, S. Karlin, & P. Suppes (Eds.), Mathematical methods in the social sciences 1959. Stanford: Stanford University Press, 1960.

Fishburn, P. C. The theory of social choice. Princeton: Princeton University Press, 1973.

Fishburn, P. C. A probabilistic model of social choice: Comment. Review of Economic Studies, 1975, 42, 297-301.

Fishburn, P. C., & Gehrlein, W. V. Win probabilities and simple majorities in probabilistic voting situations. Mathematical Programming, 1976, 11, 28-41.

Fishburn, P. C., & Gehrlein, W. V. Towards a theory of elections with probabilistic preferences. Econometrica, 1977, 45, 1907-1924.

Hammond, P. J. Dual interpersonal comparisons of utility and the welfare economics of income distribution. Journal of Public Economics, 1977, 7, 51-71.

Harsanyi, J. Cardinal welfare, individualistic ethics, and interpersonal comparisons of utility. Journal of Political Economy, 1955, 63, 309-321.

Intriligator, M. D. Mathematical optimization and economic theory. Englewood Cliffs, NJ: Prentice-Hall, 1971.

Intriligator, M. D. A probabilistic model of social choice. Review of Economic Studies, 1973, 40, 553-560.

Intriligator, M. D. Econometric models, techniques, and applications. Englewood Cliffs, NJ: Prentice-Hall, and Amsterdam: North-Holland Publishing, 1978.

Intriligator, M. D. Income redistribution: A probabilistic approach. American Economic Review, 1979, 69, 97-105.

Luce, R. D. A probabilistic theory of utility. Econometrica, 1958, 26, 193-224.

Luce, R. D., & Raiffa, H. Games and decisions. New York: John Wiley & Sons, 1957.

May, K. O. A set of independent necessary and

sufficient conditions for simply majority decision. Econometrica, 1952, 20, 680-684.

May, K. O. Intransitivity, utility, and the aggregation of preference patterns. Econometrica, 1954, 22, 1-13.

Mirrlees, J. A. An exploration in the theory of optimal income taxation. Review of Economic Studies, 1971, 38, 175-208.

Phelps, E. S. Taxation of wage income for economic justice. Quarterly Journal of Economics, 1973, 87, 331-354.

Phelps, E. S. Recent developments in welfare economics: Justice et equité. In M. D. Intriligator (Ed.), Frontiers of quantitative economics, Vol. III. Amsterdam: North-Holland Publishing, 1977.

Phlips, L. Applied consumption analysis. Amsterdam: North-Holland Publishing, 1974.

Raiffa, H. Decision analysis. Reading, Massachusetts: Addison-Wesley, 1968.

Sadka, E. On income distribution, incentive effects, and optimal income taxation. Review of Economic Studies, 1976, 43, 261-267.

Sen, A. K. Collective choice and social welfare. San Francisco: Holden-Day, currently distributed by North-Holland Publishing, Amsterdam, 1970.

Sen, A. K. On economic inequality. Oxford: Clarendon Press, 1973.

Sen, A. K. On weights and measures: Informational constraints in social welfare analysis. Econometrica, 1977, 45, 1539-1572.

Sen, A. K. Social choice theory, In K. J. Arrow & M. D. Intriligator (Eds.), Handbook of mathematical economics, Vol. III, Amsterdam: North-Holland Publishing (in press).

Sheshinski, E. The optimal linear income tax. Review of Economic Studies, 1972, 39, 297-302.

Sheshinski, E. Income inequality and growth. In M. D. Intriligator (Ed.), Frontiers of quantitative economics, Vol. III, Amsterdam: North-Holland Publishing, 1977.

Suppes, P. Behavioristic foundation of utility. Econometrica, 1961, 29, 186-202.

Vickrey, W. S. Utility, strategy, and social decision rules. Quarterly Journal of Economics, 1960, 74, 507-535.

Part IV

THE MEANING AND MEASURE OF INCOME INEQUALITY

Rae and Fessler strive to develop a viable conception of the "degree" of income inequality; while

Menchik explores the practical parameters of its measurement.

Thurow's comparative analysis of incomes policies and their consequences challenges the notion of a "great tradeoff" between justice and efficiency.

9. The Varieties of Equality

Douglas W. Rae and Carol Fessler

Frequent appeal is made to equality as a principle of distribution. Turn-of-the century suffragists demanded an equal distribution of voting rights; the more recent civil rights movement demanded, among other things, an equal distribution of opportunities in employment and education. Proponents of progressive taxation, of minimum wage legislation, and of a socialist economic structure demand, in different degrees, an equalization in the distribution of income and wealth. Although the issue may often be stated as "equality or not equality," most people actually find themselves somewhere in between, supporting measures that offer relatively greater equality, but not adhering to a policy that would distribute perfectly equal shares of everything to everyone. The question of equality in the distribution of income is not a dichotomous issue.

In a dichotomous logic, all propositions are either wholly true or wholly false without shades of differentiation. Just as people are or are not women, they are or are not tall, intelligent, or honest. Just as political societies are or are not members of the European Economic Community, they are or are not prosperous, just, or free. This type of thinking simplifies the transformation of any ideal into practice by reducing its existence to a yes or no proposition: freedom or its absence, prosperity or the lack of it, justice or no justice--and equality or not equality. Here, for instance, are some possible divisions of 100 apples between two persons:

	I	II	III	IV	V
Person I	100	99	75	51	50
Person J	0	1	25	49	50

Dichotomous thinking would sort these alternatives

by labeling V equal, and I, II, III, and IV unequal--and, in effect, equally unequal. It would fail to distinguish between absolute inequality (I) and progressively increasing equality as we move along toward IV. But distributive issues usually turn on the distinction between more and less equality. If equality is to provide a coherent principle of distribution, that distinction must be analyzed and its implications considered.(1) That is the task of this essay.

In this essay we examine three main items. We begin by briefly discussing the difference between absolute and relative equality. Second, we identify several distinct notions of relative equality, different ways of determining whether one allocation is more equal than another, as in the following table:

	I	II
Person J	100	7,000
Person K	50	5,000

Depending on which notion of relative equality is applied, each allocation is more equal than the other. We examine the ways in which the different notions of relative equality are related to each other, investigate the possibility of ordering these notions according to their stringency or fidelity to a root notion of equality, and look for a single notion of equality that can yield a complete ordering of all possible allocations according to their relative equality.

Third and last, we look at the relation between a commitment to equality and the level at which equality is to be established. Is our egalitarianism strict enough to prefer V in the following series?

	I	II	III	IV	V
Person I	2,000	200	20	2	0
Person J	1,000	100	10	1	0

If not, then it is apparently necessary to embed equality in a larger system of allocative principles, or to embrace some theory that does this for us.

ABSOLUTE VS. RELATIVE EQUALITIES

By absolute equality we mean that every pair of individuals (or races, or classes, or mugs of beer) who are supposed to be equal at all are fully equal. Absolute equality has a twofold character: (1) Every pair of subjects must be covered, and (2) every such pair must be fully equal. The former governs extent and the latter governs degree. One might thus complain that some equals had not been made equal, or that some equals had not been equal enough. The two complaints are independent and both must be answered by absolute equality. Notice that this relation of absolute equality may cover only a narrow marginal allocation, or it may cover only a tiny group of equals.

Within the limits mapped out by the definitions of a subject class of equality and the domain of equality (what is to be divided equally among whom), we may identify a particular distribution as one of absolute equality. One could thus have absolute equality in the division of a packet of chocolates between a pauper and a titan of industry, even if only the titan liked chocolate, even if all other aspects of life conspired to compound the pauper's misery: The absolute equality would be absolutely trivial, but absolute nonetheless.

By relative equality we mean that one allocation is more nearly equal than another, by being more extensive or more intensive or both. More extensive means covering more of the subjects who are supposed to be equal. More intensive means that, for a given pair of would-be equals, something closer to absolute equality has been attained. Again, these are independent considerations to which we will momentarily give independent consideration. They are also capable of interactive complexity when one has sufficient hubris to attempt to construct an index for relative equality in all its aspects (see "Relative Equality in General," below).

Relative equality is far more frequently at issue than absolute equality. Absolute equality is often impossible, or is possible only at a very low level. Some goods, like praise, victory, or distinction, can only be divided unequally, if they can even be divided at all. But more important, society may want relative equality without wanting so much as to contemplate absolute equality. This is surely true in taxation and incomes policy for most if not all Western systems, as well as in policies to mitigate inequalities in health, education, transportation, and housing. And we may embrace equality on the margin--say, in the allocation of political rights or minimal incomes--conceiving this as a way of making the global condition of life more equal than it once was, yet without seeking the eventual attainment of absolute global equality.

RELATIVE EQUALITIES

A typical subject for egalitarian reform is a not-so-equal allocation and a demand for some alternative that will be more nearly equal. But what is to count as more nearly equal? This may hinge on the number of putative equals made actually equal ("The Extent of Equality" below), or on the degree to which pairs of equals approach absolute equality ("The Degree of Equality Between Two Subjects"), or on some combination of these ("Relative Equality in General").

The Extent of Equality

Suppose we have N putative equals. Then an allocation becomes more and more equal as the number of actual equals approaches N. To begin with, suppose a society claims that all adults should have the right to vote, but intimidation prevents 15% of the adult population from exercising this right. If this number is cut to 14% (or even to 14.999%), relative equality may be claimed for the new arrangement. This is the first and simplest version of relative equality: the more equals, the more equal.

A different way to think about the problem is to think of pairwise relations among putative equals. Suppose the class of such equals consists of Mssrs. J, K, L, and M. Absolute equality exists since, say, each receives the same bundle of goods. Each pairwise relation is an equal one: J is equal with K, K is equal with L, and so on. We can develop a tableau as follows, with 1 denoting a pairwise equality and 0 a pairwise inequality:

	J	K	L	M
J		1	1	1
K			1	1
L				1
M				

The blanks are redundant comparisons, and the implied measure is the number of 1s divided by the number of nonredundant comparisons (vis., $n!/2[(n - 2)!]$ for n putative equals). Here the answer is 6/6 = 1.0, which is the maximum value and corresponds to absolute equality.

Now suppose we rearrange things so that Mr. K is privileged while J, L, and M remain one another's equals. We get:

	J	K	L	M
J		1	0	0
K			0	0
L				1
M				

with the result 2/6 = 1/3. If each person received a different size bundle of goods, then every pair would be unequal, and the minimum for this measure would thus be defined as zero. This is in fact a well-known measure of homogeneity used in political science, economics, biology, and other subjects.(2) It may be as good a definition for the extent of relative equality as will be found, but like all other such definitions, it is subject to a decisive critique.

These measures rest on an overly simple, indeed dichotomizing, view of allocation. Compare the following distributions:

	I	II
J	10	1
K	11	1
L	12	1,000,000

Thinking in merely nominal terms, I contains no equality and II contains some equality (since J and K are equals). In the measure described above, I = 0, and II = 1/3. But surely I is more nearly equal than II. The problem is, of course, that we have so far failed to note the degree of equality or inequality within given pairs of putative equals.

The degree of equality between two subjects

Now we examine just one pair of individuals who are supposed to be equals, and ask how equally they are treated under two allocative outcomes, so as to decide which outcome is more equal. The rules we use to answer such a question constitute criteria of relative equality, and four such rules command our attention:

1. Maximin criterion
2. Ratio criterion
3. Least difference criterion
4. Minimax criterion

We will take up each singly, commenting briefly upon its peculiarities, and then bring the four together to see how they relate to one another within shrinking, constant (or redistributive), and expanding economies.

The first test is:

(1) Maximum criterion: Any allocation that improves the position of the less advantaged subject is more equal (maximin: maximizing the minimum).

This criterion, praised elsewhere as a principle of justice,(3) judges relative equality by saying that what gives more to those with less must be more equal. This is the elemental feature of social democracy which most clearly links it with egalitarianism. It often corresponds to our intuitive notion of egalitarian redistributions:

Subject	Allocation I	Allocation II	Allocation III
J	80	50	80
K	20	50	50

II is more equal than I, and II would be recommended by the maximin criterion. This appears merely coincidental, since the lowering of the advantaged person's entitlement coincides with the raising of the disadvantaged person's entitlement. But note that, as in III, raising K's take from 20 to 50 while leaving J's at 80 would also be preferred under a maximin test--which seems reasonable.

Here is a second criterion:

(2) Ratio criterion: Any allocation that increases the ratio between the lesser entitlement and the greater is more equal.

The question is, by what fraction of the advantaged subject's take is the allotment of the disadvantaged subject represented? Thus, in the following sequence of allocations, the fraction in question moves from 0 to 1 as we move from absolute inequality toward absolute equality:

	I	II	III	IV	V
J	0	1	25	40	50
K	100	99	75	60	50
Ratio:	0	1/99	1/3	2/3	1/1

This corresponds very closely with our intuition, and avoids the obvious promiscuity of maximin as a criterion of equality. But notice that the ratio criterion will count each of the following allocations as more equal than its predecessor:

	I	II	III	IV	V
J	1	10	100	1000	1,000,000
K	10	90	800	7000	6,000,000
Ratio:	1/10	1/9	1/8	1/7	1/6

The ratios are improving by steady increments, while the differences expand by alarming increments. This is, in fact, an exaggerated version of what has happened to median incomes for black and white American households, as indicated in Table 1.(4) The ratio is moving fitfully up toward 1/1 (that is, the black median/white median ratio rises from 0.50 to 0.61) while the difference (even in constant, inflation-free dollars) has risen apace. Some authors, like Dorn,(4) reckon this an instance of rising inequality, while others, like James P. Smith and Finis Welch,(5) interpret it as indicating a steady trend toward relative equality between these two racial blocs.

Table 1. MEDIAN HOUSEHOLD INCOMES IN 1950 AND 1975 IN CONSTANT 1967 DOLLARS

	Median Income			
Year	Black	White	Ratio (b/w)	Difference
1950	$2,592	$4,778	0.50	$2,186
1975	$5,452	$8,860	0.61	$3,408

The net equalization of ratio for 1950-75 = 0.11.
The net disequalization of constant dollar difference = $1,222.

Which view is right depends on the difference between the ratio criterion and the following alternative to it:

(3) Least difference criterion: Any allocation that decreases the absolute difference between the greater entitlement and the lesser is more equal.

Whereas division regulates 2, subtraction regulates 3: We just subtract the amount held by a disadvantaged party from the amount held by an advantaged party, seeking to minimize the result in moving toward equality. This criterion defines our objection to 2 by asserting that absolute differences--not just ratios--are important. In absolute equalities, criteria 2 and 3 converge precisely: Any ratio of 1/1 will also have a difference of 0. But once this very rare case is breached, the two considerations are utterly distinct. We can diminish the ratio while increasing the difference, and we can increase the ratio while diminishing the difference, provided only that the ratio is not 1/1 and the difference is not 0 when we begin.

A fourth and last version of relative equality corresponds to the leveling impulse often associated with egalitarian tyranny, as in Tocqueville's analysis:

> There is indeed a manly and legitimate passion for equality which rouses in all men a desire to be strong and respected. This passion tends to elevate the little man to the rank of the great.

> But the human heart also nourishes a debased taste for equality, which leads the weak to want to drag the strong down to their level and which induces men to prefer equality in servitude to inequality in freedom.(6)

This principle requies no direct taste for tyranny,(7) and could be better said without the sexist metaphor, but it does attack advantage:

> (4) Minimax criterion: Any allocation that diminishes the entitlement of the more advantaged subject is more equal (minimax: Minimize the maximum).

This is of course the hard edge of egalitarianism, the edge most obviously fostered by envy rather than nobler sentiment. However, in one very special circumstance (constant sum allocation), this principle is equivalent to other less ungenerous ones.

Constant Sum and Redistributive Allocations

When the sum being distributed remains constant, the four criteria of relative equality are all exactly equivalent. Here is an example of this equivalence:

	I	II	III	IV	V
J	100	99	75	51	50
K	0	1	25	49	50

This is a constant sum allocation: There are always 100 units being divided. The maximin criterion (1) recommends each move from I to II to III to IV to V, since each raises the minimum. The ratio test (2) recommends each of the same moves because each pushes the ratio (K/J) toward unity. The least difference criterion (3) favors this sequence, since each move diminishes the top-to-bottom difference. Finally, the minimax criterion (4) urges the same series of choices since the advantaged subject's take declines as we move from I toward V.

But an example is not a demonstration, and for that we must turn to a diagram. In Figure 1, we represent each of these criteria by an indifference curve. These are analogous to the indifference curves of microeconomics. Rather than representing the various combinations of a collection of goods that give equal satisfaction to a consumer, our indifference curves can be seen as representing the various allocational distributions that give equal satisfaction to an ardent egalitarian whose sole consideration is the promotion of one particular species of relative equality.

FIGURE 1. FOUR PRINCIPLES OF RELATIVE EQUALITY

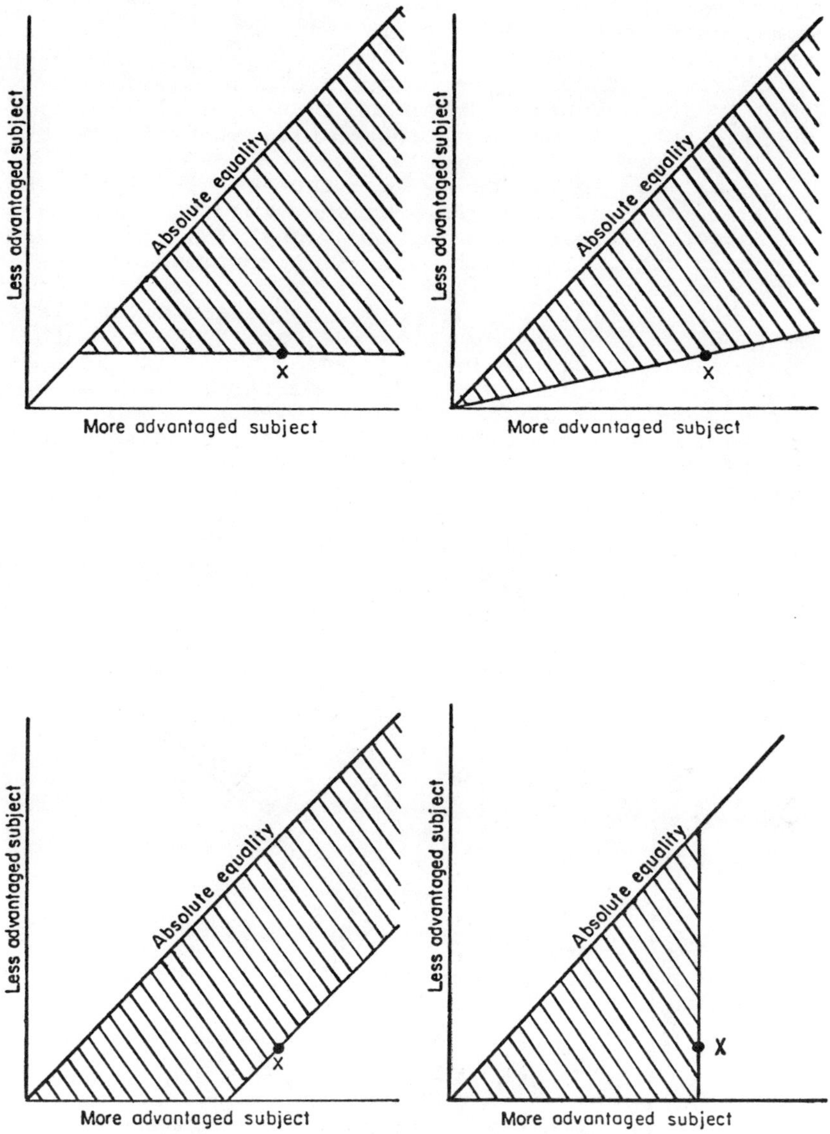

In each case the less advantaged party's entitlement is shown on the vertical axis and the more advantaged party's allocation is shown on the horizontal axis. The shaded areas lying generally above and to the left of X--between it and the line of absolute equality--constitute relatively equal policies compared to the starting point X according to the four criteria. (The area beyond absolute equality may be put aside since it would give more to the disadvantaged than to the advantaged and therefore is analytically nothing but a permutation of identities.(8) This makes our demonstration general.)

Now turn to Figure 2. Here the four indifference curves from Figure 1 have been superimposed, and a line representing the possible allocations of a constant sum has been added (broken line). All the points on this line divide the same fixed sum.

Note that all of the points above and to the left of X on the constant sum line (AX) are preferable to X according to criteria 1, 2, 3, and 4. This is shown by the fact that all four indifference curves meet at X and commend all points to its northwest (the shaded zone north of 1 and west of 4). All the constant sum points northwest of X fall into this larger set, and must therefore be preferred by all four criteria over X.

Look now to the points southeast of X on the constant sum line (XB). All of these must be inferior to X by criteria 1, 2, 3, and 4 on reasoning, mirroring the reasoning just given above. Since nothing here

FIGURE 2. THE CONVERGENCE OF CRITERIA

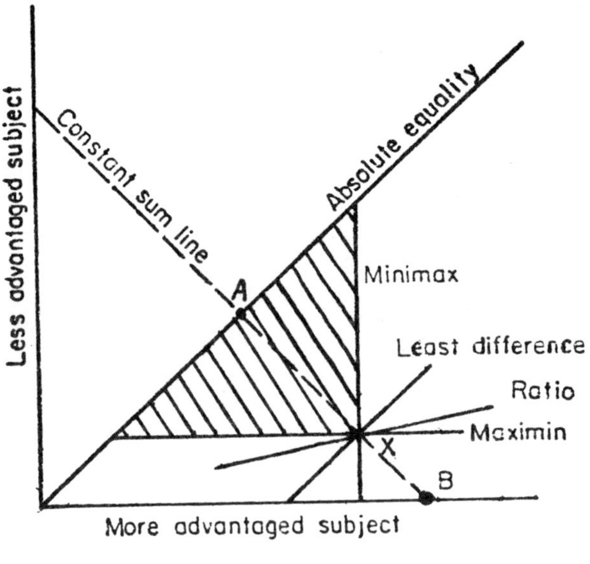

depends on the particular point (X) chosen, the demonstration is general. If (and only if) a point Y on the constant sum line is more equal than a point X according to any criterion, it must be preferable according to all four.

The convergence is actually much more general than this. Instead of the restrictive set of constant sum allocations, we can speak of all strictly redistributive outcomes. These are outcomes in which one person's entitlement is increased and the other's is decreased--though not necessarily by the same amount.(9) Thus one subject might gain 100 units while the other loses just one; or one might lose 10,000 units while the other gains 11. This class is equivalent to Pareto-undecidable allocations,(10) and is represented by the sets of points northwest and southeast of X in Figure 2. These two sets are both bounded by lines 1 and 4--maximin and minimax criteria--in that figure. Our reasoning holds good for this general class, and it would be incorrect to confine its implications to the special case of constant sum allocation. The general proposition, already demonstrated, is this:

> Consider any two allocations X and Y to be redistributive (or Pareto-undecidable) if one subject is better off in X than in Y and another subject is better off in Y than in X. Then if Y is recommended by (1) maximin, or (2) the ratio criterion, or (3) the least difference criterion, or (4) minimax, then it must also be recommended by all three of the remaining criteria. If Y is not recommended by at least one criterion, then it will be recommended by none of the other criteria.

The main interpretation of this proposition is that upward redistributions will be opposed and downward redistributions will be endorsed by all four criteria of relative equality, which simply says that these four criteria are indeed measures of equality, not of inequality. Therefore it does not really matter which criterion we choose--provided we are dealing in a two-sided redistributive economy.

Relative Equalities for Allocations with Growth or at Least without Mutual Loss

Let us turn now to a broader class of allocations than the one just analyzed, namely, to the class of allocations in which we have either redistribution or mutual gain (but not mutual loss) in a purportedly equalizing allocation. This broader class of cases is represented in Figure 3 by the unshaded area, which includes the fan of logically nested rules given by our four criteria of relative equality. Look at areas A through E in the diagram to see which criteria of relative equality approve of each:

Zone	Is More Equal Than X According To:
A	No criterion
B	(1) Maximin
C	(1) Maximin and (2) ratio criterion
D	(1) Maximin, (2) ratio criterion, and (3) least difference
E	(1) Maximin, (2) ratio criterion, (3) least difference, and (4) minimax

Every outcome not involving mutual loss falls into one of these five zones. (Again, we can ignore the area beyond absolute equality.) This tabulation is equivalent to a Venn diagram with the form of a bullseye:

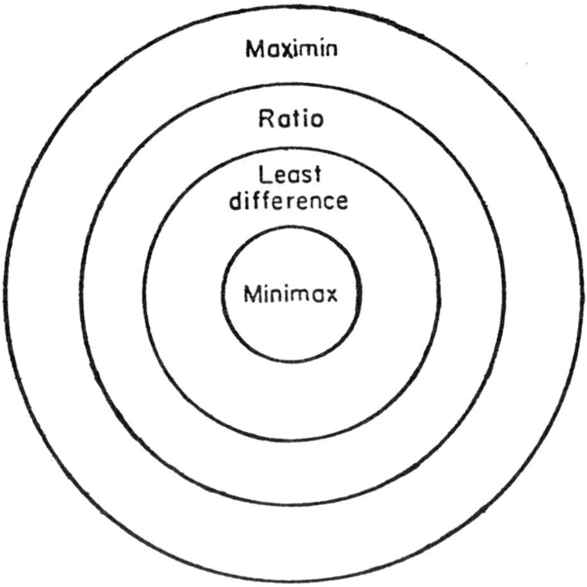

This warrants the following general conclusion:

> Consider any two allocations X and Y such that Y is not worse for both subjects. Then if Y is more equal than X according to (4) minimax, it must also be more equal according to (3) least

FIGURE 3. ALLOCATION WITHOUT MUTUAL LOSS

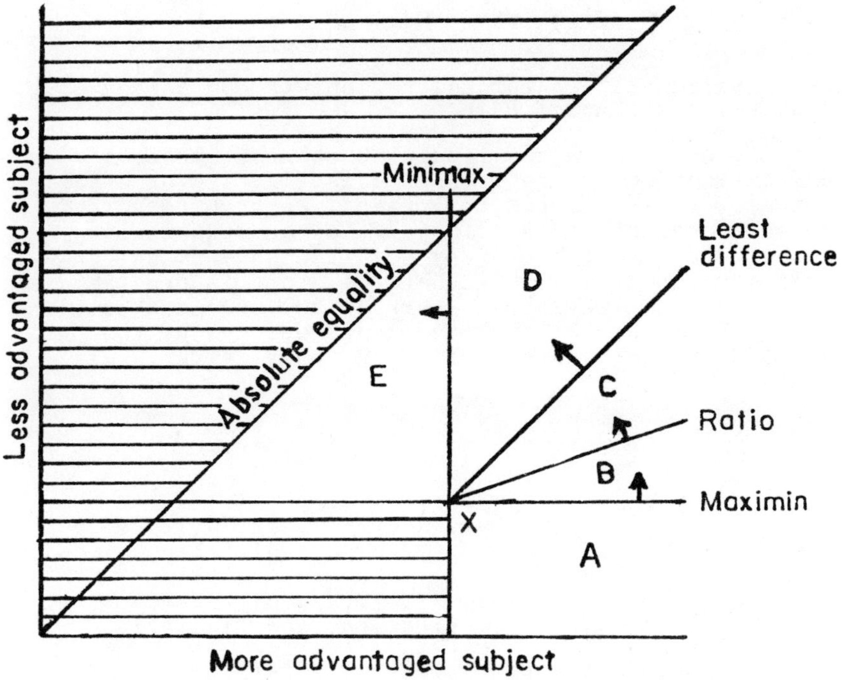

difference; and if it is more equal according to (3) least difference, it must also be more equal according to (2) the ratio criterion; and if it is more equal to (2) the ratio criterion, it must also be more equal according to (1) maximin; and if it does not satisfy (1) maximin, then it does not satisfy any of the four criteria.

The most important implication of this conclusion is that "leveling up"--using growth to bring up the bottom while avoiding painful redistribution down from the top(11)--is a very weak form of relative equality. As the table below illustrates, one can satisfy this urge, thus fulfill maximin, and still have less equal ratios than before, greater differences than before, and larger entitlements for the previously advantaged.

	I	II
J	100	1,000
K	90	100

This may not seem very likely, but it illustrates the general point, and a vast number of other examples could instead be supplied. The key to this finding is, of course, the prospect of mutual gain; when that is gone, everything is reversed.

Relative Equalities for Allocation with Shrinkage or at Least without Mutual Gain

We now consider a final and obverse class of allocations which are either redistributive or entail mutual loss (but not mutual gain). We wish to demonstrate that this allocative circumstance also produces a strict hierarchy of stringency among relative equalities, but that the order is precisely reversed from that above. Look at the unshaded portion of Figure 4, and at the five zones defined by the indifference curves depicting our four criteria of relative equality:

Zone	Is More Equal According To:
A	No criterion
B	(4) Minimax
C	(4) Minimax, and (3) least difference
D	(4) Minimax, (3) least difference, and (2) ratio criterion
E	(4) Minimax, (3) least difference, (2) ratio criterion, and (1) maximin

This follows by reasoning that is literally and exactly the mirror image of the reasoning just given for expansive allocative circumstances, and it precisely turns the bullseye inside out:

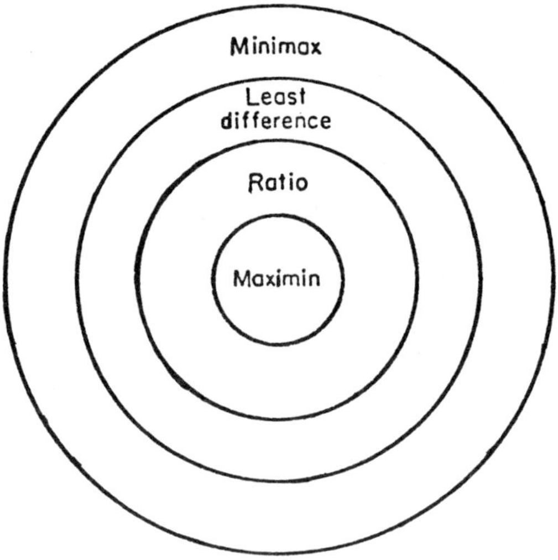

FIGURE 4. ALLOCATION WITHOUT MUTUAL GAIN

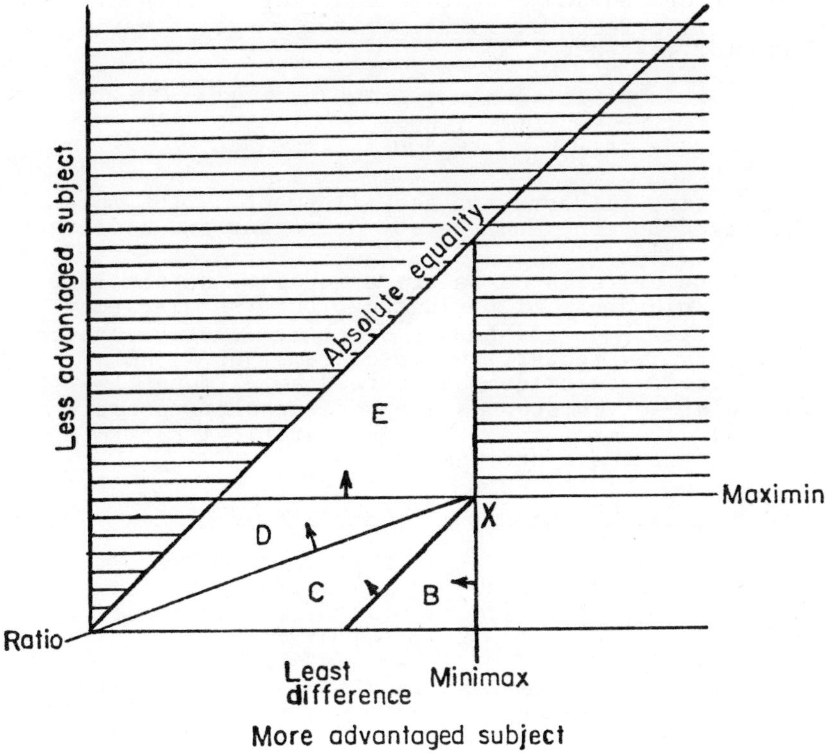

Thus the general conclusion is, not surprisingly, inverted.

> Consider any two allocations X and Y such that Y is not better for both subjects. Then if Y is more equal than X according to (1) maximin, it must also be more equal according to (2) the ratio criterion; and if it is more equal according to (2) the ratio criterion, it must also be more equal according to (3) least difference; and if it is more equal according to (3) least difference, it must also be more equal according to (4) minimax; and if it does not satisfy (4) minimax, then it does not satisfy any of the criteria.

In short, the maximin criterion is no longer permissive but restrictive, and what satisfies this test under an economy without mutual gain must satisfy all the other criteria as well. Indeed, in a shrinking economy, if the entire loss is located in the allocation of the more advantaged subject, the resulting distribution is relatively more equal by all criteria except maximin X. Thus, for instance:

	I	II
J	1,000	900
K	500	500

Distribution II decreases the allotment of the more advantaged person, and thereby decreases the difference and the ratio.

These criteria of relative equality do not lack a coherent hierarchy of stringency, but the hierarchy wholly depends on the nature of the allocative choice. Under strictly redistributive circumstances, all four criteria coincide. Under favorable (mutually beneficial) circumstances and unfavorable (mutually harmful) circumstances, their hierarchical rankings, from most to least stringent, are:

Mutually beneficial	Mutually harmful
(4) Minimax	(1) Maximin
(3) Least difference	(2) Ratio criterion
(2) Ratio criterion	(3) Least difference
(1) Maximin	(4) Minimax

How Social Scientists Resolve all of the Above by Means Well-Known to Ostriches

These interactions among the principles of relative equality depend on the possibility of mutual gain or loss, which depends in turn on the possibility of fluctuation in the total to be divided. If we wanted to simplify matters by setting up a single and universal index of relative (in)equality, we would need to hide fluctuations in the total from our own attention. To do this, we simply normalize everyone's entitlement, treating it as a proportion of the total or (what does the same work) as a proportion of the mean entitlement. Thus a 7:3 division and a 7,000:3,000 division are alike reduced to being divisions in the proportion: 0.7:0.3 or 70%:30%. Every allocative choice then looks like the constant sum case discussed under "Constant Sum and Redistributive Allocations" (and indeed, every allocation does distribute the constant sum of 100% of the goods to be divided). This has the result that all four criteria of relative equality coincide.

This maneuver underlies just about every important analytic index for relative equality or inequality known to economic and social science.(12) Its apparent purpose is to simplify analysis without putting aside any useful information, and it does exactly that. It does it, however, in the style of ostriches. On the normalized data, all rules of relative equality will agree. In the one case where the normalization changes nothing (constant sum allocation), this apparent agreement represents an actual agreement of judgements; in all other cases it masks conflicts among the criteria by removing the information needed to see conflict. Thus, for example, we might be shown the following move from I to II as an instance of relative equalization:

	I	II
J	0.33 (33%)	0.35 (35%)
K	0.67 (67%)	0.65 (65%)

We will agree that this modest alteration is to be counted as an increase of the minimum, an improvement of the ratio, a decrease in the difference, and a diminution of the maximum--all of these at once, and all because of each. But it may not increase the minimum if the total shrinks from I to II:

	I	II
J	330	175
K	670	325
Total	1000	500

It may not diminish differences, or lower the maximum, if the total expands from I to II:

	I	II
J	330	700
K	670	1300
Total	1000	2000

Only the ratio is preserved in this normalized conception, and the remaining criteria are forced to function as if they were surrogates for the ratio. Thus conflicting notions of relative equality continue to conflict in an unnormalized world but coincide happily in a normalized analysis of it.

An Invariant but Partial Notion of Relative Equality

All the criteria so far discussed silently ask us to conceive of the idea "more equal than" as a complete ordering: For any pair of allocations X and Y, either X is more equal or Y is more equal or the two are equally (un)equal. But as others have already suggested, this may be a distortion. Here, for instance, is Amartya Sen: "The very idea of inequality seems to have a quasi-ordering framework. The concept is not geared to making fine distinctions and comes into its own with sharper contrasts."(13)

We have remained captives of dichotomous thought at a second level of abstraction, assuming that just the right idea of relative equality would produce a universally applicable and categorical series of answers. It is quite likely that this cannot be attained, and that a partial or quasi-ordering idea of relative equality is what we should expect.

One could assert that relative equality exists only when all four criteria point in the same direction. This would be equivalent to saying that both maximin and minimax must be met if an allocation is to count as more equal, no matter what the economic circumstances (expansion, constancy, shrinkage). As we have seen, any outcome meeting both of these criteria will meet the remaining criteria of differences and ratios.

In Figures 3 and 4 this maximin-minimax test tells us that Zone E is always preferable to Zone A. Both the remaining principles must then agree in their judgements of these two zones. A slightly less rigid (but equivalent) test would require that the maximum be diminished without the minimum being diminished, or that the minimum be increased without the maximum being increased. This would mean that many or even most allocative choices would lead to <u>no</u> judgement about relative equality. The Pareto principle and equality would divide life between them: Equality would say nothing about mutual gain or loss while the Pareto principle continued its silence about redistribution. Equality could speak to Pareto-undecidable choices, and the Pareto principle could speak to equality-undecidable choices, with the following division of a two-dimensional commodity space:

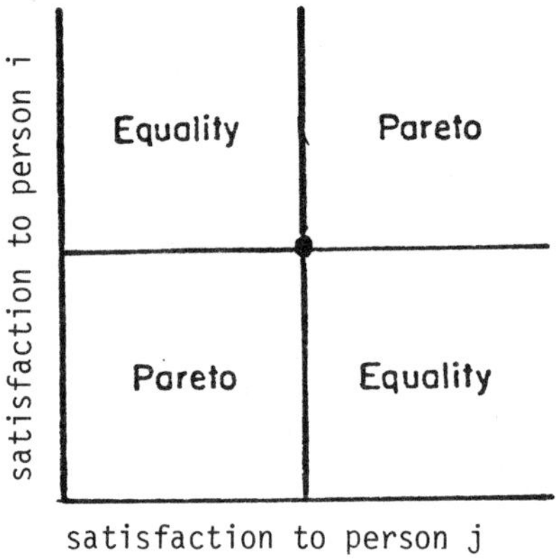

Relative Equality in General

Equality seems two-sided: this group being equal with that group, this person equal with that person. This two-sidedness is symbolized in the conventional notation of arithmetic with one term on each side of "=". One seldom sees a three-sided equality expression.

 , to say nothing of 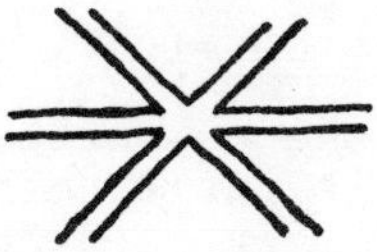

Three or more terms may be equal, each with all the rest, but this will be interpreted as a claim about pairs of terms--it will be decomposable into an array of binary relations. Combining pairwise equalities to form more elaborate ones presents no difficulty, so long as equality is conceived of dichotomously, as holding or not holding in each pair.

But the general problem of relative equality involves degrees of equality; it therefore requires extension beyond the simple pairwise relation to which the notion applied itself so nicely. We are compelled to consider two things at once: (1) the degree to which any given pairs approach equality, and (2) the extent to which any given degree of equality is spread over the putatively equal pairs of subjects. This requires us to combine two independent desiderata in judging the relative equality of any two distributions, for instance:

	I	II
J	60	80
K	60	50
L	60	40
M	0	10

Which *is* more equal? Or is neither more equal than the other? The difficulty is that I is more equal when we consider degrees of equality in given pairs, and II is more equal when we consider the spread of equality among pairs. I offers great equality to fewer people; II offers less equality spread a bit further. This problem faces all general ideas of relative equality, and it suggests that no fully general idea will prove satisfactory. Still, let us examine the problem a little further.

The usual approach is to construct an index of equality or inequality which first measures (in)equality between each pair of subjects and then averages over all pairs. A main example is the Gini index of inequality, which nicely illustrates the best and worst of its genre. While the Gini index is often depicted as an extension of the Lorenz curve,(14) its fundamental structure is actually based on pairwise comparisons. Following Sen's notation,(15)

$$G = \frac{1}{2\underline{n}^2 . \underline{u}} \sum_{\underline{i}=1}^{n} \sum_{\underline{j}=1}^{n} \underline{y_i} - \underline{y_j}$$

where n is the number of subjects, u is the arithmetic mean of their entitlements, and $\underline{y}_i$ and $\underline{y}_j$ are the entitlements of persons i and j. We begin by constructing a tableau of all absolute pairwise differences. Thus, for instance, we might begin with allocation II above, and arrive at the following pairwise differences:

	J	K	L	M
II				
J	0	30	40	70
80				
K	30	0	10	40
50				
L	40	10	0	30
40				
M	70	40	30	0
10				

The grand total of pairwise differences amounts to 440 units. Given four subjects, with a mean entitlement of 45 units, the arithmetic is:

$$\frac{1}{2 \ . \ 4^2 \ . \ 45} \ 0.440 = \frac{440}{1{,}440} = 0.305$$

This is a function of the ratio between the average pairwise difference and the mean. If we conduct this calculation for distribution I above, it turns out that its Gini index value is 0.250--considerably lower than the value for II just calculated. This lower value tells us to think that I is less unequal or more equal than II.

But imagine that we are hired as consulting magicians by Mr. J, whose 80-unit entitlement inclines him to favor allocation II. He would like us to defend that allocation in the name of equality: to reverse the judgement just given against it by the Gini index. The task is easy, for we need only propose that relative inequality is properly defined by the mean difference from the mean entitlement, yielding:

I has a mean difference from the mean of 22.5 units, which normalizes .500 when divided by the mean entitlement.

II has a mean difference from the mean of 20 units, which normalizes to 0.444 when divided by the mean entitlement.

While the first (Gini) measure told us one thing, this one tells us another. The implication should be obvious--it is easy to engage in moral gerrymandering of this sort, and it is impossible to say categorically which of the two views of relative equality is best or which distribution is most equal. A difficult problem in the simplified case of two-sided comparisons becomes an intractable one in the many-sided case.

The ease of this gerrymandering is alarming only if one takes the indices in question as serious definitions of (in)equality, and not as tentative hints about the shape of an overall distribution. If we take them in this lighter way, and are willing to renounce for equality any claims to universal scope, we can accept Amartya Sen's wise conclusion:

> . . . inequality as a notion does not have any innate property of 'completeness'. In a trivial sense it is, of course, the case that one can define 'inequality' precisely as one likes, and as long as one is explicit and consistent one may think that one is above criticism. But the force of the expression 'inequality', and indeed our interest in the concept, derive from the meaning that is associated with the term, and we are not really free to define it purely arbitrarily. And--as it happens--the concept of inequality has different facets which may point in different directions, and sometimes a total ranking can not be expected to emerge. However, each of the standard measures does yield a complete chain, and arbitrariness is bound to slip into the process of stretching a partial ranking into a complete ordering. It is arguable that each of these measures leads to some rather absurd results precisely because each of them aims at giving a complete-ordering representation to a concept that is essentially one of partial ranking.(17)

We must, then, restrict the concept of relative equality; we must look askance at the many efforts to devise a single, best index of equality,(18) and focus on those cases in which we can make unambiguously equalizing changes, typically by redistributing things from the top toward the bottom of society.(19) But we will in any case need to ask ourselves about the level at which equality is to be achieved.

THE LEVEL AT WHICH EQUALITY IS TO BE ATTAINED

Imagine a hopeless cripple who yearns to play soccer as an equal in a crowd of healthy soccer-loving athletes. We give him special training and special equipment (say, an electric wheelchair with pneumatic kicking devices) so as to increase his mobility, but every such effort to equalize athletic abilities fails. Is equality therefore unattainable? Not at all: we could cripple the healthy athletes since we cannot uncripple the cripple. This will implement equality. Our cripple will play on even terms with the others, even though the level of soccer played may be greatly diminished.(20) By slight extension, equality of some sort might be attainable under any circumstances. Equality of a more final sort will be attained for all of us; in Colonel George Mason's well-worn epigram, "We came equals into this world and equals we shall go out of it."(21)

However, most advocates of equality would not promote equality at just any level. If I have an income of 10¢ and you have an income of $100,000, my advocacy of equality very likely entails an increase in my income. Yet, strictly speaking, my advocacy of equality alone would compel me to choose I and not II:

	(1)	(II)
You	$0	$60,000
Me	$0	$40,000

This is because almost every standard of relative equality will pick out I as more equal than II. Since this is surely not what egalitarianism really seeks, we must conclude that some aggregative principles are at least implicitly mixed with any direct demand for equality.(22)

The maximin criterion for relative equality is this sort of compromise and has been proposed as a criterion of social justice by John Rawls.(23) It constitutes both Rawls's basic concept of justice and his specific rule for material allocation (as the "difference principle"). One way to interpret this principle is to say that we should pursue equality until it begins to hurt those it should help most--those who are least advantaged by existing inequalities. Another (complementary) interpretation is to say that society should let inequalities stand, but only if they are advantageous to their victims. Thus we might allow certain inequalities of income if these appeared to offer incentives for work, risk taking, or capital accumulation that would actually promote the welfare of society's least advantaged members--those without work, without assets to risk, without the possibility of accumulating capital. To attack such inequalities would be (for Rawls) unjust and (for the poor) unprofitable.

If, instead, we leave equality a purely distributive notion,(24) the problem of the level of equality presents itself as a trade-off or conflict of values pitting equality against utilitarian maximization. In the framework of market economics, it thus appears to Arthur Okun that, "We can't have our cake of market efficiency and share it equally."(25) He suggests that more equality usually means more governmental drag on production, lessened incentives for risk, work, and investment, and so on. Yet, as Okun recognizes, more equality may imply more efficiency, and it is often argued that (for a fixed total of commodities or wealth) an equal or nearly equal distribution maximizes total welfare.

While the analytical and empirical complexities of this point are great, they need no resolution here--for our point is simple: No generous or humane view of equality can be merely a view of equality. It must see equality within constraints, above some floor. Equality itself is as well pleased by graveyards as by vineyards.

NOTES

1. A great many useful points on this subject are to be found in Amartya K. Sen, On Economic Inequality (New York: W. W. Norton, 1973), esp. pp. 24-76.

2. See Douglas Rae and Michael Taylor, The Analysis of Political Cleavages (New Haven: Yale University Press, 1971), Chapter 2. For critical discussion, see Mogens N. Pedersen, "On Measuring Party System Change: A Methodological Critique and a Suggestion," Comparative Political Studies 12, No. 4, pp. 387-403.

3. John Rawls, A Theory of Justice (Cambridge, MA: Harvard University Press, 1971).

4. Edwin Dorn, Rules and Racial Equality (New Haven: Yale University Press, 1979), pp. 34-35.

5. James P. Smith and Finis Welch, "Race Differences in Earnings: A Survey and New Evidence," Rand Corporation, 1978. Prepared with the support of a grant from the National Science Foundation.

6. Alexis de Tocqueville, Democracy in America, trans. George Lawrence, ed. J. P. Mayer (Garden City, New York: Doubleday, 1969), p. 57.

7. It would, however, entail tyranny in the sense of doing harm to some when it would have been possible to harm none. For a development of tyranny in this sense see James S. Fishkin, Tyranny and Legitimacy: A Critique of Political Theories (Baltimore: Johns Hopkins University Press, 1979). On this definition, all four principles of relative equality entail tyranny; 4 is just the most obvious case.

8. Note that we could perform the same analysis with twice as many lines by labeling the axes with names (like Mr. I or Ms. J) instead of with ranks like more and less advantaged. It seems best to count people's noses instead of counting their feet and dividing by two.

9. See Arthur Okun's discussion of the "leaky bucket" in redistributive policies in Equality and Efficiency: The Big Trade-Off (Washington, DC: Brookings Institution, 1975), pp. 91-95.

10. The Pareto principle states that any move that increases the utility of at least one person while decreasing the utility of no one increases the aggregate welfare and is therefore preferred to the status quo. In Figure 12, any move to the northeast of X (shaded area) is Pareto-preferred to X. Similarly, moves in the opposite (southwest) direction are clearly undesirable by the Pareto principle. Moves to the northwest and southeast, however, are redistributive moves, involving a gain in utility to one person and a simultaneous (but not necessarily corresponding) loss in utility to the other. Utility is not inter-personally comparable, so we cannot know whether these moves increase or decrease aggregate welfare, whether the gainer gained more than the loser lost. Such moves are therefore Pareto-undecidable.

FIGURE 12. THE PARETO PRINCIPLE.

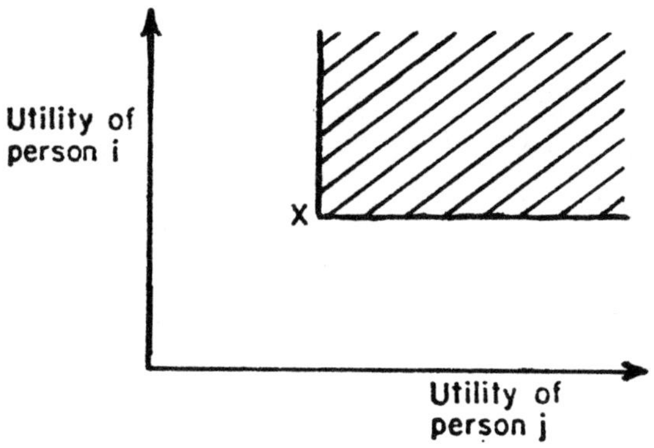

11. See David Potter, People of Plenty (Chicago: University of Chicago Press, 1954).

12. Including: the Gini index, variance and coefficient of variation, standard deviation, various logarithmic indices, and the whole series of normative indices used in welfare economics. See Sen, Economic Inequality, p. 36. See also Malcolm Sawyer, Income Distribution in O.E.C.D. Countries (Washington, DC: Organization for Economic Cooperation and Development, Occasional Studies, 1976), pp. 6-11.

13. Sen, Economic Inequality, pp. 75-76.

14. Al olgive, or cumulative curve, showing what proportion of a total domain is held by each given proportion of a population. In Figure 13, for example, is a composite curve on household incomes for OECD countries. The figure is based on data for Australia, Canada, France, West Germany, Japan, the Netherlands, Norway, Spain, Sweden, the UK and the USA. The curve is for an unweighted average of post-tax income based on standardized household sizes. The bottom-to-top income shares by decile are: 2.2, 8.8, 5.3, 6.7, 8.1, 9.4, 10.8, 12.7, 15.6, 25.4, as given in Table 10 of Sawyer, Income Distribution. The Gini index may be interpreted as the ratio of area (A) to area (A plus B) in the Lorenz diagram.

FIGURE 13. OLGIVE, OR CUMULATIVE, CURVE.

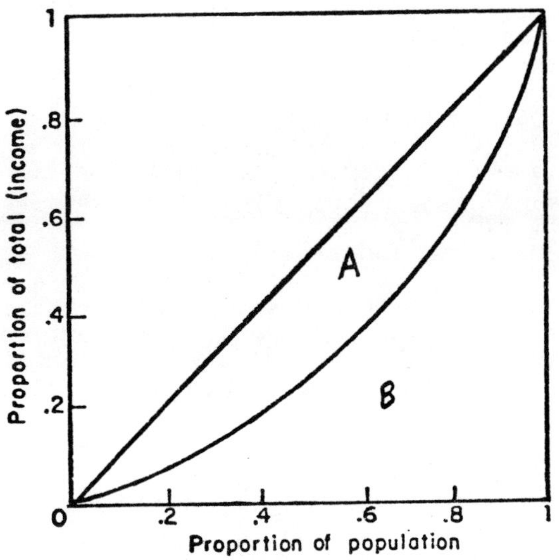

15. Sen, Economic Inequality, p. 31.

16. It is actually exactly half that ratio. Thus

the value 0.305 implies that the average pairwise difference was (2 · 0.305 =) 0.610 of the mean (27.5 units mean difference, divided by 45 units mean entitlement = 0.610).

17. Sen, Economic Inequality, p. 48.

18. For useful surveys of such efforts see: Sen, Economic Inequality; Sawyer, Income Distribution; D. G. Champernowne, The Distribution of Income Between Persons (Cambridge: Cambridge University Press, 1973); Jan Pen, Income Distribution, trans. Trevor S. Preston (New York: Praeger, 1971); Martin Bronfenbrenner, Income Distribution Theory (Chicago: Aldine-Atherton, 1971).

19. Lester C. Thurow argues that such an approach is unavoidable for the US. See his The Zero-Sum Society (New York: Basic Books, 1980).

20. See Kurt Vonnegut, "Harrison Bergeron," reprinted in Welcome to the Monkey House (New York: Dell Publishing, 1968).

21. The Papers of George Mason, 1725-1792, ed. Robert A. Rudtland (Chapel Hill: University of North Carolina Press, 1970), Vol. I, p. 229. Cited in J. R. Pole, The Pursuit of Equality in American History (Cambridge: Cambridge University Press, 1978), p. 30.

22. We here follow Brian Barry's distinction between aggregative and distributive principles: ". . . an aggregative principle is one which mentions only the total amount of want-satisfaction among the members of a reference group, whereas a distributive principle requires for its statement a mention of the way in which want-satisfaction is to be divided among the members of a reference group." Notice that mixed principles referring both to the total and to their distribution are termed distributive. All our concepts of relative equality, including those with aggregative features (such as maximin), are thus distributive for Barry. See his Political Argument (London: Routledge & Kegan Paul, 1965), p. 43.

23. Rawls, A Theory of Justice.

24. There is no such thing in Barry's scheme, and it would be more useful to say that aggregative principles require no mention of distribution, while distributive principles require no mention of totals, and mixed principles require both. On this telling most views of equality become purely distributive while some (mainly maximin) become mixed.

25. Okun, Equality and Efficiency, p. 2.

10. Some Issues in the Measurement of Income Inequality

Paul L. Menchik

Economists have a good deal to say about the impact of the market and of public policy on income inequality; but the meaning and measure of this term are often unclear. This chapter will focus on some methodological and conceptual problems in measuring the distribution of income. We refer here to the size distribution of incomes rather than to so-called factor shares or functional distributions. Statements about functional distribution, for example, shares to workers and capitalists, tell little about income inequality, and can even be misleading.(1) In spite of its shortcomings, the factor share approach continues to be used, perhaps because of its analytical simplicity, although analytical models have been developed that use much more reasonable measures of inequality (see, for example, Stiglitz, 1969, or Becker and Tomes, 1979). The rest of this paper will be devoted to exploring problems in measuring the size distribution of income, of which there are many.

The most generally accepted definition of income is the so-called Haig-Simons definition, that is, the monetary value of a person's consumption plus the change in the value of his or her net worth over a period of time. Although this definition seems straightforward, complications arise, and questions need to be asked concerning:

1. An income concept that comprehends the value to the consumer of nontraded (or not explicitly traded) goods, both consumption goods and assets;
2. The time period--such as the instant, the lifetime (or the multigenerational continuum)--appropriate to this analysis;
3. Whether the person, the family, the household, etc., is most appropriate as the unit whose income is to be measured.

The resolution of these issues can have a significant effect on the measures selected, but before discussing them we must ask why income is the appropriate measure of relative "well-offness"?

One concept of income as a consistent measure of well-being invokes the notion of the indirect utility function. Suppose the objective of consumers is to maximize utilities implicit in the consumption of goods and services, subject to the constraint that their expenditures do not exceed their incomes. For individuals whose preferences can be represented by the direct utility function $U(\underline{X})$, the problem is to select the vector $\underline{X}^*$ that maximizes U and also satisfies the budget constraint $\underline{P} \cdot \underline{X} \quad y$. Let y designate income (or budget), $\underline{X}$ the vector of all K goods (including future consumption and bequests), $\underline{X} = (X_1, X_2, \ldots, X_K)$, and $\underline{P}$ the price or opportunity cost of consuming all K goods, $\underline{P} = (P_1, P_2, \ldots, P_K)$. The utility maximizing bundle X can also be determined if the consumer solves the dual problem of attaining the maximum level of utility attainable at a given level of income and vector of prices, for example:(2)

$$V(\underline{P}, y) = \max U(\underline{X}) \quad \text{subject to } \underline{P} \cdot \underline{X} = y$$

The indirect utility function, $V(\underline{P}, y)$ conveys consumer well-offness as both an increasing function of income, and as a decreasing function of prices. This characterization of well-offness is a useful one because it emphasizes that those with equal incomes are not necessarily equal in a meaningful sense if they face different prices. Similarly, those having unequal incomes may be equals in terms of utility if the higher income person also faces higher prices.

For example, individual X lives in colder climate but receives a higher money income than does individual Y. Since the price X pays for a comfortable indoor temperature exceeds that paid by Y, we cannot necessarily say X is better off than Y when comparing their V's. Another example arises in cases in which individuals differ by health status. Since the cost of performing tasks, in terms of one's own time and other inputs, is lower for the healthier than the less healthy person, equal incomes imply higher levels of V for the healthy than for others.

The use of an indirect utility function to order well-offness is an operational approach. The parameters of various functional forms have been estimated (see for example, Deaton and Muellbauer, 1980). When the estimated parameters are used, individual incomes and prices will yield an ordering of welfare that is firmly grounded in economic theory. Some problems in measurement to be detailed in the next section are more amenable to solution using the indirect utility function approach than others.

THE INCOME CONCEPT

Many researchers use the money income concept as reported in the Current Population Survey (CPS) of the U.S. Department of the Census. This measure contains wage and salary income, self-employment income, property income (interest, dividends, rent, trust, and estate income), private pension receipts, governmental cash transfers including Social Security, and a miscellaneous category that contains private transfers. A number of economists have detailed the shortcomings of the CPS definition and have carefully tried to correct it in order to generate a more meaningful measure (see, for example, Blinder, 1980; Taussig and Danziger, 1976; Moon and Smolensky, 1977; Reynolds and Smolensky, 1977; Smeeding, 1979; Schultz, 1975; and Browning, 1976). None of these studies has corrected for the omission of a very substantial form of income that is enjoyed by many Americans: imputed rental income from owner-occupied homes.

Imputed Rental Income

The problems associated with the nontaxation of imputed rental income are well known. It is surprising, therefore, that students of the income distribution have excluded this form of consumption from the income concept.(3) Whether the period of account is static or dynamic, imputed rental income ought to be included in the income definition. In a static model homeowners can be thought of as paying rent to themselves that can be considered unreported income. Alternatively, in a dynamic model, assume that two individuals have the same net worth and labor earnings. Individual A invests assets yielding a financial return, while B purchases a home and receives housing services (while A rents a home). Since A's property income is included in the income measure and B's imputed rent is excluded, B's income is incorrectly understated relative to A's, and these equally endowed individuals are recorded as being unequal.

How does inclusion of imputed rent alter the size distribution of income? My first response to this question would be "to make it more unequal." Table 1, from Projector and Weiss (1966), page 110, reveals that the incidence of home ownership rises monotonically across the income spectrum. Consequently, the relationship between income and imputed rent (a fraction of house value) should be positive.(4) This is not in itself sufficient to permit us to conclude that inclusion of imputed rent is disequalizing. Most measures of inequality are relative measures--for example, the Gini coefficient and coefficient of variation--and adding a greater absolute amount to the rich than to the poor will not increase the measure. Doubling of all income, for example, will leave the Gini coefficient or coefficient variation unchanged. What is relevant is whether imputed rent rises, is constant, or falls as a percentage of income as we move up the income distribution scale. And since middle income recipients might gain relative to both rich and poor, summary measures are insufficient to convey the character of change within the size distribution. Certainly, a careful study examining the bias engendered by omission of imputed rent in the measurement of the income distribution is long overdue.

Underreporting of Property Income

Another problem confronting students of income distribution is the extent to which property income is correctly measured. The CPS income definition excludes realized or unrealized capital gains, in violation of the Haig-Simons principle. Furthermore, property income that is included in the CPS definition is grossly understated,(5) for example, only 38% of total interest income is accounted for. This is why it has been said that "the CPS comes close to being a distribution of earnings plus social security payments" (Budd, 1970, p. 256).

Property income is distributed a good deal more unequally than is total factor income. In a recent paper (David & Menchik, 1979) the distribution of "permanent" property income is contrasted with the distribution of "permanent" income for a sample of 1,297 male Wisconsin State Income Tax payers.(6) Since income tax records were used, property income (such as the sum of interest, dividends, rent, trust income, and realized capital gains) can be separated from total factor income (property plus wage and salary income). Applying the coefficient of variation, the ratio of standard deviation and mean, as the index of inequality, shows that permanent property income is distributed over six times more unequally than is permanent income in the cross-section.(7) Since wealth-to-income ratios (as well as liquid and investment wealth-to-income ratios) appear to rise as income increases (Projector & Weiss, pp. 110-111), full inclusion of property income is likely to increase measured income inequality.

TABLE 1 PERCENTAGE OF GROUPS WITH EQUITY ON A HOME ACCORDING TO INCOME CLASS

	Income Class in 1962 (in thousands of dollars)									
	0-3	3-5	5-7.5	7.5-10	10-15	15-25	25-50	50-100	≥100	Total
Percentage of group having equity in a home	40	45	60	73	80	86	92	94	96	57

Source: Projector and Weiss 1966, page 110.

Capital Gains

The appropriate treatment of capital gains presents us with some interesting conceptual and practical difficulties. One would expect inclusion of capital gains to have a disequalizing effect on the income distribution, since wealth holdings are concentrated among those with high incomes. Furthermore, because of a preferential tax treatment that confers greater advantages as one's income tax bracket increases, capital gains should form a larger part among the income sources of the rich than other forms of property income. Moreover, unrealized capital gains, dollar for dollar, should be the most disequalizing source of property income. Since unrealized capital gains are forgiven at death, the tax price of this form of bequest is lower than for alternative instruments of inheritance, and its advantages become greater as the sum to be bequeathed grows larger.

Browning (1976) and Smeeding (1979) attempt to take the treatment of capital gains into account in the measurement of income. Browning (1976) is not clear on how he manages to produce an estimate of the 1972 distribution of capital gains to families that assigns the poorest 40% a larger proportionate share of total gains than they receive by way of money income. Smeeding supposes that capital gains income is distributed proportionally with other forms of property income,(8) failing to take into account that the tax incentive to take property income in the form of capital gains instead of dividends increases as one moves to higher income levels. For that reason, Smeeding certainly understates the gains accruing at the top of the income distribution scale.

On a conceptual level, capital gains that have accrued in recent years may not be income in the Haig-Simons sense, but instead a maintenance of principle in real dollars. If an asset that pays interest or dividends increases at the same rate as prices in general, we can hardly say that the nominal gain in its values represents Haig-Simons income. A study by Eisner (1980) finds that from 1946 through 1977, $3 trillion of nominal gains evaporate when compared to the general rise in prices. Adjusting for inflation, he finds that real gains are transformed into a $6 billion loss.

Of course simply ignoring capital gains entirely because they amounted to a negligible (in fact negative) amount in aggregate is hazardous since some assets may have experienced substantial positive real gains while others suffered large losses. To correctly allocate real gains (losses) among income classes, it is necessary to know real rates of return on a range of asset types and the distribution of these asset types by income distribution categories. If, for example, real estate and collectibles (paintings, precious metals, sculpture, and so on) outstripped inflation while shares on the New York Stock Exchange failed to do so, real capital gains (losses) may have had important distributional effects depending on different allocation of such assets between income categories. To the best of my knowledge, there exist no studies of income distribution that include real capital gains by asset type.(9)

The Underground Economy

Recently economists have written about a potentially enormous segment of the economy, a growing sector that may engender significant biases in the measurement of both the size and the distribution of national income: the so-called underground economy. This sector includes income from such illegal activities as prostitution, gambling, loansharking, narcotics, and the fencing of stolen goods excluded from GNP accounts. These and other activities that GNP accounts are designed to include are either underreported or totally excluded (Feige, 1979, p. 2); among them are moonlighting, the skimming of retail sales, employment that is off the books, illegal alien employment, suspect inventory evaluations, covert rentals, and barter. This underground, or "irregular" economy as Feige calls it, is an international phenomenon. It is argued that this sector exists because of the illegality of some of the activities, a desire to evade taxes and the costs of regulation, and "a growing sense of cynicism and disillusionment, which has promoted individuals to circumvent the economic and legal conventions of society."(10)

Gutmann (1977) estimated the size of the underground economy in 1976 to be $176 billion. But this figure is based on certain rather questionable propositions concerning the stability of the currency/demand-deposit ratio, the exclusive use of currency, and the velocity of money in this sector. More careful analysis by Feige (1979) suggests that the underground sector is even larger than Gutmann estimates. Depending on the number of physical transfers a unit of currency could perform before retirement, Feige (Table 2) estimates the sector to be between $225 and $369 billion in 1976, and between $542 and $704 billion in 1978.(11)

What is the effect of underground income on the total income distribution? Even if Feige's estimates are an overstatement by a factor of four, underground income may significantly alter the distribution of total income. Assuming that the sense of cynicism, disillusionment, and lawless behavior is uniform across the income distribution, we may ask who it is that has the incentive to generate underground income. My answer would be: those facing high positive marginal tax rates--the rich--and those facing high negative tax (benefit reduction) rates--the poor. Individuals in the upper tail of the income distribution would have large financial incentives to barter services and otherwise generate income that is not reported to tax authorities. Likewise, poor individuals who face substantial benefit reduction rates (see Schiller, 1980, chapter 12) often in excess of 100%,(12) would have large incentives to earn nonreported income. Because, by this logic, underground income would increase disproportionately at the two ends of the distribution, it is unclear what the effect of its inclusion would be on an overall measure of income inequality.(13)

Income In-Kind

People receive compensation both in money and in-kind. The measurement of in-kind income presents us with both practical and conceptual difficulties. Suppose two individuals have an opportunity to earn the same wage rate working at identical jobs, but one works for a lower wage at a job that offers a pleasant and safe working environment, while the other earns a higher wage working in an unsafe, unpleasant environment. If the difference in wage rates is the amount necessary to induce the high-wage worker to accept unpleasant working conditions, we might argue that their total incomes are really equal. The high wage worker receives negative in-kind income, equivalent to worker's evaluation of the disutility of an unpleasant job. The nonpecuniary aspects of compensation can of course be either equalizing or disequalizing. In the case just mentioned, equals were perceived as being unequals when only pecuniary compensation was measured. On the other hand those receiving the same pay may be unequals because in-kind compensations differ, and inequalities in pay may be further augmented by the inequalities inherent in the character and conditions of work. Thus Okun (1975, pp. 71-73) claimed that nonmonetary compensation, broadly defined, is generally disequalizing:

> In actual practice, the income premiums that are equalizing--compensating for the lower attractiveness of a job--are swamped by income

TABLE 2. ESTIMATES OF THE UNDERGROUND ECONOMY IN 1976 AND 1978

Year	Estimation Official Plus Irregular Income (billions of dollars)	First Approximation of Irregular Economy (assuming 125 turnovers per unit of currency)	Second Approximation of Irregular Economy (assuming 225 turnovers)	Percentage of Irregular to Total Economy (assuming 225 turnovers)
1976	1932.0	225.5	369.1	19.1
1978	2648.3	541.7	704.4	26.6

Source: Feige (1979, p. 13).

> differentials that accentuate such nonmonetary differentials as social status and recognition.(p. 72)

Measuring intangible in-kind income is, like measuring status and recognition, very difficult. Although it is conceptually possible to do so, the measurement of tangible employer-subsidized "perks" like the use of a company car, free food and travel, and so on, have not been included in studies of income distribution.(14) Certain fringe benefits, such as health and life insurance, and vested private, federal, state, and local pensions, have proven more amenable to measurement.(15)

The issue of appropriate valuation of in-kind income is one in which the indirect utility function method (discussed above) may be successfully employed. Individuals who receive subsidized health care, for example, face lower prices for health services than do those who don't receive such benefits.(16) Given the estimated parameters of an indirect utility function, one can deduce the value to the recipient of such a price-reducing benefit.

Evaluation of In-Kind Public Transfers

The appropriate valuation of in-kind public transfers has been hotly debated. Smeeding (1979) argues that only the cash equivalent value to the recipient should be counted, while Browning says in-kind transfers should be valued at cost. A careful study by Smolensky and coworkers (1977) found that a dollar of food stamps or rent supplements is worth a full dollar to the recipient, while a dollar of Medicare, Medicaid, and public housing is valued at less than one dollar. Browning (1979) argued that, if in-kind public transfers are valued at less than their cost, the political ramifications of the undervaluation (in Browning's view) of the share of income received by the poor will lead to the further expansion of these antipoverty programs. Since Browning believes that in-kind transfers are economically inefficient, expansion of such programs will create greater waste, and by valuing such transfers at cost instead of cash-equivalent value, wasteful expansion may be averted.(17) Whatever one's political preferences, the positive economist should recognize that a one dollar transfer in-kind will (almost) always be valued less by the donee than a one dollar cash transfer.(18) Hence when aggregating in-kind income, we should, as Smolensky suggests, discount certain forms of in-kind income.

Whether in-kind transfers are valued at cost or at cash-equivalent value, their inclusion certainly increases the income of the poor and reduces measured inequality. There may be, however, a partial offsetting effect working in the case of transfers to the poor. It has been observed that many people eligible for transfer income fail to collect their benefits. In a careful study of the food stamp program, MacDonald (1977) observed that in 1974 under 40% of all persons entitled to food stamps actually received them. By 1976 the proportion participating had risen somewhat, but was still less than 50%.(19) Why is the participation rate so low?

Suppose we rank those eligible for the benefits of a transfer program by the amount (in dollars) they can receive by participating. This benefit distribution is graphically represented in Figure 1 by the line ADB. The eligible individual entitled to the greatest benefit can receive OA dollars. Moving down the schedule, individual entitlement falls until point B, where the individual is entitled to the fewest dollars--a small positive amount. The horizontal axis

FIGURE 1. THE DEMAND AND SUPPLY FOR IN-KIND TRANSFERS

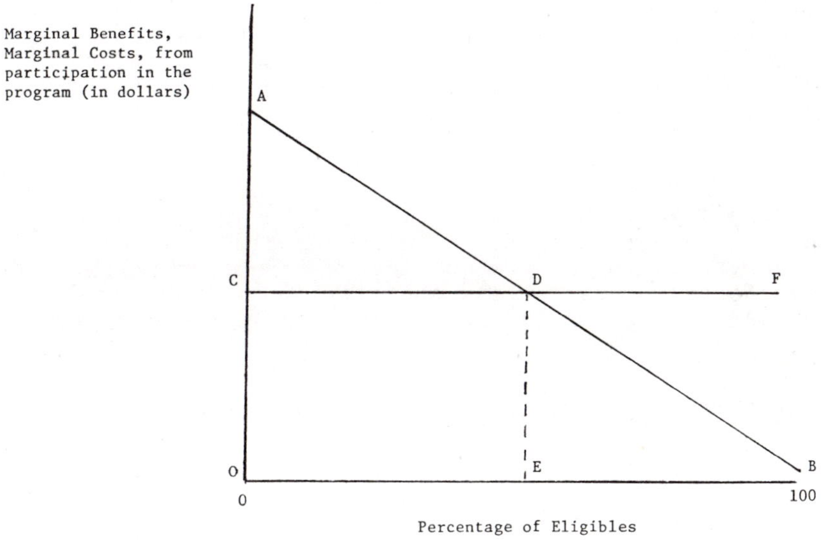

represents the proportion of eligibles, from zero to 100, entitled to receive an amount equal to or greater than the number of dollars indicated by the height of the ADB schedule. We might call ADB the "demand" for transfers.

Suppose that only a proportion, for example, that represented by the point E, of eligibles participates in the program, and that the incidence of participation varies directly with the amount one expects to receive.(20) One possible explanation for this pattern is that there is a marginal cost that one must be compensated for before agreeing to participate in the program. For simplicity let us represent this marginal cost or "supply" function as the horizontal line CDF. Only individuals expecting to receive an amount in excess of C will choose to participate in the program, because only those people receive a positive net benefit from the program.

What costs are represented by the supply function? According to MacDonald the costs of participating in the food stamp program include the time and trouble it takes to get on the program, and the stigma cost of being a participant.(21) The so-called stigma cost, according to Weisbrod (1970), is due to the loss of dignity and self-respect that individuals suffer when making their poverty known to others so that they can receive welfare benefits. This public exhibition of poverty status is particularly germane to the food stamp program, since the stamps are spent in public. The cost of participation in a transfer program, including the stigma cost, is a form of negative in-kind income that can be measured by the height of CPF. If should therefore be clear that the total income resulting from the program, both monetary and nonmonetary, is the area ACD, not AOED as a person looking only at budget size might conclude. If one accepts this logic, the equalizing effect of certain transfer programs is less than is commonly believed due to the failure to measure all in-kind (in this case negative) income.

Evaluation of Leisure Time

The measurement of the value of leisure time poses another challenge to students of income distribution. If two individuals face the same hourly wage rate, but one chooses to work longer while the other chooses to enjoy more leisure or engage in other nonmarket activities, can we really call these people unequals in a full income sense?

One way of approaching this question is to use the standard neoclassical model of labor supply, in which individuals treat their wage rate as the price of leisure and are free to consume as much of it, or work as many hours, as they please. At the margin, individuals would then be valuing an hour of leisure at their hourly wage rate. Consequently one could add to measured income the product of wage rate and hours of leisure (or some arbitrary number of annual hours less hours worked) and derive one's full or potential income.

It is true that inframarginal hours of leisure, like inframarginal of other goods, may be worth more to the consumer than the wage rate or purchase price. However, it would be incorrect to include the consumer surplus from leisure if consumer surplus derived from the consumption of other goods were not included; hence leisure should be valued at the market wage rate.

This approach can be criticized on several counts. First, it is assumed that the demand for each person's labor is infinitely elastic at one's wage rate. The presence of involuntary unemployment tends to belie that assumption. Second, for salaried individuals an hourly wage rate may not be a well-defined concept. One can certainly divide one's annual earnings by hours worked and derive earnings per hour. It is by no means clear, however, that earnings per hour is the price of leisure time, since the last hour of work may increase one's future earnings by either a substantial or negligible amount. Finally, among those outside the labor force, the assignment of a potential wage may be little more than guesswork, since attributes that lead to nonparticipation may be unknown to the researcher. In spite of these reservations, hours of leisure time do seem to be more equally distributed than dollars of income (Sirageldin, 1969) and appear to be negatively correlated with income (Morgan & Smith, 1969), and for these reasons I would suspect that including leisure into the income definition has an equalizing effect.

Browning (1976) attempted to incorporate the value of leisure time into the income concept. He estimated the number of adults who are not earners by income quintile and multiplied that number by the average earnings per earner for each quintile. The total was then added to the income of each quintile.

This approach has several deficiencies: (1) It estimates only the value of one component of the value of leisure time, ignoring the leisure enjoyed by earners. (2) It is implicitly assumed, of course, that all unemployment is voluntary. (3) The approach assumes that the potential earnings of those not working are as large as the actual earnings of those who do. Even if all unemployment was voluntary this third deficiency leads us far off the mark. Heckman (1976) pointed out that the decision to participate in the labor market is very different from the decision governing the number of hours of work. Consequently, economists who estimate the potential wage of individuals not working or participating in the market have used the two-step method pioneered by Heckman. First the probability of working (given one's personal attributes) is estimated, and second the market wage rate is estimated (given both one's attributes and the probability of participating at all). If the probability of participation is directly related to one's potential wage, then using the earnings of those who actually work overestimates the potential earnings of those who choose not to work.(23)

The interaction of this bias, and the effects of minimum wage legislation exacerbate the bias in Browning's procedure. Let us suppose that the demand for one's labor is in fact perfectly elastic at one's own wage. Also assume that one's wage rate is a correct measure of one's marginal productivity. If those who don't work fail to because their rate of productivity is less than the minimum wage rate, we are assigning to them a wage rate they could not legally be earning. It is often argued that minimum wages create welfare losses; Browning is in effect adding these welfare losses to the income of the poor.

Treatment of Personal Taxes

If we care about the distribution of net income, we should deduct taxes paid in addition to adding transfers received.(24) Taussig (1973) estimated that deducting federal personal income taxes reduces the Gini coefficient measure of inequality by about 4%. The payroll tax in the short run should be disequalizing, and so would the state and local sales taxes.(25) Most state income tax structures are progressive and would therefore add to measured equality, if taken into account.

THE APPROPRIATE PERIOD OF ACCOUNT

Measured income inequality is sensitive to the accounting period used. As the accounting period is shortened, the quantitative significance of transitory deviations from permanent income magnifies the degree of measured inequality. In addition, as people age income has been observed to follow a life cycle pattern. Note that if this life cycle path is expected, and individuals can borrow and loan at their rate of time preference, the normative significance of life cycle inequality is much different from that which unexpected stochastic variations or interpersonal differences convey.(26)

For both of these reasons we would expect the measure of annual income inequality to exceed the measure of permanent income inequality (where permanent income is computed as a multiyear average). Table 3, taken from David and Menchik (1979), presents statistics on the mean and variation of adjusted gross income among Wisconsin men for whom income tax return data are available. The measure of income inequality used is the coefficient of variation computed both within and across birth cohorts for three years, 1948, 1954, and 1958. The coefficient of variation of permanent income, computed as a multiyear average of about eight years, is shown in the last row.

The coefficient of variation is independent of mean income level. And unlike some other measures, for example, the variance of logarithm, it satisfies the Pigou-Dalton property that transfers from poorer to richer people increase measured inequality (see Sen, 1973). The coefficient of variation is equally sensitive to transfers of a given size between people at different income levels, whereas a competing measure, the Gini coefficient, does not have this property.

Several points can be made in reference to Table 3. Comparing the permanent income row to annual data for all men in column 7 reveals that the overall permanent income inequality is lower, by about 14%, than the average of the three annual measures of income inequality. This reduction in measured inequality is in approximate agreement with Kravis's (1962) finding thatannual Gini coefficients exceeded permanent or lifetime Ginis by about 10%. Within birth cohorts, annual overall inequality exceeds within-group inequality for the younger cohorts. However, we find that in five of the six cells within-group inequality exceeds annual inequality for the two oldest groups. Hence, whether purging of life cycle income variation (by age-group disaggregation) actually results in lower measured inequality depends on the age group that is analyzed.

Reading down columns 1 to 6 reveals that income means and variances increase as birth cohort members age (except for the mean income of the oldest cohort). The real rate of increase is overstated somewhat, since incomes are stated in current dollars, and over the 10-year period prices increased by 20%. Comparing 1948 to 1958 suggests some increase in income inequality as the cohorts age 10 years. However, the relationship between age and inequality is somewhat confounded by the time or period effect; for example, the cross-section measure of inequality peaked in 1954 for the period from 1948 to 1959.

The average of single-year inequality within cohorts generally exceeds cohort permanent inequality, with the notable and somewhat puzzling exception of the 1895-1904 cohort. It is important to note that permanent income inequality varies substantially over the life cycle (assuming that cohort differences can be taken to represent a life cycle proxy). Consequently, even with long accounting periods economists should be very careful about reporting an index of lifetime income inequality, since the measure depends on the age distribution of the sample.

Since income inequality in a given year depends on the age distribution of the population, one might want to ask what measured inequality would be after purging out all age effects. Paglin (1975) has tried to answer this question by decomposing the Gini coefficient into inequality attributable to differences in age, and inequality attributable to all other factors. It appears, however (Danziger, Haveman, & Smolensky, 1977), that his method of decomposition is invalid. There is the additional conceptual question of whether people experiencing the lifetime incomes ex post were really equals in an economic sense, or only in an accounting sense. This question is not addressed by

TABLE 3. MEAN, STANDARD DEVIATION, AND COEFFICIENT OF VARIATION FOR ADJUSTED GROSS INCOME--1948, 1954, AND 1958 (WISCONSIN MALE TAXPAYERS)

		Birth Year						
Year	Statistic	1930-1934 (1)	1925-1929 (2)	1915-1924 (3)	1905-1914 (4)	1895-1904 (5)	Before 1895 (6)	Total (7)
1948	$\bar{X}$	$1690	$2150	$3120	$3860	$4390	$3850	$358[illegible]
	$\sigma\bar{X}$	500	110	2400	3180	5200	3630	364[illegible]
	CV	0.296	0.512	0.769	0.824	1.18	0.942	1.0[illegible]
1954	$\bar{X}$	2310	3330	4200	4560	4750	3590	402[illegible]
	$\sigma\bar{X}$	1560	2140	3550	4640	5720	4722	433[illegible]
	CV	0.675	0.643	0.845	1.02	1.20	1.32	1.0[illegible]
1958	$\bar{X}$	4020	4990	5680	5610	5350	3670	488[illegible]
	$\sigma\bar{X}$	2220	3360	4730	5450	5770	5830	487[illegible]
	CV	0.552	0.672	0.832	0.971	1.08	1.58	0.99[illegible]
Permanent	CV	0.499	0.412	0.592	0.759	1.24	1.05	0.88[illegible]

Source: David and Menchik (1979).

Paglin and should be examined carefully if the issue of lifetime income distribution is to have normative content.

THE INCOME UNIT

The final measurement issue to be discussed is the concept of the unit of account. Should the family, the individual, the household, etc., be the unit for which income is to be measured? If we are interested only in how the market passes out rewards, perhaps the earnings of individuals is most appropriate. However, given that individuals living together will choose to divide up total effort so that one specializing in market work and the other in nonmarket work (homework for example), should we treat the income of the latter as zero?(27) This approach would lead to a larger measure of income inequality than a measure that, say, uses the average of the incomes of those living together.

Some might argue that the result of this division of labor, due perhaps to the gains from specializing in one's area of comparative advantage, should not be to increase inequality in any meaningful sense. Economists and others have made the point that since it takes a larger budget for a large family to maintain the same standard of living as a small family, one must correct for differences in family size when comparing the income of families. Kuznets (1950) ranked all units by their per capita (as opposed to total) income. In defining the level of income that constitutes poverty, the Social Security Administration has used equivalence scales to generate a measure of family welfare. This method can be thought of as an intermediate position between the per capita approach and the approach that makes no adjustments for differences in family size.

A possible argument against making any adjustments at all is that in a world of efficient contraception, family size is endogenous, like the number of consumer durables one holds. If one pair of adults spends their income on purchasing and maintaining consumer durables while the other spends the same amount of income raising children, instead of declaring the second family more needy we should only say they have different tastes. The problem with this logic is that once they have arrived, we must also count the children, not just the parents, as members of the relevant population, and members of larger families will have a smaller share of income to consume than members of smaller families, given the same income.

The census family--all people who live in the same household who are related by blood, marriage, or adoption--can be criticized as too narrow a definition of the appropriate consumption unit; we might want to include unrelated individuals living together in the definition of family. However, if income transfers are made between families, say from grown children to their parents, even this definition may be too narrow. Suppose that as a family prospers it can afford to have a retired member live apart from the rest. If all members prefer this arrangement we can say, employing the Pareto principle, that total family welfare has been improved. If, however, the retired member is largely being supported by others, the census might claim there has been an increase in inequality even though this is only true in the most narrow sense.

I think that the issue of the appropriate unit is unresolved. Economists should be very careful to make clear the unit used in their research, since the measure of inequality appears to be sensitive to the choice of unit (Danziger & Taussig, 1978). Perhaps it is best to present separate measures of inequality for families of different size instead of one all-inclusive measure.

CONCLUSION

The purpose of this chapter is to elucidate the many difficulties one can encounter in measuring income distribution. It may serve perhaps as a warning against the absolute acceptance of quantitative or qualitative statements about _the_ distribution of income, and as an aid to the reader in the intelligent assessment of research findings.

NOTES

In writing this paper, I have benefited from discussions with Ronald Fisher and John Goddeeris.

1. For example, it has been argued that an increase in the nation's capital stock, driving down the rate of return to capital, will (if the elasticity of substitution between labor and capital is less than unity) increase the relative share of total output received by labor (and reduce the share to capitalists) and consequently reduce income inequality. The conclusion following the words "and consequently" is suspect. Although capitalists may have, on the average, higher incomes than workers, the classification of the president of General Motors as a worker and a poor farmer or widow living off of an annuity as a capitalist is not terribly appealing. Moreover, increasing the share of total output received by workers need not decrease inequality. Most income recipients, including even capitalists, work for pay; and the issue revolves rather around the question of

whose pay it is that increases. Say we have two classes of labor, high skill and low skill, and high skill labor exhibits complementarity in production with respect to capital, while low skill labor and capital are substitutes (Hamermesh & Grant, 1979). In such a case increasing the capital stock will tend to increase the degree of dispersion in labor earnings and may very well increase total income inequality, not decrease it as the two-factor model predicts.

2. Assuming nonsatiation.

3. Recall that the services of housing add to one's consumption and consequently to one's Haig-Simons income.

4. Assuming, of course, that housing is a normal good.

5. See Budd (1970).

6. Permanent income means income averaged over a period ranging from 5 to 13 years.

7. The coefficients of variation of permanent income and permanent property income are 0.886 and 5.84 respectively, in the cross section. Breaking the sample into age cohorts, the ratio of property income CVs to income CVs falls as people age, the youngest group having a ratio of 22 and the oldest group a ratio of 3.

8. In Browning's (1979) subsequent work he adopts Smeeding's technique.

9. Blinder's (1980) careful study assigns real capital gains (actually losses) for the periods 1970-1977 and 1960-1977 to income quintiles using Smeeding's approach, but it makes no distinction among asset types.

10. Feige (1979), p. 3.

11. A recent paper (Kenadjian, 1980) written by the Chief Economist in the Compliance Division of the U.S. Internal Revenue Services estimated that in 1976 unreported income from legal sources was from $75 to $100 billion, and that $25 to $35 billion of unreported income was earned from three illegal sources: gambling, prostitution, and narcotics.

12. This is due to the counterproductive way in which one's means for public transfer payments are tested.

13. This situation may be an example of a case in which the two Lorenz curves cross. In such a case deducing overall effects from a change in the magnitude of any particular indicator is arbitrary and misleading (Atkinson, 1970).

14. To the extent that these benefits are not taxed, individuals in higher tax brackets might prefer to be taxed in cash compensation. Hence these forms of compensation should be correlated with income.

15. See the (differing) findings of Smeeding (1979) and Browning (1979).

16. Assuming, of course, that the providers of

health care fail to behave as discriminating monopolists would.

17. Garfinkle (1973) has in fact shown that since societal economic welfare is a function of the utilities of both the donee and the donor, transfers in-kind may be more efficient than transfers in cash.

18. The donee will be indifferent between the two forms if either (1) the donee can costlessly convert the good into cash, or (2) the donee, if given cash, would have purchased exactly the same bundle of goods that he consumes in the presence of the in-kind transfer.

19. Work in progress by Jennifer Warlick reveals a similar participation rate for the SSI (supplementary security income) program.

20. The positive correlation between benefit level and participation has been observed in the food stamp program by MacDonald (1977, p. 107).

21. I have benefited from a discussion with John Bishop on this issue.

22. Garfinkel and Haveman (1977) compute "earnings capacity," a new measure of economic status. Earnings capacity is the amount of income a household would generate if its capabilities were fully used. They estimate that the distribution of earnings capacity is about four-fifths as unequal as measured income.

23. The problem is one of selectivity bias. Browning, in trying to estimate potential earnings for everyone in the quintile is not drawing from a random sample when using average earnings of those who do work.

24. CPS includes transfers, for example, Social Security and welfare payments, but does not exclude tax payments.

25. Browning (1978) asserts that the incidence of sales taxation is proportional over a lifetime accounting period. Menchik and David (1980) have shown this is not so. The wealthy do, in fact, suffer a smaller proportionate burden than the nonwealthy under a lifetime consumption tax.

26. If these conditions are satisfied, two individuals with the same present discounted value of lifetime income, but differently shaped income paths, are equally well-off in a lifetime sense, even though their annual incomes might differ considerably.

27. One might want to count household production as in-kind income. However, measuring this income is an extremely difficult task.

REFERENCES

Atkinson, A. On the measurement of inequality. Journal of Economic Theory, 2, 244-263.

Becker, G. & Tomes, N. An equilibrium theory of the distribution of income and intergenerational mobility. Journal of Political Economy, 1979, 87, 1153-1189.

Blinder, A. The level and distribution of economic well-being. NBER Working Paper #480. In M. Feldstein (Ed.), The American economy in transition. Chicago: University of Chicago Press, 1980.

Browning, E. The trend toward equality in the distribution of net income. Southern Economic Journal, 1976, 43, 912-923.

Browning, E. The burden of taxation. Journal of Political Economy, 1978, 86, 649-671.

Browning, E. On the distribution of net income: Reply. Southern Economic Journal, 1979, 45, 945-959.

Budd, E. Postwar changes in the size distribution of income in the U.S. American Economic Review, 1970, 60, 249-260.

Danziger, S., & Taussig, M. The Income Unit and the Anatomy of Income Distribution. Institute for Research on Poverty Discussion Paper 516, University of Wisconsin, 1978.

Danziger, S., Haveman, R., & Smolensky, E. The measurement and trend of inequality: Comment. American Economic Review, 1977, 67, 505-512.

David, M., & Menchik, P. Aspects of the lifetime distribution of income and wealth. Presented at a meeting of the Eastern Economic Association, May 11, 1979.

Deaton, A., & Muellbauer, J. An almost ideal demand system. American Economic Review, 1980, 70, 312-326.

Eisner, R. Capital gains and income: Real changes in the value of capital in the United States, 1946-1977. In The measurement of capital, studies in income and wealth, Vol. 45. Chicago: University of Chicago Press for N.B.E.R., 1980.

Feige, E. The irregular economy. Its size and macroeconomic implications. SSRI Workshop Paper #7916, 1979.

Garfinkle, I. Is in-kind redistribution efficient? Quarterly Journal of Economics, 1973, 87, 320-330.

Garfinkle, I., & Haveman, R. Earnings capacity, poverty, and inequality. New York: Academic Press, 1977.

Gutmann, P. The subterranean economy. Financial Analyst Journal, 1977, November/December.

Hamermesh, D., & Grant, J. Econometric studies of labor-labor substitution and their implications for policy. Journal of Human Resources, 1979, 14, 518-542.

Heckman, J. The common structure of statistical models of truncation, sample selection and limited dependent variables and a simple estimator for such models. Annuals of Economic and Social Measurement, 1976, 5, 475-492.

Kenadjian, B. The direct approach to measuring the underground economy: IRS estimates of unreported income. Presented at the meetings of the American Economic Association, September 6, 1980.

Kravis, I. The structure of income: some quantitative essays. Philadelphia: University of Pennsylvania Press, 1962.

Kuznets, S. Shares of upper income group in income and saving. Occasional Paper 35. New York: National Bureau of Economic Research, 1950.

MacDonald, M. Food, stamps, and income maintenance. New York: Academic Press, 1977.

Menchik, P., & David, M. The effect of income distribution and redistribution on lifetime saving and bequests. Econometrics Workshop Paper #7915, Michigan State University, 1980.

Moon, M., & Smolensky, E. Improving measures of economic well-being. New York: Academic Press, 1977.

Morgan, J., & Smith, J. Measures of economic welloffness and their correlates. American Economic Review, 1969, 59, 450-462.

Okun, A. Equality and efficiency: The big tradeoff. Washington, DC: The Brookings Institution, 1975.

Paglin, M. The measurement and trend of inequality: A basic revision. American Economic Review, 1975, 65, 598-609.

Projector, D., & Weiss, G. Survey of financial characteristics of consumers. Washington, D.C.: Federal Reserve Board, 1966.

Reynolds, M., & Smolensky, E. Public expenditure, taxes, and the distribution of income: The U.S., 1950, 1961, 1970. New York: Academic Press, 1977.

Schiller, B. The economics of poverty and discrimination, 3rd Ed. Englewood Cliffs, NJ: Prentice-Hall, 1980.

Schultz, T. Long-term change in personal income distribution: Theoretical approaches, evidence, and explanations. In D. M. Levine & M. J. Bane (Eds.), The "inequality" controversy. New York: Basic Books, 1975.

Sen, A. On economic inequality. Oxford: Clarendon Press, 1973.

Sirageldin, I. Nonmarket components of national income. Ann Arbor: University of Michigan, Survey Research Center, 1969.

Smeeding, T. On the distribution of net income: Comment. Southern Economic Journal, 1979, 45, 932-944.

Smolensky, E., Stiefel, L., Schmundt, M., & Plotwick, R. Adding in-kind transfers to the personal income and outlay account: Implications for the size distribution of income. In The distribution of economic well-being, Vol. 41 in Studies of Income and Wealth, NBER, 1977.

Stiglitz, J. The distribution of income and wealth among individuals. Econometrica, 1969, 37, 382-397.

Taussig, M. Alternative measures of the distribution of economic welfare. Princeton, NJ: Industrial Relations Section, Princeton University, 1973.

Taussig, M., & Danziger, S. Conference on the trend in income inequality in the U.S. Institute for Research on Poverty. Special report #11, University of Wisconsin, 1976.

Weisbrod, B. On the stigma effect and demand for welfare programs: a theoretical note. Institute for Research on Poverty. Discussion paper 82, University of Wisconsin, 1970.

11. The Illusion of Economic Necessity

Lester C. Thurow

The just distribution of economic resources has always been a contentious political issue. But it is an issue that very few countries, and certainly not the United States, are willing to face directly. Instead of engaging in the philosophical discussions and political debates necessary to determine the just distribution of economic resources, there is a strong desire to hide behind economic necessity.

According to the argument, economic growth requires a specific distribution of economic resources (usually the current distribution, sometimes a more unequal distribution, but never a more equal distribution), and therefore it is impossible to have a political or philosophical discussion about the just distribution of economic resources. Harsh economic realities just won't permit the country to alter the distribution of economic resources.

Historically both liberals and conservatives have used economic growth to avoid making distributional judgements. The hard necessities of economic growth make it impossible to alter the distribution of economic resources, but they also make it unnecessary. If the country just has more growth, then it will have more good jobs and high incomes for everyone, and it won't have to worry about the distribution of those jobs or incomes. Individuals will be happy with their new higher incomes regardless of their relative status, and society won't have to address the divisive issue of equity. And in any case the distribution of economic resources will automatically become more equal in the process of economic growth.

We now know that almost all of the implicit assumptions in the second and third part of this social consensus are false. When talking about incomes above the range of physiological necessities, individual perceptions of the adequacy of their economic performance depend almost solely on relative as opposed to absolute position. The poor in the United States might be rich in India, but they actually live in the United States and feel poor. The middle class may have fresh fruits and vegetables that the richest kings could not afford in the Middle Ages, but they feel deprived relative to the upper middle class who can afford things that they cannot afford. There is no minimum absolute standard of living that will make people content. Individual wants are not satiated as incomes rise. If their incomes rise less rapidly than someone else's, or less rapidly than they expect, they may even feel poorer as their incomes rise.

In the past there was also a widespread optimistic belief that the distribution of market incomes would automatically become more equal with economic growth. Minorities would automatically catch up with majorities, and the poor would close the gap between themselves and the rich. Here again we know now that this is not true. From 1948 to 1978 the distribution of market earnings has become more unequal (see Table 1). In 1939 the average year-round full-time female worker earned just 61% of what the equivalent male made. By 1978 she made just 57% as much. After 40 years of rapid economic growth, women are farther behind at the end than at the beginning.

TABLE 1. DISTRIBUTION OF EARNINGS(1)

Quintile	1948	1977
1	2.6%	1.7%
2	8.1	7.7
3	16.6	16.1
4	23.4	26.4
5	49.3	48.1

With the demise of the belief that no one would care about the distribution of income as long as their absolute incomes were rising and the demise of the belief that the distribution of income would automatically become more equal with economic growth, those who wish to maintain that the society should not interfere with the market distribution of economic resources are forced to retreat to the position that the harsh realities of economic growth require more inequality to stimulate savings and investment. But is it true that any movement toward more equality automatically lowers the rate of growth and leads to lower absolute incomes for everyone?

Even a perfectly competitive static neoclassical market economy operating at 100% efficiency does not face a direct trade-off between equity and efficiency. Whatever the initial distribution of economic resources, equal or unequal, the market will generate the selfsame pressures for efficiency. Whatever the starting point, an efficient distribution of marginal products will be produced. As a result every society must make a conscious decision at least once about the distribution of economic resources. What is a fair starting point? Each initial distribution of resources, however, will produce a different set of marginal products and a different set of incomes.

Suppose the initial distribution of resources allocates incomes to those that love classical music. Then the marginal products and incomes of classical musicians will be high. If no resources had been allocated to those who love classical music, then there would have been neither the product nor any income for classical musicians.

But the role of equity decisions in a perfectly functioning static neoclassical economy is basically beside the point. Dynamic real-world economies do not operate at 100% efficiency. They may have reached political limits, but most of them have not reached any harsh economic limits upon income redistribution.

INTERNATIONAL COMPARISONS OF EQUALITY AND EFFICIENCY

Table 2 ranks various countries according to their economic performance from 1960 to 1977. The Japanese were most efficient with a 7.5% rate of growth of per capita Gross Domestic Product, while the British were least efficient with a 1.9% rate of growth of per capita GDP. The rest of the data in Table 2 indicate the degree of inequality in each country and the extent of the redistribution efforts. As one can quickly see, there is no rank order correlation between performance, the degree of equality, or the extent of the redistributional effort. Different data sets would present slightly different rankings in the degree of inequality and extent of redistributional effort, but they would not alter the conclusion that there is little or no rank order correlation between these variables and economic performance.

The country with the most equal pre-tax distribution of income, Japan, has the best performance, whereas the country with the most unequal distribution of income, the United States, is near the bottom of the performance distribution.

TABLE 2. PERFORMANCE AND REDISTRIBUTIONAL EFFORT(2)

Country	Real Per Capita GDP Growth 1960-1977	Distribution of Income (Income top 20%/income bottom 20%) Pre-Tax	Post-tax	Government Final Consumption (Percent of GDP)	Income Maintenance (Percent of GDP)
Japan	7.5%*	5.6	5.2	10%	3%
Spain	5.0	--	7.1	10	--
France	4.1	8.6	10.9	15	12
Norway	4.0	8.3	5.9	19	10
Italy	3.8*	--	9.1	14	10
Canada	3.4	10.1	8.2	20	7
Netherlands	3.4	7.8	6.6	18	19
Germany	3.1	7.9	7.1	20	12
Sweden	2.7	6.8	5.6	28	9
Australia	2.6*	5.9	5.9	16	4
United States	2.5	11.8	9.5	18	7
United Kingdom	1.9	7.5	6.1	21	8

*1960-1976

Wide differences exist in the extent to which countries succeed in redistributing income. Norway, the country with the largest pre-tax to post-tax movement toward equality, has a relatively good economic performance, but so has France, a country that is making the distribution of income more unequal with taxes and transfers. Countries at the bottom of the performance distribution do not systematically make larger redistributional efforts.

Similar conclusions can be reached by looking at the proportion of GDP going to government consumption or the proportion of GDP going to income maintenance activities. Except for Japan, the three countries that spend the least on income maintenance are at the bottom of the performance distribution. High proportions of government consumption seem more correlated with economic performance, but the differences mainly reflect military spending. If defense spending is removed from the totals, the differences in final consumption are small. U.S. final consumption, for example, drops to 13%. If any conclusions were to be drawn (and I believe that it cannot), one would have to conclude that military spending is antithetical to economic growth.

Some good performers have a high degree of inequality and no redistribution; others have a low degree of inequality and substantial redistribution. Poor economic performers are equally mixed in terms of the degree of inequality and the extent of their redistributional effort. Whatever the connection between equity and efficiency, it is not a simple one in which the willingness to tolerate inequality guarantees efficiency or is necessary to achieve efficiency.

If you look at a country like Japan, with its superb economic performance and high degree of equality, it becomes clear that the willingness to tolerate inequality is not necessary to achieve economic growth. The Japanese have one-half as much income inequality as the United States, yet three times its growth rate. There are sets of human institutions that can produce both more equality and more growth.

THE AMERICAN WHITE MALE

But it is not necessary to look at foreign cultures to reach such conclusions. Compare the distribution of earnings for fully employed white males with that for the rest of the labor force (see Table 3). Unless you believe that the culture in which women, minorities, and unemployed white males exist is different from that of employed white males, there is every reason to believe that a reward structure that is capable of keeping white males on their economic toes is also capable of keeping other Americans on their economic toes.

Yet, as the data show, white males have a much more equal distribution of earnings than the rest of the population. There is a 5 to 1 gap in earnings between the top and bottom quintiles for fully employed white males, but a 27 to 1 gap for everyone else. Can economic efficiency really require 5 times as much inequality among minorities and women to keep them working?

The 5 to 1 gap of white males is approximately the same gap as that in Japan. If the Japanese have a peculiar culture that allows them to have more equality and high economic growth, then it is a culture shared with American white males. In terms of reward structures, American white males and the Japanese play a very similar economic game. Presumably there is no economic reason why the entire American work force could not play the same economic game that is now being played by the major group in the work force.

TABLE 3. DISTRIBUTION OF EARNINGS IN 1977(3)

Quintiles	Full-Time Full-Year White Males	All Other
1	7.7%	1.8%
2	13.9	7.2
3	18.2	15.8
4	23.5	27.0
5	36.7	48.2
Mean Earnings	$16,568	$5,843

ANALYSIS OF SAVINGS AND WORK

The economic profession has devoted substantial efforts to analyzing the impacts of progressive taxes on savings and work behavior. These studies generally find that within the range of taxes imposed in the United States adverse effects have been small to nonexistent. The public discussion of incentive proceeds as if these studies had never been done, but even if substantial adverse effects had been found the studies would not prove that redistributive taxes and transfers were impossible. There are always alternative policies that could be imposed to offset any adverse incentive effects.

Consider the problem of generating more savings. A more unequal distribution of income probably would produce more savings, but it is equally clear that there are many ways to raise a society's savings rate. Japan, a country with one of the world's highest savings rates, is also a country with one of the most equal distributions of income. Its personal savings rate is high for a variety of reasons. Consumer and mortgage credit is less available. This forces individuals to save to buy the goods and services they want. And while individuals are saving to buy a car or a house, Japanese industry can use their savings to build industrial plants and equipment. And one person's savings do not have to go to finance the consumer or mortgage credit of another.

Institutions can also save. Governments can run surpluses in their budgets. Corporations and governments can be required to fully fund their pension plans. The list of possibilities is almost endless. If a society chooses to raise the savings rate with more income inequality rather than one of these other options, that is a political decision and not an economic necessity.

Individual work incentives are more of a real social problem since there is no option to individual work effort. But we have already seen the much more equal distribution of potential economic rewards that now exists for white males. America could cut its total inequality in half before it even reached the distribution of earnings that now exists for white males.

The work behavior of married females also demonstrates that the U.S. tax-transfer system does not have an adverse effect on work effort. Under U.S. tax laws married women enter the labor force at the marginal tax rates of their husbands. Implicitly, women pay the highest tax rates in the economy, yet they are entering the labor force very rapidly. And at the moment the women who are married to men in the highest income brackets are entering the labor force even more rapidly than those married to low-income husbands. If marginal tax rates were high enough to have an adverse work effect, women should not be entering the labor force in record numbers, yet this is precisely what they are doing.

Not surprisingly, these facts about American work behavior are confirmed in the analytical studies of work behavior. Three kinds of work effort studies have been done in the United States. One set of interview studies focuses on the work effort effect of high taxes on high-income individuals.(4) These studies have uniformly found that even when taxes were much higher than those now in place (there is now a 50% maximum tax rate on earnings), there was no adverse effect on work effort. Two factors accounted for this result. For the types of individuals who actually pay high tax rates, income effects (with a lower take-home income you must work harder to achieve some standard of living) dominate substitution effects (with a lower take-home wage rate leisure becomes more attractive), and such individuals face a wide variety of nonmonetary incentive systems. Power, prestige, promotions, fame--they all help to keep high-income individuals working hard in the face of high marginal tax rates.

The second set of econometric studies focuses on aggregate labor supply functions and is dominated by the labor supply characteristics of the average worker. Aggregate labor supply functions consistently show either that taxes have no impact on work effort, or that the labor supply curve is actually backward-bending.(5)

The third set of studies focuses on the work behavior of those on welfare. In negative income tax experiments, families were given higher incomes and higher marginal tax rates. Since income and substitution effects work in the same direction, it is not surprising that a small adverse work effort resulted.(6) (Marginal tax rates of 70 to 80% and poverty line income grants--now $6600 for a family of four--seem to result in a 10% reduction in work effort.) Alternative reward systems are also much less important for workers at this level. But what attracted an adverse political reaction was not the small reduction in work effort, but the fact that the poor used their higher incomes to get divorced. Divorce seems to be a superior good that the middle class wants for itself but is unwilling to give to the poor.

The underground economy is also advanced as evidence that income redistribution has reached its economic limits. But here again the evidence does not necessarily lead to that conclusion. Underground economic activity is still economic activity. It contributes to output and well-being. When production leaves the taxable sphere it may affront our political institutions, but the only economic penalty is a reduction in government revenue. The real GNP has not become smaller and people are not working less. They simply aren't paying taxes.

In the United States the growth in the underground economy, if it has grown, is supposed to have taken place since the late 1960s. But this has been a period with a substantial reduction in the progressivity of the tax system. The maximum rates are lower on both earnings and capital income than they were in the

1940s, 50s, and early 60s. If the underground economy is growing it is clearly related to changes in other cultural mores or to the examples set by national leaders. If Presidents can legally or illegally avoid paying taxes, the average citizen will do the same. If legal loopholes are not "fairly" distributed, the average citizen can simply go underground and make some loopholes of his own.

If governments want to stop the underground economy, there are also many enforcement procedures that can be employed. Reducing the level or progressivity of taxation is only one of many options. If taxes are reduced to solve the problem, that is a political decision and not one required by economic necessity.

While economic growth is often advanced as an argument for limiting further movements toward equality, this argument is a smoke screen that cannot be backed up with hard economic data. Advanced industrial societies may not wish to increase income equality, but this has to be argued as an ethical proposition. Economic growth does not require it.

OFFSETTING INEQUALITY WITH EDUCATION

In the early 1960s there was an easy answer to the problem of inequality. If there was too much inequality, there was no need to address the issue directly. Inequality in the distribution of market earnings could be counteracted with rising equality in the distribution of human capital and appropriate macroeconomic policies. Pump a more equal distribution of human capital into a full employment economy, and a more equal distribution of earnings will automatically flow out of the system. This strategy was followed, but we now know that it did not work.

Using education as a measure of human capital, government programs were successful in pumping a more equal distribution of human capital into the economy (see Table 4). From 1965 to 1976 the proportion of the work force with less than a high school degree fell from 50 to 25% and the proportion with more than a higher school degree rose from 11 to 35%. But a more equal distribution of earnings did not flow out of the economy. This was true for the entire economy (see Table 1) and for more homogeneous subgroups within the economy.

Among men 24 to 34 years of age who work full-time full-year, the percentage with less than a high school degree has fallen from 26 to 12% while the percentage with more than a high school degree has risen from 34 to 52% (see Table 5). In the face of this enormous change in the distribution of education, the relative earnings of the bottom three educational classes rose 5% and the relative earnings of the top three educational classes fell 6%. To close the earnings gap between top and bottom quintiles by 11% required 13 million man-years of education above that which would have been necessary to hold the distribution of education constant at 1968 levels. Using direct costs of $3000 per man-year of education, $39 billion was necessary to achieve this change. If such a program were expanded to the entire labor force, an expenditure of $365 billion (or 21% of the Gross National Product) would have been needed to make the same improvement.

TABLE 4. DISTRIBUTION OF MAN-YEARS OF EDUCATION OF THE WORK FORCE(7)

Years of Education	1965	1976
0-7	17.4%	5.3%
8	15.0	5.3
9-11	17.7	14.3
12	29.8	40.4
13-15	8.9	17.7
16	6.8	10.1
≥17	4.2	7.0

But there is every reason to believe that the effects of a more equal distribution of education disappear with age. Among those 55 to 64 years of age, the changes in the distribution of education were, if anything, more dramatic. Those with less than a high school degree fell from 59 to 27% and those with more than a high school degree rose from 18 to 28%. Yet the net reduction in relative earnings was only 6%, or half as large as that for the younger group.

While there was a modest reduction in the income differences among educational classes and a much more equal distribution of education, these changes did not show up in a more equal distribution of earnings (see Table 1). Even among the most preferred group, white males who work full-time full-year, the distribution of earnings did not become more equal (see Table 6). Although average earnings differentials for different educational classes were falling, the variance in earnings within each education subclass was growing, so there was no overall improvement in the distribution of earnings.

TABLE 5. DISTRIBUTION OF RELATIVE EARNINGS FOR MALES BY EDUCATIONAL ATTAINMENT FOR THOSE WHO WORK FULL-TIME FULL-YEAR(8)

Educational Attainment	25-34 Years of Age				55-64 Years of Age			
	Relative Earnings		Percent of Labor Force		Relative Earnings		Percent of Labor Force	
(years)	1968	1976	1968	1976	1968	1976	1968	1976
0-7	63%	70%	5.2%	2.0%	63%	62%	21.5%	10.3%
8	78	85	5.3	1.6	75	75	20.3	11.2
9-11	85	86	15.5	8.8	86	87	17.6	14.8
12	100	100	39.8	35.7	100	100	22.8	35.5
13-15	111	109	14.8	21.4	114	122	7.9	12.7
16	138	122	10.6	18.0	199	157	5.3	7.7
17	143	137	8.8	12.4	190	190	4.7	7.9

TABLE 6. DISTRIBUTION OF EARNINGS FOR FULL-TIME FULL-YEAR WHITE MALES(9)

Quintile	1968	1976
1	7.7%	7.7%
2	14.3	13.9
3	18.2	18.2
4	23.5	23.5
5	36.3	36.7

This occurs because education quickly ceases to be human capital and becomes a desirable background characteristic as the average level of education increases. The relevant form of human capital is that acquired on the job. Different individuals receive different on-the-job experience and training. As a result they earn different incomes, even though their formal education is identical. But this creates a severe problem if governmental programs are to alter the market distribution of earnings, because the distribution of human capital or potential earning power now lies outside the traditional domain of government. The job becomes the focus of human capital acquisition as well as the place where employment and wages are acquired.

But even if you believe that education can have an equalizing impact on market wages, there is going to be less of that impact in the 1980s than in the preceding decades. In the 1970s there was an enormous difference in the educational attainments of the cohorts entering and leaving the labor force. Those entering the labor force were educated in the post-World War II environment, and those leaving the labor force were educated in a very different environment before the war. But the 1980s will be a period when both those entering and leaving the labor force will have been educated after World War II. While there has been some further equalization of educational attainments since World War II, the changes are very small compared with changes before and after the war. Thus education is going to offset fewer of the other factors leading to inequality in the 1980s than it did in the 1970s.

It is also unlikely that there will be any effort to increase or equalize average educational attainments. Age cohorts have reached an educational plateau where there are no longer year-to-year improvements. Rates of return on educational investments have also fallen far below those available on riskless bonds. More education is no longer a good private investment, and it is unlikely that governments will regard it as a good social investment. And even if they did, it would be difficult to persuade private individuals to sacrifice current earnings for more education. They know that it is not a good private investment, even if their government has not yet reached this social conclusion.

As a result education is not going to alleviate the need to decide what is fair or unfair. That issue is going to have to be addressed directly.

THE SOCIAL CONSENSUS

Redistribution tax-transfer programs are on the defensive because there has been a breakdown in the social consensus on how government should help different income classes. While there has never been an explicit income redistribution consensus in the United States, there has been an implicit consensus that ran something like this:

Income transfer payments and in-kind consumption goods should be used to deliver benefits to the poor and the lower middle class. Large human capital investments and government jobs should provide strong underpinnings for the middle class. The rich should benefit from a tax system that provides many opportunities for paying little or no taxes if one's affairs can be arranged properly, and government should act to support business profits. Minorities should receive the support of government through direct employment and affirmative action. Everyone should get something to help raise their absolute incomes, but government should give more aid to low-income groups so as to reduce gradually any relative income differences.

The strategy flowing from this consensus worked and produced a significant movement toward a more equal distribution of per capita household income at a time when market earnings have been becoming more unequal (see Tables 1 and 7). What was an 11 to 1 difference in incomes between the first and fifth quintiles fell to a 7 to 1 difference, while the same gap in earnings was rising from 19 to 1 in 1948 to 28 to 1 in 1977. Government made these conflicting trends possible. In 1977 government income transfer payments provided 60% of the income going to the bottom quintile, and wages in its manpower training programs directly accounted for another 14% of the earnings going to the bottom 40% of the labor force.

In the United States the per capita mean income of the elderly has also reached parity with that of the nonelderly, and the percentage of the elderly living in poverty (14%) is only slightly higher than that of the entire population (11.4%). In contrast in 1967, 30% of the elderly were in poverty while only 14% of the entire population were under the poverty line. Almost all of the reduction in poverty in the 1970s has occurred among the elderly. Median per capita elderly incomes still lag behind slightly, but if in-kind consumption goods are considered, the median elderly household has also reached parity.

TABLE 7. DISTRIBUTION OF PER CAPITA HOUSEHOLD INCOMES(10)

Quintile	1948	1977
1	4.1%	5.6%
2	10.5	11.7
3	16.0	18.1
4	23.5	26.5
5	45.9	38.1

Working wives were the other factor that allowed a more unequal distribution of earnings to become a more equal distribution of household incomes. In the 1950s, 60s, and early 70s women who were in households in the second and third quintiles of the income distribution were going to work more rapidly than women in other income classes. By working they kept their family incomes rising in pace with those of the upper two quintiles, even though their husband's earnings were not rising as rapidly as those of husbands in higher income classes.

America's social consensus is breaking down for a number of reasons, but probably the most important is inflation. In inflationary periods middle- and upper-income groups feel that their real income is falling. As a result they are no longer willing to support increases in transfer payments and may even demand cutbacks. There is no doubt that such a feeling is widespread in the United States, but the feeling is at variance with the facts.

In the 1970s real per capita disposable income rose 28% in the United States. This is slightly less than the 30% rise of the 1960s, but much more than the 20% rise of the 1950s.(11) Nor were there any adverse shifts in the distribution of household incomes in the 1970s. Real income gains were evenly spread across the population. Then why the feeling of economic gloom?

The feeling is probably produced by a form of money illusion. This is a disease that never afflicts a rational "homo economicus" but burdens most real human beings. While real per capita incomes were growing 28%, money incomes were growing 134%. Suppose a money man were to deliver $134, but were to then change his mind and take $106 back. Would you consider yourself better off or worse off? Objectively you are $28 better off, but you have seen the $134 and can imagine what life would have been like if you had really gotten $134 in increased purchasing power. You may even be able to persuade yourself that your real standard of living has fallen. And in some psychological sense you may be worse off.

This money illusion is compounded by a form of intrinsic puritanism. Everyone believes that their income is rising because of their own personal merit and that inflation then takes these hard-earned gains away from them. No one gives inflation credit for raising their income, yet inflation cannot occur unless it is raising someone's income.

Inflation also converts personal or industrial problems into what seem to be social problems. At any point in time in a dynamic growing economy, millions of incomes are rising and millions of incomes are falling. Without inflation, those suffering income cuts see this in the form of wage reductions. Since others are getting wage gains, they cannot argue that the system is failing everyone. But in an inflationary period everyone is apt to be getting wage gains. Some of those gains are simply smaller than the rate of inflation. But now the losers can believe that if only inflation stopped they would have had real income gains. Many college professors in the United States, for example, blame their falling real incomes on inflation when the real cause is to be found in a downturn in the population and a large supply of new Ph.Ds.

Whatever the cause and regardless of the truth, the middle and upper classes feel that they are worse off and can no longer afford income transfer payments. This feeling is partly due to inflation, but there is another problem.

As has already been mentioned, the second and third quintiles held onto their relative income position in the 1960s and 70s by virtue of their wives going into the work force in greater numbers than wives in other income classes. This source of income equality has already vanished. Female participation rates are now rising most rapidly for wives with high-income husbands. If you believe in selective mating (that is, that men are married to women who would make the same amount in an equal opportunity world), then the effects of higher participation are going to be magnified by higher earnings for these women. Because of working wives the incomes of high-income households are apt to be rising much faster than those of the rest of the population in the early 1980s, as they did in the late 1970s.

But this means falling relative earnings for the second and third quintiles. With the gap between themselves and higher income classes growing, they have a strong feeling that their real standard of living is falling. The effect of inflation may be subjective rather than objective, but their relative income is falling and this leads to very real feelings of economic deprivation. The net result is that the middle and lower middle classes are less willing to pay for the transfer payments necessary to keep the income of the bottom quintile rising in pace with the rest of the nation.

But if productivity continues falling, as it did in 1979, and OPEC continues to increase its share of the American GNP, as it did in 1979, then real incomes will actually be falling in the 1980s. With widespread feelings of economic deprivation and the onset of a period of real declines, the social consensus on redistributing economic goods and services dissolves. Everyone feels that the country's major problem is raising their own personal income and that their taxes should be reduced. No one has any extra income to help anyone else. But this feeling and its political consequences often lead to reflexive actions that make the problem worse rather than better.

Nowhere is this more likely than in the idea that the middle class does not benefit from government, and that it would be better off if only it could reduce the size of government. This stance ignores the enormous expenditures on roads, schools, parks, and other benefits that go principally to the middle class, but more importantly it ignores the incomes earned in the process of producing government goods and services.

In 1976 American governments (federal, state, and local) directly employed 18.4% of the labor force or 19.7 million people.(12) Of these, 14.2 million were state and local government employees. In addition government indirectly employed another 9.8 million employees who worked in the private economy but produced goods and services bought by government.

The data in Table 8 shows the distribution of earnings for government employees, indirect government employees (those working in private industry but producing goods and services bought by government), and private-private employees (those working in private industry and producing goods and services purchased by private firms or individuals).

Government is basically a producer of middle- and

upper-middle-class jobs. Without government there would be many fewer middle-class families. Governments, for example, directly employ 50% of all professional female workers. When government's indirect demands are included, two-thirds of all women professional workers work for government. Government also pays white women a 28% premium over what they would make in the private economy. If government were to contract and the private economy were to expand by the same amount, the number of middle-class jobs would fall. The private-private economy provides more low-income jobs and more high-income jobs, but fewer middle-income jobs.

The U.S. government is both a principal employer of minority groups and an employer who pays minorities groups higher wages than those they receive in the private economy. Government is the principal route for minorities to enter the middle classes. While 18% of the entire population is employed by government, government employs 25% of all blacks. Black males receive a 17% premium in government, and black females receive a 36% premium. Middle-class minority incomes would fall sharply in any contraction of government.

Cutting government expenditures to alleviate middle-class feelings of economic deprivation is in the end apt to intensify the feeling it was designed to eliminate. Middle-class incomes will fall more than middle-class tax payments.

With all of these factors leading to either imagined or real declines in absolute or relative incomes, it is not surprising that the social consensus has broken down. The feelings of affluence that allowed the vast expansion of transfer payments during the 1970s have disappeared and been replaced by feelings of deprivation that will inhibit the expansion of social welfare programs in the 1980s.

THE DISTRIBUTION OF INCOME IN THE 1980s

The 1980s are apt to be a decade of rising inequality in the United States. Some of the factors leading to this result have already been seen in the breakdown of the social consensus on how government should aid different income classes. Government is not apt to play the equalizing role in the 1980s that it played in the 1970s. The market distribution of earnings is growing more unequal. This trend can be expected to continue and will be augmented by the pattern of female labor force participation. Because of female work and changes in wage patterns, high-income households are going to be recording much higher income gains than low-income households.

To the extent that the 1980s witness a continuation and expansion of the current policies for

TABLE 8. DISTRIBUTION OF GOVERNMENT AND PRIVATE EARNINGS(13)
1976

Earnings ($1000s)	Military	Federal Civilian	State and Local	Indirect Government	Government (Direct and Indirect)	Private-Private
0-3	2.2%	12.4%	25.2%	24.3%	21.8%	30.5%
3-6	20.1	8.7	15.1	15.0	14.7	16.5
6-9	36.3	13.2	17.9	15.7	17.9	14.9
9-12	17.7	17.5	16.9	18.6	15.9	11.2
12-15	11.5	20.6	10.7	11.4	12.1	8.8
15-20	8.1	15.7	9.5	11.0	10.6	9.5
20-25	2.2	5.7	3.0	4.7	3.8	4.1
25-30	1.9	6.2	1.7	3.6	2.9	3.6
⩾ 50	--	0.1	--	0.7	0.3	0.8
Mean Earnings	$10,670	$12,929	$8,714	$9,367	$9,553	$8,431
Number of Workers (millions)	2.1	3.4	14.2	9.8	29.4	77.6

fighting inflation, unemployment is going to be very high by historic standards. Since most of this unemployment will be concentrated among low-wage workers, this will further lower their income relative to upper-income groups.

The progressivity of the tax system is also apt to decline during the 1980s. Even without further additions to social welfare programs, regressive social insurance taxes will be growing relative to progressive income taxes. But there is also strong pressure to reduce the progressivity of the income tax on the grounds that this will stimulate savings, investment, and economic growth. A more inegalitarian tax system is necessary, we are told, to achieve higher, if more unequal incomes in the future. More inequality today and tomorrow is the price that must be paid to raise the general income level.

In the context of rising market inequalities, smaller increases in transfer payments, and more regressive taxes, redistributional issues are unlikely to disappear but to focus on market earnings. Income and employment conditions alike will focus social attention on the unemployed. If high unemployment rates continue into the future, the jobless will no longer be made content with unemployment insurance and the expectation that macroeconomic stimulation will quickly restore their earnings status.

The programs that generated greater equality in the 1960s and 70s have ceased to grow, and the market is moving in the direction of more inequality. America must overtly face a period of rising inequality for the first time. Income distribution data was first collected in the 1930 census. Never since then has the distribution of income grown more unequal. The 1930s and 40s were periods of rapidly rising equality. The 1950s and early 1960s were periods of stability in the distribution of income. And the late 1960s and early 1970s were periods of modest growth in equality. While presumably there were periods of rising inequality before 1930, no one knew what was happening in the economy, or at least no one had hard data to prove what was happening. But rising income inequality in the decade ahead cannot be hidden from public view. It will enter as a fact into the political discourse. And with that fact before us, it is hardly likely that we can avoid a debate on what constitutes a fair distribution of economic resources and what policies should be used to bring this distribution about.

PROBLEMS WITH SOCIAL JUSTICE

During the 1960s and 70s attention was focused on income transfer payments. The 1980s will be a decade of renewed interest in the distribution of market incomes, where major redistributional questions will revolve around the market distribution of earnings. This is likely to be so because there are already large articulate ethnic groups that have been, are, and will be demanding parity in their income-earning opportunities. Blacks, Hispanics, women--each wants a larger share of the available job opportunities, and each wants a larger share of the good job opportunities. Other countries do not have America's large ethnic groups, and female workers abroad do not seem to be quite so militant, but regional demands for income parity are growing everywhere.

The whole concept of group, as opposed to individual, justice is one that Western societies find difficult to handle. Individual blacks may have been unfairly treated, but each and every black has not been unfairly treated. Consequently, remedies must come at the individual level (a case by case fight against discrimination or remedial programs for individuals) and not at the group level. Affirmative action programs or quotas that create special preferences for minorities are often fought on the grounds that they are unfair, even if everyone agrees that many of the members of that group have suffered from unfair practices in the past. The Western tradition is one of justice for individuals and not social justice for groups. Individuals are awarded voting rights and individuals are to have equal opportunities to achieve economic success.

But at the same time ours is an age of group consciousness. Economic minorities argue that group parity is a fundamental consideration in the achievement of economic justice, and that the calculus of a just or optimal distribution of income cannot be fairly reckoned on the basis of individual comparisons alone. In doing so they argue that they are not advocating something new, but merely extending the old doctrines that were used to invoke aid for farmers or other industries and regions. Since group demands are apt to become more extensive, organized, and powerful, it behooves us to understand the rationale of their argument.

While Americans try to fend off group demands with the concept of equal opportunities for individuals, this defense is difficult because equal opportunity suffers from some fundamental problems. At the level of the individual, no one can tell whether equal opportunity does or does not exist. In a deterministic world the problem would be simple. Each individual's economic life could be examined to see whether they did or did not reach a level of economic achievement consistent with their inputs (talents, efforts, human capital, and so on). Individuals could be identified as receiving less than equal treatment.

But the real world is highly stochastic, not deterministic. Since everyone is subject to a variety of random shocks--good and bad--no individual-to-individual variations in income can establish unfairness or discrimination. Two individuals may have participated in the same economic lottery. They may have stood side by side and plucked their number out of the same turning tumbler. One lost and the other won. But the resulting income inequality signals no inequality of opportunity, no unfairness of treatment. One was lucky and the other was not.

Since those variables normally thought of as the deterministic variables--education, skills, age, and so on--explain only 20 to 30% of the variance in individual earnings, the economy is one in which the stochastic shocks (or unknown factors) are very large relative to the deterministic (or known) part of the system.(14) The more that the stochastic portion prevails, the less possible it is to identify systematic inequalities by reference to individual income variations. Who can say, using economic data, that a particular individual was the victim of discrimination or suffered from bad luck? This is a judgement that can be made only at the level of the group.

This can be seen in the standard tests for the existence of discrimination. Earnings data are collected for different groups of individuals, and a statistical equation is estimated to show the relationship between earnings and the normal human capital factors for each group. These equations are then examined to see if they are significantly different. If they are, the different groups do not participate in the same economic lottery.

But the measurement problem creates a remedy problem. If a systematic denial of opportunity can be identified only at the level of the group, then remedies can also only be addressed to the group. Societies can attempt to create an economy in which everyone participates in the same economic lottery, but they cannot create an economy in which everyone is treated equally. If you believe current earnings functions, 70 to 80% of the variance in individual earnings is outside the control of even perfect government economic policies. Only groups can be treated equally.

But this immediately raises a tension between group fairness and individual efficiency. Suppose the dean of a medical school is charged with the task of maximizing the number of doctors for some given budget. In the process of carrying out this mandate the dean notices that 99% of all male admissions complete medical school, and that 99% of these go on to become lifetime doctors. But he also notices that the same percentages are 98 for women. As a consequence each male admissions represents 0.98 (0.99 x 0.99) lifetime doctors, and each female admission represents 0.96 (0.98 x 0.98) lifetime doctors. Seeking to be efficient and obey the mandate to maximize the number of practicing physicians, the dean establishes a "male only" admissions policy.

The dean of this medical school would be practicing statistical discrimination. He would be treating each group fairly based on its objective characteristics, but unfairly treating 96% of all women who would have gone on to become practicing doctors. The problem is that he has no technique for identifying which 4% of all women will fail to become practicing physicians, and he therefore expands a very small difference in objective characteristics into a zero-to-one decision rule that excludes all women. Is the dean acting fairly or unfairly, efficiently or inefficiently? To be efficient is to be unfair to individuals. But where is the balance to be struck?

Since most Americans have a desire to be efficient and to deliver individual justice, there is a dilemma. Individuals have to be judged on grouped data, yet all systems of grouping will result in unfair treatment to some individuals. Most of us would be unwilling to let the dean exclude women on a 1 percentage point difference in the relevant probabilities, but what if the difference were 50 percentage points or 90 percentage points. Whatever the allowed differential, it would result in the unfair treatment of some individuals.

What this problem illustrates is that every society has to have a theory of legitimate or illegitimate groups. When can individuals be judged by reference to the groups of which they are nominally a part? And when would it be illegitimate to do so?

At first thought, mobility (or the lack of mobility) would seem to be an easy way to determine what groups are legitimate. If it is easy for an individual to leave any group, then individuals in that group cannot claim to be unfairly treated. When individuals can freely choose whether or not to be affiliated with the group, then presumably the value of belonging must exceed the costs of so doing, or they would not belong. It is precisely this argument that leads to the standard economic conclusion that governments should not have programs to aid farmers, particular industries, or regions of the country. Farmers may have lower incomes than urban dwellers, but they could always cease to be farmers and become urban dwellers. Therefore farmers cannot be unfairly treated economically regardless of their relative income.

While this argument sounds reasonable to those of us that are not farmers, it is equally applicable to regions or religions. Technically, it is just as easy, if not easier, and less costly to shift religions as it is to shift regions. Yet most would not be willing to argue that someone should be required to change his or her religion to receive economic parity. Why?

Unfortunately, any negative group discrimination in the past also creates a need for positive group discrimination in the present. Consider a race run between two equally fast groups of individuals. One group, however, has been given a heavy load to carry. They suffer from discrimination. As the race progresses the group without the load gradually gains a lead over the group carrying the load. Now discrimination is abolished and the loads are removed from the backs of the group being discriminated against. The race continues. The group that has been discriminated against is no longer falling behind, but neither is it catching up. The two sets of runners are equally fast when neither carries a load. The group that has been discriminated against in the past can catch up only if one of three things is done: (1) The race can be stopped and started over, (2) the group that is ahead can be required to carry a heavy load, or (3) the group that is behind can be given special help in catching up. Given discrimination in the past, the creation of equal opportunity in the present does not create a fair race. Only positive discrimination in the present can create a fair race. But this is the affirmative action that many Americans find unfair.

Whatever the reason, it is clear that most countries are undergoing a process of balkanization. More and more groups are forming and asserting that they have been discriminated against in the past, and that government should intervene to bring their income up to parity with the majority or reference group. However it is done, each society is going to have to establish rules on when it will recognize the group's demand for parity and when it will resist that demand. If everyone is guaranteed employment and earnings protection, the economy will be frozen into an impossible situation. Economic change and growth will have become impossible since no one will be willing to suffer the risks and at least temporary income losses associated with economic change. Yet these risks and income losses are a necessary part of economic growth.

Developing a theory of legitimate groups is going to be important, not only to determine which of the many new groups demanding recognition should be recognized, but also to determine which of the many groups now being recognized--farmers, steel-workers --should no longer be recognized. Probably the most fundamental issue facing advanced industrial societies is the ability to decide when it should or should not intervene in the market to protect or raise some group incomes.

MAKING AND ENFORCING SOCIAL JUDGEMENTS

In most industrial countries marginality has been used to avoid having to decide what is ultimately fair or unfair. Instead of arguing about the nature of a just distribution of income, there is agreement on marginal programs to help this or that group or to make the distribution of income a little less unequal. This escape from having to face the issue--What is economic justice?--is probably drawing to a close. Industrial societies are now facing a period when they must decide what groups do and do not merit parity with the rest of the society, and what is or is not a fair distribution of household income.

Long before they reach complete equality, most societies will decide that they now have a distribution of income that is "equal enough" and will shift their attention to other social problems. Long before every group has parity, society will have to learn how to make decisions that some group does not deserve to reach parity.

In most countries the major redistributional effort has focused on the elderly. At least in the United States these programs have succeeded. Per capita elderly incomes have reached parity with those of the rest of the population. Economic deprivation is no longer automatically associated with old age. Income transfer payments are the only solution for those that are out of the labor force, but they are not the solution for the remaining groups that are in the labor force. If these groups are to be helped, the aid will have to take the form of the more contentious policies designed to intervene in the market distribution of earnings.

The most dramatic change that has ever occurred in the American market distribution of earnings occurred during World War II. As part of the war effort and the widespread belief that the resulting burdens should be more equally shared, government wage regulations were used to narrow wage differentials. After a five-year war effort these government-imposed wage differentials were so embedded in the structure of wages that they continued even after the regulations ordering them had been removed. Only recently have wages started to drift toward greater inequality.

The heart of this change was not the government regulations ordering wage differentials to be reduced but the widespread social opinion that wages should be narrowed as part of an egalitarian war effort. It is this social opinion and not the government regulations that allowed wage differentials to be reduced. Similarly, it will be the presence or absence of this opinion in the future that will allow government to intervene to narrow wage differentials. The technical problems of exactly what programs are to be used to narrow the differentials are relatively minor in comparison with the social decision that the differentials should be narrowed.

In the United States the relative earnings of blacks rose in the late 1960s and early 1970s when there was a consensus that black earnings should rise. When the consensus disappeared in the mid-1970s, black earnings quit rising. But government programs did not change. The same laws and institutions existed. They just quit working in a different social context.

America does not face the big trade-off between equity and efficiency. It may someday face that trade-off, but as can be seen by looking at either Japan or white males, the country has not yet reached that day. Inequality could be cut in half without going beyond the degree of equality that now exists in the economic game played by white males. Even then there would be alternative policies that could be used to offset the adverse work or savings incentives of "too much" equality.

Although it has no doubt done so in the past, the illusion of economic necessity can hardly stifle philosophical and political debates about the just distribution of income in the future. As this paper has shown, inequality is not necessary for economic growth. Even if the argument is believed to be true, it is politically acceptable only in the context of a distribution of resources that is not becoming more unequal. With rising inequality in the 1980s, the losers will demand a justification for their deteriorating position. What justification is to be given to them?

NOTES

1. U.S. Bureau of the Census, Current Population Reports, Consumer Income. #118, Series P-60. March 1979. p. 237.

2. United Nations, 1978 Statistical Yearbook. New York, 1979. pp. 698-702. Malcom Sawyer, "Income Distribution in OECD Countries," OECD Occasional Studies. July 1976. Paris. p. 14. OECD, "Development

and Trends in Social Security Expenditures and the Distribution of Social Benefits." Oct. 1979, pp. 3, 6.

3. U.S. Bureau of the Census, Current Population Reports, Consumer Income. #118, Series P-60. March 1979. pp. 237-240.

4. Daniel M. Holland, "The Effects of Taxation on Effort," Proceedings of the 62nd National Tax Association. Oct. 1969. p. 428.

5. See labor supply sectors in any of the major macroeconomic models of the country--DRI, Wharton, or Chase Econometrics.

6. Articles reviewing the results of the negative income tax experiments have appeared regularly in the Journal of Human Resources.

7. U.S. Bureau of the Census, Current Population Reports, Consumer Income. #118, Series P-60. March 1979. p. 194.

8. Ibid.

9. U.S. Bureau of the Census, Current Population Reports, Consumer Income. #118, Series P-60. March 1979. p. 238.

10. U.S. Bureau of the Census, Current Population Reports, Consumer Income. #117, Series P-60. Dec. 1978. p. 19.

11. Economic Report of the President. Washington, DC. Jan. 1980.

12. Lester C. Thurow, "The Indirect Incidence of Government Expenditures," American Economic Review. May 1980.

13. Ibid. Calculated from Census Bureau tapes and input-output tables of the U.S. Bureau of Labor.

14. Jacob Mincer, Schooling, Experience, and Earnings. New York: National Bureau of Economic Research, 1974. p. 112.

Part V

INCOMES POLICY
What is being done?
What can be done?
What should be done?

Page asks and tries to answer this question: why doesn't the government promote income equality?

Marmor takes the welfare state as it has existed in the United States and Canada as subject of a comparative inquiry; and asks how, given a plethora of criteria, we are to evaluate their experience and judge them to be successes or failures.

Witte considers taxation as an instrument normally intended to reconcile the criterion of efficiency in resource allocation with the commitment to distributive justice and equity. He surveys the evolution of tax theory and critiques that theory, indicating its irrelevance for realistic policy choices.

Solo in a note proposes that novel use of the progressive expenditure tax as a means of achieving a more equitable system of income distribution.

12. Why Doesn't the Government Promote Equality?

Benjamin I. Page

There is reason to expect that a democratic government, under popular control, would redistribute income to increase equality among its citizens. Yet in the United States little effective redistribution has taken place. Inequality remains very great. The puzzle I want to address is why this is so. Do our democratic forms conceal a fundamentally undemocratic reality?

I will first outline some normative arguments for equality and note the extreme inequality of private incomes in the United States. Next I will examine U.S. government actions in four spheres--taxation, social welfare policy, public goods spending, and regulation--reviewing evidence about the distributional impacts of policy and discussing the political reasons why programs take the shape they do. I will argue that in each sphere the net redistributive effects are limited or even negative, and that certain political factors, including interest group power and the structure of the economy, have prevented extensive redistribution.(1)

INEQUALITY AND THE STATE

Of course not everyone favors equality. Many Americans believe that their federal and state governments do engage in a vast redistribution of income, extracting billions of tax dollars from the rich and the middle class for handouts to the poor, and many dislike the idea. As this is written, in fact, egalitarianism seems to be altogether out of fashion. Newspapers and television are full of lamentations that we have been spending too much on inefficient welfare schemes and not enough on finding energy sources or arming against the Russians.

Upon reflection, however, most people will

acknowledge that extreme inequality of income is likely to interfere with fundamental values they cherish, whether they call themselves liberal, radical, or conservative. The conservative values of order, stability, and community, for example, are threatened by the resentment that inequality creates. In the twentieth century the deprived cannot be expected to accept their lot as God-given or to ignore the material abundance around them. While equality encourages a sense of fellowship and solidarity, inequality can breed crime and violence and, in the ultimate case, revolution.

Liberty too requires a degree of material equality. The very poor are not very free. Nor are one man's liberties safe when another lacks them. Similarly, the ideals of self-fulfillment and personal development are hard to achieve for those with empty stomachs.

The liberal notions of equal opportunity and fair reward, so dear to Americans, also turn out to depend for their moral force upon substantial equality of result. How can a child have a fair start in the competitive race if his parents collapsed after the previous heat? Inherited wealth, good nutrition, intellectual stimulation, and a thousand other advantages accrue to the fortunate children of winners. Fairness requires equality, at least at the start, but it is hard to define any single starting line. And society cannot easily equalize the chances of young runners unless it equalizes the condition of their parents--that is, unless it equalizes practically everyone.

Moreover, the idea of a just but unequal reward does not stand up well under close examination. Even in a perfect labor market with wages exactly equal to marginal products (a mythical labor market, as far as one can tell), a worker's income would depend on uncontrollable aspects of consumer demand and the supply of labor and other factors, quite apart from his own skills or efforts. For that matter, why try to reward the lucky people who are blessed with superior skills and motivation from superior genes or superior environments? Why not compensate the unlucky instead? The only persuasive reason for giving achievement-based rewards is to encourage work. But such pragmatic logic is a far cry from reliance on fairness; it can justify inequality only insofar as needed to accomplish the purpose, which becomes an empirical question. As we will see, there is considerable doubt that extreme inequality is necessary.

A difficult approach that also leads in an egalitarian direction begins with the utilitarian aim of maximizing the happiness (or satisfaction or utility) of mankind. As Pigou put it:

> . . . it is evident that any transference of income from a relatively rich man to a relatively poor man of similar temperament, since it enables more intense wants to be satisfied at the expense of less intense wants, must increase the aggregate sum of satisfactions.(2)

That is, suppose we share the classical utilitarian impulse that society ought to be arranged so as to maximize the total amount (the sum) of happiness of the individuals in it. Implicit in this goal is an acceptance of the possibility, in principle, of adding up and comparing the happiness of different individuals. (Many ordinalist economists flinch at this thought, but to deny such a possibility is to deny any hope of talking about justice or equality, a denial which amounts in practice to ratifying the status quo.) Suppose further that a given amount of total income would bring the same amount of happiness to each individual--or at least that we must proceed upon that assumption in the absence of evidence to the contrary. Finally, suppose (quite plausibly) that money has declining marginal utility for everyone. A dollar brings more happiness when one is penniless than when one already has millions, and the amount of happiness brought by an extra dollar declines steadily with increasing income.

Under these assumptions, if we treat people only as consumers and posit that there is a fixed amount of income to distribute, simple mathematics shows that happiness is maximized by a completely equal distribution of income.

To be sure, some steps in this argument are controversial, and such utilitarian thinkers as Bentham, J. S. Mill, Edgeworth, and even Pigou pulled back from endorsing complete equality. The chief problem is that since people are actually producers as well as consumers, the expectation of redistribution could reduce the amount of income available to be shared. If redistribution cut production sharply enough, it might reduce rather than increase total happiness.

This qualification must be put into perspective, however. First, as we noted in connection with fair rewards, it calls into question only the feasibility, not the ultimate desirability of redistribution. It leads us to inquire whether people can be persuaded to work hard for reasons other than unequal money, either under our own or a different economic system. Second, as an empirical matter the disincentive effects upon work and investment in our current economy are probably smaller than is commonly believed. There can be little doubt that the optimum distribution of income would require considerably more equality than is found in the contemporary United States.(3)

The private marketplace has produced very unequal incomes in this country. Since World War II the census has regularly found that the bottom fifth of all families and unrelated individuals receives only 3 to 4% of the total money income, while the top fifth gets 43 to 45%--ten times as much.(4) None of the great political or economic changes of the 1950s, 60s, or 70s reduced this inequality.

The census figures do not tell the whole story. Self-employed businessmen and doctors with relatively high incomes tend to underreport their earnings in such surveys; so do those with very low incomes who do housework or odd jobs. Capital gains are not fully taken into account. Expense accounts, fringe benefits, and the imputed rental value of their homes are omitted from the income of the rich. Moreover, money figures include government cash transfers like social security, and conceal the loss of income to indirect taxes (sales, property) in the form of higher prices and higher rents. We would like to know how unequal private incomes are, setting aside the effects of government, so we can later judge how government affects the distribution of income.

Pechman and Okner, with some unusually good data from 1966, attempted to calculate such an income distribution using a broad definition of income that included unrealized capital gains, imputed rents, indirect taxes, and (unfortunately for our purposes) transfer payments. They adjusted for nonreporting and underreporting. Their findings, much like those of the census, were that the bottom fifth of all families got less than 4% of the income in the country, while the top fifth got nearly half the income. In fact they found that the top 1% of families got 10% of the income. On the average each of them received nearly 60 times as much as a family in the bottom fifth.(5)

These figures may tend to understate pregovernment inequality since they include transfer payments. But on balance they probably somewhat overstate the extent of inequality by relying on annual statistics. When earnings are averaged over people's lifetimes, smoothing over good and bad times and youth and age, inequality is less sharp.(6) Similarly, if family income is measured relative to need (for example, number of dependents), inequality appears somewhat less stark.(7) In any case, however, it remains substantial.

Wealth, with all the power and status it brings, is even more unequally distributed than income. The top 1% of wealth-holders own one-quarter to one-third of all the wealth in the United States, while those on the bottom hold no wealth at all or are in debt. There has been virtually no change since World War II.(8)

The cold statistics of inequality alone do not convey the human meaning of poverty. Poor people eat badly, are sick often, and die young. They live in crowded run-down housing. Work, if they can find it, is dull and unpleasant. For those stuck in urban ghettos, crime and filth are inescapable. The affluent society, flaunting its luxuries, broadcasts contempt for those who are left out, and relative deprivation is painful even for those above a minimum standard of living.

Government action would appear to offer the main hope. Public finance economists posit a distributive function for the modern state, transferring income from rich to poor in order to redress the inequalities created by the private economy.(9) In a democracy one might well expect that the low-income majority would vote to have the state take money from the rich and give it to those in the bottom half. To be sure, such a prediction might be upset by the problem of cyclical majorities.(10) But presuming that some vote-determined equilibrium distribution exists, it is hard to see why it should be a highly unequal one.

What, then, does the U.S. government actually do in the way of redistributing income?

THE EFFECTS OF TAXATION

If redistribution is to occur, half the job can be done by taxes. Progressive income taxes, falling proportionately harder on high incomes than low, could presumably be used to take money from the rich to give it to the poor.

In the United States the federal income tax has long been seen in just this light. The scheduled rates have looked very progressive, in recent years ranging from just 14% on taxable income below $500 to 70% on income over $100,000.(11) Yet its redistributive effects have been limited. Actual tax payments, as a proportion of total income, have been much less progressive than the nominal rates. And the mild progressivity of the income tax has lost impact as other, more regressive taxes have begun to provide more and more of the revenue.

In 1976 income taxes as a proportion of total money income (IRS adjusted gross income plus excludable dividends, moving expenses, sick pay, and such tax preference items as excluded capital gains) started near zero and rose to about 10% for incomes around $14,000, and to 24% for incomes in the $50,000 to $75,000 range. They reached a high of only 33% for incomes between $200,000 and $500,000, and actually declined to 28% for incomes of $1 million and over.(12) That is, effective tax rates were progressive up to about $75,000, but then leveled off at a rate far below the schedule's 70%. Equality could hardly be achieved by taking away only one-quarter of incomes over $1 million.

As a percentage of more broadly defined adjusted family income, including imputed rent and unrealized capital gains and the like, income tax rates look even less progressive. Goode found that the top 1% of income earners paid only 18% of their income in taxes. Their share of all the after-tax income in the country, 8.3%, was not much smaller than their before-tax share of 9.2%.(13)

The reason for the big gap between nominal and effective tax rates is that much that comes in is not defined as income under the tax code, or is excluded, exempted, deducted, or taxed at special low rates. A large part of this favored income goes to the rich, especially capital gains, imputed rent, expense account meals and travel, and municipal bond dividends. Special treatment of capital gains alone was sufficient in 1976 to reduce the highest nominal tax rate of 69% to an effective rate of 50% on total income;(14) and it has subsequently been made even more lenient.

Tax breaks that are popular with the middle class, such as income splitting between husband and wife and deductions for charity and interest payments and property taxes, actually are more help to the rich. A one dollar deduction saves more taxes for a person in a high tax bracket than a low one. Pechman has estimated that deductions cut the nominal tax rates of those in the highest brackets by more than one-quarter.(15) In particular, tax shelters involving accelerated depreciation and interest deductions that create artificial losses to offset ordinary income (later recouped as lightly taxed capital gains) are widely used for cutting the taxes of the wealthy.

Although the income tax still provides some 40 to 45% of federal revenue, it is rapidly being overtaken by payroll taxes, which now produce about 30% of all receipts. Payroll taxes are strongly regressive at high income levels because they are levied at a flat rate up to a certain income ceiling and then stop. (Economists generally agree that the employer's share as well as the employee's is paid by workers, in the form of lower wages.) The tax constitutes a much larger proportion of total income for those with wages at or below the ceiling than for those above it. Moreover, nonwage income like dividends, interest, rent, and capital gains, which accrue mostly to the wealthy, are not subject to the tax at all.

Since the very poor earn little in taxable wages, payroll taxes as of 1977 were somewhat progressive for incomes up to $12,000; roughly proportional from $12,000 to $22,000, the range where the flat rate applied; and regressive thereafter. The peak was about 11% on comprehensively defined family incomes of $15,000, falling to 6% on $45,000, and approaching 0% on the highest incomes.(16) As payroll tax rates have risen, this regressive effect becomes more and more important. Because of wage inflation the rises in the dollar ceiling for income subject to the tax have not much reduced regressivity.

The corporation income tax provides a declining share of federal revenues, now around 12%. Which income classes actually bear how much of the burden of this tax is a matter of controversy, since some economists argue that it comes out of shareholders' profits or indirectly reduces returns on capital generally, while others claim it is shifted to consumers in the form of higher prices or to employees as lower wages. If the tax is shifted to consumers or workers, it is regressive; but if it falls entirely on the owners of capital, it is a very progressive tax. If it is partly shifted it may be nearly proportional to income.(17)

Since the corporate income tax raises only a small amount of revenue, however, these drastic differences in possible incidence have only a moderate impact on assessments of how all taxes together affect the distribution of income. The same is true of estate and gift taxes, which fall mainly on the rich but at low rates and in easily avoidable fashion. Federal excise taxes on alcohol, gasoline, tobacco, and the like hurt low-income citizens most, but they are too small to affect the overall picture.

The combined impact of all federal taxes, then, is progressive, with the regressive payroll tax diluting the progressivity of the individual income tax. Total rates range from about 14% up to 24% of adjusted family income. If we accept the optimistic assumption that corporate taxes fall entirely on the owners of capital, total federal taxes are more progressive, ranging from some 9% on the lowest incomes to more than 35% on the highest.(18) Even so, of course, a top rate of 35% on incomes over $1 million would not be sufficient to produce anything like equality of incomes.

State and local taxes, on the other hand, are probably so regressive that they largely or totally nullify federal progressivity. More than one-third of state and local revenue comes from sales taxes. Sales taxes are very regressive because consumption of the goods that are taxed at a flat rate takes up a much larger proportion of income of the poor than the rich. Browning has come up with an ingenious argument that sales taxes are actually progressive with respect to post-transfer income, because the poor get much of their income in untaxed in-kind benefits. But this conclusion rests on very dubious assumptions--for example, that in-kind benefits maintain a constant value regardless of price levels, and that the poor spend no higher a proportion of their incomes on taxed goods than the rich do.(19)

According to Pechman and Okner, sales and excise taxes are regressive throughout the income scale, taking 9% of the incomes of those at the bottom and only 1% of incomes over $1 million.(20) Sales taxes, like regressive payroll taxes, have been growing rapidly.

Property taxes, the other major source of state and local revenue, are subject to dispute about incidence. The traditional view has been that property taxes are shifted from apartment owners to renters in the form of higher rents, and from the owners of business property to consumers in higher prices. If so, property taxes are substantially regressive, ranging from 6 or 7% on very low incomes to less than 1% on incomes over $1 million.(21) (On the other hand Aaron claims that even under the traditional assumptions the tax is roughly proportional rather than progressive, if normal [weighted average] incomes instead of annual incomes are considered and varying value/rent ratios are taken into account.(22))

Recently, however, some economists have argued (assuming, perhaps implausibly, that the total quantity of capital including land is fixed) that a tax on real property is borne by the owners of property generally.(23) If so, the property tax is rather progressive, ranging from 2 to 3% on low incomes to 10% on incomes over $1 million.(24)

The matter is complicated by inequities in tax administration. The most valuable homes tend to be assessed, and therefore taxed, at a lower proportion of their value than are less expensive homes. And tax rates tend to be higher in central cities, where average incomes are low, than in affluent suburbs.(25)

Income taxes produce only about one-sixth of state and local revenue. In most states they are less progressive than the federal income tax because their nominal progressivity generally ends at a low point on the income scale and a moderate flat rate is imposed thereafter. Corporation income tax rates are low and the effects minor.

The total effect of state and local taxes depends on who pays the property tax. If it falls on property income, effective state and local tax rates follow a U curve, starting at about 10% on the lowest incomes, dropping to 6.5% in the middle, and rising again to a peak of about 14% on incomes of $1 million and over. But if the property tax is shifted to renters and consumers, total state and local taxes are sharply regressive throughout the income range. They decline from 14% on the lowest incomes to just over 4% on incomes of $1 million and more.(26)

Even at best, then, state and local taxes are regressive or proportional over the range of most Americans' incomes and do not reach a very high rate on the highest incomes. At worst, and there is reason to suspect the worst, they are quite regressive.

When all federal, state, and local taxes are taken together, the net effects again depend somewhat on incidence assumptions. Under Pechman and Okner's regressive ("3b") assumptions, the total effect of all taxes is almost exactly proportional, taking 24 to 26% of income at virtually all levels. Under their progressive ("1c") assumptions the rates rise at the top of the income scale, reaching a peak of nearly 50%. But for the vast majority of Americans the rates are very nearly proportional, varying only from 22 to 25%, and even the very top income earners need not fear confiscation(27) (see Table 1).

TABLE 1. TOTAL EFFECTIVE RATE OF ALL FEDERAL, STATE, AND LOCAL TAXES IN 1966

Adjusted Family Income (Thousands of Dollars)	Effective Rate (%)	
	Under Progressive (1c) Incidence Assumptions	Under Regressive (3b) Incidence Assumptions
0-3	18.7	28.1
3-5	20.4	25.3
5-10	22.6	25.9
10-15	22.8	25.5
15-20	23.2	25.3
20-25	24.0	25.1
25-30	25.1	24.3
30-50	26.4	24.4
50-100	31.5	26.4
100-500	41.8	30.3
500-1,000	48.0	30.3
1,000	49.3	29.0

Source: Pechman and Okner, Who Bears the Tax Burden?, p. 49.

In short, regardless of incidence assumptions taxes are mostly proportional to income. They do not accomplish much redistribution, reducing the Gini coefficient of income inequality by only 5% at best.(28)

Why is this so? A political explanation must consider the possibility that the will of the people is thwarted, that our democratic machinery is malfunctioning.

One might at the outset look to chairmen of the House Ways and Means and Senate Finance Committees, like Wilbur Mills and Russell Long, as powerful opponents of progressive taxation. Opponents they have been, but powerful, perhaps not. It turns out that over the years the chairmen have kept closely in tune with their committees; their voting records are no more conservative.(29)

It might then be argued that the committees themselves are influential and unrepresentative, swayed by lobbying and corporate campaign contributions.(30) In fact Senate Finance has tended to be more conservative than the Senate as a whole, loading tax bills with loopholes, but it has often been reversed on the floor. The more successful Ways and Means Committee has been virtually a microcosm of the House.(31)

More fundamentally, it is possible that congressmen as a whole, themselves having high incomes and being elected in low-visibility circumstances where money counts, are less enthusiastic about progressive taxation than is the public generally. Certainly party differences have been modest, as even Democratic congressmen and presidents fall far short of advocating strongly redistributive taxes.(32) It is also true that implementation of tax policy is given a pro-rich thrust by the ingenuity of high-priced tax lawyers for hire: As soon as one tax shelter is eliminated, a new one is invented, from cattle herds to airplane leasing to pornographic movies.

Lobbying, even since the rise of public interest groups, remains very heavily oriented toward the wealthy, especially commercial, industrial, and professional interests. Transaction costs and the free rider problem inhibit representation of diffuse taxpayer interests.(33) As Stanley Surrey has pointed out, special interests gain power from their expertise and control of information; often only the Treasury provides any counterbalance to their onslaught.(34) Occasionally, as with the notorious Ross Perot amendment, campaign contributions can be directly linked to passage of a regressive loophole that would likely be opposed by the public if it were known.(35)

The plausibility of an interest group explanation for tax regressivity is increased by the fact that technical complexity is great and information costs unusually high; lacking awareness of tax issues, the average citizen may be powerless to influence policy.(36) The "scope of conflict" is narrow and interest groups may be able to operate unhindered.(37)

This is particularly true in state politics, where, as we have seen, taxes turn out to be most regressive.(38)

Yet evidence of interest group influence is only anecdotal and circumstantial, not conclusive. Moreover, groups do not simply thwart the will of an unaware majority. Survey data indicate widespread public agreement with the nonprogressive structure of taxes and with various specific loopholes.(39) If interest groups do exert influence, therefore, they must manipulate public opinion along with policy, in the fashion described by Edelman or Miliband.(40)

In support of this possibility, it is true that a great deal of misinformation about taxes is fed to the public. The nominal rates on tax schedules themselves give a false impression of progressivity. Deductions for mortgage interest and charitable contributions sound good and don't reveal on the surface that they favor the rich. Alarming talk about "capital shortages" frightens the average man into approving easy treatment of capital gains. The property tax revolt gathered steam after the new economics convinced owners of capital that they bear the burden of the tax, but proposed reductions were not portrayed in those terms to renters.

On the other hand nonprogressive taxation may in fact be optimal, given our economic system. Structural constraints may determine both tax policy and public opinion. Perhaps in a capitalist system wide income variations are necessary as incentives for work and investment and production. Conservative economists and Marxian structuralists tend to agree on this point, while differing about whether a socialist system would be superior.(41) There is substantial evidence that U.S. tax policy since the time of Andrew Mellon has been strongly influenced by the belief that too much progressivity would cut production and hurt everyone.(42)

Clearly the use of material incentives does impose some limits on redistribution. Those who work only for the sake of cash will undoubtedly slow down if all the fruits of extra effort are taxed away. The real questions are (1) just how tight those limits are, and (2) whether alternative incentive systems could loosen them.

The second question is a hard one, requiring comparative research where comparable data are scarce or (in the case of hypothetical systems) nonexistent. To be conclusive, experiments with nonmaterial incentives would probably have to be undertaken on a national or international basis, and sustained for several generations. The attempts by China and Cuba to promote production along with equality show promise but have so far met with only partial success. Both countries have recently re-emphasized differential material rewards.(43)

The first question cannot be answered conclusively either, but it is somewhat easier to deal with. The evidence so far does not in fact indicate that people in Western countries work substantially less when they are taxed at high rates.(44) Work motivation even in capitalist systems may be largely noneconomic. Or, up to fairly high tax levels, the income effect of needing to work harder for the same standard of living may cancel out the substitution effect of choosing more leisure over less-rewarded work.

Similarly, there has been more noise than hard evidence to support the notion that production will dry up because of reduced savings and investment if taxes are too progressive. The role of investment itself in growth is not well understood; technological change may be more important, and excessive investment at times of slack demand may actually be harmful. So much capital is derived from retained earnings that the importance of private savings to investment is unclear. Nor is it obvious that progressive taxation reduces savings.(45) Almost certainly, lenient treatment of capital gains is an inefficient way to increase investment. More sharply targeted (but still regressive) measures like accelerated depreciation and investment tax credits are of disputed effect.(46)

The United States, then, does not presently appear to be anywhere near the structural limits of possible redistribution. There is leeway for more progressive taxes with little if any loss in production. For a full political explanation of nonprogressivity, we must probably return to the hypotheses of interest group influence and manipulation of opinion.

SOCIAL WELFARE POLICY

In a thoroughgoing income redistribution scheme, the government would return much of its tax revenue to low-income people. It is widely believed that the U.S. government does exactly that; and in fact about half the federal budget does go to social welfare programs involving income assistance, jobs, food, medical care, housing, and education. Yet the total amount is not great enough, nor the allocation sufficiently pro-poor, to accomplish a major redistribution of income.

By far the largest federal social welfare program is old age, survivors, and disability insurance, including Social Security and the Railroad Retirement and federal employee plans. These take up more than one-quarter of the entire federal budget. In one sense they represent an enormous transfer of income to the poor, with some 60% of the payments going to those whose annual incomes, subtracting government transfers, fall below the poverty line(47) (see Table 2).

But the actual redistributive impact of Social Security has been limited. Nearly half of the beneficiaries are not poor at all. Most of the others are poor only in the sense that they have retired after having worked and earned substantial lifetime incomes. If Social Security didn't exist, they would have saved more or kept working longer.(48) Social Security, and (even more so) federal employee plans, have acted mostly as compulsory insurance or forced savings schemes, imposing a regressive tax on workers and returning the proceeds at retirement. They protect against disability and smooth out each worker's lifetime income--worthy purposes--but they do not equalize lifetime incomes with one another. (The bonus of benefits exceeding average contributions in the early years of the program went to high-income people as well as low and did not much reduce inequality in lifetime incomes.(49))

Federal unemployment insurance is another large program with less redistributive impact than one might expect. It mainly covers temporary jobless episodes for those usually working at good wages, not the long-term joblessness of people at the bottom of the economic heap. (Expected unemployment, for example, in construction work, is presumably compensated for by higher wages. The UI program may actually increase unemployment by subsidizing layoffs in cyclical industries.(50)) Only about one-fifth of unemployment insurance payments go to the pretransfer poor.

Cash transfer programs that do go to the very poor, like Aid to Families with Dependent Children and Supplemental Security Income for the aged, blind, and disabled, are relatively small (Table 2). Together they amount to only about 3% of the federal budget. Not nearly as much money reaches welfare mothers as the casual newspaper reader might think. Much more has been spent on programs like veterans benefits, which are not particularly pro-poor and amount to deferred military compensation; or agricultural price supports, which go overwhelmingly to the wealthiest farmers.(51)

States and localities devote a high proportion of their income assistance budgets to the poor through public aid and contributions to AFDC and the like, but the amount spent does not quite match the modest federal total.

In-kind benefit programs, which have grown rapidly in recent years, suffer from the same defects of not focusing on low-income people or else being rather small. In addition they are often not worth to the recipients what is spent on them, and they enrich the high-income providers of goods and services.

TABLE 2. MAJOR INCOME TRANSFER PROGRAMS AND BENEFITS TO TH
PRETRANSFER POOR IN 1965 AND 1974
(IN MILLIONS OF DOLLARS)

	1965 Expenditures	1974 Expenditures	Percentag Spent on Pretransf Poor in 19
Federal Programs			
A. Social Security	$16,488	$53,564	58.8%
B. Railroad retirement	1,118	2,671	58.8
C. Railroad disability	44	28	58.8
D. Public employee retirement	3,216	10,776	40.5
E. Unemployment Insurance	2,506	5,316	20.8
F. Workers Compensation	73	1,237	45.2
1. Regular	73	271	--
2. Black lung	--	966	45.2
G. Public assistance	2,614	6,925	85.9
1. AFDC	956	4,009	91.8
2. OAA, AB, APTD, and Emergency Assistance	1,658	1,047	77.8
3. SSI	--	1,869	77.8
H. Veterans' income support	4,108	6,763	43.0
1. Compensation and pensions	4,042	6,616	--
2. Other	57	103	--
I. Food Stamps	36	2,718	83.0
J. Housing assistance	227	1,968	65.0
1. Public housing	219	1,233	73.0
2. Rent supplements	--	137	77.0
3. Home ownership and rental housing assistance, sec. 236	--	523	46.0
4. Other	2	59	89.0
K. Health	1,990	15,120	58.0
1. Medicare	--	9,557	59.0
2. Medicaid	271	5,563	73.0

State and Local Programs			
A. Public employee retirement	$1,861	$5,682	40.5%
B. Temporary disability insurance	253	481	27.0
C. Workers Compensation	1,690	4,152	45.2
D. Public assistance	2,148	5,658	86.1
1. AFDC	768	3,362	91.8
2. OAA, AB, APTD, and General Assistance	1,379	1,652	77.8
3. SSI	--	643	77.8
E. Veterans' bonuses and compensation	20	156	43.0
F. Housing assistance	80	545	73.0
G. Medicaid, vendor medical payments	252	4,174	73.0

Source: Sheldon Danziger and Robert Plotnick. Has the War on Income Poverty Been Won? (in preparation); Sheldon Danziger, Robert Haveman and Robert Plotnick, "Income Transfer Programs in the United States: An Analysis of Their Structure and Impacts," p. 20.

The food stamp program, the most pro-poor in-kind program and the one whose benefits are most nearly equivalent to cash, remains small in size at around 1% of the federal budget. The use of coupon funny money instead of cash causes some inefficiency and leads to stigma at the grocery store counter. Still, food stamps are as close as we come to having a general, noncategorical income support program. They at least provide minimal nourishment and give a small push in the direction of equalizing incomes.(52)

Medical care programs, by contrast, are quite large (about 10% of the budget) but very inefficient and of limited redistributional effect. Medicare covers virtually all old Americans, not just those of low income. Like Social Security, it is a compulsory insurance program funded by regressive taxes, and it does not do much to redistribute lifetime incomes. Moreover, a large part of the money has gone to hospitals and doctors in the form of higher fees rather than toward buying more or better medical care.

Medicaid, on the other hand, is aimed at the poor and has accomplished a substantial redistribution of medical services.(53) Still, much of what is spent doesn't reach the intended recipients because of administrative overhead, fraud (mainly by providers), and inflated fees. What does reach patients is worth less to them than its cost--perhaps only 68 cents on a dollar.(54) Hospitals and doctors have been the big winners.

Housing programs, too, have not been aimed primarily at the poor and have been less efficient than cash would be in redistributing income. Public housing has produced some of the worst slums in America, and a dollar spent on public housing is worth only some 56 cents to the average tenant.(55) The construction industry has prospered. Rent supplements approach the virtues of cash transfers but remain a very small budget item. Home mortgage assistance has gone mainly to the middle class; efforts after 1968 to help low-income home buyers resulted in massive defaults and abandonments and windfall profits to realtors and lenders.(56) The largest single housing program has been tax deductions for mortgage interest and property taxes, worth billions of dollars to the upper middle-class owners of expensive homes.(57)

The most promising field for in-kind programs is job training and employment. Jobs are much superior to cash transfers in that they can encourage productivity and self-fulfillment along with income equality. But efforts to date have been halfhearted and the results have been disappointing. Early Job Corps and retraining programs proved to be very expensive and were ineffective in raising earnings.(58) Work requirements in welfare programs failed since many of the poor couldn't work and jobs didn't exist for others. Elaborate tax incentive schemes for hiring the unemployed merely displaced other workers and subsidized employers.

By the mid-1970s it was clear that neither training nor requirements nor incentives made sense if jobs weren't available at decent wages. The Comprehensive Employment and Training Act (CETA) sensibly turned to direct funding of public service jobs, but it left administration to the states and localities. Not all the federal money actually creates useful new jobs; much of it merely pays for things the states would do anyway, while some is frittered away on make-work. And total federal outlays for employment remain small, around 2% of the budget. The government has done little to insure everyone productive work at good pay. This may be the greatest failure of the U.S. welfare state.

Education is especially important to the liberal vision of equal opportunity. State and local governments spend more on schools than anything else, and redistribute a lot of income in the process; universal public education has been a major achievement of the last century. Still, universal access to schools does not necessarily mean equal education. In most states more resources go into wealthy neighborhoods than poor, accentuating the advantages of having high-income parents and peers.(59) Schooling has not done much to overcome the great lead that children of the wealthy have in the race to get ahead.(60) School may in fact reinforce inequality by training working-class children to be obedient workers and by teaching everyone to accept as fair the unequal rewards dispensed by the capitalist economy.(61)

Since 1965 the federal government has spent substantial sums trying to help educate the disadvantaged at all levels of schooling, although not always with success.(62) Higher education expenditures by states are much less egalitarian, since children of upper-income families more often go to college.(63) (If property taxes are linked to the expenditures and presumed to be progressive, however, higher education spending looks less pro-rich; and complex lifetime effects also dilute the pro-rich thrust.(64))

Taken together the billions of dollars spent on social welfare programs have a definite impact. They have provided at least minimal food, medical care, and schooling, and have lifted nearly all Americans above the meager officially defined poverty level. But this does not mean they have done much to reduce income inequality.

Claims by Browning(65) and others that there has been a massive redistribution of income rest upon fanciful assumptions: that in-kind benefits are worth to the recipients every penny it costs to provide them; that education expenditures go equally to children of the poor and the rich; that the leisure of the unemployed represents income equal to their potential earnings; that regressive sales taxes and the employer share of payroll taxes can be ignored.(66) Similar though less blatant errors have probably also led other economists(67) to overstate the extent of social welfare redistribution.

When programs are examined in more detail, as in Table 2, it is clear that even on an annual income basis the largest--like Social Security and Medicare--go mainly to the middle class. Redistribution is limited. According to Plotnick and Skidmore's estimate, social welfare expenditures in 1972 cut the proportion of officially poor in the population from a pregovernment 20% to a postgovernment 12% or even (taking account of in-kind transfers and underreporting of income) 6%. Yet relative poverty or inequality (measured by the proportion of families with "welfare ratios" below half the median) decreased not one bit between 1965 and 1972, before and after the Great Society.(68)

Similarly, Danziger and others found that in 1976 only 6.5% of the population remained officially poor after government transfers. But in relative terms, about 15% of all Americans were poor, virtually the same proportion in 1976 as in 1965 (see Table 3). Inequality was as great after the War on Poverty as before. The post-transfer Gini coefficient of inequality, which takes on values of 0.0 for complete equality and 1.0 for total concentration of income, actually rose from 0.392 in 1965 to 0.408 in 1976.(69)

Political parties play an important part in the making of social welfare policies. Since the New Deal era, Democratic presidents and legislators have consistently pushed for more spending of an egalitarian sort than Republicans have.(70) On welfare matters the parties, competing for votes, do not take identical stands at the midpoint of public opinion. Instead there are systematic differences between the platforms, the candidates' stands, and the proposed bills and roll call votes of the two parties.(71)

TABLE 3. INCOME TRANSFERS AND THE PROPORTION OF POOR PEOPLE IN THE U.S. POPULATION FROM 1965 THROUGH 1976

	Income Concept		
Type of Poverty Measure, Year	Pretransfer Income	Post-transfer Income	Adjusted Post-transfer Income
Absolute Measure			
1965	21.3%	15.6%	12.1%
1968	18.2	12.8	10.1
1970	18.8	12.6	9.4
1972	19.2	11.9	6.2
1974	20.3	11.6	7.8
1976	21.0	11.8	6.5
Relative Measure			
1965	21.3%	15.6%	
1968	19.7	14.6	
1970	20.8	15.1	
1972	22.2	14.9	
1974	22.9	14.9	
1976	24.1	15.4	

Source: Danziger, Haveman, and Plotnick, "Income Transfer Programs," p. 31.

These differences, stemming from differing socioeconomic constituencies and the need to appeal to activists and money givers as well as to ordinary voters, lead to zigzags in policy as the parties alternate in power. They also increase the visibility of social welfare policy and help mobilize low-income citizens to better awareness of their interests. Still, the Democratic party does not have the kind of egalitarian commitment we associate with the socialist parties of Europe. For historical reasons the United States lacks any real leftist party for workers and the poor. Even the moderate party differences that exist may be decreasing in a gradual process of party dealignment or disintegration.(72)

With active parties and fairly high public visibility, the scope of conflict is relatively broad and interest groups play a less dominant part. Yet they do matter. The AMA lost the Medicare battle but won the war, getting high fees for doctors' services. For years, farm interests, working through friendly congressional Agriculture committees, blocked food stamps for the poor and kept the more profitable commodity distribution program. Mortgage lenders lobbied hard for the boondoggle of home purchase guarantees and subsidies. The construction industry has obtained large bricks-and-mortar expenditures for schools and hospitals. Above all, organized labor has focused on programs like social insurance and the minimum wage which benefit their workers more than the poor. Organized groups of service providers may be responsible for the patchwork of in-kind rather than cash assistance programs.(73)

The public, attentive to bread-and-butter matters of jobs, food, housing, and medical care, has gradually insisted on government amelioration of the rough edges of capitalism. By the same token, however, Americans believe in meritocracy and Lockean liberalism. They have resisted any massive redistribution of income.(74) Again, we must ask whether public opinion has been manipulated by the rich and well organized, or whether it reflects the reality of economic structure.

No doubt at some point large cash transfers would undermine the work incentives of low-income people and cut production. The poor do, however, express strong desires to work rather than accept welfare.(75) Econometric studies of labor supply indicate only moderate disincentive effects for experimental income guarantees and even for current programs with their perverse notches and high implicit tax rates.(76) Lampman has estimated that the whole panoply of programs since 1930 has cut the labor supply by only about 7% from what it would have been without them.(77) The Seattle-Denver income maintenance experiments indicate that it would be possible to offer a guaranteed income equal to the full official poverty level--taking away 70 cents of benefits for each dollar earned above that--and to lose less than 1 to 2% of total U.S. production.(78)

While we do not yet know the precise terms of what Okun called the "big trade-off" between equality and efficiency,(79) it does seem clear that much more redistribution could be achieved in the United States without great loss of productivity, even if cash transfers were used. High-paying public service jobs could do still better, producing valuable goods and services while they redistributed income, and ending our cruel trick of imbuing people with the Protestant ethic but then providing no jobs for them to fill. The American voter may have been fooled into his fear of equality.

SPENDING ON PUBLIC GOODS

About half the federal budget goes to provide things that more or less fit the definition of public goods.(80) Their distributional effects, while difficult to calculate,(81) probably favor high- and middle-income citizens more than low. In addition, their very magnitude reduces the funds available for redistributive programs.

The military takes up an enormous amount of money, about one-quarter of the budget. Economists sometimes talk as if defense benefited every citizen equally, but depending on the enemy of the moment, some citizens obviously have far more at stake than others. Defense against the Soviet Union is much more valuable to the owners of factories and banks and oil companies, whose property could be expropriated or destroyed, than to low-income people who have less to lose and conceivably something to gain from imposition of a socialist system.

Moreover, U.S. military forces are oriented less toward strategic defense of the homeland (which could probably be accomplished with a small number of nearly invulnerable submarines armed with nuclear missiles), than toward enforcement of American influence throughout the world and resistance to Communist or leftist regimes everywhere.(82) This has undoubtedly reinforced the inequality of worldwide incomes. For Americans the protection of U.S. raw materials and markets and investments certainly benefits consumers, but more than that it helps the high-income owners of transnational corporations.

The military draft is an in-kind tax that probably falls most heavily on those of low income. The poor and blacks have been no more likely than others to serve in the armed forces (and have less income to be deprived of during service), but they have more often been conscripted into infantry combat positions and more often killed or wounded, especially in Vietnam.(83) High pay and perquisites and retirement benefits for officers also contribute to inequality. A peacetime volunteer army, on the other hand, amounts to a huge public service job program that clearly helps the poor. (Current opposition to the volunteer army may reflect unease about this as well as reluctance to pay the full cost of attracting and training skilled manpower.) Wars themselves, hardly the ideal path to equality, have in our economy tended to promote full employment and raise workers' share of the national income.(84)

The procurement of military material benefits the rich, producing fewer jobs but higher salaries than civilian spending does and going mostly to wealthier regions of the country.(85) The design and production of sophisticated weapons systems in particular raise returns to capital and increase the incomes of well-paid scientists and engineers. With cost-plus contracts the profits of defense contractors often run high.(86) Finally, since total public spending is widely regarded as fixed, money devoted to the military tends to come out of social welfare programs like education and health.(87)

Foreign aid is too small to reduce noticeably worldwide income inequality, if that were its aim. But it is subordinate to foreign policy and has gone largely to support friendly despots, thus upholding inequality. It too probably most benefits the high-income Americans who own property abroad.

Science and technology spending goes mostly to the space program, much of it with military implications. Space exploration, for all its grandeur, is a luxury good of more interest to the comfortable than to the undernourished. High-income engineers and the owners of capital-intensive electronics and aerospace firms gain from government demand for their products.

Law and order is mainly the responsibility of state and local governments. Police manpower, according to at least one study, is assigned on roughly an equal basis (proportional to need) to poor neighborhoods and others.(88) To the extent that enforcement efforts go where crimes of violence and petty theft are, the predominately low-income victims benefit most. But the criminal justice system as a whole is heavily oriented toward combating major crimes against property (bank robbery, grand theft) that chiefly threaten high-income people. Protection of private property is, in a sense, protection of inequality. Further, political uses of law enforcement machinery to repress the Left have discouraged and destroyed some egalitarian movements.(89)

Energy-related spending by the federal government

has risen markedly since the oil embargo and price rises of 1973-1974. Most energy subsidies have probably increased the returns to nuclear, coal, and oil companies and thereby enriched high-income individuals. In the long run, however, they may benefit people in proportion to their use of energy, which is more nearly equal than the overall income distribution.

Federal spending on the environment and natural resources has gone largely to build municipal sewage treatment plants. While everyone presumably gains more or less equally from consequent reductions in disease, the aesthetic and recreational benefits are generally of more interest to high-income people.(90) The substantial sums spent on dams and water projects, often inefficient,(91) have helped contractors and skilled labor in the construction process and have provided cheap irrigation for agribusinesses. U.S. public lands have been run largely to the profit of lumber and ranching interests,(92) and national parks please suburban campers more than the urban poor. Local parks, on the other hand, may often favor those of low income.(93)

Transportation money comes mostly from state and local governments and goes mainly for local roads, which probably tend to be maintained better in upper-income areas than in low.(94) Mass transit, which can have pro-poor effects--though not if suburban commuter rail lines are emphasized(95)--has received some local, but very little federal subsidy. Instead the federal government has devoted billions of dollars to the interstate highway system. Highways benefit upper-income car owners, who take long trips more than others, and they help the cement, construction, automobile, and oil and gas industries and ultimately the consumers who pay lower prices for transported goods. Net benefits may well be nearly proportional to income.

The traditional rationale for agricultural subsidies has been to encourage the virtues of family farming, but most of the money has gone to rich farmers and has probably accelerated the demise of noncompetitive small farms.(96)

Federal revenue sharing and community development grants to state and local governments have complex distributional consequences determined mainly by those governments. In some cases the use of poverty criteria in allocation formulas insures that much of the money goes to poor communities, but in other cases high-income, low-growth counties have been favored.(97) Even money delivered to high-poverty areas, of course, does not necessarily reach low-income people.

Spending for government operations, interest expenses, and the like presumably affects the income distribution in the same way as the totality of government programs it supports, with perhaps some extra subsidy to upper middle-class officials' incomes.

Several economists have attempted to estimate the net distributional impact of all federal, state, and local taxes and spending, including public goods, by calculating the pregovernment income distribution and then adding to each income group its share of the benefits from each spending program and subtracting its share of each tax, to arrive at a postgovernment distribution.

The results depend on what assumptions are made about the allocation of various tax and spending programs, some of which are quite controversial. Under the more plausible assumptions, such as those used to calculate lines 3 or 4 of Table 4, government appears to have a moderately equalizing effect. The pro-poor effects of social welfare spending and federal taxes outweigh the regressiveness of state and local taxes, and public goods spending is seen as neutral. Reynolds and Smolensky estimate that in 1970 the Gini index of inequality for postgovernment incomes was 0.384 or 0.375, somewhat lower than the pregovernment inequality of 0.446 (see Table 4).(98)

TABLE 4. ESTIMATES OF INCOME INEQUALITIY BEFORE AND AFTER GOVERNMENT TAXES AND SPENDING

Distribution	Gini Coefficient of Inequality		
	1950	1961	1970
Pregovernment			
1. Private factor income	0.436	0.436	0.446
Postgovernment			
2. Income after taxes and spending (standard incidence assumptions)	0.363	0.342	0.339
3. (Standard assumptions except general expenditures by income)	0.384	0.378	0.375
4. (Regressive assumptions)	0.394	0.388	0.384
5. (Progressive assumptions)	0.328	0.289	0.284

Source: Reynolds and Smolensky, Public Expenditures, p. 67.

I would argue that even this modest estimate of equalizing effects is overstated. As Reynolds and Smolensky themselves point out, the contrast between pre- and post-government distributions can be a very misleading indicator of government impact, because the pre- figures already include many effects of government on private earnings. Government displacement of private savings by Social Security and of private wages by unemployment insurance and AFDC and food stamps, as well as government subsidy of the incomes of defense contractors and highway builders and the like, probably make private incomes look more unequal than they would actually have been without government action. Thus in the pre-post comparison government appears more egalitarian than it actually is. (Of course the counterfactual of incomes in the absence of government is itself scarcely conceivable in a modern society.)

When we focus on the more reliable post- figures alone, not attempting to disentangle governmental from private influences on incomes, it is clear that the level of inequality after all government action is taken into account remains high, with a Gini coefficient of 0.384 or 0.375. And even these figures probably understate the degree of inequality. They assume that public goods benefits are proportional to income, whereas many of them (such as those from military spending) actually go to the very high-income owners of property. They also neglect the difference between the values of in-kind benefits (such as medical care) and their costs, thus overstating the income of the poor. On the other hand, by using annual data they treat as low income earners many people (for example, the aged) with substantial lifetime incomes.

Most striking is that under all but the least plausible (line 5) of Reynolds and Smolensky's alternative assumptions, there was no appreciable decline in inequality from 1950 through 1970. Americans' incomes were no closer to equal after the New Frontier and the Great Society than before.

Turning back to the more narrow topic of public goods, special features of their politics help explain why they don't much benefit the poor. Public goods generally involve lower visibility, fewer conflicts along party lines, and more unchallenged influence by interest groups than is the case with social welfare policy.

The New Deal party alignments have simply not differed much about public goods.(99) Post-World War II foreign policy is the classic case of bipartisanship, with only occasional disagreements over tactics as at the end of the Vietnam War. Nor have the parties divided much over space or highways or the environment, although certain aspects of energy policy have recently become partisan.

Partly because of their nonparty character, public goods issues usually have low public visibility. Information costs are high and popular control limited. The scope of conflict is narrow.(100)

By the same token, interest groups can often prevail unopposed. Public goods like post offices, dams, and military bases and contracts come in geographically divisible distributive packages, which can be doled out pork-barrel fashion to congressional districts.(101) Local contractors and other interests get concentrated benefits, for which they reward congressmen, while the general public is unaware of the diffuse costs.

Similarly, the space and highway programs respond to monolithic lobbying by contractors and manufacturers. Energy policy has long been dominated by the biggest oil companies, and land and water policy by lumber and livestock companies and agribusinesses. The well-organized among farmers know how to get subsidies.(102) Underfunded programs like basic research, mass transit, and foreign aid have lacked such powerful advocates.

The familiar lobbying techniques of campaign contributions, close personal relations with legislators, help with speeches and bills and research, media campaigns, and stimulation of grass-roots contacts are apparently effective in these cases (conclusive evidence is hard to come by) because the public is relatively inert. Information costs weaken public control. Transaction costs and free rider problems limit the extent to which consumers and low-income citizens are organized. Interest group politics has a pro-rich bias.(103)

Structural factors may influence policy as well. The great magnitude of public goods programs, which displace pro-poor programs in the budget, may be largely determined by the fact that a market economy requires patching up by the government to function acceptably. The particularly pro-rich form that many of these programs take may result in part from the need for work and investment incentives in a capitalist economy. And substantial military spending may be dictated by the fact of international anarchy, which compels self-interested nations to engage in arms races.(104) Just how far structural explanations can take us is not clear, but our review of specific programs suggests that there exists much inefficiency and overspending for the wealthy which is best accounted for in interest group terms.

LAW AND REGULATION

Countless government regulations and laws and even the Constitution affect the pregovernment distribution of income in the United States. The effects are complex. On balance they appear to increase or reinforce inequality.

Research on the effects of regulation has shown that it is frequently inefficient and favorable to the regulated, forcing consumers to pay higher prices than a free market would bear. State and local licensing of occupations is a conspicuous example. AMA-dominated licensing of physicians and accreditation of medical schools keeps the supply of doctors low and their fees high. Bar examinations and law school accreditation do much the same thing for lawyers. Barbers, optometrists, taxicab drivers, plumbers, and a host of other occupations benefit from similar barriers to entry.(105)

State and local regulation of prices and quality has tended to enforce monopoly pricing of gas and electricity, telephone service, taxi fares, and intrastate trucking. Building codes require expensive materials and wasteful techniques. Restrictions on advertising for doctors, lawyers, drugs, and eyeglasses dampen competition and raise prices.(106)

Several federal regulatory commissions, created amidst cries for consumer protection, have turned out to benefit the regulated. The Interstate Commerce Commission (ICC) set rates and rules favorable to railroads and, later, to trucks. The FCC restricted the number of usable radio and television frequencies and parceled out valuable station rights without charge. The CAB failed to license any new trunk airline carriers for many years and set fares at high levels. The FDIC limited the number of new banks. The AEC approved commercial development of nuclear energy at the expense of safety and the environment.(107)

Tariffs and quotas, restricting imports of Italian shoes and Japanese stainless steel and Argentinian beef and many other goods, have increased the prices obtained by domestic industries and paid by consumers. Agricultural price supports, together with acreage limitations, inflate the prices received by agri-business. Milk marketing orders keep dairy prices high.

On the other hand OSHA in recent years has promulgated safety rules favorable to workers rather than industry. The EPA has imposed fairly strict standards against air and water pollution. HEW has laid down sweeping antidiscrimination rules for minorities and women. The NRC has gotten tougher with the nuclear industry. Even the FTC roused itself from lethargy and cracked down on noncompetitive industries and deceptive advertising.(108) It is too early to tell whether all this represents a permanent new antibusiness thrust or a passing phase.

Recent years have also seen a movement toward deregulation, the effects of which are difficult to assess. Loosening restrictions by the old agencies (for example, on air fares and trucking rates) may help consumers.(109) Much of the deregulatory zeal, however, has been aimed against proconsumer or proworker regulations by OSHA and EPA.

The overall picture has been one of much regulation favoring producers and some benefiting workers or consumers.(110) The income distributional effects are complicated. Regulation that favors producers undoubtedly tends to increase profits and thereby increases the already high incomes of owners of capital while lowering real incomes of ordinary consumers. But some of the increased revenue is competed away, for example, by airlines offering food and entertainment and frequent underused flights.(111) This reduces the gains to capital while increasing deadweight losses to society. Some regulation, such as equal employment opportunity rules for minorities, clearly benefits people of low income. At the same time much environmental and consumerist regulation hurts the poor by increasing the prices of goods, including necessities, and by reducing employment.(112)

Regulatory politics practically demand an interest group interpretation. Visibility to the public is extremely low, reducing the possibility of public control. The average citizen is easily fooled by symbols of regulatory rigor when industry clients are actually being protected.(113) The scope of conflict is particularly narrow; organized interests are often able to capture the regulatory process or win powers of self-regulation. This is especially true at the state and local levels, where politics operates obscurely among small constituencies.(114)

The general tendency for regulation to be pro-industry, then, is easily accounted for; but what of recent environmentalist and consumerist victories? There is no real contradiction, because interest group politics has simply continued with a modified lineup of players as public interest groups have entered the fray.(115) These groups are still underorganized compared to business, and their current liveliness may be only part of a cycle in which the public spotlight will fade and industry recapture control.(116) In any event it cannot be assumed that public interest groups represent people of low income. Quite the contrary, they have a heavily upper middle-class orientation. The high-income bias of group activity continues in a different form.

The deregulation movement attests to, among other things, the power of economic theory when it is skillfully disseminated. It also attests to the economic and political power of businesses upset about OSHA and EPA.

Macroeconomic policy, involving government efforts

to affect employment and inflation and economic growth and stability, is pursued chiefly through fiscal and monetary instruments. Among advanced industrial nations, the United States has had unusually high rates of unemployment and low rates of inflation.(117) A tight money supply, high interest rates, limited public employment, restricted government spending and debt, and a host of lesser policies like the minimum wage (which eliminates low-paying jobs) all conspire to hold inflation down and keep unemployment high. At the same time easy tax treatment of capital gains, depreciation, and investment encourages growth and profits at the expense of current consumption.

Unemployment is the scourge of low-income people, many of whom face the prospect of periodic or long-term joblessness. The so-called new unemployment especially affects women, the young, and marginal workers. This does not mean they don't need the income; most of the unemployed are chief wage earners for their families, and suffer serious harm. Unemployment is much less a problem at high-income levels.(118)

Inflation, on the other hand, may disproportionately penalize owners of capital, or (more likely) may have little net income-distributional effect. The days of erosion of the fixed incomes of the aged poor ended when Social Security was indexed. Relative price rises for food, gasoline, and heating, which do hurt those of low income, cannot be attributed to inflation in the true sense and are not helped by stringent macroeconomic policies.(119) U.S. macroeconomic policy, when it prefers unemployment to inflation, is distinctly antipoor.

The political parties differ somewhat about macroeconomics, with Democratic administrations less friendly to unemployment than are Republicans,(120) but these differences are modest. American labor is not militant. There is no potent leftist workers party, perhaps for reasons reaching back to the nonfeudal open-frontier origins of the country, our early Lockean liberal ideology, and ethnic divisions within the working class.

Since capitalist countries vary greatly in their unemployment rates, the economic structure of capitalism does not offer a promising explanation for high U.S. joblessness. The political power of business groups is the likely cause. Through the need to encourage growth for everyone's future consumption, however, economic structure may in part account for policies that give a high rate of return to capital relative to labor. The logic of the capitalist system compels workers to allow the capitalists profits if they and their children want to eat more in the future.(121)

Among the most profound government influences on the distribution of income is the legal system. The Constitution itself enshrines private ownership of property, forbidding government takings without compensation and thus imposing a barrier against any major redistribution of wealth. The Constitution also upholds the sanctity of contracts against state infringement and forbids relief to debtors through state issuance of cheap paper money. The federal government was designed as a bulwark of sound money, firm contracts, and free trade. State laws protecting property against theft and fraud, enforcing contracts, and (later) permitting general incorporation and recognizing corporations as persons at law, completed the legal infrastructure of capitalism.(122)

The distributional consequences of this legal structure depend on an assessment of whether capitalism is inherently less egalitarian than alternative forms of social and economic organization. This is no easy assessment to make, given the paucity of alternative systems in existence. The case of China, for all of its mixed lessons, suggests that greater equality may be possible in socialist systems and that nonmaterial incentives have some promise.

Charles Beard's acccount of the Constitution as a product of the self-interested rich has proved too simple. Still, the document was drafted by lawyers and merchants and large landowners, not by mechanics or yeoman farmers, and it was ratified by a minority of Americans.(123) The Constitutional and other legal underpinnings of capitalism undoubtedly reflected growing bourgeois power and organization, as well as the demands of an emerging economic structure. Their later maintenance and enhancement have been largely dictated by the structure of the economy, which has been perceived as working reasonably well and which could be damaged (to everyone's grief) by careless tinkering. The wholesale abandonment of capitalism, even if beneficial in the long run, would likely require a painful descent through the valley of transition to socialism, in which today's workers would have to sacrifice for their children's children.(124) It is not hard to understand why America's proletariat has not revolted.

CONCLUSION

I have emphasized two types of explanation for the failure of government to do much about income inequality. One, the interest group analysis (alleging biased pluralism or imperfect political competition), sees organized groups with an upper-income bias as exerting political power over and above the formal one-man-vote standard of democracy. The other, the structuralist view, points to inherent features of a capitalist economy which compel rational actors, even those of low income, to accept inequality for the sake of a bigger pie for everyone. Both types of explanation can accommodate the fact of public acquiescence, one explaining it in terms of ignorance and deception and the other in terms of correct calculations of self-interest.

For each type of explanation there is substantial evidence. It is not possible to judge with complete confidence how true each is; that remains an important task for political and economic research. But it does seem safe to conclude that both have some validity. The capitalist system, or any economic system based on material incentives, no doubt imposes bounds on redistribution unless society as a whole is willing to sacrifice consumption for the sake of equality. On the other hand the bounds are surely not so tight as to prevent any reduction in inequality from its present high level. Interest group power has probably kept the government from pushing close to its structural limits.

Quite different policy implications follow from the two types of explanation. To the extent that structural constraints are important, serious egalitarian ought to consider working toward an alternative economic and social system. A humanistic socialism, built on motives of cooperation and self-development rather than greed, might achieve a high degree of equality along with productivity and growth. The design of such a system and of methods of transition to it deserve careful thought. The economic shocks that have recently shaken American complacency may offer us an unusually good chance to explore alternative futures.

To the extent that interest groups rather than structural factors maintain inequality, it makes sense to consider mild political reforms of the sort congenial to American liberals. One approach would be to increase the public visibility of the distributive aspects of policy, raising a hue and cry about each regressive tax or pro-rich subsidy. Egalitarians could try to educate the citizenry about who pays for and who benefits from government programs, as well as how much redistribution is structurally possible, so people will demand the equality that would be in their interest. And efforts could be made to arouse and organize those of low income to attain a degree of political effectiveness matching their numbers. Another line of reform would be to reduce the political power of money as much as possible by severely limiting campaign contributions, prosecuting bribery, preventing conflicts of interest, eliminating tax deductions for lobbying, and the like.

The central point is that egalitarian results require political changes. Policy proposals can be helpful as banners to rally around, but a carefully crafted income redistribution plan is of little use if it dies in Congress. Only changes in the political equation can avert continued repetitions of that fate.

We should have no illusions about the ease of making even modest changes. The problem of information and transaction costs that inhibit public participation will not simply vanish. Money and organization can do much to maintain their power, working through Congress, the executive branch, and the courts. The ability to translate wealth into political power may itself be a structural fact in a capitalist democracy, since (for example) money affects what sort of information is and isn't transmitted to the public. After years of work by Surrey and Pechman and others to educate the populace about tax expenditures and loopholes, the tide was suddenly reversed in the late 1970s by a media blitz about a bogus capital shortage. For every pro-equality article in the scholarly journal or *Working Papers*, there seem to be 10 against equality in the *Public Interest* and the *Wall Street Journal* and in the publications of private-enterprise-funded institutions. There is money opposing equality.

NOTES

1. For a more detailed discussion, see Benjamin I. Page, *Who Gets What From Government*, forthcoming.

I am grateful to a number of political science and economics colleagues at the University of Wisconsin and the University of Chicago for criticisms and suggestions; to Scott Milliman, Candice Hoke, and Michael Galati for research assistance; and to HEW (through the Institute for Research on Poverty, University of Wisconsin, Madison) and the Social Science Divisional Research Committee of the University of Chicago for support. The views expressed are entirely my own.

2. Arthur C. Pigou, *The Economics of Welfare*, 4th ed. (London: Macmillan, 1938), p. 89.

3. Benjamin I. Page, "Utilitarian Arguments for Equality," Discussion Paper #547-579, Institute for Research on Poverty, University of Wisconsin, Madison, August 1979.

4. United States, Bureau of the Census, *Current Population Reports: Consumer Income*, Series P-60, n. 114 and 116, July 1978; Edward C. Budd, "Postwar Changes in the Size Distribution of Income in the U.S.," *American Economic Review* 60 (1970): 247-260.

5. Joseph A. Pechman and Benjamin A. Okner, Who Bears the Tax Burden? (Washington, DC: Brookings, 1974), p. 46.

6. Morton Paglin, "The Measurement and Trend of Equality: A Basic Revision," American Economic Review 65 (September 1975): 598-609; Lee Lillard, "Inequality: Earnings vs. Human Wealth," American Economic Review 67 (March 1977): 42-53; but see Sheldon Danziger, Robert Havemen, and Eugene Smolensky, "The Measurement and Trend of Equality: Comment," American Economic Review 67 (June 1967): 505-512; and Martin David and Paul Menchik, "Aspects of the Lifetime Distribution of Income and Wealth," paper presented at the meeting of the Eastern Economic Association, May 11, 1979.

7. Sheldon Danziger and Michael K. Taussig, "The Income Unit and the Anatomy of Income Distribution," Review of Income and Wealth, forthcoming, 1980.

8. Dorothy S. Projector and Gertrude S. Weiss, Survey of Financial Characteristics of Consumers (Washington, DC: Federal Reserve System, 1966); Robert J. Lampman, The Share of Top Wealth-Holders in National Weath (Princeton: National Bureau of Economic Research, 1962); James D. Smith and Stephen D. Franklin, "The Concentration of Personal Wealth, 1922-1969," American Economic Review 64 (May 1974): 162-167.

9. Richard A. Musgrave and Peggy B. Musgrave, Public Finance in Theory and Practice, 2nd ed. (New York: McGraw-Hill, 1976).

10. Kenneth J. Arrow, Social Choice and Individual Values, 2nd ed. (New York: Wiley, 1963); Koichi Hamada, "A Simple Majority Rule on the Distribution of Income," Journal of Economic Theory 6 (1973): 243-264. Joe Oppenheimer, "The Democratic Politics of Distributive Justice: Theory and Practice," paper delivered at the annual meeting of the American Political Science Association, Septemeber, 1979; sees redistributional politics as heavily influenced by lack of a majority rule equilibrium.

11. Joseph A. Pechman, Federal Tax Policy, 3rd ed. (Washington, DC: Brookings, 1977), pp. 298, 301.

12. Pechman, Federal Tax Policy, pp. 349-350.

13. Richard B. Goode, The Individual Income Tax, rev. ed. (Washington, DC: Brookings, 1976), pp. 248-251.

14. Pechman, Federal Tax Policy, p. 350.

15. Pechman, pp. 83-92, 350.

16. Pechman, pp. 201-209.

17. The three contending positions are taken by Marian Krzyzaniak and Richard Musgrave, The Shifting of the Corporation Income Tax (Baltimore: Johns Hopkins University Press, 1963); Arnold C. Harberger, "The Incidence of the Corporation Income Tax," Journal of Political Economy 70 (June 1962): 215-240, together

with John G. Cragg, Arnold C. Harberger, and Peter Mieszkowski, "Empirical Evidence on the Incidence of the Corporation Income Tax," Journal of Political Economy 75 (December 1967): 811-821; and Pechman, Federal Tax Policy, pp. 129-136, respectively.

18. Pechman and Okner, Who Bears The Tax Burden? pp. 38, 62.

19. Edgar K. Browning, "The Burden of Taxation," Journal of Political Economy 86 (August 1978): 649-671; see Timothy M. Smeeding, "Are Sales Taxes Progressive?" unpublished, Institute for Research on Poverty, University of Wisconsin, Madison, 1979.

20. Pechman and Okner, Who Bears the Tax Burden? p. 59.

21. Dick Netzer, Economics of the Property Tax (Washington, DC: Brookings, 1966); Pechman and Okner, p. 59, variant 3b; Henry J. Aaron, Who Pays the Property Tax? (Washington, DC: Brookings, 1975), pp. 20-27.

22. Aaron, pp. 25-38.

23. Peter Mieszkowski, "The Property Tax: An Excise Tax or a Profits Tax?," Journal of Public Economics 1 (1972): 73-96; Aaron, Who Pays the Property Tax?

24. Pechman and Okner, p. 59, variant 1c.

25. Aaron, pp. 56-70.

26. Pechman and Okner, p. 62.

27. Pechman and Okner, p. 49.

28. Pechman and Okner, p. 56.

29. John F. Manley, The Politics of Finance (Boston: Little Brown, 1970); Benjamin I. Page, "Federal Tax Policy and Inequality," paper delivered at the annual meeting of the Midwest Political Science Association, Chicago, Illinois, April 21-23, 1977.

30. Philip M. Stern, The Rape of the Taxpayer (New York: Random House, 1973); Robert M. Brandon, Jonathan Rowe, and Thomas H. Stanton, Tax Politics (New York: Random House, 1976); Ralph Nader Congress Project, The Revenue Committees (New York: Grossman, 1975).

31. Manley, The Politics of Finance; Page, "Federal Tax Policy."

32. But see Susan B. Hansen, "Partisan Realignment and Tax Policy 1789-1970," in Realignment in American Politics ed. Bruce A. Campbell and Richard J. Trilling (Austin: University of Texas Press, 1980).

33. Mancur Olson, Jr., The Logic of Collective Action (Cambridge: Harvard University Press, 1965); Russell Hardin, Collective Action, forthcoming, 1981.

34. Stanley S. Surrey, "The Congress and the Tax Lobbyist: How Special Tax Provisions Get Enacted," Harvard Law Review 70 (1957): 1145-1181.

35. Wall Street Journal, November 7, 1975, p. 1.

36. Anthony Downs, An Economic Theory of Democracy (New York: Harper & Row, 1957).

37. E. E. Schattschneider, The Semisovereign People (New York: Holt, 1960).

38. Grant McConnell, Private Power and American Democracy (New York: Knopf, 1966), Chap. 6.

39. Benjamin I. Page, "Taxes and Inequality: Do the Voters Get What They Want?" Discussion Paper #432-77, Institute for Research on Poverty, University of Wisconsin, Madison, August 1977.

40. Murray Edelman, The Symbolic Uses of Politics (Urbana: University of Illinois Press, 1964); Ralph Miliband, The State in Capitalist Society (New York: Basic Books, 1969), Chaps. 7-8.

41. Milton Friedman, Capitalism and Freedom (Chicago: University of Chicago Press, 1962); Adam Przeworski, "Material Bases of Consent: Economics and Politics in a Hegemonic System," Political Power and Social Theory 1 (1979), and Adam Przeworski and Michael Wallerstein, "The Structure of Class Conflict in Advanced Capitalist Societies," paper delivered at the annual meeting of the American Political Science Association, Washington, DC, August 1980.

42. Andrew Mellon, Taxation: The People's Business (New York: Macmillan, 1924); Ronald Frederick King, "From Redistributive to Hegemonic Logic: The Transformation of American Tax Politics, 1893-1954," paper delivered at the annual meeting of the American Political Science Association, New York, August 31-September 3, 1978.

43. Ding Chen, "The Economic Development of China," Scientific American 243 (September 1980): 152-165. Contrast the egalitarianism of Barry Reckord, Does Fidel Eat More than Your Father? (New York: New American Library, 1972), with the salary reforms announced in Granma 16 #73 (March 25, 1980), pp. 1, 4-5. Cuba, of course, faces the special problems of small size, few resources, and a hostile capitalist neighbor.

44. Thomas H. Sanders, Effects of Taxation on Executives (Boston: Harvard University Graduate School of Business Administration, 1951); George F. Break, "Income Taxes and Incentives to Work: An Empirical Study," American Economic Review 47 (September, 1957): 529-549; Robin Barlow, Harvey E. Brazer, and James N. Morgan, Economic Behavior of the Affluent (Washington, DC: Brookings, 1966).

45. Dale W. Jorgenson, "Econometric Studies of Investment Behavior: A Survey," Journal of Economic Literature 9 (December 1971): 1111-1147.

46. Gary Fromm, ed., Tax Incentives and Capital Spending (Washington, DC: Brookings, 1971), presents markedly conflicting findings by different

econometricians. See also E. Cary Brown, "Tax Incentives for Investment," American Economic Review 52 (May 1962): 335-345.

47. This and subsequent references to proportions of various programs going to the pretransfer poor are drawn from Sheldon Danziger, Robert Haveman, and Robert Plotnick, "Income Transfer Programs in the United States: An Analysis of Their Structure and Impacts," prepared for the Joint Economic Committee of the United States, Special Study on Economic Change, University of Wisconsin, Madison, May 1979; and from Robert D. Plotnick and Felicity Skidmore, Progress Against Poverty (New York: Academic Press, 1976). Federal spending figures are taken from United States, Office of Management and Budget, The Budget of the United States Government, Fiscal Year 1981 (Washington, DC: U.S. Government Printing Office, 1980), and recalculated by the present author as proportions of total outlays.

48. Martin Feldstein, "Social Security, Induced Retirement, and Aggregate Capital Formation," Journal of Political Economy 82 (October 1974): 905-926; Alicia Munnell, The Future of Social Security (Washington, DC: Brookings, 1977); but see Robert J. Barro, The Impact of Social Security on Private Saving (Washington, DC: American Enterprise Institute, 1978).

49. Richard V. Burkhauser and Jennifer L. Warlick, "Disentangling the Annuity from the Reidstributive Aspects of Social Security," unpublished, Institute for Research on Poverty, University of Wisconsin, Madison, December 1978.

50. Martin Feldstein, "Temporary Layoffs in the Theory of Unemployment," Journal of Political Economy 84 (October 1976): 937-957, and "The Effect of Unemployment Insurance on Temporary Layoff Unemployment," American Economic Review 68 (December 1978): 834-846.

51. Charles L. Schultze, The Distribution of Farm Subsidies (Washington, DC: Brookings, 1971).

52. Maurice MacDonald, Food, Stamps, and Income Maintenance (New York: Academic Press, 1977); Timothy M. Smeeding, "The Anti-poverty Effectiveness of In-kind Transfers," Journal of Human Resources 12 (Summer 1977): 360-378.

53. Karen Davis and Cathy Schoen, Health and the War on Poverty (Washington, DC: Brookings, 1978).

54. Smeeding, "Antipoverty Effectiveness."

55. Lee Rainwater, Behind Ghetto Walls (Chicago: Aldine, 1970); Smeeding, "Antipoverty Effectiveness."

56. Brian D. Boyer, Cities Destroyed for Cash (Chicago: Follett, 1973).

57. Henry J. Aaron, Shelter and Subsidies (Washington, DC: Brookings, 1972).

58. United States, Congressional Budget Office, Public Employment and Training Assistance (Washington, DC: U.S. Government Printing Office, 1977).

59. John D. Owen, School Inequality and the Welfare State (Baltimore: Johns Hopkins University Press, 1974); Murray Milner, Jr., The Illusion of Equality (San Francisco: Jossey Bass, 1972).

60. Christopher Jencks and others, Who Gets Ahead? (New York: Basic Books, 1979).

61. Samuel Bowles and Herbert Gintis, Schooling in Capitalist America (New York: Basic Books, 1976); Miliband, The State in Capitalist Society, Chaps. 7-8.

62. Victor G. Cicirelli and others, The Impact of Head Start (Westinghouse Learning Corporation, 1962); Burt S. Barnow and Glen G. Cain, "A Reanalysis of the Effect of Head Start on Cognitive Development: Methodology and Empirical Findings," Journal of Human Resources 12 (1977): 177-197; Henry M. Levin, "A Decade of Policy Developments in Improving Education and Training for Low-Income Populations," in A Decade of Federal Antipoverty Programs, ed. Robert H. Haveman (New York: Academic Press, 1977), pp. 123-188.

63. W. Lee Hansen and Burton A. Weisbrod, "The Distribution of Costs and Direct Benefits of Public Higher Education: The Case of California," Journal of Human Resources 4 (1969): 176-191.

64. Joseph A. Pechman, "The Distribution Effects of Public Higher Education in California," Journal of Human Resources 5 (Summer 1970): 361-370; John Conlisk, "A Further Look at the Hansen-Weisbrod-Pechman Debate," Journal of Human Resources 12 (1977): 147-163.

65. Edgar K. Browning, "How Much More Equality Can We Afford?" Public Interest 43 (Spring 1976): 90-110; and "The Trend Toward Equality in the Distribution of Net Income," Southern Economic Journal 43 (July 1976): 912-923.

66. See Timothy M. Smeeding, "On The Distribution of Net Income: Comment," Southern Economic Journal (January 1979): 932-944.

67. For example, W. Irwin Gillespie, "Effect of Public Expenditures on the Distribution of Income," in Essays in Fiscal Federalism, ed. Richard A. Musgrave (Washington, DC: Brookings, 1965), pp. 122-186; Richard A. Musgrave, Karl E. Case, and Herman Leonard, "The Distribution of Fiscal Burdens and Benefits," Public Finance Quarterly 2 (July 1974): 259-311; and Morgan Reynolds and Eugene Smolensky, Public Expenditures, Taxes, and the Distribution of Income (New York: Academic Press, 1977).

68. Plotnick and Skidmore, Progress Against Poverty, pp. 42, 82, 85, 112.

69. Danziger, Haveman, and Plotnick, "Income Transfer Programs"; Sheldon Danziger and Robert Plotnick, Has The War on Poverty Been Won? forthcoming.

70. James L. Sundquist, *Politics and Policy: The Eisenhower, Kennedy and Johnson Years* (Washington, DC: Brookings, 1968).

71. Benjamin I. Page, *Choices and Echoes in Presidential Elections* (Chicago: University of Chicago Press, 1978), Chap. 4.

72. Walter Dean Burnham, *Critical Elections and the Mainsprings of American Politics* (New York: Norton, 1970).

73. Schattschneider, *The Semisovereign People*; Theodore R. Marmor, *The Politics of Medicare* (Chicago: Aldine, 1973); Nick Kotz, *Let Them Eat Promises* (Garden City, NY: Doubleday, 1971); Sundquist, *Politics and Policy*; Daniel P. Moynihan, *The Politics of a Guaranteed Income* (New York: Random House, 1973).

74. Louis Hartz, *The Liberal Tradition in America* (New York: Harcourt Brace, 1955); Robert E. Lane, "The Fear of Equality," in *Political Ideology* (New York: Free Press, 1962), Chap. 4; American Institute of Public Opinion, *The Gallup Poll,* 3 vols. (New York: Random House, 1972).

75. Leonard Goodwin, *Do the Poor Want to Work?* (Washington, DC: Brookings, 1972).

76. Harold Watts and Albert Rees, *The New Jersey Income-Maintenance Experiment: Volume II, Labor Supply Responses* (New York: Academic Press, 1977); Stanley Masters and Irwin Garfinkel, *Estimating the Labor-Supply Effects of Income Maintenance Alternatives* (New York: Academic Press, 1977).

77. Robert J. Lampman, *Labor Supply and Social Welfare Benefits in the United States,* Special Report #22, Institute for Research on Poverty, University of Wisconsin, Madison, October 1978.

78. Michael C. Keeley, Philip K. Robins, Robert G. Spiegelman, and Richard W. West, "The Estimation of Labor Supply Models Using Experimental Data," *American Economic Review* 68 (December 1978): 873-887.

79. Arthur M. Okun, *Equality and Efficiency: The Big Tradeoff* (Washington, DC: Brookings, 1975).

80. Paul A. Samuelson, "The Pure Theory of Public Expenditure," *Review of Economics and Statistics* 36 (1954): 387-389; and "Diagrammatic Exposition of a Theory of Public Expenditure," *Review of Economics and Statistics* 37 (1955): 350-356; Musgrave and Musgrave, *Public Finance.*

81. Henry J. Aaron and Martin McGuire, "Public Goods and Income Distribution," *Econometrica* 38 (November 1970): 907-920; Geoffrey Brennan, "The Distributional Implications of Public Goods," *Econometrica* 44 (March 1976): 391-399.

82. See Charles A. Sorrels and others, "Defense Policy," in *Setting National Priorities: The 1979 Budget,* ed. Joseph A. Pechman (Washington, DC: Brookings, 1978), pp. 233-273; Kevin N. Lewis, "The

Prompt and Delayed Effects of Nuclear War," *Scientific American* 241 (July 1979): 35-47; Arthur Macy Cox, "The CIA's Tragic Error," *New York Review of Books,* Nov. 6, 1980, pp. 21-24.

83. Neil D. Fligstein, "Who Served in the Military, 1940-73," *Armed Forces and Society* 6 (Winter 1980): 297-312; R. Berney and D. Leigh, "The Socioeconomic Distribution of American Casualties in the Indochina War: Implications for Tax Equity," *Public Finance Quarterly* 2 (April 1974): 223-235; Maurice Zeitlin, Kenneth Lutterman, and James Russell, "Death in Vietnam: Class, Poverty, and the Risks of War," in *The Politics and Society Reader,* ed. Ira Katznelson and others (New York: McKay, 1974), pp. 53-68.

84. Jeffrey G. Williamson, "The Sources of American Inequality, 1896-1948," *Review of Economics and Statistics* 58 (November 1976): 387-397.

85. Wassily Leontieff and Marvin Hoffenberg, "The Economic Effect of Disarmament," *Scientific American* (April 1961); Leontieff and others, "The Economic Effect--Industrial and Regional--of an Arms Cut," *Review of Econòmics and Statistics* 47 (August 1965): 217-241.

86. Murray Weidenbaum, "Arms and the American Economy," *American Economic Review* 58 (May 1968): 428-445; Richard F. Kaufman, *The War Profiteers* (Indianapolis: Bobbs-Merrill, 1970).

87. Bruce M. Russett, *What Price Vigilance?* (New Haven: Yale University Press, 1970), Chap. 5.

88. Robert L. Lineberry, *Equality and Urban Policy: The Distribution of Municipal Public Services* (Beverly Hills: Sage, 1977).

89. Athan Theoharis, *Spying on Americans* (Philadelphia: Temple University Press, 1978); David Wise, *The American Police State* (New York: Random House, 1977); Alan Wolfe, *The Seamy Side of Democracy* (New York: David McKay and Co., 1973).

90. Robert Dorfman, "Incidence of the Benefits and Costs of Environmental Programs," *American Economic Review* 67 (February 1977): 333-340.

91. John A. Ferejohn, *Pork Barrel Politics* (Stanford: Stanford University Press, 1974).

92. McConnell, *Private Power,* Chap. 7.

93. Lineberry, *Equality and Urban Policy.*

94. Frank Levy, Arnold J. Meltsner, and Aaron Wildavsky, *Urban Outcomes: Schools, Streets, and Libraries* (Berkeley: University of California Press, 1974).

95. Mark Frankena, "Income Distributional Effects of Urban Transit Subsidies," *Journal of Transport Economics and Policy* 7 (September 1973): 215-230.

96. Schultze, *The Distribution of Farm Subsidies.*

97. United States, Congress, House Committee on Banking, Finance, and Urban Affairs, Subcommittee on the City, 95th Congress, Second Session, City Need and the Responsiveness of Federal Grants Programs (Washington, DC: U.S. Government Printing Office, August, 1978); U.S. Congressional Budget Office, Troubled Local Economies and the Distribution of Federal Dollars (Washington, DC: U.S. Government Printing Office, 1977).

98. Reynolds and Smolensky, Public Expenditures, p. 67. See also Musgrave et al., "The Distribution of Fiscal Burdens and Benefits," and Gillespie, "The Effect of Public Expenditures."

99. Page, Choices and Echoes, Chap. 3.

100. Downs, An Economic Theory of Democracy; Schattschneider, The Semisovereign People.

101. Theodore J. Lowi, "American Business, Public Policy, Case Studies and Political Theory," World Politics 16 (July 1964); David R. Mayhew, Congress: The Electoral Connection (New Haven: Yale University Press, 1974); Morris P. Fiorina, Congress: Keystone of the Washington Establishment (New Haven: Yale University Press, 1977); Lewis Anthony Dexter, "Congressmen and the Making of Military Policy," in New Perspectives on the House of Representatives, ed. Robert L. Peabody and Nelson W. Polsby (Chicago: Rand McNally, 1963), pp. 305-324; Ferejohn, Pork Barrel Politics; Barry S. Rundquist, Political Benefits (Lexington, MA: Lexington, 1979); R. Douglas Arnold, Congress and the Bureaucracy (New Haven: Yale University Press, 1979).

102. David Hapgood, "The Highwaymen," in Inside the System, ed. Charles Peters and John Rothschild (New York: Praeger, 1973), pp. 214-229; Robert Engler, The Politics of Oil (Chicago: University of Chicago Press, 1961); Bruce I. Oppenheimer, Oil and the Congressional Process (Lexington, MA: Lexington, 1974); McConnell, Private Power, Chap. 7; Theodore J. Lowi, "How Farmers Get What They Want," The Reporter (September 14, 1964): 34-37.

103. Downs, An Economic Theory of Democracy; Olson, The Logic of Collective Action; Hardin, Collective Action; Schattschneider, The Semisovereign People, Chap. 2.

104. Lewis F. Richardson, Arms and Insecurity (Pittsburgh: Boxwood Press, 1960).

105. Reuben Kessel, "The A.M.A. and the Supply of Physicians," Law and Contemporary Problems 35 (Spring 1970): 267-283; Thomas G. Moore, "The Purpose of Licensing," Journal of Law and Economics 4 (October 1961): 93-117; George J. Stigler, "The Theory of Economic Regulation," Bell Journal of Economics 2 (Spring 1971): 3-21.

106. E.g., George J. Stigler and Claire

Friedland, "What Can Regulators Regulate? The Case of Electricity," Journal of Law and Economics 5 (October 1962): 1-16; Lee Benham, "The Effect of Advertising on the Price of Eyeglasses," Journal of Law and Economics 15 (October 1972): 337-352.

107. Paul W. MacAvoy, The Economic Effects of Regulation (Cambridge: Massachusetts Institute of Technology Press, 1965); Richard Caves, Air Transport and Its Regulators (Cambridge: Harvard University Press, 1962); Sam Pelzman, "Entry in Commercial Banking," Journal of Law and Economics 8 (October 1965): 11-50; Irvin C. Bupp and Jean-Claude Derian, Light Water (New York: Basic Books, 1978).

108. Nina W. Cornell, Roger G. Noll, and Barry Weingast, "Safety Regulation," in Setting National Priorities: The Next Ten Years, ed. Joseph A. Pechman (Washington, DC: Brookings, 1976), pp. 457-504; W. David Montgomery and James P. Quirk, "Cost Escalation in Nuclear Power," in Perspectives on Energy, 2nd ed. (New York: Oxford University Press, forthcoming).

109. Michael E. Levine, "Revisionism Revised? Airline Deregulation and the Public Interest," Law and Contemporary Problems, forthcoming.

110. Paul L. Joskow and Roger G. Noll, "Regulation in Theory and Practice: An Overview," Social Science Working Paper #213, California Institute of Technology, May, 1978; Roger G. Noll, Reforming Regulation (Washington, DC: Brookings, 1971); Richard A. Posner, "Theories of Economic Regulation," Bell Journal of Economics 5 (1974): 335-358.

111. George Douglas and James Miller III, Economic Regulation of Domestic Air Transport (Washington, DC: Brookings, 1974).

112. E.g., Myrick Freeman III, "The Incidence of the Costs of Controlling Automotive Air Pollution," in The Distribution of Economic Well-Being, ed. P. Thomas Juster (Cambridge, MA: Ballinger, 1977), pp. 163-199.

113. Edelman, Symbolic Uses of Politics, Chap. 3.

114. Louis L. Jaffe, "The Effective Limits of the Administrative Process," Harvard Law Review 67 (May 1954); Marver H. Bernstein, Regulating Business by Independent Commission (Princeton: Princeton University Press, 1955); McConnell, Private Power.

115. Andrew S. MacFarland, Public Interest Lobbies: Decision Making on Energy (Washington, DC: American Enterprise Institute, 1976) and Common Cause, forthcoming; Norman J. Ornstein and Shirley Elder, Interest Groups, Lobbying and Policymaking (Washington, DC: Congressional Quarterly, 1978).

116. Hardin, Collective Action; Bernstein, Regulating Business.

117. Douglas A. Hibbs, Jr., "Economic Interest and the Politics of Macroeconomic Policy," Center for

International Studies, M.I.T. Cambridge, MA, 1975; abridged version in American Political Science Review 71 (December 1977).

118. John L. Palmer and Michael C. Barth, "The Distributional Effects of Inflation and Higher Unemployment," in Improving Economic Measures of Well-Being, ed. Marilyn Moon and Eugene Smolensky (New York: Academic Press, 1977), pp. 201-239; Kay Lehman Schlozman and Sidney Verba, "The New Unemployment: Does It Hurt?" Public Policy 26 (Summer 1978): 333-358.

119. Harold T. Shapiro, "Inflation in the United States," in Worldwide Inflation, ed. Lawrence B. Krause and Walter S. Salant (Washington, DC: Brookings, 1977), pp. 267-294; Helmut Frisch, "Inflation Theory, 1963-1975: A 'Second Generation' Survey," Journal of Economic Literature 15 (December 1977): 1289-1317; Christopher Jencks, "Why Worry About Inflation?", Working Papers (September-October 1978): 8-11, 75-78; G. L. Bach and James B. Stephenson, "Inflation and the Redistribution of Wealth," Review of Economics and Statistics 56 (February 1974): 1-13.

120. Hibbs, "Economic Interest."

121. Przeworski, "Material Bases of Consent"; Przeworski and Wallerstein, "The Structure of Class Conflict."

122. See Morton J. Horwitz, The Transformation of American Law, 1780-1860 (Cambridge: Harvard University Press, 1977).

123. Charles A. Beard, An Economic Interpretation of the Constitution (New York: Macmillan, 1913); Robert E. Brown, Charles Beard and the American Constitution (Princeton: Princeton University Press, 1956); Forrest McDonald, We the People: The Economic Origins of the Constitution (Chicago: University of Chicago Press, 1958).

124. See Przeworski and Wallerstein.

13. The North American Welfare State: Social Science and Evaluation

Theodore R. Marmor

This essay is about the North American welfare state in the period since the great depression. Its aim is to clarify the issues involved in appraising Canadian and American programs; its method is to set out the course of development and the quite different standards by which social welfare programs are justified and evaluated. The effort proceeds from the premise that policy analysts can contribute to both tasks, and it takes for granted that clarifying the sources of appraisal is as crucial and difficult as description and explanation. There are some who treat this subject as if it were trivially easy to appraise once the facts are in, but hard to get the facts. Such a view supports the demand for more policy analysis, but confuses the task of evaluation. Showing how that is so is the underlying theme of this work.

The essay proceeds in three parts. The first sets out a number of different views about what social welfare programs are meant to achieve. These views--roughly grouped into the residualist, the social democratic, and the Marxist--provide sharply differing standards of appraisal both for the origins of the welfare state and its condition in the 1980s.

The second part applies these evaluative perspectives to North American developments since the 1930s. It summarizes what the history of the major programs has been, concentrating on the three largest areas of expenditure: pensions, family benefits, and public financing of health insurance.

Part three reconsiders the issue of appraisal. It offers alternative evaluations in the light of competing perspectives on the welfare state. It seeks to narrow the factual disputes over what effects the North American welfare state has had. And it tentatively discusses the problem of political feasibility, suggesting the way the tension between political understanding of how programs arise and change, and the evaluation of those programs, accompanies almost all policy analysis. All together, the three parts constitute a critical judgement on the technocratic conception of how policy analysis and the welfare state should join.

COMPETING PERSPECTIVES

Policy analysts--and the political actors they address--bring sharply different notions of purpose to the programs that comprise the contemporary welfare state. Whether the concept of the welfare state is itself normatively adequate will not be addressed; for the moment we use the term to describe a group of programs in health, education, and social security that have received very substantial and growing public subsidy since roughly the mid-1930s. The term itself entered our policy vocabulary at about the time of the World War II(1) and the programs' major period of growth came long after the label became part of the popular lexicon. From the time of their establishment, there have been underlying differences in what such public programs were meant to achieve.

One perspective on the programs' objectives--called here residualist--characterizes the welfare state as a safety net. The net of social welfare was intended to rescue the victims of capitalism, provide a cushion against certain contingencies (unemployment, sickness, large numbers of children, widowhood), and give subsistence level relief to those unable to provide for their own needs.(2) This view of purpose, originating as it does in the European poor laws, is ubiquitous in modern capitalist nations. Though the popularity of such views differs among those nations, the criteria for judging the efficacy of the welfare state is everywhere affected by these themes. In North America, and in Australia as well, this residualist conception is the staple not only of business and financial elites, but of large proportions of middle- and lower-income populations as well.

Most of those who describe the welfare role as residual believe that management of the welfare system should be highly decentralized. In federal regimes diffusion of authority for social welfare to states and provinces has been the rallying slogan of the residualists. In the United States public assistance programs such as the federal-state program of Aid to Dependent Children (later Aid to Families with Dependent Children, AFDC), which was part of the original Social Security Act of 1935, exemplify this ideal. In Canada similar developments took place, reinforced with constitutional requirements that the provinces be responsible for social programs except as provided by constitutional amendment.(3) Advocacy of decentralization presumes that individual families will typically assure the welfare of their members. When that fails, institutions close to those families--charitable groups, then local and provincial or state programs--will constitute the safety net protecting against destitution.

The metaphor of the safety net suggests the key features of the appropriate welfare policy design. The net is close to the ground and the benefits are accordingly modest--a subsistence that might well vary widely in connection with community standards of adequacy. The clientele are the down and out; the eligibility criteria--whether tests of needs or means--are designed to sort out the truly needy from the rest. There is an implicit notion of potential waste: aid to those who do not need the net to survive. Minimal adequacy, selectivity, localism, and tests of need--these constitute the residualist's controlling notions for evaluating the welfare state.

So stated, the conception of welfare as residual sharply differs from what I term the social insurance model. The basic purpose of social insurance is to prevent destitution, although a multitude of questions regarding the desirability of redistribution of income and power arise when considering the role of social insurance in the welfare state. Is the welfare state designed to bring about adequacy, equity, or equality? Is it to compensate for past social injustice and misfortune or perhaps to invest in the future? Is it designed to supplement or replace income, to allocate cash, services, or power, and with what balance among them?(4) What links the social insurance advocates, despite their variance in answering these questions, is the rejection of the residualist conception of welfare on the one hand, and hesitancy about how much notions of redistribution of income and power should be the basis of evaluating the welfare state on the other.

The central metaphor of social insurance is the insurance card (or book). If the net of welfare is to catch those who have failed, the card of social insurance is to prevent destitution. The aim is simple: the universalization of the financial security presumed in the higher civil service and among economic elites. The threats to economic security include some obvious ones--involuntary unemployment, widowhood, sickness, injury, or retirement--as well as less obvious ones such as a large family. Welfare states have provided for these eventualities at different times, in different orders, and with considerable variation in generosity and terms of administration. Yet, irrespective of form and levels of payment, social insurance programs have rejected as inferior the machinery of selective, means-tested programs, the more universal the entitlement, the closer to the model.

Contributions during working life, the theory states, "entitle" one to "protection" against the risks of low income. Sometimes the contributions are participation in the larger society's general tax arrangements, as is the case in Canada. Or, as in Britain, contributions are in the form of weekly social insurance payments. These arrangements differ sharply from the percentage of payroll taxes (contributions) of the United States' Old Age and Survivor's Insurance program. Yet overall the idea is to contribute to future protection. Equitable treatment, not the equalizing of incomes, is the model.

Clearly redistribution of income is one consequence of such programs, but it is not the primary aim. And the model of redistribution is not intended to be between socioeconomic classes, but over the life cycle of individuals and their families. The relevant question for the proponent of social insurance pertains to the adequacy of preparation of the citizenry for the predictable risks of modern industrial society. Looked at this way, the welfare state is simply the extension of the principles of private insurance to markets where either the risks are uninsurable or the distribution of income unlikely to engender widespread insurance purchase.

Such a broad characterization is bound to miss the details of one or another nation's mix of programs. Moreover, no nation has only social insurance programs; everywhere both residual and social insurance strategies are mixed in actual social welfare programs. But variation and mixture do not preclude recognition of the evaluative differences in the perspectives. For in the answers to questions about who gets what, when, and where, it makes considerable difference whether the issue is subsistence or fairness with respect to past effort and earnings. Similarly, it counts whether the standard is appropriate levels of assistance for the downtrodden or adequate compensation for losses of earning power. And, when the aim is to replace past earnings, the in-kind payments--food, housing, special transport cards--are presumed inferior to cash payments.

So far we have not mentioned redistribution of power in our discussion of welfare states. In the residualist's notion of the welfare state, the powerful take care of the weak, and the state apparatus supplements the limited possibilities of private charity.

Social insurance extends the protection available earlier only to tiny economic elites, but does not transform the structure that created those elites. From a more radical perspective, aims of help and compensation are themselves questionable, since they constitute adjustments to the harsh realities of industrial society, and not means of transforming society. The standard for the Marxist theorist is equalization, not equity or adequacy of cash payments. The aim is social change, not evening the distribution of income over the life cycle. And the mechanisms are not ameliorative social programs for the people, but institutions that redistribute status, power, and income to the less privileged. What social insurance advocates count as generous provision is, for the most critical Marxist, illusory, a way to gloss over the contradictions of modern capitalism.(5)

Thus far Marxist theorists have not produced a metaphor that competes with either the safety net or the insurance card. But the image of this revolutionary collective suggests the difference. The aim of programs by the people, not for the people, expresses the compelling notion. And that means a rejection of the charitable societies as well as the harsh administrators of the dole, of the social security office as well as the "helping" professions. Professionalism and paternalism alike evoke the wrath of the Marxist, as well as of some social democratic reformers who have grown weary of the routines and restraints of mature welfare states.

UNDERSTANDING THE NORTH AMERICAN WELFARE STATE

Separating the evaluative standards for welfare states does not commit one to any particular interpretation of the origins and character of particular welfare states. But in practice the tasks of description, explanation, and appraisal are quite connected. To illustrate, I want to turn to three of North America's most prominent programs in social welfare: pensions, family allowances, and government health insurance. Each manifests somewhat different features of the perspectives on welfare discussed in the first section of this essay. Discussing only three reduces the task of explication to manageable proportions.

Old Age Security

The average Canadian retiring in the early 1970s received government pension benefits comparable in terms of preretirement income to those of his American counterpart. Nevertheless, both present pension programs and the chain of developments leading to them differ strikingly.

The difference in timing of the introduction of national pensions can scarcely be regarded as accidental. In Canada pension programs were introduced during a period of relative prosperity, while in the United States the depths of the depression stimulated new policy. The Liberals, the dominant party in Canada in the twentieth century, went on record as favoring national pensions as early as 1915. Although it wasn't until 1922 that the Liberal government enacted a means-tested flat grant pension scheme, the idea had encountered little ideological opposition.

In contrast, only Theodore Roosevelt's 1912 campaign presented social insurance as a national issue in the United States, and until the Social Security Act passed in 1935, a national pension policy was actively opposed by most major politicians and trade union leaders. This was largely because the state appeared to be competing with the unions as agents of economic improvement for the working class.(6) Not until the 1920s did organized labor declare its willingness to press at the state level for public pensions to assist the needy.

In Canada what opposition existed stemmed largely from specific vested interests, such as private insurance, not from ideological hostility or broad interest groups. After World War I there was considerable discussion in the provinces about pension schemes. But, as in the United States, a major new tax program at the subnational level was held to be destructive of the governmental unit's competitive position in the economy.

From the mid-1920s onward various pension schemes were broadly discussed in Canada, but only a flat-rate, means-tested program was regarded as both constitutionally possible and fiscally reasonable.(7) Several provinces favored a joint federal-provincial scheme, and this was provided for by the 1927 plan. In fact it was the first jointly funded public program in Canada and the first major activity of the federal government in the field of social welfare. After the Liberals--with Socialist support--introduced the program, the Conservatives moved to increase their strength by pledging to increase benefits.(8) The maximum Canadian pension was first set at $20 per month and was reduced by the amount of outside income between $125 and the limit of $365 a year.

By 1950 the basic payment had increased to $40, but widespread dissatisfaction was engendered by the means-test and its assumption that one could live comfortably on a bit over a dollar a day. Furthermore, by this time per capita income had made the pension scheme increasingly irrelevant for a large part of the population. As early as 1931 the Conservative Party had favored contributory pensions, and the Liberal Party government of the early 1940s "had always been for the contributory principle."(9) But despite both popular and party sentiment, this reform was by no means imminent.

The Liberals had anticipated contributory pensions when they proposed the reform of 1951, but they were thwarted and instead witnessed the passage of the Old Age Security and Old Age Assistance Acts. The former simply took the maximum benefit level from the existing means-tested scheme and made it a demogrant for those over 70, while the Assistance Act retained the old system for those between 65 and 69.

The immediate appeal of demogrant pensions, as proposed by the tiny Cooperative Commonwealth Federation (CCF), was a factor leading to this compromise legislation. However, the constitutional problems of a contribution scheme appeared insolvable. According to the deputy minister, "pensions financed out of general revenues clearly were intra vires and contributory pensions clearly were not, while earmarked taxes constituted a grey area."(10) Thus a constitutional amendment had to be designed which explicitly provided that both the provinces and the federal government would have authority for administering contributory "old age pensions."

For another decade and more, legislators struggled to enact some kind of earnings-related scheme. The Canadian Congress of Labor continued its attack on the inadequacy of the demogrant plan, while the Conservatives won a landslide victory in 1957 by campaigning on a platform that included the introduction of earnings-related pensions. Massive electoral pressure might then have contributed to reform, were it not for John Diefenbacker's determination that any revision should include survivors' and disability benefits which had not been allowed by the 1951 amendment. Not until the Liberals returned to office in 1965--and after several provincial-federal conferences at which pensions were only one of several major issues--was the earnings-related scheme including survivors' and disability benefits introduced.

Subsequent pension developments included the phasing out of Old Age Assistance as the eligibility age for now earnings-related Old Age Security was lowered to 65, and the enactment of the Guaranteed Income Supplement which provided a means-tested increase of up to 40% over the Old Age security payment.(11)

In contrast to the Canadian programs, which evolved over time, the original plan of the U.S. Social

Security Act of 1935 remains basically intact. Under pressure from the vast success of the grassroots Townsend Movement,(12) the Roosevelt Administration established a means-tested Old Age Assistance program financed jointly by the federal government and the states, and a contributory, federally administered pension scheme. In 1939 coverage of the self-financed pension scheme was expanded to include the survivors and dependents of those insured.

The contributory part of the OASI system had a very long gestation period. It was not until the early 1950s that even half the aged in the United States were receiving any benefits at all from the programs initiated in 1935. And, until about the time of Canada's 1951 reforms, Old Age Assistance--about two-thirds financed by the federal government from general revenues, with the rest from state taxes--provided for a larger number of the aged in the United States than did OASDI. During most of this period increases in the average levels of payment per beneficiary numbers, however, have been dramatic. By 1975 support of some kind for the old was virtually universal, and Supplementary Social Insurance (SSI), the 1972 federal successor to OAA, provided full support for only a few percent of the elderly population.

In 1975 the United States spent $62.6 billion on OASDI and an estimated $3.3 billion to support the aged under SSI. This was 4.6% of the GNP, up sharply from 3.7% in 1972. In Canada the payments from the Old Age Security and Guaranteed Income Supplement Program totaled $3.4 billion in 1975, and the Canadian and Quebec Pension Plans in that year paid $0.5 billion. The total proportion of the 1974-1975 GNP was 2.8% compared with 2.6% three years earlier.

A detailed comparison of benefits per recipient reveals little average difference between the nations. Two factors, however, explain the far greater U.S. total expenditure. First, the Canadian population is younger. If 10.7% of Canada's population had been 65 and over, as in the United States, instead of only 8%, the Canadian pension share of GNP would have been 3.8% in 1975.(13) Virtually all of the rest of the difference in expenditures is explained by the additional beneficiaries under the OASDI system: the survivors and the disabled. Thirty-two million Americans received some benefits from the system in 1975, although only 22.7 million were 65 or over.(14)

Family Allowances

The Canadian system of family allowances introduced in 1945 is wholly without a direct American counterpart. Unfortunately, no very satisfactory account of the genesis of the law has been made, although the discussion of family allowances over a year earlier in the British Parliament was undoubtedly influential. The usual rationale for family allowances is simple enough: An income sufficient for a single person or a couple may not be sufficient for a family with children. As William Beveridge explained at the time, "it would be absurd and even dangerous to give subsistence benefits on a family basis, to try to abolish want when earning were interrupted by sickness or accident, unemployment or old age, without taking steps to see that want was abolished also for all people when earning."(15)

However compelling the Beveridge argument might have been, several sources claim that it was not the principal reason family allowances were introduced in Canada. Rather, family allowances were "seen as a socially desirable means of distributing resources collected for war purposes in a way that might stimulate the purchase of available consumer goods when other forms of semidurable and durable goods were in short supply and when the release of tax resources to other members of the community might have set up inflationary trends."(16) This original intent was wholly unnecessary as it turned out, but it was in keeping with the fears of the simple Keynesian thinking about underconsumption which dominated policy circles in both the United States and Canada.

This observation is consistent with the extent to which real benefits per child were allowed to fall over later years. The $6 per month payment for the lowest age group was retained from 1946 to 1972.(17) Never a very generous payment, it was effectively almost halved by inflation.(18) The official justification was that the allowances had become increasingly unnecessary with the growth in real incomes and other social services--particularly Medicare (government health insurance) and the Canada Assistance Plan (income support).(19)

By the early 1970s many Canadian observers were predicting the virtual demise through neglect of the family allowance. Expert federal opinion strongly favored such an abolition because of the seeming irrationality of paying without regard to need and then taxing back only part of the payment even for the wealthiest families.(20) Instead the Family Allowances Act, which went into force in 1974, boosted monthly payments from $7.48 to $20 per child.

What explains the sudden and unexpected change? First, the payment figures overstate the fiscal reality; the new scheme provides taxable benefits while the older grants were largely tax-free. Second, the entire family allowance program is federally funded, yet has always had greatest popularity in the province of Quebec. To view the introduction of the family allowances as a "gesture to French Canadians," as Moynihan does,(21) may be overly simple, but pronatalism has always been a powerful sentiment in French Canada. Quebec is the only province that uses the fixed total of federal support to give increasing allowances for each successive child, and only Quebec and tiny Prince Edward Island provide additional family supplements out of provincial funds.(22)

If the ruling Liberal Party turned around on family allowances to shore up its political strength in Quebec, as many Canadians believe, it would scarcely have been the first time.(23) The details of the decision to change government policy are not yet known. Whatever the causes, the fiscal impact of family allowances is now substantial. In 1974 and 1975 family allowances amounted to 1.3% of the Canadian GNP.(24)

While the impact of family allowances on the birth rate has never been firmly established in other countries, a desire to increase the population has often resulted in program initiation and revision.(25) The potential for increases in the birth rate among the poor was certainly a factor when family allowances came to be regarded with suspicion in the United States, although its fiscal inefficiency, which taxation reduces but cannot eliminate, would have been a more reasonable basis for opposing the program. Even many favoring family allowances over the negative income tax as the beginning (or the end) of a solution to America's poverty problem did so mainly because of its allegedly greater political acceptability--the logical complement of its inefficiency.(26)

The connections between America's welfare state and family allowances are complex. On the one hand there is no direct counterpart to the child cash benefits of Canada. That alone marks America's development as somewhat special, setting it off from the great bulk of OECD countries. Neither weekly nor monthly do American families have their disposable income altered by the arrival of government checks reflecting the number of children in their household. Yet the tax system provides another form of child allowance that cannot be ignored.

Children, for tax purposes, produce exemptions from income tax of $750 each. In 1976 child tax adjustments accounted for an estimated $10 billion in foregone government revenues, approximately 0.5% of the GNP.(27) A program of that magnitude, though not conventionally grouped with social welfare expenditures, is nonetheless part of the American welfare state. And because family tax allowances work through the tax system, their distributive properties differ from equal direct cash payments per child.

Medical Care

Evaluating international developments in government health policy is complicated by the widely varying medical care systems of the countries being compared. When one compares U.S. and Canadian health policy, however, the striking underlying similarity of the medical care systems simplifies the task. American and Canadian hospitals are largely voluntary, not publicly owned; typically physicians in both countries are paid under a fee-for-service system. The similarities extend even to the training and outlook among physicians and nurses. As one Canadian national official said, the principal hospital officials and physicians belong to "sister associations. They read the same journals, attend the same meetings, [and] prescribe the same drugs."(28)

In both systems the government has used the model of private health insurance and has socialized its costs. While most Western European health insurance programs were parts of the social insurance institutions labor unions helped to manage, the North American pattern differs markedly. Private health insurance sets the example for what the government might more equally distribute.

In the United States the anticipated outcry from conservative sectors and, in particular, from organized medicine caused President Roosevelt to delete any mention of national health insurance from the original Social Security Act. In the early postwar years, the Truman administration tried to revive national health insurance, but the proposal met with strong congressional resistance. The American Medical Association, starting in earnest with the congressional elections of 1950, conducted a sustained campaign against so-called socialized medicine, one that appears to have been extraordinarily successful. Supporters of government health insurance were obliged to shift their attention to an especially attractive subgroup, the aged, but even this change in tactics was unsuccessful until the Kerr-Mills Act of 1960, which provided federal-state cost sharing for the medical expenses of the indigent elderly.

Throughout the early 1960s pressure for more comprehensive coverage of the aged continued, along with concern about improved access to care for the poor. After the Democratic landslide of 1964, these demands were translated into the legislation creating Medicare and Medicaid. The former was an entirely federal effort that provided hospitalization insurance for the elderly under Social Security; it also provided heavily subsidized but elective coverage for outpatient services. Both subplans required patient cost sharing. Medicaid was to provide for the poor and to retain the joint federal-state control, financing, and varying benefits characterizing the federal-state AFDC program. Most state programs employed minimum cost sharing.(29) The American debate still rages over whether government health insurance, which is now partial and pays for some 40% of health expenditures, should become universal.

The absence of national health insurance scarcely means that the U.S. federal government was idle in the health policy field during the 1950s. A number of research, construction subsidy, and categorically specialized disease and population programs were established: the National Institutes of Medicine, the Hill-Burton hospital construction and modernization program, and the program for poor mothers and children (Title V of the Social Security Act) are examples of programmatic activity.

In Canada public policy as well as popular and professional opinion developed along somewhat different lines. It is difficult to find complete rejection of government action in the health insurance field among virtually any group in postwar Canada. The American Medical Association, which in the early part of the century had briefly considered the idea of public health insurance,(30) stood in firm opposition to virtually any government action in the field for 50 years.(31) In sharp contrast the Canadian Medical Association began issuing policy statements quite favorable to government action as early as 1934. A 1943 statement supported a plan that would be "compulsory for persons having an annual income below a level which proves to be insufficient to meet the cost of adequate medical care," and that "payment of the premium should be made by the employee, employer, and government."(32)

There is striking similarity between this early Canadian thinking and the AMA's Medicredit national health plan introduced into the U.S. Congress in the 1970s. Medicredit "would have astonished AMA critics a decade ago and generated complaint within the medical profession for its encouragement of more third party medical financing."(33) Canadian physicians shared many concerns with their colleagues to the south: third party control, the freedom of relationship between doctor and patient, adequate remuneration and fears about the impact of government participation on quality. What differed, however, was the timing and tone of the Canadians' responses.

We cannot know how much these differences reflect

the differing views of Canadian doctors, and how much they reflect a different reading by them of political realities. Surely both have played a part. Presumably Canadian physicians as a group are somewhat less anxious about the negative consequences of state action. Most likely Canadian federal legislation such as the 1935 Employment and Social Insurance Act (which, while found to be unconstitutional, envisioned health benefits financed by compulsory premiums as part of a general improvement in Social Security) was seen as unassailable evidence that the government would eventually promote national health insurance.

In the immediate postwar years--again in vivid contrast to the American situation--several provinces began to develop health insurance schemes. By 1947 CCF-controlled Saskatchewan, a particularly left-leaning province for which there is no U.S. analogue, had almost universal, compulsory hospitalization insurance. By the mid-1950s there was strong provincial pressure for the federal government to become involved in hospital insurance. In April of 1957, with little opposition from organized medicine, the federal parliament passed the Hospital Insurance and Diagnostic Services Act. Hospital insurance was recognized by virtually everyone as being but a first step. One year after the 1964 report of the Hall Commission, the government proposed to the provinces the outlines of the Medical Care Act which provided for a comprehensive range of medical services jointly financed under federal government guidelines. It was passed with only two opposing votes, and was fully implemented.(34) While the medical profession announced opposition to many aspects of the 1966 legislation, Saskatchewan's abortive doctors' strike(35) several years earlier rendered that opposition largely ineffective.

As U.S. policymakers consider the future of government health insurance, they will naturally consider the Canadian experiences, especially since the full operation of Canadian "Medicare." Until very recently both countries appeared unable to control the astronomical growth of what is called the medical care industry. All indicators were that more real resources would be devoted to medical care, a higher rate of inflation would prevail in that sector, patient utilization would increase, and services would intensify, particularly in the hospital. The rates of overall health expenditure increases during the 1960s were remarkably similar: Between 1960 and 1971 total Canadian health expenditure rose by 11.8% per year, while the comparable U.S. rate was 11.1% per year. Furthermore, the North American countries were the leading spenders among all of the industrial countries until 1969.

What is striking is the different response of Canada and the United States to the apparent problem. From the vantage point of 1971, both countries were spending leaders. Only five years later, however, the picture had changed considerably. Canada spent a smaller share of its GNP on health in 1976 than in 1971: roughly 7.1% versus 7.3%. The United States spent approximately 8.6% of its GNP in 1976, as opposed to 7.6% in 1971.

APPRAISING THE COMPLEXITIES OF THE NORTH AMERICAN WELFARE STATE

The first two parts of this essay have separately sketched the criteria for appraising social welfare programs and the major spending programs of the North American welfare state. Distinguishing the evaluative standards, while not closed to argument, is far less controversial than evaluating the programs themselves. And characterizing the programs, while subject to disagreement, is far easier than appropriately applying the relevant standards to the current state of affairs. In this part I want to turn to selected elements in evaluative controversies of the contemporary welfare state in North America. The subject is obviously large and no brief treatment will satisfy the participants in current debates. Here I want to address what would be widely accepted as part of the relevant debate--namely, to what extent are evaluations of the North American welfare state inappropriate, misdirected, or misleading?

The American literature on Social Security of the last decade and a half illustrates one way in which welfare states are inappropriately evaluated. Essentially the problem is one of applying a simple standard to complex programs. In the case of pensions the typical form of appraisal is to stipulate a major purpose for governmental pensions and to measure the extent to which Social Security has satisfied that aim. In the American debate the claim is that social insurance is intended to produce an adequate income in old age through contributions during one's working life, essentially the socialization of private insurance. Welfare programs are, by contrast, supposed to be selective, redistributing income only to those who need it but do not deserve transfers on insurance grounds.

So understood, American Social Security payments to the elderly are bound to fail in evaluation on one or the other grounds, since the program itself has mixed objectives. In this sense the origins of Social Security get lost in the specification of one or another dominant social objective. What is inappropriate is the failure to recognize that American

Social Security grew as a means to reduce the separate treatment of the elderly poor; its promoters sought to blur the sharp line between insurance and welfare aims. Invoking a clear standard--helpful in clarifying one's own thought--is inappropriate when social support for an institution depends on a complex mix of purposes.

There is another obvious way in which social complexity and evaluative simplicity produce inappropriate conclusions. When social patterns change over time, standards have to be adjusted. Consider, for instance, the assumptions about family circumstances in the 1930s and the provisions for a spouse's benefit in pension plans. Social Security experts assumed during the depression that most beneficiaries stayed married to the same spouse and that most wives did not work for extended periods outside the home. Changes in both family structure and female participation in the labor force make spouse's benefits problematic today. But what is problematic is the relation between the contemporary social facts and the program's factual premises, not the issue of whether Social Security has worked well. In this respect it is inappropriate to regard adjustments of the spouse's benefit as a problem <u>of</u> Social Security; it is now an issue <u>for</u> Social Security to address.

There is a second respect in which evaluations of the North American welfare state confuse rather than clarify. In the first instance we noted the mismatch between simplicity and complexity. Here we have in mind evaluations that do not address the conflicts among the purposes social welfare programs are meant to serve, or the problem of misdirected evaluation. Consider, for instance, the enthusiasm for broad social insurance programs that would redistribute family income over the life cycle without the stigma of "relief." In the jargon of the welfare state, this issue is usually thought of as selectivity versus universality. Applied to family allowances, the goals of reducing family poverty efficiently and adjusting income to family size obviously conflict in any given budget for income transfers. To use general child allowances as an antipoverty measure is inefficient. But the antipoverty aim--and the metaphor of the safety net associated with it--is but one of the purposes Canada serves with child allowances and the United States with tax deductions for children.

The clash of aims is equally vivid in some disputes over Social Security pensions. A vocal group of economists have insisted that there are two mutually exclusive standards by which to judge cash transfer programs for the elderly--those of insurance and those of welfare. In practice there are both returns on past contributions and explicit redistribution within the pension programs of North America. The fusion of elements constitutes for Milton Friedman the "triumph of imaginative packaging."(36) Others refer to the "myth" of Social Security as pure insurance, lamenting either its failure to treat equal contributions equally or to function as a socially adequate net under the incomes of the poor elderly.

This exercise in stipulating aims and distinctions among them has little to do with what most Americans know or believe about Social Security. Rather it is the evaluation of a complex, mixed program by standards of orthodox public finance. Just how great a gulf there is between professional opinion among economists and the broader public appraisals of Social Security is suggested by George Break's reluctant defense of present arrangements in a volume about Social Security's crisis:

> Preposterous as the logic may seem to some economists, a successful tax structure must be grounded in faith and in a sense of equity. If the concept of earned entitlements inspires confidence and a sense of equity, it cannot simply be dropped as a basic premise of social security without putting the whole structure in serious jeopardy.(37)

And, as our discussion of North American pension development showed, mixing social insurance justifications with antipoverty objectives is precisely what took place over time. Looked at from the standpoint of reducing the separate treatment of the aged poor, the withering of public assistance for the elderly stands as an accomplishment. Only misdirected criticism would regard public support for a blurring of welfare and social insurance purposes as preposterous.

At times the North American welfare state is subjected to simply misleading evaluation wrapped in the mantle of social science. Typically, such judgements arise unselfconsciously out of what are presented as quite obvious inferences from descriptions of welfare state programs. "The Social Security system" in the United States, we are told, is not only "the major source of retirement income for millions of Americans," but, "for millions more it is the source of their greatest tax burdens." Indeed, Social Security's taxes and benefits are "the second largest and most rapidly growing item in their respective parts of the federal budget." From description there is the leap to appraisal, but unmediated by either explication or defense of the basis for evaluation. Social Security, "despite impressive accomplishments" we are informed, "is in serious trouble." Not only are the "so-called trust funds paying out more than they are taking in" but, most importantly, an "enormous long-term deficit lurks on the horizon."(38)

The misdirection here involves the confusion of states of affairs with important problems. Both the relationship between current Social Security taxes and payments on the one hand, and their connection to the projected long-term deficit on the other, are matters of explicit political choice. We can change the tax rates to reduce the projected deficit or the present balance between taxes and payments. The hidden premise is that radically altering tax burdens for current and prospective American workers is difficult. As a result, considerations of political feasibility are introduced without explicit, or at least extensive attention. Indeed, when the policy adjustments are outlined--increase general revenues, increase social security taxes, or diminish outlays--the option of reduced benefits, we are again told, is not worth considering. "Political realism" should, in this view, "direct the students of Social Security policy to devote little time and effort" to such an alternative.(39)

This brief discussion of evaluation was meant to raise, but not resolve, the sorts of problems that a serious appraisal of the American welfare state entails. Common criticisms--some inappropriate, misleading, or misdirected--were cited to suggest how far we are from a serious review of the major institutions of the welfare state. In no case did I turn to mistaken accounts of these institutions, presuming instead that accurate description is not the major problem of evaluation. There are some, like Sherwin Rosen, who think "most of the points of issue" about programs like Social Security can "only be resolved empirically," through "more definitive answers" about the effects of Social Security on private savings, the effects of the work retirement test, and the like.(40)

Such a view, from the standpoint of this essay, is twice misguided. Not only would such findings not settle the debates, but even sorting out the standards to evaluate such empirical findings would be insufficient. And the reason is not complicated. What the welfare state is to accomplish has always been contentious--at its origins, during its most rapid growth, and currently. There are substantial differences between evaluating the success of social welfare policies in terms of their original intentions and justifications on the one hand, and in the light of all the additional criteria that, on the other hand, might be applied over time. When we look at the welfare state from alternative angles, the appraisals must remain controversial, simply not subject to a determinative combination of standards and results. To be sure, it might well be possible to regard the North American welfare state as reasonably successful in the light of aspirations during the depression. But when we now consider the size of the public budget, or the additional programs for social redistribution, the new considerations dislodge older appraisal and the problem of evaluation shifts markedly.

As the first part of this essay argued, the justifications for social welfare programs can be understood to reflect three quite different programmatic conceptions. Even agreeing on an appropriate conception would not determine the appropriate level of effort, outlay, and sacrifice warranted by the welfare state in its contemporary setting. In this respect neither social science nor political philosophy can adequately appraise the North American welfare state. In the end that task requires politicians. And those politicians have to choose the relevant considerations as well as reflect on the connections between original aspirations and programmatic fates.

NOTES

1. Ian Gough, Political Economy of the Welfare State (London: Macmillan Publishers, 1979).
2. Adam Graycar, Welfare Politics in Australia: A Study in Policy Analysis (Melbourne: Macmillan, 1979), p. 20.
3. Christopher Leman, The Collapse of Welfare Reform: Political Institutions, Policy, and the Poor in Canada and the United States (Cambridge, Ma: MIT Press, 1980).
4. Graycar, Welfare Politics.
5. Gough, Political Economy of the Welfare State.
6. Gaston V. Rimlinger, Welfare Policy and Industrialization in Europe and America (New York: John Wiley and Sons, 1971), pp. 80-81.
7. Kenneth Bryden, Old Age Pensions and Policy-Making in Canada (Montreal and London: McGill-Queen's University Press, 1974), pp. 77-78.
8. Ibid, p. 74.
9. Ibid, p. 115.
10. Ibid, p. 123.
11. Bryden, Old Age Pensions, presents a very detailed discussion of the pattern of negotiations and the positions taken by several of the provinces. See pp. 129-146.
12. See Rimlinger, Welfare Policy, for a discussion of the free pension movement, pp. 195-196.

13. Cf Canadian Bureau of Statistics, Canada Year Book, 1974 (Ottawa, Canada: Canadian Census and Statistics Office, 1974).

14. Council of Economic Advisors, Economic Report to the President (Washington, DC: U.S. Government Printing Office, 1976).

15. Quoted by Eleanor Rathbone, Family Allowances (London: George Allen and Unwin, 1949), p. 274.

16. John S. Morgan, "An Emerging System of Income Maintenance: Canada in Transition" in Shirley Jenkins (ed.) Social Security in International Perspective: Essays in Honor of Eveline M. Burns (New York: Columbia University Press, 1969), p. 113: Bryden, Old Age Pensions, p. 110; Joseph W. Willard, "Family Allowances in Canada" in Eveline M. Burns (ed.) Children's Allowances and the Economic Welfare of Children: The Report of a Conference (New York: Citizens Committee for Children of New York, 1968), p. 113.

17. A slightly higher payment was made for older children from 9 to 16 (and 17- and 18-year-olds were added to the scheme in 1964).

18. Statistics Canada, Social Security: National Programs (Ottawa: Statistics Canada, 1976), p. 249.

19. Willard, "Family Allowances," p.66.

20. Christopher Leman, "Patterns of Policy Development: Social Security in the United States and Canada," Public Policy (Spring 1977), pp. 67-70.

21. Daniel P. Moynihan, The Politics of a Guaranteed Income: The Nixon Administration and the Family Assistance Plan (New York: Vintage Books, 1973), p. 48.

22. Statistics Canada, Social Security, 1976, pp. 211, 214.

23. Ibid, p. 247.

24. Ibid, p. 247.

25. Theodore R. Marmor and Martin Rein, with the assistance of Sally Van Til, "Post-war European Experience with Cash Transfers: Pensions, Child Allowances, and Public Assistance," Technical Study of the President's Commission of Income Maintenance Programs (Washington, D.C.: U.S. Government Printing Office, 1969), p. 273; Moynihan, Politics of the Guaranteed Income, p. 48.

26. Moynihan, Politics of a Guaranteed Income, pp. 125-126.

27. Roughly estimated. Personal communication by Wayne Hoffman, The Urban Institute, Washington, D.C., December 1980.

28. Maurice LeClair, "The Canadian Health Care System" in Spyros Andreopoulos (ed.) National Health Insurance: Can We Learn From Canada? (New York: John Wiley and Sons, 1975), p. 11.

29. See Theodore R. Marmor, The Politics of Medicare (Chicago: Aldine, 1973).

30. Ibid, p. 7.

31. For a detailed account of the pre-World War II activities of the AMA, see Oliver Garceau, Political Life of the AMA (Cambridge: Harvard University Press, 1941); for the postwar period through the passage of the 1965 legislation, see Marmor, The Politics of Medicare.

32. LeClair, "The Canadian Health Care System," p. 19.

33. Kenneth Bowler, Robert Kudrle, and Theodore Marmor, "The Political Economy of National Health Insurance: Policy Analysis and Political Evaluation" in Kenneth Frideman and Stuart Rakoff (eds.) Toward a National Health Policy (Lexington: D.C. Heath and Company, 1977), p. 164.

34. See LeClair, "The Canadian Health Care System," pp. 11-18.

35. For a discussion of the generally unsatisfactory results of attempting to use flat rate copayments in the provincial schemes, see Robert Evans, "Beyond the Medical Marketplace: Expenditure, Utilization and Pricing of Insured Health Care in Canada" in Andreopoulos (ed.) National Health Insurance, pp. 130-132.

36. Milton Friedman, "Payroll Taxes, No; General Revenues, Yes" in Michael Boskin (ed.) The Crisis in Social Security: Problems and Politics (San Francisco: Institute for Contemporary Studies, 1978), p. 28.

37. George Break, "Social Security as a Tax" in Boskin (ed.) The Crisis in Social Security, pp. 122-123.

38. Michael Boskin, "Introduction" in Boskin (ed.) The Crisis in Social Security, p. xi.

39. Edward Cowan, "Background and History: The Crisis in Public Finances and Social Security" in Boskin (ed.) The Crisis in Social Security, p. 11.

40. Sherwin Rosen, "Social Security and the Economy" in Boskin (ed.) The Crisis in Social Security, pp. 87-106.

14. Tax Philosophy and Income Equality

John F. Witte

Taxation and the problem of equality have rarely been separated. Particularly since the advent of income taxation, the issue has been a primary consideration of tax theorists. While the concern of many theorists has been to establish a just formula for the extraction of an unpleasant burden, income redistribution has always been a central concern. And although a number of theories reviewed in this paper are ancient by social science standards, the recent interest in "principles" of justice and equality following publication of John Rawls's A Theory of Justice, justifies at least their momentary rebirth. Reviewing the history of these theories and their limitations should clarify the difficulties of establishing rigorous principles of income equality through the tax system.

There are three relatively distinct periods in modern income tax theory. The first, which I will call classical tax theory, extends from the last half of the nineteenth century to about 1930. The theories created during this formative period for income taxation were primarily efforts to establish deductive principles of taxation that would either serve as an exact formula, or at least provide a general guide to the proper rate of taxation. By the 1930s, with income tax a reality in the United States and pragmatic philosophy dominating social science, tax philosophy had changed. Beginning with Henry Simons, tax experts shifted from a quest for deductive principles to a concern over the definitional problem of the tax base, and to lengthy arguments over important but narrow provisions of the tax code.

This comprehensive tax base argument is still going on. However, the last decade has seen a return to the search for more precise tax theory. Although this new optimal tax theory displays many of the characteristics of the classical approach, it can also be interpreted as something of a combination of the earlier prescriptive theories and the more pragmatic strategies that have evolved since.

This chapter will describe the evolution of these theories, explain their content, and evaluate their advantages and limitations. Although I will be particularly interested in those aspects that bear on the question of income equality, the framework of evaluation is more general. Thus the first section below discusses the two basic approaches to tax policy, pragmatism and prescription, and the criteria on which each can be judged. Although no effort is made to extend this discussion beyond the field of taxation, the evaluative criteria discussed would seem to apply to other policy fields and to general theories of equity.

The argument of this paper will be that all efforts to establish a solid theory of equity in taxation have major flaws, and that therefore the equality issue must be decided prior to and apart from the tax code. In the final section I offer two suggestions on what might be critical factors in establishing such a prior position.

EVALUATING THEORIES OF TAXATION

The Pragmatic Approach

The pragmatic approach to tax policy assumes no general theory of taxation against which proposals can be rigorously evaluated. Rather, basic policy innovation, such as the current controversy over a value-added tax, as well as adjustments of existing provisions are treated on a case-by-case basis. Policies are analyzed relative to sets of desirable and undesirable consequences. No effort is made in advance to weight these factors or to rank them by priority. It is assumed that the relevance of various criteria will vary from policy to policy, and thus their relevance is left to the political system to sort out at the appropriate time.

Evaluation takes the form of a series of learned discussions about the advantages and disadvantages of proposal X, or of proposal X versus Y and Z. For those who follow Congressional committee discussions, staff reports, and so on, this approach is recognizable as the primary form of evaluation of tax policy in the political arena.(1)

A classic example of this approach is George Break and Joseph Pechman's analysis of various tax reform proposals in the mid-1970s.(2) They begin by discussing five principles or goals of taxation: equity, economic efficiency, fiscal efficiency, simplicity, and certainty. They then review a broad range of tax proposals and apply these principles in a relatively ad hoc manner, although incidence (vertical equity) is an omnipresent consideration. The influence of this book on tax policy and the tax reform act of 1976 was immense, although some of the changes they recommended were short-lived.

Another example of the pragmatic approach can be found in the writing of Harold Groves. Following his criticism of prescriptive theories of taxation, Groves suggests that the case for progression actually rests on

> . . . what progressive taxation will do to serve or disserve such widely accepted national objectives as an increase in per capita real income, minimum economic fluctuations, a workable tax system producing adequate revenue, political stability under representative government, international independence or security, elimination of extreme want, and perhaps mitigation of social disorders, such as crime, divorce, mental illness and the like.(3)

An impressive list indeed, but as with the criteria considered by Break and Pechman, there is no guide to the precedence of one consequence over another. What we have in this and the earlier example is little more than a checklist of policy considerations.

Pragmatic policy evaluation then becomes a series of arguments over the competing advantages and disadvantages of alternatives. And the arguments are guided by a loose set of criteria which are brought into play as circumstances dictate. This does not necessarily mean that these arguments are wholly arbitrary. They may be judged for the validity of their empirical assumptions, and for the clarity, consistency, and relevancy of the internal arguments.(4) However, because of the octopus-like approach, where there are multiple lines of argument, pragmatic positions are by their nature less susceptible to the type of fatal flaws that can occur in deductive theories bent on deriving single general principles. This should be kept in mind in the following section on theories of income taxation.

The argument given for this approach is that it tends to fit the complexity of the subject and is well adapted to a pluralist political system, where consensus is constantly shifting and difficult to identify. This is so because the values associated with various consequences of a policy are not immediately clear, and there is no procedure other than political agreement on how values should be aggregated. Thus the best that can be hoped for is an open and thorough policy debate, and the final test of a decision becomes the lack of long-term political resistance.(5) Manley's work on the politics of the Ways and Means Committee clearly indicates the dominance of this approach in the real world of tax policymaking.(6)

However, the reduction of policy evaluation to a series of disjointed arguments concerning separate provisions, relatively unconstrained by guiding principles, has its costs, and theorists have therefore attempted to create more comprehensive philosophies. Those who support a pragmatic approach to public policy often cite the conservation of time and resources required for decision making as a major advantage of their approach. Their arguments are based on a comparison between the pragmatic approach and either massive planning efforts or the creation of social welfare functions that require the incorporation of broad sets of values.(7)

While I leave you to judge for yourself if such a comparison is appropriate in a general sense, it is surely erroneous for theories of taxation. The aim of the tax philosopher is much more limited. Their sights are set on such modest goals as arguing for a flat or progressive rate structure, or for what forms of income should be included in the tax base.

If such principles could be agreed on, they would undoubtedly present less difficulty and not complicate the decision process. If, for example, a dominant principle of progressivity were accepted, not only would it be possible to eliminate entire types of regressive tax systems, but it would also greatly increase the difficulty of sustaining arguments for extremely regressive provisions in the income tax (thus presumably discouraging their introduction). Admittedly, without an exact specification of progressive rates, there would remain a great deal to discuss. However, the decision space would be less extensive with an operative principle than without one.

The pragmatic approach may also strain the legitimacy of the political system. Legitimacy may be affected either because alternatives are not adequately considered (because of the time problem described above), or because decisions cannot be explained appropriately to opinion leaders or the public. The complicated arguments and elaborate trade-offs that are involved may simply be so complex that even intelligent, well-informed observers will be mystified at how or why decisions are reached. A cynic might even wonder if those making the decisions can reconstruct reasonable explanations. In any event there is this uncomfortable feeling that tax provisions may suddenly and unpredictably appear. It is not unreasonable to explain the tax act of 1978 in exactly these terms.

While this mild schizophrenia tarnishes the legitimacy of tax policy, it also creates uncertainty that is a major deterrent to individual or corporate economic planning.

Finally, there is also the more traditional problem of legitimacy based on the complaint that the discussions and deliberations, so important to the pragmatic approach, will not fairly represent affected interests. In taxation this complaint comes from both ends of the political spectrum. Liberals claim that wealthy individuals and business get special treatment and consideration far beyond their numbers or rights, while conservatives point to the progressive rates and claim majority tyranny. Both question the legitimacy of the process.

A final objection against pragmatism might be raised by the idealist, if one is yet to be found. The objection is simply, even naively, that if we wish to radically alter the status quo, pragmatism, with its balancing, compromising, and general normative wheeling and dealing, is very unlikely to achieve our purposes. To create such change is the role of philosophy and hence political principles. This is perhaps the most disturbing problem with pragmatism, for an infusion of idealism, and at least the appearance of changing direction from time to time, is certainly beneficial and may even be a necessary condition of a healthy democracy.

The Prescriptive Approach

Prescriptive tax theories attempt to determine a general philosophy of taxation that serves as a dominant guide in policy choices. Whereas the pragmatist begins with the assumption that circumstances will and should dictate which sets of taxing devices will be employed at any time, the prescriptive theorist argues that a basic tax formula is superior and should serve as the baseline from which policy deviations and exceptions may be drawn. The general form of prescriptive theories is relatively simple and does not differ significantly from the more discrete arguments employed in the pragmatic approach. What differs, as will be explained below, is the generality or robustness of the prescriptions, and the value claims they make.

A prescriptive theory can be thought of as a series of statements of the following form:

> Given a set of conditions, X_i,
> and a set of circumstances, C_i,
> apply alternatives A_i.

Conditions consist of empirical statements (or assumptions) about the nature of the real world. Familiar examples might be that marginal utility declines with increasing income, or that work effort is reduced in proportion to increasing marginal taxes. These conditions are the bedrock upon which tax prescriptions are formed. Standing alone, conditions, being empirical statements, must be true in the sense that they can be verified by observing the real world. To the degree that evidence is mixed or unattainable, the prescriptive theory is weakened.

Circumstances describe either sets of conditions that modify or refine general conditions, or identifiable categories of individuals for which policy alternatives apply or from which they are excepted. An example of the former might be that the marginal propensity to save increases with income once a certain minimal level of consumption is achieved. Examples of the latter might be that tax treatment of individuals with earned versus unearned income should be treated differently, or that special tax dispensation should be granted to the blind, aged, crippled, or possibly those engaged in low-paying though socially desirable intellectual endeavors.

Circumstances thus serve as a bridge between generalizable empirical assumptions and normative prescriptions of policy alternatives. If they take the form of excepting or refining conditional statements, they must be judged on the empirical grounds described above. Conversely, if they serve to except or refine the prescription of alternatives, they must be judged in accordance with normative standards applicable to the selection of alternatives to be discussed below.

The decomposition of prescriptive theories can do without the circumstances category, because a separate theory can be devised linking a complex set of conditions (including exceptions) with a possibly equally complex set of alternatives. However, in so doing we tend to lose sight of the basic propositions in the underlying general theory. The use of the circumstances category allows for the clear statement of a general theory, but accepts the fallibility of that theory when applied to the diversity of personal and economic situations encountered in the real world.

Alternatives are general prescriptive rules that can be either positive alternative sets (do A_i), negative constraints (do not do A_i), or an indifference set. While complex priority schemes might be allowed, as we will see (with the possible exception of the recent optimal tax theory), the prescriptive alternatives that are offered in tax theories are usually quite simple.

Granting that the statements of conditions are

accurate, we judge alternatives by requiring a convincing argument that the alternative selected produces a desirable outcome. These arguments are either causal chain arguments which specify that if we do A it will lead to further action which will have valuable consequences, or that A is simply valuable in its own right. Harold Groves discusses equality in relation to taxes in exactly these terms:

> Egalitarianism may be espoused as a pure value judgement on the score that the ethic of distribution associated with the private family is preferred to that which comes out of the market place. This was the egalitarianism of Henry Simons. But egalitarianism may also be supported in terms of its by-products. One of these, in the reviewer's view, is a viable and stable democracy. Egalitarianism within limits is both a means and a goal in a democratic society and government.(8)

To judge the selection of alternatives that are linked to further outcomes again requires justification of an empirical claim (that is, for the above, is some degree of equality indeed necessary for a stable democracy?) as well as an argument for the value of the final outcome.

Up to this point, in theory, evaluation of prescriptive theories seems reasonably straightforward. Conditions and circumstances need to be separated from the specification of alternatives; the validity of these assumptions can be analyzed following something like a scientific method, however humbled in application to social phenomena; and finally, if the argument for an alternative set involves causal chains that lead to ultimately valuable outcomes, these causal chains can be probed for logical consistency and empirical validity.

However, at this point we must face the question: Why is one set of outcomes preferred to another? For example, Why should equality of income be preferred to economic growth? Or why should a tax that is costly to administer but direct and visible be preferred to a tax that is simple but indirect? The diehard logical positivist at this point closes the argument by postulating that there is no answer to this question, that values are merely beliefs, which are subject to change, circumstances, and so on, and therefore that any external validation of preferences is an impossibility.

Although it is difficult to quarrel with this position in the extreme, unless one is prepared to offer a convincing theory of values to serve as an alternative, there are several tests that weigh on our judgement of the prescription of final outcomes. The most rudimentary is that a clear argument is advanced for a final outcome--that is, that an appeal to a clearly specified value is offered as a rationalization. Beyond requiring clarity in specifying values, this means that an argument that offers a positive case for an outcome can be judged superior to one that arrives at an alternative by eliminating all other alternatives as undesirable. While in some instances this elimination procedure may be necessary and valid, if the status quo as an alternative is adequately evaluated, the case is weaker than one in which a positive claim is advanced.(9)

A second factor affecting the judgement of alternatives is the extent to which the consequences predicted are universally valued. This is a difficult problem to discuss in theory, but it is often not as difficult to apply in practice as it might appear. The theoretical problem is to define a method for determining what is valued and what is not. Although this is a central issue in the historical development of ethics, it is difficult--given that taxation is a public policy emerging from a supposedly democratic government--to adopt any definition other than judging values on the basis of what people desire. With this definition, however, we immediately generate several problems.

First, determining what people desire is an inexact art at best. Empirical attitude research is some help, although there are limitations when questions turn to tax issues, or to more general beliefs about equality.(10) What this means in practice is that we combine observations of attitudes and reactions with intuitive assumptions about how the average man might react. While intuition implies mystification for the modern positivists, in fact little else has been used in tax theories in the last century. And surprisingly this combination of intuition and observation is not too difficult to apply in many circumstances.

For example, is it unreasonable to suggest that most people would agree that individuals living on the very edge of subsistence should not be heavily taxed, or not taxed at all? Similarly, at the other extreme, would many people agree to a 100% tax rate at some income level without other methods of recognition and reward being introduced? The problem is admittedly somewhat more difficult when consequences are less specific and the values associated with these consequences are unclear. As we will see in some detail, when applied to taxation the classical utilitarian notion of happiness suffers this confusion.

A second problem has to do with balancing or aggregating valued outcomes. What can really be said, for example, about the great trade-off between equity and efficiency that is so much a part of tax policy? In any precise way, I think not much, although optimal tax theorists are currently making great efforts. However, if our purpose is to judge the degree of universal appeal of a tax principle, the very existence of such trade-offs may be extremely relevant. One of the great problems with classical theories, for example, is that they claim universality, and indeed usually appeal to a widely shared set of vaues, but ignore or greatly discount negative consequences. The realization of this in the early 1900s drove tax theory in the pragmatic direction.

Decomposing prescriptive theories into statements of conditions, circumstances, and alternatives facilitates the examination of the individual parts of an argument based on the criteria I have described. However, there are several further factors that apply to the prescriptive system as a whole. The first of these is clarity, or the degree to which the arguments accurately specify and link the various components of the system. Arguments may fail to specify accurate conditional assumptions, or they may insufficiently link ultimate consequences with prescribed alternatives. An example of the latter is the current concern over tax effects on capital formation. The majority of these debates concentrate on empirical assessments of various forms of taxation on the accumulation and investment of capital. A more complete argument would clarify the underlying consequences involved (few argue that capital formation in itself is to be valued), and the additional required causal links between capital formation and these outcomes. This is important because it is not at all difficult to get swept up in the cry for greater capital, without considering the certainty of the effects on economic growth, or the ramifications for equity.

It seems to me, however, that one aspect of the problem of clarity needs to be approached with a degree of tolerance. I am referring to the exact specification of alternatives. Tolerance is required because, unlike some commentators on tax philosophy, I believe there is benefit in theories that prescribe a general direction to be followed in a policy area, even if an alternative set cannot be exactly formulated. Thus, for example, as discussed above, I would not consider theories useless if they prescribe progressivity but fail to define how much. There is, however, a limit. That limit is reached when the theory becomes so vague that it fails to distinguish or confuses two or more critical alternative sets. An example of this, to be discussed below, is the famous confusion of John Stuart Mill between equal and proportional sacrifice theories.

An important final criterion for evaluating tax theories, and the one that ultimately distinguishes prescriptive theories from pragmatic arguments, is the degree of robustness of the theory.(11) Intuitively, a theory is robust to the extent that it prescribes a narrow alternative set for a general population. Thus theory A is robust relative to theory B to the degree that conditional assumptions and circumstantial requirements are minimized, and either the range of positive or indifferent alternatives is restricted, or the set of negative alternatives is maximized. Robustness has nothing to do with the validity of a theory; rather it is a measure of its utility.

To use a previous example, establishing a principle of tax exemption for subsistence level incomes is undoubtedly a principle accepted by most. However, the theory in itself is very weak because it says nothing about the taxation of incomes beyond that level. To take a more general case, the Rawls difference principle, in allowing any distribution of goods as long as the most marginal group in society benefits, is an extremely weak theory.(12) If, for example, we were to use his principle to judge the justice of societies over a period of time, the only truly unjust society would be one that increasingly and intentionally impoverishes its poorest members. Historically there may be some such societies, but their number must be quite limited.

With some exceptions for the work of Henry Simons, who bridges the gap between classical deductive theories of taxation and the modern pragmatists, the criteria and tests suggested by this method of thinking about prescriptive policy theories will provide the framework for analyzing the major classes of income tax theories.

THEORIES OF INCOME TAXATION

The Classical Theories

As the issue of equality exploded in the industrialized world of the nineteenth century, there was a parallel expansion in theories of income taxation. While some of these theories, particularly the earlier ones, proposed equal or proportional taxation, all were acutely aware of the impending prospect of progressive, and hence redistributive tax rates. It is safe to say that none of the principles developed have sustained the test of time and policy development. The world of the twentieth century simply created too many complexities, too much knowledge, and too great a deference to science. But their failure is more than a matter of historical interest, it is instructive in the current debates concerning redistribution, and what we might expect from them.

In what follows I will concentrate on the two major and currently most relevant approaches: the approach linking utility with equity in taxation, and the argument for the so-called faculty approach, later to be crudely merged into the idea of ability to pay. This leaves out the benefit theory of taxation which was relegated to the status of "historical interest only" as early as 1894 by E. R. Seligman, and given very short treatment by Simons in 1938 and Blum and Kalven in 1952. Its resurrection by Richard Musgrave in 1959 is important; however, the inherent problems of determining a general theory describing who benefits from government and the difficulty of applying any such theory to an income tax seem insurmountable.(13)

Theories linking utility and taxation are important not only because of their sheer volume, but also because of the importance of utilitarian principles in classical and neoclassical economics. The link is more than simply a natural theoretical extension. The importance of these theories is that they attempted to appeal to values of equality (of various constructions), while at the same time taking into consideration the not unreasonable idea that different amounts of happiness were created from different income increments. Indeed, the most prominent of these theories, the minimum sacrifice theory, offers the powerful combination of greater equality and maximum happiness. Since taxation considered apart from benefits constitutes lost utility, utilitarian-based theories are expressed in terms of sacrifice.

My concern will be with three theories: equal, proportional, and minimal sacrifice. Equal sacrifice is defined as an equal loss of utility for each taxpayer. Proportional sacrifice is defined as a loss of utility that insures that the ratio of after-tax utility between taxpayers is equivalent to the pre-tax ratio. Finally, minimal sacrifice theory specifies that tax rate which minimizes the amount of utility lost, thus maximizing total after-tax utility. In mathematical terms, the following definitions apply:

Given a general utility function $U = f(z)$, utility loss at any income level z can be expressed as

$$z \,.\, t.\, f'(z)$$

where t is the value of the tax rate function at income level z (o t 1), and $f'(z)$ is the rate of change of the utility with respect to income. Assuming C and K are constants:

Definition 1. Equal sacrifice is that tax rate for which $z \cdot t \cdot f'(z) = C$ for each taxpayer.

Definition 2. Proportional sacrifice is that tax rate for which $z \cdot t \cdot f'(z) = K.1\ (z)$ for each taxpayer.

Definition 3. Minimum sacrifice is that tax rate which minimizes for <u>n</u> taxpayers. $\sum_{i=1}^{n} z_i \cdot t_i \cdot f'(z_i)$

These formulas are critically dependent on the specification of the utility function, f(z). A minimal assumption is that the marginal utility of income declines as income increases, or put another way, that total utility does not increase in proportion to an increase in income. Writing in 1889, following the mathematical work of Cohen-Stuart some years earlier, F. Y. Edgeworth used this minimum conditional assumption to strike a fatal blow against both equal and proportional sacrifice while making a strident argument for minimum sacrifice.

Cohen-Stuart, a Dutch mathematical economist, had demonstrated that if the utility curve is thought to follow a rectangular form, U = log(z) (the so-called Bernoulli curve), then the marginal rate of decline (the first derivative), was simply the inverse of income (du/dz = 1/z). Given this assumption, Cohen-Stuart demonstrated that equal sacrifice would lead to a flat or constant tax rate, while proportional sacrifice would specify a progressive rate. These results are reproduced in column 1 of Table 1. Cohen-Stuart's conclusion was that proportional sacrifice should be the guiding principle of taxation.(14)

To the extent that his analysis is correct, it appeals to universal values in that it combines an outcome of increased absolute equality with a principle of equal treatment that leaves relative utility unchanged. Up until the late nineteenth century, this latter principle, the so-called leave-them-as-you-found-them ideal, was the most widely accepted principle of taxation.(15)

Edgeworth quickly destroyed Cohen-Stuart's elegant formulation by demonstrating very simply that if other utility functions are selected--functions that still fall within the class of decreasing marginal utility--equal and proportional sacrifice theories will produce totally inconsistent directions in tax rates. This is shown by comparing columns 1 and 2 in Table 1 for a simple example. As is evident, equal sacrifice may lead to either a constant or a regressive rate, and proportional sacrifice to a progressive or flat rate

TABLE 1. TAX RATES FOR EQUAL AND PROPORTIONAL SACRIFICE THEORIES GIVEN DIFFERENT DECREASING RATES OF MARGINAL UTILITY

	(1)* $U = \log(z)$	(2)+ $U = \sqrt{z}$
Equal Sacrifice	$t = c$	$t = \frac{2C}{\sqrt{z}}$
Proportional Sacrifice	$t = k \log(z)$ (progressive)	$t = k$ (flat rate)

*For $U = \log(z)$, $\frac{dU}{dz} = \frac{1}{z}$.

$$\text{Equal sacrifice} = t \cdot z \cdot \frac{1}{z} = c, \text{ or } t = c.$$

$$\text{Proportional sacrifice} = t \cdot z \cdot \frac{1}{z} = k \cdot \log(z), \text{ or } t = k . \log(z).$$

+For $U = z$, $\frac{dU}{dz} = 1/2z^{-1/2}$.

$$\text{Equal sacrifice} = t \cdot z\,(1/2z^{-1/2}) = c, \text{ or } t = \frac{2}{z}.$$

$$\text{Proportional sacrifice} = t \cdot z(1/2z^{-1/2}) = k \cdot z^{1/2}, \text{ or } t = 2k.$$

depending on the assumed utility function. With more complex functions it can be shown that equal sacrifice may lead to progressive rates, and that proportionality may be regressive.(16)

A moment's reflection on the definition of minimal sacrifice, with the assumption of decreasing marginal utility, will demonstrate that this inconsistency is not relevant for minimal sacrifice. If utility decreases with income, the smallest amount of utility per dollar will be lost by always taxing the highest incomes. In the words of Edgeworth, "the principle of least sacrifice in trumpet tones proclaims that the rate of taxation ought to be progressive; except so far as this distributional presumption is cut into by productional and other utilitarian conditions."(17)

Given the assumed general conditions of decreasing utility, Edgeworth's argument is compelling, and it would appear that only the minimal sacrifice doctrine survives even the weakest test of clarity. However, before we concentrate on that theory, I would note that the proportional sacrifice principle seems to have more desirable characteristics than equal sacrifice. For all classes of decreasing marginal utility functions, proportional sacrifice does appeal to an identifiable sense of equality in that it leaves the relative differences between individuals unchanged. On the other hand, equal sacrifice increases relative inequality conceived in terms of utility.

The only justification for this type of equality would be that all should share in the finances of government in absolutely equal terms. But what justification can there be for this, other than a benefit theory that proposes that all share equally in the fruits of government action? Although arguments about benefits can be made to favor either the rich (by posing that government protects property and upholds contracts), or the poor (by emphasizing expenditures for need-based programs), I find an assumption of equal benefit as equally arbitrary and untestable as the others.(18) However, without this assumption there seems to be no case to be made for equal sacrifice.

Minimal sacrifice theory is not without significant flaws. Unfortunately, a number of the criticisms that have been made seem to be in error and greatly confuse the issues. These criticisms, to use my terms, are questions addressing both the clarity and robustness of the theory. The most prominent critique in terms of clarity is the argument that utility is such a vague concept that it can neither be quantified nor compared between individuals. Blum and Kalven specifically concede that the idea of declining marginal utility makes intuitive sense and would be accepted as valid by most individuals, but then declare that "The error lies in trying to translate money, which can be measured in definite units, into corresponding units of satisfaction or wellbeing. In the end satisfaction in the sense of happiness defies quantification."(19)

This is not an uncommon criticism of utilitarianism and one I personally sympathize with. However, while this problem of "cardinal, interpersonal comparisons" of utility creates havoc for most theories of welfare economics, it does not affect the clarity of the minimal sacrifice theory as Blum and Kalven, Simons, Groves, and others suggest. All that is required is the intuitive acceptance of continuous declining marginal utility of income for the vast majority.

If this is accepted, whether we know the exact shape of that curve or not, a specific prescription for a progressive tax system is forthcoming and that fact makes minimal sacrifice a dominant theory relative to equal or proportional sacrifice. Indeed it is precisely because we cannot measure utility exactly that minimal sacrifice becomes dominant. The prescription that follows from a rigorous application of minimal sacrifice is that required taxes are extracted exclusively from the wealthiest individuals in society, and that group is continuously expanded as incomes are reduced. Given any continuous function that fulfills the requirement of decreasing marginal utility, the income thus extracted will represent a minimal loss of utility. Whether or not utility is quantifiable in practice, the prescription is exact.

Another variant of this argument is that the vagueness of the utility concept and the lack of specification for utility functions leads to such a broad array of possible alternatives that the theory is useless. This challenge in terms of robustness is an appropriate critique of equal and proportional sacrifice theories as has been shown, but not of minimal sacrifice as it has so far been conceived. In fact the opposite is true: It is because the minimal sacrifice theory is so devastatingly robust that it is open to criticism.

There are two basic weaknesses of the minimal sacrifice theory and they both follow from what has been said above. The first arises from the prescription that it leads to. Essentially, the tax is born only by the wealthiest members of society, continuously bringing them down to a level equal with at least some of their fellows. The extreme nature of this outcome led even the most dedicated proponents of minimal sacrifice to suggest that the rates should stop somewhere below the 100% level. Cohen-Stuart, along with many other theorists, argued for a subsistence exemption with subsequent progressive rates that eventually became proportional. He couched his argument in an elaborate theory that for the very rich, who have satisfied all personal wants, the utility of incomes ceases to marginally decline, suddenly and mysteriously providing constant utility (at a presumed very low level).

Edgeworth is not at all convinced by this as he coyly comments, "The mathematical reader who is not convinced by Mr. Cohen-Stuart on this point will hardly defer to others."(20) He then goes on to state: "Practical reasons, not deductions from any form of the first principle, would thus lead to a 'digressive progression' culminating in a simply proportionate tax of the higher incomes, such as in fact seems to be coming into vogue."(21) The practical reasons he discusses are the consideration for "other disutilities" such as disincentives to work, produce, or invest.

His fellow utilitarian, T. N. Carver, elaborated this argument in a famous article entitled "The Ethical Basis of Distribution and its Application to Taxation":

> The evils of taxation are of two kinds: (1) the sacrifice to the one who pays the taxes; (2) the repressive effect which a tax may have on industry and enterprise. Therefore in accordance with the principle of utility, the burdens of taxation should be so distributed that the sum of these two forms of evil--should be as small as possible.(22)

Carver then goes on to argue that a dilemma emerges because the minimal sacrifice theory minimizes the first evil, while equal sacrifice minimizes the second. Before we consider this trade-off with efficiency, which is the ultimate problem with utilitarian theories, several comments on the modification of this minimal sacrifice theory are in order.

First, obviously, when the theory is augmented to include a low-income exemption and an upper-income flat rate, it loses a great deal of clarity and robustness. Although Edgeworth went on to create "Formulae" for aiding policy makers in setting tax rates (formulae they did not particularly welcome),(23) there is no convincing analysis for either the break points or the steepness of the progressive rates. Once the anchor of minimal sacrifice is raised, the ship quickly begins to flounder.

A further point concerns the values to be considered. True utilitarians of the mold of Cohen-Stuart, Edgeworth, and Carver are absolutely ingenious in their efforts to relate all values to utilitarianism, variously defined to include individual, community, past, present, and future well-being, and in Edgeworth's terms (quoted above), "other utilitarian considerations." But there is more than utility when it comes to taxation, and one of the great problems with the minimal sacrifice prescription applied in its true form is that for classical liberals, weaned on Adam Smith and J. S. Mill, the idea of taxing only a few, and taxing them to a point of equality, overrides any consideration of meritorious reward or concern for the idea that it is unjust for the few to bear alone the burden of a government that provides some measure of common benefit. In other words it seems reasonable to question what these utilitarian tax theorists never doubted--that the appeal of their theories could be related to a single, truly universal value.

The final difficulty with the minimal sacrifice

theory, and all other utilitarian-based efforts, is the common critique that a steeply progressive tax may minimize the loss of short-term individual utility, but that it will undoubtedly have an effect on work effort and production, which will presumably affect future well-being. If we agree with Carver that these two elements must be summed, minimal sacrifice, taking efficiency into consideration, now either requires measurement or becomes indeterminate because the minimal assumption of declining marginal utility loses a great deal of its intuitive appeal. What is at issue is our fundamental knowledge of the utility function.

It is at this point that the common attacks on utility as a nonempirical, nonquantifiable, and inherently vague concept are appropriate. Without some measure of the trade-off between the evils Carver describes, utility theories provide absolutely no guide to an appropriate tax rate--reggressive, constant, or progressive rates with endless combinations and kinks are all reasonably possible. As we will see below, this problem is not solved, although it is being directly addressed for the first time by the optimal tax theorists.

The second classical tax theory to be discussed is the faculty theory, associated in modern times with E. R. Seligman.(24) Actually, as Seligman himself documents, the faculty theory predates utilitarian theories. It follows utilitarian theories in this presentation because Seligman's important modification is premised in part on the failure of sacrifice theories. As Seligman reports, the concept of faculty or ability, which was first associated with property, was employed in England and France and was the basic concept in the tax laws of the American colonies. As the theory developed, particularly in America, there was a gradual shift from an emphasis on property to an emphasis on income. A significant intellectual boost and a decisive prescription was established in a famous maxim by Adam Smith that "the subjects of every state ought to contribute . . . as nearly as possible in proportion to their respective abilities, that is in proportion to the revenues that they respectively enjoy under protection of the state."(25)

Up to this point "ability" was uncomplicated by the philosopher; it meant simply property or income, which was taxed at a flat rate. As Seligman notes, this was changed when the idea was accepted that only that part of income above a minimum existence level should be subject to taxation. With this change ability shifted from being solely a measure of production to include consumption as a factor. And with this entering wedge (Seligman's phrase), tax theory quickly shifted to the idea of sacrifice and all that was to entail.

Seligman's contribution was first to call attention to the distinction in faculty theory between these consumption and production components, but most importantly to associate the productive element with the power to produce. His basic proposition was

> that the possession of large fortunes or large incomes in itself affords the possessor a decided advantage in augmenting his possession. The facility of increasing production often grows in more than arithmetical proportion. A rich man may be said to be subject in some sense to the law of increasing returns. The more he has the easier it is for him to acquire still more.(26)

From this Seligman cautiously endorsed progressivity based on the logic that the consumptive side of faculty was indeterminant but that "the productive element of taxable capacity would not illogically result in a more than proportional rate of taxation."(27)

He admitted that this principle led to an indefinite rate of progression (an argument he had used against sacrifice theories), but then made the interesting qualification that, "An uncertain rate, if it be in the general direction of justice, may nevertheless be preferable to a rate which, like that of proportion, may be more certain without being so equitable."(28)

Playing the advantage he acquired through this statement, he went on to suggest that in fact a "digressive rate of progression" (progression at a decreasing rate) that ended significantly below 100% would be desirable--thus cutting off a basic criticism of minimal sacrifice theory.

There is clearly something appealing in this theory of progressive taxation. That wealth creates a disproportionate degree of market power is an idea that appeals to common sense and has been often used as a way to attack the fairness of the market. However, as a prescriptive theory that taxes should therefore be levied progressively, it suffers several flaws. First it is apparent that Seligman has replaced the nebulous concept of utility with a concept that is equally difficult to identify and measure. As I argued in the last section of this chapter, that this leads to a theory that is relatively unrobust does not concern me as much as it does other critics such as Blum and Kalven.(29) On the other hand the basic condition he proposes is an empirical statement, and it matters greatly for the specific prescription he offers whether power does actually increase in more than arithmetical proportion. Does it? Who is to say? More importantly, how would one even set out to determine if it does?

While the nonempiricist may shrug off this criticism as rigid positivism, there is a further problem: Why should we favor a result that consciously curtails productive power? One answer might be that productive power is not valued. It is not only utilitarians who would object to this notion. Indeed, other things being equal, few would support such a supposition. But this is a clear result of the Seligman theory.

The rationalization that must be given is that market power should be made more equal either because the added increment that accrues to the well-off is unearned (the distinction between natural and acquired power), or because the equalization of market power is to be valued regardless of how it is achieved. The former argument requires even more refined proof than the basic proposition (Blum and Kalven's comments are particularly relevant here, see note 29), whereas the latter argument requires significant elaboration in that it flies directly in the face of a concern for merit and just deserts. Thus at best the faculty theory must be judged in terms of a series of complex value trade-offs--trade-offs that are ignored in the effort to establish a firm principle of progressivity.

In reading these various theories one is struck by theorists' abilities to arrive by different routes at a similar conclusion concerning the ideal income tax. And that conclusion is a low-income subsistence exemption, followed by progressive rates that become a flat rate at some level. One can speculate that they arrived at this common conclusion either because tax systems were already developing along these lines, or perhaps because it is what a less rigorous, more practical, and more intuitive analysis would discern. Following this latter tack, one might argue that it is not only costly but somewhat repugnant to extract taxes that jeopardize subsistence. Similarly, it is efficient (in terms of total revenue) as well as intuitively fair to tax those above subsistence in relation to their means, but detrimental to incentives and begging for resistance if this progressivity is carried to an extreme. This is more the reasoning of the politician than the philosopher, but it is a fact that all countries that have an income tax have adopted some variant of this rate formula.

In reading these theories one gets the feeling that the deductive method is distorted, beginning with an agreed conclusion and working back to premises. Whether this speculation is accurate or not, the influence of these theories on the creation of income taxes is probably of some significance, although the path of such influence is impossible to trace. However, by the

1930s tax theory and debate had significantly changed, and prescriptive theories of taxation based on grand principles were forgotten. The argument turns rather to a more pragmatic problem of defining the income base, and the debate over equality becomes concerned primarily with horizontal equity, or the dictum that equals be treated equally.

Simons and the Comprehensive Tax Base Theory

Henry Simons's Personal Income Taxation, written in 1938, altered not only the substantive issues in taxation, but also the method of reasoning that had been dominant for the prior 70 years. In terms of both substance and approach, Simons provided the framework for the major tax debates since that time. No other work in public finance has had such impact on the policy agenda.(30) For Simons the task was not to create a deductive principle of taxation that would lead to prescriptive formulae like those proposed by utilitarian or faculty theorists, but rather to determine the appropriate basis for taxation in general. In accordance with the pragmatism that had become dominant in American universities at this time, he scornfully dismissed these prior theories:

> Whereas the question is as to how taxes should be allocated with respect to income, consumption, or net worth, the answer is that they should be proportional to ability or faculty, which cannot be conceived quantitatively or defined in terms of any procedure of measurement. Such an answer indicates that the writer prefers the kind of taxation which he prefers; that he is unwilling to reveal his tastes or examine them critically; and that he finds useful in his profession a basic 'principle' from which, as from a conjurer's hat, anything may be drawn at will.(31)

Again in the best traditions of pragmatism, Simons believed that the problem with taxation, as with other policies, "is that of weighing one set of effects against the other."(32) While Simons favored progressivity, the argument was made by proclamation as a simple personal belief based "on the ethical or aesthetic judgment that the prevailing distribution of wealth and income reveals a degree (and/or kind) of inequality which is distnctly evil or unlovely."(33) Simons did devote several paragraphs to a renunciation of the just deserts principle as it applied to market outcomes, but essentially he felt that the discussion of vertical equity in taxation could go no further than this simple expression of faith and belief. He turned rather to the task of defining the appropriate basis for taxation and then to analyzing specific tax provisions that had become, and remain, highly divisive political issues. Thus, although Simons offers a theory of sorts, it is certainly of a different class than that of his distinguished predecessors.

The accretion definition of income that is jointly associated with his name and that of Robert Haig was based on the notion of market power or rights. In Simons's words, "personal income may be defined as the algebraic sum of (1) the market value of rights exercised in consumption and (2) the change in the value of the store of property rights between the beginning and end of the period in question."(34) This definition is very broad, and in contrast to the leading competing theory of the time, Fisher's consumption theory, it fully included earnings and growth or loss of savings and investments, whether they be personal or corporate, distributed or undistributed. He also emphasized the inclusion of income-in-kind (including imputed rent of owner-occupied dwellings), tax-exempt security interest, charitable contributions, and earnings on life insurance. Simons considered these and other exemptions and exclusions as special privileges that destroyed horizontal and vertical equity.(35)

There has been some misunderstanding over the objectivity of Simons's famous accretion definition of income. Some commentators have implied that the argument defining this base is neutral in that once the base is established, the question of progressivity can be resolved by political consensus.(36) Simons was well aware that this was not so. By including certain forms of income, he knew very well that the result would directly affect progressivity. Given the vehement tax battles in Congress in the years immediately preceding his book,(37) he would never have been able to get away with a claim of objectivity in the standard. Rather the appeal he made was based on his simple desire for redistribution and on the argument that excluding many forms of income from taxation violated horizontal equity. The theory must stand or fall on this basis and not on concocted arguments of political neutrality.

As to why income should be redistributed through progressive taxation, Simons says very little beyond stating that inequality is "distinctly evil or unlovely." That phrase is interesting in that, unlike the rigorous logical and economic arguments related to specific provisions that he presents later, it seems to suggest that the case for general vertical equity cannot be made using these "rational" methods of evaluation. Rather, much more in the tradition of Hume, equality should be preferred because of the sentiment and passion evoked by conditions of inequality. Simons thus offers really little more than an assumption that progressivity is desirable. His treatment of this question implies either that debates over equality must end in unassailable confessions of belief, or possibly that progressivity in taxation is to be accepted as a mere fact of life. In either event prolonged rational arguments would be a waste of time. Thus we are left with little to evaluate in terms of considerations of vertical equity--exactly, I suspect, as Professor Simons planned.

Simons's theory, however, cannot evade the issue of horizontal equity, which he, and later numerous advocates, put forward as its major strength. The value to which this appeals is an ancient and rudimentary principle that we can reasonably expect to be widely accepted. Thus Simons's standard for taxation, while admittedly a partial standard, would be extremely powerful if it fulfilled its promise as a basis for establishing equal treatment in taxation.

However, it does not provide an adequate standard for horizontal equity unless a very narrow view of the tax system is adopted--a view to which Simons himself did not subscribe. Horizontal equity must appeal not only to market rights or power, but to equity as overall economic well-being. Simons's pragmatism leads him to discuss taxation in terms of effects, but to be at all ethically appealing this must mean ultimate economic effects and not simply an accountant's measurement of consumption and changes in wealth. The difficulty with this expanded conception of what is fair between individuals is that not only market power, but also varying needs must be taken into consideration. The issue ultimately is what counts as being in a similar, or different, economic situation; who in fact are equals from the point of view of tax policy and who are not. To put this in the extreme, it simply does not strike one as fair to suggest that horizontal equity is achieved by taxing equally a young healthy, educated, single individual, and a perhaps disabled widow with several children, no job, and large medical bills, even if by some fortuitous event their incomes turn out to be the same.

Tax policy has always taken such conditions into effect, and it is more than a symptom of special privilege. While Simons remained uncompromising, more contemporary supporters of the comprehensive tax base have allowed exceptions to the original definition based on the need argument. For example, at one point in a defense of the exclusion of insurance payments and disaster losses from the comprehensive tax base, Musgrave argued that "The purpose is not to exclude specific income sources but to allow for situations where taxpayers with equal incomes and family size have strikingly different needs. . . . By allowing for disaster situations, the equity goal, far from being offended, can be achieved more fully."(38) Similarly, Joseph Pechman and Harvey Brazer readily admit that exceptions to the Haig-Simons definition are allowed and required. In fact, Pechman and Musgrave chide Boris Bittker, a critic of the comprehensive tax base approach, for claiming the definition admits no exceptions.(39)

A potential answer to the problem of incorporating need considerations in the tax system is to reason, with Stanley Surrey, that these considerations can best be met by government subsidy programs, thus maintaining the purity of the comprehensive tax base.(40) This is a logical possibility, but it faces monumental political problems. If, as I have argued, horizontal equity implies a consideration of economic well-being, not just market rights, the link between the tax system and countervailing subsidies would have to be assured and made very explicit. Politicians, accustomed to providing particularistic benefits,(41) will eagerly promote need arguments and will be wary of subsidies separated in time and procedure from decisions that remove existing benefits. In addition, for those who suggest that taxation should aid in the promotion of income redistribution (including both Simons and Surrey), there is a narrow logical thread that must be maintained, separating need from a justification for progression. This is a difficult path to follow, and it may be only by Simons's vague admonition that "inequality is unlovely" that such a position can be maintained.

Historically, what has happened is that the number of deductions, exclusions, exemptions, and special treatment categories has expanded dramatically. Part of this expansion is unrelated to need as the tax code is conceived more and more as a versatile policy tool that can be used to induce desirable forms of economic behavior. However, provisions promoted on the basis of special needs still make up the majority of what Surrey terms "tax expenditure" items. Because Simons's theory provides no clue to what would be a relevant need concern, different comprehensive tax bases have been proposed in recent years in what can only be described as an ad hoc approach based on political judgements concerning specific provisions. Once Simons's rigid line is relaxed, the comprehensive tax base crumbles as increasing numbers of special circumstances are brought forward for unequal treatment.

Without some theory or prescription of need, what is not that robust a theory in the first place dissolves into little more than a series of detailed arguments over specific income tax provisions. What we have then is a nonargument for progressivity, a certainly questionable standard for horizontal equity, but an excellent agenda for pragmatic tax debate. Simons's immense contribution can be measured by the fact that in the United States and many other countries, income tax debates are still influenced by the definition of income he proposed, and deal with many of the arguments he advanced on specific provisions. What is striking, perhaps, is how often he is referred to, and how little the arguments seem to have advanced in the last 40 years.

Optimal Tax Theory

The recent research efforts that fall under the general rubric of optimal tax theory have the potential of combining the rigorous deductive prescriptions of classical income tax theories with value trade-offs that are the mark of pragmatic analysis. In so doing, optimal tax theory resurrects the utilitarian method of analysis, but in a much more complex manner. Because this research is so new (the first important paper was written in 1971), and because it is expanding in so many directions, I will attempt only to outline the general methods being applied. The limitations that I note must be viewed with the adolescent nature of the field in mind. In the brief description of the various approaches and uses of optimal tax theory below, I have focused on a few of the most widely cited papers. The discussion will be aimed more at explaining the methods of the author than the specific conclusions they reach about the proper rates and levels of taxation. This is appropriate because specific conclusions at this stage are really of little importance in that the string of assumptions that are made are so elaborate that none of the authors suggest immediate policy relevance.

Optimal tax theory begins where classical tax theory left off. The classical theory is expressed, following Atkinson, as

$$W = U_n [Z(n) - T(n)] f(n) dn$$

where individuals of type n are differentiated by their earnings ability. Both before-tax earnings ability, Z(n), and the taxes paid, T(n), are conceived as functions of ability. f(n) is a function representing the frequency distribution of people of type n, and W is the sum of individual utilities after taxes.(42) The object of the Edgeworth minimum sacrifice theory was, given a total tax to be raised, to choose a function T(n) to maximize W. The answer (described previously) is that the wealthiest are taxed until ultimately all incomes are equalized. As argued above, the two major criticisms of this theory were the drastic nature of the solution and the problem of calculating overall utility, including possible disincentives of taxation. Optimal tax theories try to correct each of these problems.

The first effort was that of Mirrlees, who introduced one type of disincentive, that taxation can effect the choice for leisure over work, but that leisure also has a utility value. The general utility function is

$$W = \int_0^\infty U\,[x(n),\ y(n)]\ f(n)dn$$

where y(n) is the proportion of each day spent at work for individual of type n, and where x(n) is after-tax income, or

$$x(n) = z(n) - T[z(n)]\ .$$

Before tax income, z(n) is a direct function of n (n being thought of as a wage rate per unit time for each type of ability) and y(n); thus,

$$z(n) - n\ y(n).$$

Mirrlees found it impossible to arrive at any very clear conclusions about the general properties of T(n) because "The optimum tax schedule depends upon the distribution of skills within the population . . . in such a complicated way that it is not possible to say in general whether marginal tax rates should be higher for high-income, low-income, or intermediate income groups."(43) He was able to come to definite conclusions only if he made a number of simplifying assumptions about the shape of f(n) and U(n). The utility function he explored in detail is the classical log function expanded to include both income and leisure, the importance of each to be weighted through the use of a parameter. Using this special case represented as $U = \log_e [x^a (1 - y)]$, and assuming a lognormal function for f(n), he was able to work through some numerical examples, calculating T[z(n)] to maximize total utility W for several values of a.

Mirrlees readily admitted that the results are very sensitive to these assumptions, and he used the term "heroic" to describe the rate at which leisure replaces work as tax rates are changed. While this is certainly so, he accomplished two things that eluded classical theorists: (1) He introduced one element of lost efficiency due to taxation, that is, the disincentive to work, and (2) he expressed the utility formulation with reference to variables susceptible to measurement: wage levels and hours worked. Although the ultimate shape of the individual utility curve remains a question when conceived in these terms, empirical research may help clarify its basic nature.(44) In the meantime simulations can be generated by varying the assumed functional relationship and the value for a.

Subsequent authors have added considerably to this general model. Fair added the proposition that earnings are a function of both ability and education, and incorporated education in his model.(45) He also built in a guaranteed minimum income and thus allowed for negative tax rates. Since his effort was aimed at finding an optimal income distribution, he made very restricted assumptions concerning the tax rate. However, adding education brought into play another potential source of empirical information (although he used a rather crude approximation in his analysis).

Other complexities have also been added to the general model. Atkinson, creating a model restricted to consideration of a flat tax rate, also incorporated the notion of education affecting earnings, but did so in the context of maximizing lifetime income.(46) His model, which he admitted is very simple, assumes that working hours are constant and that the critical choice that people make will be their level of education--a choice dependent on one's ability and on expected tax rates. Following a "suggestion" by Becker, he assumed (simply) that $z(n,E) = nE^2$, where n is the wage rate index of ability as before, and E is the years of education. To this he adds an assumption concerning the distribution of abilities (a Pareto distribution) and a revenue constraint of zero net revenue (assuming the only function of taxation is redistribution). This is obviously a very specialized model, but it gives the reader an idea of how optimal tax theory can expand in a number of different directions.

In an article in 1973, Feldstein added three further ideas.(47) First he attacked the assumption that wage rates are considered constant as tax rates vary (the n in the previous models). Second he rejected the notion that the revenue constraint should be zero, incorporating rather a lump-sum government subsidy that enters the utility function. And third he considered, for the first time, the impact on optimal tax rates of different assumptions concerning capital accumulation. Based again on very simple labor and capital supply models, he determined that fixed or variable wage rates have surprisingly little effect on optimal tax rates, but that elasticity of substitution between labor and leisure, the size of a fixed government revenue demand (apart from that used for redistribution), and the effect of taxes on capital accumulation, all significantly alter the optimal tax solutions.

Before commenting on these developments in modern tax theory, one further idea attributable to A. B. Atkinson is very important. In an early paper on equality, Atkinson stated that the social welfare function might be generalized as

$$W = (\Sigma U_i^p)^{\frac{1}{p}}$$

where W is social welfare and p is a parameter that represents the egalitarian preference of society. This is a transformation of the original utilitarian calculation, in that for $p < 1$, higher weights are given to the increments of those with less utility. The classical utilitarian model, $W = \Sigma U_i$, is achieved when $p = 1$, while for $p = -\infty$, social welfare depends only on the utility of the worst-off in society.(48) Atkinson revived this idea in reviewing the work of Mirrlees to demonstrate that Mirrlees's results were very sensitive not only to the work/leisure trade-off, but also to his selection of the classical utility model, or the equivalent of $p = 1$. He concluded that as p decreased, "the marginal utility of income diminishes more rapidly and the 'cost' of inequality (in terms of the loss of aggregate utility) increases."(49)

This idea represents both something new and something old. By weighting individuals differently, Atkinson really is merely varying the utility function in a different way. Thus the statement quoted above is not at all new, but merely a restatement of what Cohen-Stuart and Edgeworth discovered 70 years earlier. In other words Atkinson re-established that tax rates are very sensitive to assumptions concerning utility functions. And to the extent that the utility function is indeterminant, optimal tax theory is subject to the same type of criticisms as classical utilitarian theories.

However, Atkinson's formulation introduces several interesting possibilities. In the first place, by precisely specifying a parameter representing equality, various ranges of solutions can be generated and models can be compared for roughly equivalent notions of intended equality. This type of exercise, used in the cited articles by Atkinson (1973), Feldstein, and Rosen, could prove to be a useful policy-making tool. If credible models could be developed, decision makers could select the value of equality desired, and the models would then crank out the appropriate tax rates. Stating this possibility in this way introduces the second idea in that by allowing for a weighting parameter, p, the welfare function is transformed from a mere counting operation, in which each individual's utility is counted equally, to a political or social calculus for arriving at p.

Atkinson also took the next step, and reformulating an earlier proposal of Musgrave, suggested that this same calculation can be done simply using income, thus placing a social value on different incomes dependent on "the degree of aversion to inequality in society."(50) This idea would shake classical utilitarians like Jeremy Bentham and James Mill, who found the strength and revolutionary appeal of utilitarianism in considering equally the happiness of all (their concern being the disproportionate weighting for the aristocracy). However, it would avoid the subjectivism of the utilitarian notion, and although it seems very possible that a different realm of subjectivism may be introduced (how after all do we set P?), it is not a totally unreasonable possibility given that the modern state appears to have much more responsibility for such things as equality than in the nineteenth century.

It is difficult to evaluate optimal tax theory at this early date, but several comments are in order. First, while one of the obvious strengths of optimal tax theory is the effort to merge concerns for equity and efficiency, several prominent tax experts, including Feldstein and Musgrave, who are sympathetic to the cause, have noted the complete disregard for considerations of horizontal equity. Using different approaches they have demonstrated that in certain, not unlikely circumstances, optimal tax solutions directly violate reasonable definitions of this not always clear concept.(51)

Another problem which even this brief review makes apparent is that optimal tax theory already exhibits overwhelming complexity. The mathematical models employed require numerous assumptions and produce complicated arrays of conditional alternatives. At the simplest level this makes it difficult even to understand when different prescriptions should apply. If one wishes to go further and make judgements concerning the certainty of the various conclusions, substantial knowledge of mathematics, economics, and statistics is required. Optimal tax theory cannot yet claim the relatively simple translation into logical prinicples that classical theories and the comprehensive tax base approach offered those unschooled in these advanced arts--politicians being not the least important in this category. Furthermore, if the history to date is any indication, the theory will become more, not less complex, as additions and adjustments to the models are added.

A third possible limitation of optimal tax theories

is that they lack robustness in that they apply to a very restrictive set of conditions and produce a wide choice of alternative sets. Currently both of these problems are obviously present, although the restrictive modeling is more troublesome to me than the ranges of alternatives produced. In fact, if optimal tax theory is viewed as a combination of prescription and pragmatism, providing ranges of solutions given various assumptions, this diversity may be considered an advantage.

The restrictiveness of the models is another matter. As of this writing, there is no question, and little debate, that the models used are too specialized and simple to provide estimates that could be used as specific policy recommendations.(52) However, at this stage of research this may not be critical, because more general models might not yield results specific enough to guide further research.(53) If there is one conclusion that has emerged so far, it is that the tax rates derived are extremely sensitive to assumptions concerning the elasticity of substitution of labor for leisure, capital accumulation, and so on. These conclusions emerge from relatively narrow models and serve to focus attention on areas in which empirical research is needed. Thus while the lack of robustness is detrimental in the policy sense, it may be less harmful if the objective is to establish a future research agenda.

The general conclusion that optimal tax rates are very sensitive to critical conditional assumptions implies a further and potentially fatal flaw--one largely responsible for the destruction of classical tax theory. The modeling assumptions that define both the environment (for example, revenue demands, or assumptions concerning capital stocks) and economic behavior (for example, the utility of work and leisure, or the income value of education) are empirical in nature, and at some point, if the models are to be taken seriously as a guide for policy, they must be more than assumptions: There has to be some hard evidence as a basis. Unfortunately, there are many indications that modeling labor and capital supply behavior is very difficult and dependent on complicated sets of factors about which little is known. There is also no guarantee that whatever empirical relationships that are established will not be temporary--dependent on the tastes and social and economic environments at a given point in time. Thus while the prospect and advances of optimal tax theory are exciting, and the work to date is certainly imaginative and offers several clear paths for future research, to promote it as the future salvation of tax policy requires a great deal of faith.

CONCLUSION AND SOME ALTERNATIVE APPROACHES TO INCOME EQUALITY

For all the talk of principles in taxation, when the subject is analyzed carefully there really are none that provide a rigorous guide for equity. Arguments for principles of vertical equity have never been fully accepted, and the basic flaws seem impervious to conclusive resolution. Empirically, the trade-off between equity and efficiency, be it through work disincentives, misallocation of labor, or reduced investments, is very difficult to assess. While optimal tax theorists are again working on this problem, to date they have merely reaffirmed the complexities involved. Prescribing a proper utility function is also ultimately an empirical problem that would seem to defy rigorous analysis. Further, optimal tax theory has in this regard reinforced the arguments of Edgeworth to the conclusion that how this assumption is made makes all the difference. Even if these perplexing empirical problems could be overcome, there still remains the problem of aggregating values. It strikes me as wholly unreasonable to believe that a set of principles could ever be devised to determine adequately how equality, efficiency, and just deserts should be sorted out. For this reason optimal tax theorists have had the foresight to offer ranges of solutions, which I have suggested could lead to an effort to build policy tools, not principles.

The problems of establishing a principle of horizontal equity, or the equal treatment of equals, are also significant. As I argued in reviewing the comprehensive tax base theory, this seemingly simple principle is greatly complicated in practice by desires to treat different types of income differently (for example, earned and unearned), and most importantly by the problem of specifying an adequate theory of need. To do so in any comprehensive sense would undoubtedly lead to utilitarian-like calculations, with all their inherent drawbacks. In practice what happens is that the comprehensive tax base is riddled by exceptional cases because no line can be drawn between legitimate and illegitimate claims for special treatment.

Thus it would appear that income taxation cannot be reduced to rigorous principles of equity, and that if the case for equality is to be made, it must be made prior to and apart from the tax system. If this is correct, the issue of equality will depend on other factors, on other theoretical and practical approaches.

Although no attempt has been made to extend the argument to cover more general efforts to derive convincing deductive theories of equality, it would seem that the obstacles that arise in the specific context of taxation will also affect general theories of equality. The Rawls maxi-min principle exemplifies the problem. Rawls's method in posing what reasonable individuals would decide in a prior position of ignorance ingeniously gets around the difficulties of detailed assumptions concerning utility, income, and value trade-offs. In so doing, he is able to take advantage of the general assumption that individuals act primarily in their own self-interest, but he avoids all the complicated baggage of utilitarianism. However, granting the genius of this device, it has never been clear to me that the supposition that these blind commoners appointed such a Platonic task will arrive at a maxi-min solution is any less metaphysical in its derivation than the problems of rigorously establishing utility functions. However, more importantly, as pointed out earlier, Rawls's prescription is extremely unrobust (which may explain its appeal), and it is fair to ask how a more robust principle of equality could possibly be established without considering the elaborate utilitarian and efficiency calculations that arise and cause such problems in tax philosophy. The parallel in the history of income taxation is the fact that there is almost universal agreement on a low-income exemption, but great disagreement on what should be done beyond that point. It is for this reason that tax theories require complex arguments, and it is unclear how efforts to establish rigorous general principles can avoid this complexity.

If for the moment the reader indulges the conclusion that more than logical cunning is required to establish the case for equality, the issue (at least for those interested in promoting greater equality) becomes one of determining what type of theories and/or what practical approaches should be pursued. Several issues raised in the preceding sections are relevant to this question. One approach to the problem of equality is inherent in that nagging conclusion of Simons that income distribution is a matter of aesthetics. I interpret this to mean that the level of equality has and will be determined by appealing to conscience religious precepts, empathy, a sense of community, or other primarily emotional impulses.

The famous argument by R. H. Tawney is reminiscent of this form of appeal:

> What is repulsive is not that one man should earn more than others, for where community of environment, and common education and a habit of life have bred a common tradition of respect and consideration, these details of the countinghouse are forgotten or ignored. It is that some classes should be excluded from the heritage of

> civilization which others enjoy, and that the fact of human fellowship, which is ultimate and profound, should be obscured by economic contrasts, which are trivial and superficial.(54)

Why should some classes not be so excluded? Answers could consider any of a number of consequences: long-term disutilities, distorted systems of reward, and so on. Or one might respond with Simons that "the prospect is simply unlovely." This is not a response of the head, but of the heart. It is a response that implies that scientific reasoning applies elsewhere. Thoughts about equality can be considered essentially beliefs that are generated and transmitted by ideology, religion, and the major social and economic institutions of society. While logical deduction and empirical analysis of consequences may have an impact on detailed pragmatic decisions on narrow issues, they will not have a guiding influence, or even establish limits as to the approximate degree of equality that should be achieved. Those interested in promoting equality would do better to turn to an analysis of the meritocratic systems that guide our education, work, and play. If the norms generated in these structures are not changed, an army of optimal tax theorists will make little difference.

A final problem in establishing an ethic of equality and a direction for future theory lies in the idea promoted by Musgrave and Atkinson that the state should be involved in establishing welfare criteria. For the welfare economist the assumption that the state should perform such a role is commonplace. However, I see this as an heroic assumption in that what is necessary is a much more positive role for the state than I would argue is currently practiced in the United States. On the one hand it is obvious that the laissez-faire role of the state has been abrogated, if it ever existed. While it still can be argued that the state is subservient to the private sector at least in the United States, it has regulated the activities of business in many areas, and increasingly has taken responsibility for insuring investment and capital formation. At the same time the state has made significant efforts to ameliorate the harshest outcomes of the market for those near the bottom of the income distribution. However, concern for equality extends beyond the bottom of the income distribution, and this concern leads to two aspects of the modern state that are persistent remnants of the classical liberal tradition and provide major obstacles to greater income equality.

The first is the right to property and the right to

accumulate the rewards derived from property ownership. This right, protected by layers of legal armor, has meant historical transfer of the original sanctity of private lands, farms, and small business to modern corporations.(55) In the United States it has also meant a nearly absolute ban on government ownership of productive enterprises. Further, as analysis of tax incidence emphasizes, it is the right to rewards from property ownership that most directly affects equality. While some of the most flamboyant political speeches and mountains of expert analysis have attempted to distinguish earned and unearned income and to treat them separately, the net result in the United States has been, if anything, to treat unearned income preferentially. This income, which accrues primarily to the wealthy, is so amenable to shelter that a minimum tax (10%) was added for a range of so-called preference items to insure that at least some tax is paid. The special treatment of capital gains (60% excluded) is of course the major privilege for unearned income in terms of total revenue.

The second remanant of classical liberalism is that in general the state should not take responsibility for altering the natural rewards of institutional competition and market outcomes. This does not mean that the state does not interfere with the market; it does so in numerous ways and must be considered a permanent actor in most industries. However, it has not as yet made any significant effort to structure or control systems of advancement or reward other than through some recent compensatory actions for minorities, which I would add have been met by fierce opposition from diversified interests, including some traditionally liberal groups. The implications of this for efforts to redistribute income are fairly obvious. Although exceptional cases (the aged, blind, handicapped, etc.) may serve as the basis for special pleading, a principle of just deserts becomes the rule.(56)

The purpose of this brief exercise is to reinforce the idea of Atkinson and Musgrave that inequality is ultimately a matter for state intervention and that appropriate tax policy will follow from that action. However, I am not at all certain that the assumption of a redistributive state is as obvious as they imply. While more positive theories are available,(57) they are far from accepted in this country. Without such a positive theory, the combination of beliefs supporting meritocracy and differential rewards and the acceptance that the state should not overrule institutional and market outcomes will insure the degree of income inequality that has sustained itself throughout this century.

NOTES

1. I considered using the word "incremental" in conjunction with pragmatic, but rejected the idea because of the confusing problem of defining the degrees of change. Also, while the concepts are clearly somewhat related, pragmatism is a term historically associated with philosophy and evaluation, while incrementalism defines a process of reaching decisions.

2. George F. Break and Joseph A. Pechman, Federal Tax Reform (Washington, DC: The Brookings Institution, 1975).

3. Harold Groves, "Toward a Theory of Taxation," National Tax Journal 27 (1956), p. 31. For a more complete treatment of tax philosophy, which is liberally sprinkled with pragmatic conclusions, see his Tax Philosophers (Madison: The University of Wisconsin Press, 1970).

4. For an interesting discussion of criteria applicable to policy evaluation see Brian Barry and Douglas W. Rae, "Political Evaluation," in Fred I. Greenstein and Nelson W. Polsby (eds.), Handbook of Political Science, Vol. 1 (Reading, MA: Addison-Wesley, 1975), pp. 337-401.

5. For the applicability of the pragmatic approach to tax policy see Charles E. Lindblom, "Decision Making in Taxation and Expenditure," Public Finances: Needs, Sources and Utilization (Princeton: National Bureau of Economic Resources, 1960); and John F. Manley, The Politics of Finance (Boston: Little Brown, 1970).

6. Manley puts it as follows: "Tax law, infinitely complex, is infinitely reducible small decisions that affect a few people, as the trade issue used to be. . . . with no widely accepted philosophy to guide them in responding to special requests, the committee members respond in the same way that the committee did on trade legislation: positively." Manley, ibid, p. 326.

7. See Charles E. Lindblom, "The Science of Muddling Through," Public Administration Review 19 (Spring, 1959), pp. 79-88; and David Braybrooke and Charles E. Lindblom, A Strategy of Decision (New York: Free Press, 1962).

8. Groves, Tax Philosophers, pp. 149-150.

9. See Douglas W. Rae, "The Limits of Consensual Decision," The American Political Science Review LXIX (December, 1975), pp. 1270-1295, for an interesting commentary on the importance and problem of including the status quo as a relevant policy alternative.

10. See Benjamin I. Page, "Taxes and Inequality: Do Voters Get What They Want?" (Madison: Institute of Research on Poverty, #423-77, 1977).

11. This should not be confused with Douglas Rae's use of the term "robust" in relation to authority structures, although I profited from his conceptualization. See Rae, op cit, pp. 1279-1280.

12. John Rawls, A Theory of Justice (Cambridge, Ma: Harvard University Press, 1971).

13. E. R. A. Seligman, Progressive Taxation in Theory and Practice (Baltimore, Guggenheimer, Weil, 1894), pp. 79-126; Henry Simons, Personal Income Taxation (Chicago: The University of Chicago Press, 1938), pp. 3-5; and Walter J. Blum and Harry Kalven, Jr., The Uneasy Case for Progressive Taxation (Chicago: The University of Chicago Press, 1952), pp. 35-39, 100-103.

14. Arnold Jacob Cohen-Stuart, A Contribution to the Theory of the Progressive Income Tax, 1889 (Manuscript translated, Te Velde, University of Chicago Libraries, 1936), pp. 53-60.

15. See, for example, J. R. McCulloch, Taxation and the Funding System (London: Longman, Brown, Green and Longmans, 1845). J. S. Mill, Sidgewick and other utilitarians also promoted proportional tax schemes of one sort or another.

16. F. Y. Edgeworth, "Minimum Sacrifice Versus Equal Sacrifice," in his Papers Relating to Political Economy (London: Macmillan, 1925), pp. 239-240.

17. Ibid, p. 240.

18. In this I disagree with the totally unexplained conclusion of Blum and Kalven that "In either case the difficulties of isolating and measuring particular benefits are for the most part insurmountable. If, as a result, resort is had to some general assumption about the distribution of the highly diffuse benefits of government, the most plausible one is that all citizens benefit approximately alike." (My emphasis). Blum and Kalven, op cit, p. 39.

19. Ibid, p. 63. The general discussion of this problem is on pp. 60-63.

20. F. Y. Edgeworth, "The Pure Theory of Taxation," in his Papers Relating to Political Economy, op cit, p. 110.

21. Ibid, p. 112.

22. T. N. Carver, "The Ethical Basis of Distribution and Its Application to Taxation," Annals of the American Academy of Political and Social Sciences 6 (July, 1895), p. 95.

23. For a classic example of such a confrontation see Edgeworth's article, "Formulae for Graduating Taxation," in his Papers Relating to Political Economy, pp. 260-270.

24. The discussion to follow is based on Seligman's, Progressive Taxation in Theory and Practice, op cit, 127-200.

25. Adam Smith, The Wealth of Nations, Book V, Chapter 2, Part 2. Smith unfortunately creates considerable ambiguity a few pages later by stating: "It is not very unreasonable that the rich should contribute to the public expense, not only in proportion to their revenue, but something more in proportion." Whether he actually endorsed proportional or progressive taxation was intensely debated by nineteenth century tax theorists.
26. Seligman, op cit, p. 191.
27. Ibid, p. 192.
28. Ibid, p. 194.
29. Blum and Kalven, op cit, pp. 65-67.
30. For a revealing example of Simons's continuing influence see the latest major "reform" proposal by the Treasury Department, Blueprint for Tax Reform (Washington, DC: U.S. Government Printing Office, January, 1977).
31. Henry Simons, Personal Income Taxation (Chicago: The University of Chicago Press, 1938), p. 17.
32. Ibid, p. 19.
33. Ibid.
34. Ibid, p. 50.
35. This formula extended to the inclusion of other special treatment categories as well. For example, mineral depletion allowances were a favorite target that raised Simons to his caustic best: "Legend has it that this was originally a ransom paid by Congress to a gang of prospectors, drillers and option-hawkers who rode right into the Capitol and threatened to shoot the place up if ransom was not paid. The legislation thus attained was explained to Joe Doak as a means of advancing geology." Henry Simons, Federal Tax Reform (Chicago: The University of Chicago Press, 1950), p. 96.
36. Richard A. Musgrave, "In Defense of an Income Concept," Harvard Law Review 81 (1967), p. 45.
37. The years from 1935 to 1938 produced some of the most violent tax debates in our history. The two most prominent were over Roosevelt's famous "wealth tax" of 1935, and his temporarily successful effort to tax undistributed corporate profits from 1936 to 1938. The special issues to which Simons devotes over half his book were all part of the political tax debates of the time.
38. Musgrave, "In Defense of an Income Concept," p. 56.
39. Ibid, p. 57; Harvey Brazer, "The Income Tax in the Federal Revenue System," in Richard A. Musgrave (ed.), Broad Based Taxes (Baltimore: Johns Hopkins Press, 1973), p. 7; Joseph A. Pechman, Comprehensive Income Taxation: A Comment," Harvard Law Review 81 (1967), p. 64.

40. See Stanley Surrey, *Pathways to Tax Reform* (Cambridge: Harvard University Press, 1973), and "Tax Subsidies as a Device for Implementing Government Policy: A Comparison with Direct Government Expenditures," in *Joint Economic Committee Federal Subsidy Program Papers* (Washington, DC: U.S. Government Printing Office, 1972).

41. The term belongs to David Mayhew, *Congress: The Electoral Connection* (New Haven: Yale University Press, 1974).

42. A. B. Atkinson, "How Progressive Should Income Tax Be?" in Michael Parkin and A. R. Nobay (eds.), *Essays in Modern Economics* (London: Longman, 1973), pp. 90-109.

43. J. A. Mirrlees, "An Exploration in the Theory of Optimum Income Taxation," *Review of Economic Studies* (April, 1971), p. 186.

44. An example is Harvey S. Rosen, "A Methodology for Evaluating Tax Reform Proposals," *Journal of Public Economics* 6 (1976), pp. 105-121.

45. R. C. Fair, "The Optimal Distribution of Income," *Quarterly Journal of Economics* (November, 1971), pp. 551-579.

46. Atkinson, op cit.

47. Martin Feldstein, "On the Optimal Progressivity of the Income Tax," *Journal of Public Economics* 3 (1973), pp. 56-75.

48. A. B. Atkinson, "On the Measurement of Inequality," *Journal of Economic Theory* (September, 1970), pp. 244-263.

49. Atkinson, "How Progressive Should Income Tax Be?" p. 94.

50. Ibid, p. 107. He expressed this welfare function as

$$J = H\ I(n)\ f(n)dn$$

where H(I) denotes the social valuation of income and n is the ability variable as before. The particular functional form of H that he explored was

$$H = I^{1-p}/1-p,\ p\ 0.$$

Note that $dH/dI = I^{1-p}$, so that as p increases, the marginal social value of higher incomes decreases.

51. See Martin W. Feldstein, "On the Theory of Tax Reform," *Journal of Public Economics* 6 (1976), pp. 77-104; and Richard A. Musgrave, "ET, OT and SBT," *Journal of Public Economics* 6 (1976), pp. 3-16. The same point is made by Boris Bittker, "Equity, Efficiency, and Income Tax Theory: Do Misallocations Drive Out Inequities?", *San Diego Law Review* 16 (1979), pp. 735-748.

52. For example, Atkinson concludes his article with, "The value of a model such as that discussed in this paper does not lie in the precise solutions obtained. It should indeed be obvious that the specification of the model is inadequate to provide any detailed prescriptions as to what the rate of income tax should be." Atkinson, "How Progressive Should Income Tax Be?" p. 108.

53. As Feldstein puts its, "The current paper illustrates a common dilemma in economic analysis. Examining an economic question with a more general model often yields new insights but also raises doubts about the conclusion that had been obtained by simpler models. Moreover, the greater generality of the model, the more difficult it is to obtain results that are both specific and unambiguous." Feldstein, "On the Optimal Progressivity of the Income Tax," p. 75.

54. R. H. Tawney, Equality (London, George Allen and Unwin, 1931), pp. 139-140.

55. See Robert A. Dahl, "On Removing Certain Impediments to Democracy in the United States," Political Science Quarterly 92 (Spring, 1977), pp. 1-20.

56. An interesting exercise results if we assume that taxation is an instrument of the state, and as such must conform to the role the state is thought to play in society. Following this line of reasoning the two features of state inaction described above suggest a particular type of tax system. First, if the state is neutral on rewards accruing to property or labor, the tax base would be broad, with many special provisions distinguishing earned and unearned income eliminated. There is no reason to assume, however, that the rate structure would be progessive. As a minimal requirement, taxation would not be allowed to alter the rank order that individuals have attained in the private market. Any such reordering would be considered an arbitrary infringement on individual choice and action and on the notion of just deserts, which is crucial to the workings of competitive institutions and the market system. Pushing this further can lead only to a principle of proportional taxation. If the state should not alter the rank order of individuals, why should it make an effort to alter relative distances that had been achieved before taxation? While circumstances of differential needs associated with equal incomes, and arguments that income alone is not an adequate metric of relative distance, would produce distortions in each respective principle, such arguments would be treated as exceptions requiring special pleadings. It is worthy of note that allowing what is essentially a low-income exemption, the effective tax system as a whole in the United States approximates just such a proportional rule, while the

income tax alone does not deviate that much. See Joseph A. Pechman and Benjamin A. Okner, Who Bears the Tax Burden? (Washington, DC: Brookings Institution, 1974), Chapter IV.

57. For a still interesting and relatively clear example I remind the reader of Harold J. Laski, A Grammar of Politics (London: George Allen and Unwin, 1925).

15. A Progressive Expenditure Tax Reconsidered

Robert A. Solo

Given any system of taxation that would gear itself to the ability to pay, there remains the question of how this ability should be measured. In the modern American ethos, income has been our normal mode of measurement. The higher the net income, presumably, the greater is the ability to pay: hence the progressive income tax. But one may live in luxury on great inherited wealth, while receiving no net income and paying no income tax. Under other political regimes, and today at the state and local levels in the United States, wealth, ownership, and particularly the ownership of real property have been and are taken as the clues to or measures of the ability to pay, and as the basis of taxation. Property taxes, usually proportional, could also be progressive.

There is yet another possible measure of this ability to pay, namely the sum of annual expenditures. Jones's capacity to make a contribution to the social pot could reasonably be judged to be greater because he earns more, or because he owns more, or because he spends and consumes more than Smith does. And in each case, whether on a basis of the per annum sum of incomes received, or the current value of properties owned, or the sum of annual expenditures, the tax levied could be proportional or progressive.

In 1955 Nicholas Kaldor published a book(1) urging the general adoption of a progressive expenditure tax in place of the progressive income tax, primarily on the grounds that the former would be more efficient as an "instrument for controlling the economy in the interests of economic stability and progress,"(2) on the assumption that a progressive expenditures tax would serve the purpose of limiting private consumption (which is the function of taxation) with a less depressive effect on work incentive than a progressive income tax of the same magnitude would.(3) I took strong issue with Kaldor's arguments,(4) but now I would propose a reconsideration of the progressive expenditure tax on quite different grounds: It should not replace the progressive income tax, but should be used in conjunction with it to offset certain institutionalized loopholes in the present tax system.

The first of these is the opportunity for those of great wealth to avoid all federal income taxation by holding their assets in the form of state and municipal bonds. The income on such bonds has been exempted from federal taxation on constitutional grounds, with interpretation going back to McCulloch vs. Maryland(5) in 1819, which held that neither the state nor the federal government should have the power to tax, hence to constrain or destroy the legitimate functions of the other. Those investing in such state and municipal bonds must of course sacrifice the higher earning potential of other sorts of securities. Hence the difference between state and municipal bond yields and returns from equally secure investments elsewhere constitutes a kind of tax, with revenues accruing to the state and local governments. It is a way, nevertheless, for the rich to escape progressive taxation, and a wholly irrational system for subsidizing state and local governments.

The second of these loopholes is in the tax treatment of capital gains, as described in Brian Barry's paper, an exemption that is equitable in some instances but in others opens the floodgate for evasions of the spirit and purpose of the law.

What we propose will militate against these institutionalized, legitimatized evasions of progressive taxation as well as other escapes from the ability to pay criterion. To the measure of annual income received, we would add the measure of annual consumption expenditures made; and that second test of the ability to pay would be applied only when tax obligation calculated on the income base deviated from a normative range.

Annual incomes and annual expenditures falling within (say) the upper twentieth percentile (the lower limit would be stated explicitly) would have to be fully reported (1) whenever annual consumption expenditures (including gifts as expenditures but with a system of expenditure exemptions to cover unusual needs) appeared by some normative measure to be extraordinarily high in relation to annual income, suggesting an ability to pay based on accumulated wealth or on some unreported income source, or (2) whenever the calculated income-based tax obligation, stated as a ratio of income, fell below a normative level, suggesting an evasion from tax progressivity and the spirit of the tax law. A progressive tax schedule would be applicable to annual expenditures as to annual income; and, in the aforementioned instances, the taxpayer would be obliged to pay the tax as calculated either against the income base or against the expenditure base, whichever is higher.

We are suggesting a second line of defense, a second criterion of ability to pay, to be applied in suspect cases (suspect not of cheating but of effective evasion of tax progressivity). Its application certainly has problems; nor would it eliminate all evasion. It could be a useful instrument of control nevertheless, moving actuality closer to the line of social intent. We offer it as a policy option and as an element of discourse.

REFERENCES

1. Nicholas Kaldor, An Expenditure Tax (London, Allen & Unwin, 1955).
2. Ibid, p. 14.
3. Ibid, pp. 14, 140.
4. Robert Solo, "Accumulation, Work Incentive, and the Expenditures Tax," The National Tax Journal, Vol. IX, No. 3, September 1956.
5. McCulloch vs. Maryland, 17, U.S. 316 (1819).

Part VI

THE PEDAGOGY OF VALUES

Anderson's concluding essay explores the implications of the various epistemological approaches to value judgement when the task is political education in the policy sciences.

16. Value Judgement, the Policy Sciences, and the Aims of Political Education

Charles W. Anderson

How shall we go about teaching the practical art of evaluative judgement? Any coherent philosophy of education must rest on a discipline of thought, for the aim of education is not merely to transmit inert knowledge but to set tasks and tests for the activity of the mind, to channel thought, and to give it purpose. For the policy sciences this is particularly important, since their object is not simply to teach *that,* but to teach *how.* Policy science is applied science. The goal must be in some sense to nurture ways of thinking that will presumably lead to better public decisions.

The object of education is to develop some latent power of the mind, to give it form and rigor, logic, and coherence. To achieve this some frame-work of analysis must be postulated as the path of right reason. The performances of learners are to be criticized, challenged, and perfected according to the canons of good practice that are inherent in a system of analysis. Education implies mastery of such rules of reason, and the capacity to use them with power and precision.

To adopt a paradigm of inquiry is simultaneously to commit oneself to a philosophy of education. In the contemporary social sciences the rules of scientific investigation generally structure and guide the process of education. These are the canons of reason that set the tasks, define the methods, and measure the achievements of those who would submit themselves to their discipline. Apparently, we would teach our students to think scientifically about public problems. Yet scientific investigation is not the same thing as political analysis, and the rules of scientific inquiry are not the same as the rules of political discourse. These are distinct intellectual activities. They are different realms of thought. The aim of scientific inquiry is to arrive at statements about the way things are, about the nature of the case. The aim of political discourse is to arrive at reasoned statements of commitment about desirable public purposes and the appropriate methods for achieving them. By its very nature, political analysis is simultaneously normative and practical. It has to do both with what should be done about public problems and with what can be done about them.

We should not define too narrowly the aims of a philosophy of education for the policy sciences. To confine oneself to the technical task of fitting means to designated ends would not do justice to the problem at all. What is at issue in political discourse is whether proposed public purposes and projects are to be regarded as good or bad, whether alternatives for action are to be evaluated as desirable or undesirable, whether completed programs are to be adjudged successes or failures. These are all issues of value judgement. The aim of a philosophy of education for the policy sciences is not to teach right answers to such questions, but to provide a discipline of thought that is appropriate to the activity of making such judgements.

The audience for such theory is not, in the first instance, the "community of science," nor the corps of would-be experts and advisers, but those who engage in the public debate, those who are in some sense responsible for making decisions on behalf of other people. At one level in a democracy, this includes all citizens, but especially it should be relevant to the choices of those who occupy positions of public responsibility and authority. The point and purpose of such a discipline of political judgement was well stated by Bertrand de Jouvenal.

> The mere fact of each man's involvement, in whatever capacity, in public affairs implies each asking himself what decision is good, hearing the arguments of others and giving his own opinion when he has formed it. How then has it come about that political theory seems so little concerned to help us form the opinion which we must give?(1)

In a sense the modern policy sciences are the lineal descendants of the Stoic teachers of Republican Rome, the Scholastic masters, the humanists of pre-Renaissance Italy, those who prescribed a classic education for the governing elites of Victorian England and set the curriculum of civic education for America in the period of nation building. In terms of their own pretensions, and in the light of general public understanding, the policy sciences cannot be said to be simply scientific disciplines, engaged in the quest for reliable information about human behavior and the dynamics of social institutions and processes. Nor are these basically practical arts, providing tools and techniques, useful in that they diagnose social ills and prescribe remedies for them.

The policy sciences are primarily teaching professions. They have, to a larger extent than perhaps we realize, been entrusted with the de facto responsibility of forming citizens and preparing those who would seek vocations in the conduct of public affairs. They are in this sense expected to provide a philosophy of political education for the society. Like their predecessors, they will prescribe a conception of how best to think about public affairs. It is then a policy question for the policy professions--a problem of evaluative judgement in its own right--to ask what philosophy of political education we intend to endorse.

My purpose herein is not to develop a philosophy of education for the policy sciences, but to survey the evident alternatives. What conceptions of the discipline of evaluative judgement do we in fact endorse, either explicitly or implicitly, in our teaching? What philosophy of political education is inherent in various approaches to the problem of value neutrality and value judgement in the social sciences? I shall try to weigh and assess the various approaches to the problem, and to state their implications as clearly as possible. In the end I shall want to recommend a line of thought that seems more promising than the rest, one that might provide an adequate foundation for a coherent discipline of political judgement.

WHY WE CAN'T GO HOME AGAIN: THE ENTERPRISE OF CLASSIC PHILOSOPHY AND THE NORMS OF SCIENTIFIC INQUIRY

We might very well begin with the tradition of classic political and economic thought, where the object of inquiry was to ground value judgement in some essential truths about the nature of man or the universe, or the dictates of natural reason.

Both political science and economics were seen historically as branches of moral philosophy. The classic architecture of knowledge, in lineal descent from Aristotle, distinguished between the task of pure reason, which was to establish a point of fixity in a universe of contingency and flux, and that of practical reason, or the art of judgement. The classic method was to derive an ethics and a politics from a metaphysics. In other words one reasoned from an is to an ought. For St. Thomas revelation reconciled to the natural reason of Aristotle provided a sure ground for normative inference. For Thomas Hobbes, a doctrine of man and then of politics followed from the new sciences of motion and Cartesian mathematics.

The pattern is apparent in Locke, in Kant, whose ethical and political writings follow from the epistemological critiques of pure and practical reason, and in Hegel, whose Philosophy of Mind is both chronologically and logically prior to the Philosophy of Right. For Marx a theory of praxis, of practical judgement, would be founded in the certainties of historical materialism, and in a perverse way, the same pattern is apparent in utilitarianism, where ethical and political maxims are derived from a radical skepticism of all metaphysical and epistemological absolutes, save (significantly) the desires and preferences of the individual.

Today those schooled in the presuppositions and methods of the social sciences would be quite reluctant to grant that the route to a theory of practical judgement lies first in the search for metaphysical and epistemological certainty, or self-evident axioms. We have assimilated the Humean and positivist doctrines of the logical incompatibility of is and ought propositions, and we have been instructed by the modern philosophy of science. We have learned from Kuhn and Toulmin to regard scientific theories as constructions of reality and research paradigms as artifacts of inquiry, little more than a shared consensus on problems and procedures among the practitioners of a field.

While it is true that in political science (far more than in economics) a study of the history of political philosophy is still regarded as a useful part of the process of political education (that running the gauntlet from Plato to Marx somehow contributes to moral reason), there are few among us who would urge that the proper way for policy science to come to grips with the problem of value judgement is to reopen the enterprise of classic philosophy, to seek metaphysical certainty first before attacking the problem of practical reason.

With positivism, the classic conception of right reason fell into disrepute. Yet there are remarkable similarities between the classic spirit of philosophy and the program of the modern policy sciences. If there was now skepticism of the ideal of philosophic certainty, it was nonetheless assumed that by following the method of the natural sciences one could generate "objective knowledge" that would somehow be useful in resolving public problems. Through rigorous investigation, we could discover the true causes of social problems. If we could get the facts straight, we would know with certainty which policies to adopt. Systematic research provided the basis for evaluative judgement. Once again one reasoned, in effect, from an is to an ought. The pioneers of twentieth century policy science assumed that an increase in social understanding would lead to better policy decisions. Thinking scientifically was the right way to think about policy problems.

These robust aspirations are still very much alive in the policy sciences. But increasingly a note of doubt intrudes. Today we are far from sanguine that the pursuit of the method of the natural sciences will yield a discipline of practical political judgement. The positivists were quite correct in one respect. One cannot ground evaluative judgements in metaphysical absolutes; but neither can one ground them in scientific propositions. We begin to suspect that inquiry in the social sciences is not value neutral in the positivist sense and cannot become so, that latent in our models and theories are conceptions of right order in polity and economy, that the research we undertake and the problems we regard as significant contain implicit evaluative commitments and biases.

At one level we understand all of this very well. However, such understanding leaves us in something of a quandary. We do not know exactly how to proceed. The ideals of scientific investigation do not seem to provide a sufficient foundation for a philosophy of political education. So we must go on and ask what is required of a discipline of political judgement in itself.

EMPIRICAL SOCIAL SCIENCE AND THE AIMS OF POLITICAL EDUCATION

The social sciences are not, of course, normless. They are founded on strong prescriptive canons of warranted assertion and inference, of what counts as a good argument and what is a mistake in reasoning. Not the least of these is value neutrality itself. As Arnold Brecht says, "Whoever claims scientific authority for his value system . . . is scientifically in error."(2)

The student of the social sciences is carefully inducted into the art of making a specific kind of value judgement. One evaluates the worth and merit of statements according to acknowledged standards. One learns to distinguish significant problems, valid inferences, elegant and parsimonious theories. There are rules of discourse that govern the scientific enterprise. There are criteria that are appropriate in judging the merit of scientific argument. There are grounds of legitimate criticism that must be endorsed by those who engage in the scientific enterprise.

As we have noted, the rules of scientific discourse are not directly pertinent to the tasks of political judgement. The object of scientific analysis is to provide a satisfactory account of a phenomenon. The aim of political reasoning is to determine what purposes the public should pursue. The stance of the scientist is that of detached observer, not protagonist in the public debate. Nonetheless there are those who would argue that scientific education constitutes an heuristic uniquely suited to the formation of citizens and the education of policy makers.

The norms of scientific procedure are taken as a parallel to the basic values of democratic thought. Science, like democracy, imputes no metaphysical properties, no final ends, to such abstract entities as the state, the race, or the class. Science, like democracy, entertains no a priori absolutes. Each presumes that the worth of statements must be demonstrated, in the light of reason and evidence, to the satisfaction of those who are parties to a community of discourse.

To internalize the standards of scientific inquiry is then to reinforce attitudes appropriate to democratic politics. Through scientific education, one acquires a skeptical attitude, a critical temper of mind toward argument and evidence, that is appropriate to the autonomous individual. One becomes cautious in assertion and reserved in judgement.

In the more doctrinally positivist social sciences, of course, the matter is carried somewhat further than this. The student also learns to regard value judgements as preferences and opinions rooted in the emotional predispositions of the individual. They cannot be proven or rationally justified, but they can be explained as a product of social context, or economic interest, or the cognitive formation of the individual. One comes to know thyself as a creature whose evaluative orientations reflect cultural or class bias.

The result of all of this, it might be supposed, would be the cultivation of that gentle liberal tolerance for diversity of opinion that is presumed to be the mark of the democratic citizen. Since no value judgement can be shown to be correct, if one cannot rationally justify preferences, then we are all entitled to our own opinions, and it follows logically that government should rest on the aggregation of interests or the accommodation of demands. The basic dicta of social science positivism become necessary first premises for a coherent defense of a particular conception of democracy.

Fair enough. My intention is not to reveal some latent political bias in the positivist presuppositions of social science theory. Rather, the question is whether all of this carries the matter far enough, or to its logical conclusion. It still seems in order to ask how one might best proceed in the face of a genuine quandary of decision, when one is well aware that it is possible to adopt a variety of evaluative orientations, and nonetheless one must decide. One must make up one's own mind, positivist social science perhaps counsels, but on what basis? It is no caricature to suggest that the choice might as well be impulsive, whimsical, or arbitrary. If in the end one's values are mere preferences, or emotional predilections, or the products of social and cultural conditioning, then it would seem that one can do no more than the inevitable, following the dictates of self-interest, personal passion, or inculcated belief, whatever the basis of those beliefs, whether or not they are rationally defensible, whether the social consequences of acting on them would be generally harmful or positively insane.

DECISION RATIONALITY

The policy sciences do, of course, endorse a discipline of practical reason, a conception of how one ought to proceed in the face of complex or perplexing enigmas of public choice. Most of the methods of modern technical policy analysis rest fundamentally on what might best be called a model of instrumental or strategic rationality. Given an ordered set of goals or values, one surveys an agenda of alternatives and chooses that course of action which best serves to realize the stipulated values.(3)

This is of course no more or no less than the ideal of the utility-maximizing individual, the foundation doctrine of classic economic thought, now transformed into an ideal of political rationality. The model is perfectly congruent with the fundamental norms of value neutrality of empirical social science. Values are to be regarded as the preferences of decision makers. Yet this model has some peculiar implications when considered as a discipline of political judgement, for public choice is unlike self-regarding individual choice in significant respects.

These peculiarities become fully apparent if we contemplate the lessons that a student might properly draw from a political education founded on this ideal of decision rationality. The basic point is that one ought to be very clear and cogent in the specification and scaling of one's objectives and efficient in the selection of means to achieve them. The lesson is not hard to miss. The name of the game is winning. The way one ought to confront the normative quandaries of public life is by carefully selecting a course of action designed so that one's own preferences and opinions will prevail over those who hold divergent views. Of course, to use the occasion of public responsibility to advance self-interest is precisely what one ought not to do. This defines corruption in any system of political thought, with the possible exception of crude Machiavellianism, in which the object is to husband and enhance the power of the Prince.

One possible remedy for this unfortunate state of affairs might be to then propose some formal welfare function as a test of good public policy, some rule for aggregating individual preferences, equally considered, into a conception of public purpose. Perhaps in this way the basic ethos of economic rationality can be salvaged. Yet the way we derive such a rule is edifying indeed. It quickly becomes apparent that we cannot actually show that a given policy represents a sum of personal preferences, for we cannot truly know the utility schedules that individuals might construct among an infinite variety of possible states of affairs, nor can we make intersubjective comparisons of utilities. What we will then assume instead is that any rational individual will prefer to maximize aggregate individual utility, and that therefore society should aim to maximize aggregate social utility. Pareto optimality becomes the canonical test of good public policy.

It is worth making the implications of this turn in the argument fully explicit. It is no longer assumed that policy ought to be based on the personal preferences of individuals, however they are defined. Rather we now assume that to be rational, policy makers should seek to maximize aggregate want satisfaction. A normative imperative has entered the analysis. Were someone to contend that they would prefer absolute income equality, even if the price were that no one would ever lift a plow again, that person would simply be wrong. Such a statement would not constitute a good basis for public policy, though it might be approved by consensus or affirmed by a multitude. Rather it constitutes a mistake in political reasoning. It would be irrational to invoke such a preference as a ground of public decision.

The appeal of such a welfare function is not that it is neutral among values, which it manifestly is not, but that it proposes an operational test of the public interest. To justify a public decision, it is not enough to show that it arises out of individual preference. Self-interest only appears plausible as a warrant for public action if it is coupled with some conception of how public interest will emerge from the competition or aggregation of individual interests. The burden of liberal and utilitarian thought over the past three centuries has been precisely to demonstrate that this can and should be done.

Further it is assumed that an adequate welfare criterion must serve the value of efficiency. It is always a legitimate criticism of any case or claim in political discourse to show that given ends could more appropriately be achieved by alternative means. Thus the values of the public interest and efficiency are hardly matters of preference, considerations that we are free to invoke or disregard in political judgement as we see fit. They are in some sense obligatory standards of political discourse and decision making. The question then arises whether these are the only standards that are requisite to a discipline of political judgement.

Many would argue that the test of Pareto Optimality is perfectly consistent with policies that might impose severe deprivations on specific classes, groups, or factions. One can of course improve the well-being of the better off while sustaining the mass of the population in abject poverty and meet the requirements of the criterion. It is not quite clear that such a welfare criterion is fully satisfactory unless it includes some principle of distributive justice. But in suggesting this, we are testing the worth of a principle of judgement not by asking whether it is compatible with the premises of psychological egoism, but by asking whether it accounts for certain dimensions of value that seem to be inherent in the activity of political judgement itself.

In any event it is not clear that the basic ethos of economic rationality constitutes an adequate foundation for a philosophy of political education. Most modern economists, I suspect, would endorse the view that their discipline is normatively incomplete as a guide to political judgement. They would perhaps concur with Charles Schultze in saying that the economist is fundamentally an advocate of efficiency,(4) but that there are other values that have to be taken into account in public decision making. We would do well then to move on and explore other potential approaches to the problem of political evaluation.

PRAGMATISM AS A DISCIPLINE OF JUDGEMENT

The dominant alternative to economic rationality in contemporary policy analysis is a strategy of judgement rooted in the premises and presuppositions of philosophical pragmatism. To a greater extent than is usually recognized, these have been rival paradigms for the development of policy science, and they have their homes in different intellectual specialties. The distinctiveness of political science and economics as policy sciences has much to do with the fact that the former derived much of its characteristic theoretical orientation and research method from the American pragmatic and progressive tradition, while economics is grounded in the presuppositions of classical liberalism and the utilitarian ethos.(5) In its approach to practical policy analysis, political science is more apt to endorse incrementalist strategies of decision, and to adopt a stance of tough-minded realism; economists on the other hand tend more toward the elaboration of formal models and to quest after rigorous rules of aggregation and distribution.

The two approaches differ significantly in fundamental assumptions. The tradition of classical liberalism entails a strong affirmation of the values of personal freedom and the moral autonomy of the individual. Market forces are viewed as generally benign, and the assertion of authority is treated with wariness and suspicion. Pragmatism takes a more positive view of public action. While pragmatism shares much of the liberal ethos, it was also strongly influenced by a more organic view of the community derived from nineteenth century European thought. In classical liberal and utilitarian thought, public purpose is seen to arise from a cumulative and reciprocal process of calculations of self-interest. In pragmatism the image is more one of a democratic community engaged in a sustained process of deliberation and discourse about desirable public purpose. To be sure, these are nuances of difference within a common heritage. Nonetheless the differences are significant. They lead to a different weighting of the claims of individualism and the community. In the end the ultimate test of value in pragmatic public decision making is social agreement.

Like economic rationality the method of pragmatism is deemed to be compatible with the basic norms of scientific value neutrality, though here the mysterious process of arriving at a declarative statement of legitimate values from a stance of value relativism is accomplished somewhat differently. Basically the activity of political analysis is likened to that of scientific investigation. It is a process of experimentation, exploration, and discovery. The body politic is envisioned as a community of inquiry, like that of a scientific discipline, who engage in a quest for a clearer, more coherent public philosophy through a process of trial and error, by examining the consequences and implications of always tentative adjustments in the purpose and practice of law and policy.

The disciplines of mind, the habits of thought, that go with pragmatic problem solving are identical to those that should characterize the scientific investigator. One should try to maintain a certain flexibility and agility of mind, remaining open to diverse possibilities, hypotheses, and perspectives on the problem. One should not concentrate on a narrow range of possible evaluations but formulate and consider a broad range of alternatives. One should be wary and skeptical in dealing with assumptions and evidence.

All of this is no doubt very good advice indeed. The question is whether it is to have said quite enough, whether this is a sufficient statement of what is required in public decision making. Pragmatism is by definition an open system, hence it can offer few rules of discourse, of justifiable assertion, few tests that can be applied to the actual evaluation of policy. For pragmatism the crucial imperatives are in the process, and can perhaps be fully expressed in Charles Sanders Peirce's maxim, "Do not block the way of inquiry"--which Thomas Thorson paraphrases, as a dictum of political thought, to read, "Do not block the possibility of change with respect to social goals."(6) Policy making is a process of social learning, and a process of learning must be open, exploratory, provisional.

Pragmatism, like logical positivism, does not believe that value judgements can be made a priori, but it has great confidence in value judgements made after the fact. Through experimental method we test not only the tenability of our policies, but our principles as well. Through experimentation, we find out not only what works, but what we mean by working. If adopting a certain theory of justice leads to results in practice that we regard as unjust, then we have good reason to revise our conception of justice. A value is good if it helps us to resolve a problem. It is bad if it leads to further consternation and perplexity, or to consequences that we cannot intuitively approve.

However, when we consider what actually has to be decided when we face problems of public choice, it becomes apparent that the pragmatic counsel, by itself, will not quite do the job. "Be experimental," pragmatism advises, but the question we must answer when faced with an actual dilemma of decision is which experiment to undertake. We can anticipate consequences, but we cannot wait for them. Value judgements are required before the fact as well as after. We do not just face problematic situations. We have to make an evaluative distinction between configurations of events that count as problems and those that are merely "the way things are." We have to be able to decide what will count as a "change in the right direction" and what is a matter of "making things worse." Pragmatism alone cannot tell us how to do this.

VALUE NEUTRALITY AS AN ISSUE IN THE POLICY SCIENCES

Positivism emerged as a kind of orthodoxy in all the policy sciences in the postwar period. Yet its triumph was never quite complete. There has long been a dissenting tradition in political science, economics, and sociology. In the past generation the issue has come to something of a head. Increasingly, debate on the theory and method of the social sciences has come to focus on the ideal of value neutrality. It is argued that this is both an undesirable and an untenable ideal, undesirable in that social science ought to devote its efforts not to the construction of a pure science of society, but to the generation of socially useful knowledge, untenable in that social science research inevitably contains political presuppositions and implications.

It is doubtful that value neutrality in the strict logical positivist sense ever has been an operative ideal in any social science discipline. Most modern writers on social science methodology, following Weber, admit that value judgements intrude on the process of social science research at many points. It has long been acknowledged that value commitments will influence the choice of topics and problems that social scientists choose to investigate, and that any paradigm of research contains normative implications when viewed as a framework for social understanding.(7)

From this we might derive a doctrine that many in the policy sciences would acknowledge and affirm. The researcher has an obligation to make his or her values explicit. Beyond this the basic norms of policy research are commonsense objectivity and honesty in presenting findings. One must be willing to present findings that run contrary to the preferred hypothesis. Do not stack the deck in favor of particular values or outcomes.

According to this canon no more is required than that the values that motivate and guide research be clearly and overtly stated. They need not be argued or justified. Any normative perspective is legitimate so long as the research itself meets the standards of scientific inquiry. There are no standards for judging the worth or merit of an evaluational perspective. For many this would serve adequately as a statement of fundamental norms for policy research. Yet how would it appear if translated into a philosophy of political education?

LET A THOUSAND FLOWERS BLOOM, LET A HUNDRED SCHOOLS CONTEND

The policy sciences are self-governing communities. The criteria appropriate to judging whether a person is to be certified as entitled to "profess" political science or economics are those of scientific inquiry. The right to teach is established by the scientific rigor and substantive significance of research, without regard to the value orientation of the professional. The scientific community has no standards for such a judgement. It would be normatively wrong to make a judgement on whether a PhD should be granted or tenure awarded on the basis of the values of the individual concerned. It would make no sense to say that the value judgements of the candidate did not meet so-called standards of the discipline.

These standards seem to yield few normative imperatives for the teaching mission of the policy sciences. Yet there is a philosophy of political education implicit in this understanding of the rules of the game. It is recognizable in the curricula, in the practices, in the folklore of the academy.

It becomes our responsibility to present contending approaches and doctrines. An academic discipline is not a repository for established truths. It is rather to be understood as an arena for discourse. The profession then ought not to prescribe one definitive path to right reason. It ought instead to portray the terms of the argument that exists within a discipline at a certain stage of its development as authentically as possible.

Two alternative conceptions of a practical teaching ethic would be compatible with this view. The first is of an obligation to objectivity and neutrality in portraying, as authentically as possible, an array of contending positions and doctrines. It is the duty of the Keynesian economist to assure that students are fully apprised of such relevant alternative standpoints as neoclassical orthodoxy, institutional economics, and of neo-Marxian analysis.(8)

The second conception is a commitment to an academic freedom presumed to entail the right to teach from any normative standpoint, so long as arguments are open to challenge and are not imposed as certifiable knowledge. It then falls to the academic community, the department, to assure that an array of alternative approaches is represented.

If, as much contemporary thought in the social sciences takes for granted, the ideal of strict value neutrality is questionable and unattainable, and if the scientific communities have no right to pronounce judgement on the beliefs or value commitments of their members, then one of these norms would seem to be an entailment of that deeper value relativism that derives from skepticism of positivist objectivity itself.

This is an ideal to which many would repair. Yet when carefully examined it becomes apparent that this resolution of the problem of value judgement in social science teaching leads to a quite specific philosophy of political education. The academy is now to be understood as a marketplace of ideas. The implications of this as a doctrine of pedagogy in the policy sciences must be made fully explicit.

The student now is to be presented with an array of contending frameworks for thinking about political, economic, and social arrangements. The systematic properties of each and their normative implications are to be fully articulated. On some (largely inexplicit) basis, the department or the individual instructor prescribes an array of academically respectable (or perhaps merely provocative) alternatives to which the student will be exposed, running the gamut, in economics perhaps from the Chicago school to neo-Marxism, in political science from Pluralism to power elite theory, as well as an indeterminate hodgepodge that may or may not encompass Marxist thought or the political theory of Fascism. This done, academia has acquitted its responsibility.

Now students are to make up their own minds about the merits of the contending positions.

No advice or instruction can be offered on how to perform this task. No courses on the principles of normative analysis, on political judgement, accompany this process as they do for scientific analysis itself. One can decide to become a committed liberal, or Marxist, or existentialist, or nihilist, it would seem, for any reason, or for no reason at all. If there is a philosophy of political education underlying this, it is the ideal of the marketplace. Given full information on the alternatives, the individual, always reflecting personal predispositions and proclivities, is in a position to make a rational and informed choice.

What qualities of political judgement would emerge from such an education? One has learned that it is always possible to think otherwise about a political or economic issue. The student has arrived by another route at that selfsame liberal skepticism which is taken as the mark of political sophistication in contemporary society. For many, of course, this would be quite enough. But there are other possibilities embedded in the logic of the contemporary social sciences that also deserve consideration.

THE SOCIOLOGY OF KNOWLEDGE

A closely related and eminently respectable alternative approach is to take up the problem of value judgement from the perspective of the sociology of knowledge and critical philosophy. The purpose of the teacher here is to show that our concepts, interpretations, and rational standards, in science as well as in morals and practical life, are reflections of culture, of time and place, and of habitual modes of social behavior. The pedagogic aim is to reveal the contingent character of any theoretical construct or system of evaluation, the way it arises out of historical processes, and the social function it performs--perhaps in legitimizing and reproducing the going concern. Once this is recognized, it is held, students will be liberated from socially convenient preconceptions, and capable as autonomous individuals, once again, of making up their own minds. Pure reason will be free at last to do its work. The long tradition of the sociology of knowledge, beginning in Marx and now culminating in Habermas' conception of "cognitive competence," seems to lead back to the original position or the state of nature.

The resemblance to the pedagogic ideal of the university as a perfect market is unmistakable, only now the student is choosing not among available doctrines, but without any doctrine at all. What in fact is being assumed here? Once the individual is demystified, will the resolution of the problem be obvious, or is it then the task of the individual to recreate philosophy all over again?

This perspective, taken in unadulterated form, has some strange implications. The sociologist Peter Berger speaks eloquently on the problem:

> Any such method will have to include a willingness to see the relativity business through to its end. . . . When everything has been subsumed under the relativizing categories in question (those of history, of the sociology of knowledge, or what-have-you), the question of truth reasserts itself in almost pristine simplicity. Once we know that all human affirmations are subject to

> scientifically graspable socio-historical processes, which affirmations are true and which are false? We cannot avoid the question any more than we can return to the innocence of its pre-relativizing asking.(9)

In other words, as far as the policy sciences are concerned, once all paradigms of political rationality and judgement have been revealed as human constructs, as plausibility structures emergent from culture and socially reinforced, about which it is possible to think otherwise, we still must face the problem of how we are in fact going to decide, on what basis we are going to come to conclusions about desirable public purposes and projects.

IN PARTIAL DEFENSE OF SOCRATES

It has always been an open question whether the standards of scientific inquiry were the only norms that social science needs to endorse if it is to be a coherent enterprise. There has long been a lingering suspicion that scientific models and constructs did not say all that need be said about human concerns and purposes. In recent years this issue has come to something of a head. Out of the debate over value neutrality and value judgement in the social sciences, new theoretical orientations have been proposed which in some sense extend the notion of scientific rationality beyond its historic positivist limits. These proposals need to be taken seriously, both as conceptions of methodology appropriate to social inquiry and as a potential paradigm of political education.

In these statements the inevitability of evaluation in social science research is explicitly recognized, and normative analysis is understood as a proper task of social science inquiry and analysis. More is required of social scientists than that they simply be open and explicit about their values. From this perspective scholars are also professionally responsible for the evaluative implications of their research. There are standards that the value judgements must inevitably meet in any social science inquiry.

Two political scientists, David Easton and Duncan MacRae, exemplify this approach to the evaluative element in social science research. Easton is generally regarded as one of the fathers of the behavioral revolution in American political science. His strongly prescriptive empiricism was taken as gospel by a generation that sought to develop political science squarely on the model of the natural sciences. His model of the political system was pure and general. It provided a clear alternative to the liberal and democratic presuppositions that lurked behind the paradigmatic structure dominant in political science in the 1950s. Thus when Easton spoke in his presidential address to the American Political Science Association in 1969 of a "postbehavioral" revolution in the discipline, and addressed himself to the desirability of "policy relevance" and the creation of "new ethical perspectives" as alternatives to "empiricist conservatism," a new generation of political scientists found it particularly significant that the master had so radically changed his views.

What is more noteworthy, in fact, is that Easton was remarkably consistent. Almost half of Easton's landmark book The Political System (first published in 1953) is concerned with normative analysis, and the central argument--largely ignored at the time--is that any political theory must have a normative dimension and that modern political theory, by retreating into a value-neutral historicism, had betrayed the essential heritage and function of political thought.(10)

For Easton, the central imperative of good practice in political theory is the effort to achieve "moral clarity." Facts and values are intertwined. A political theory must explicate reality, but it must also reflectively account for the normative implications of its findings of fact.

> Moral clarification requires more than the formal postulation of a few interrelated values. It requires the positive task of constructing an image of the political system flowing from these moral premises.(11)

Easton remains committed to an emotivist and positivist theory of evaluation. Values cannot be justified in any final sense. They remain the preferences of individuals. Nonetheless it is not good enough simply to be explicit about one's preferences. The social scientist is responsible for the moral consequences that would follow if the theory espoused were to be taken seriously as a guide to political thought and action. It is an error in political theory to assume that values made explicit as a guide to research need no further defense. It is legitimate in professional criticism to question not only the scientific adequacy of an investigation, but its moral implications as well.

Recently, Duncan MacRae, in his The Social Function of Social Science, has made this conception of the standards that apply to the evaluative aspect of social science research more fully explicit. MacRae envisages the policy sciences as an arena of normative discourse, and he proposes a system of standards which he takes to be consistent with the norms of scientific communication, which can stand as rigorous guidelines for evaluative argument and as criteria for judging the merit of the ethical propositions advanced by policy scientists.

The rules MacRae proposes are as follows:

1. Ethical argument is to be conducted between proponents of ethical systems that are specified in writing in advance.

2. Each discussant shall have equal opportunity to argue for his own system, and against the opposing one, by pointing out presumed shortcomings in the other system. These shortcomings can be of several kinds:

A. Lack of generality. The proposed system fails to apply to a choice about which both discussants have moral convictions and to which the critic's system does apply.

B. Internal consistency. The proposed system makes contradictory prescriptions in a situation suggested by the critic, in which the critic's system is self-consistent.

C. Inconsistency with presumably shared moral convictions. The proposed system makes a prescription which, in a specified conflict situation, conflicts with moral convictions presumably shared by the discussants, while the critic's system does not lead to such conflict.

3. After each such opportunity, the proponent of the ethical system under criticism shall decide whether he wishes to alter his ethical system or make the choice dictated by it.(12)

It is clear that MacRae is operating well within the limits of the emotivist theory of valuation which is the underpinning of positivist social science. Values remain the preferences of the individual. The question of their ultimate justification is not at issue. However, now the policy scientist is to be held responsible, almost as Max Weber might have prescribed, for the consequences that might reasonably be attributed to the value system endorsed. Furthermore, the jury of professional peers is entitled to evaluate the logical coherence of the normative presuppositions of a scholar's work according to the same criteria of generality and consistency that pertain to scientific investigation itself.

The idea of "moral clarity" suggests immediately the value of the Socratic dialogue as a method of political education. If the policy sciences are to be understood as an arena of normative discourse, as

MacRae suggests, then that ancient form of inquiry into the meaning and significance of values stands both as a method appropriate to scholarly investigation and as a technique that may be prescribed for coming to reasoned conclusions about desirable public purposes.

As an approach to political education, the Socratic dialogue has impeccable credentials. It has been a primary mode of moral and civic education for over 2000 years. As a pedagogic device it has unmistakable advantages. The student is placed in an active role. The object is practice in logical argument, nuanced judgement, clear thinking, rather than the passive acquisition of knowledge. It stimulates curiosity, and through experience, a deeper appreciation of the problems of judgement. Furthermore, the approach is completely compatible with the Weberian canons of value neutrality on the part of the instructor. In the ideal Socratic dialogue, the professor asks questions and otherwise remains inscrutable.

However, the ideal of the Socratic dialogue is not quite as innocent as it may seem. It has implications for the role of value judgement in the policy sciences which must be made explicit. Socrates, after all, is not asking questions out of idle curiosity, and his apparent ignorance is feigned. Socrates knows very well what standards a reasonable judgement must meet, and so does our hypothetically neutral instructor. For the dialogue form to be possible at all, and meaningful as a paradigm for education, the instructor must have a clear conception of what counts as a good reason for a policy decision and what does not. In the Socratic dialogue these standards are taught through discrete indirection. However, once this much is acknowledged, it is possible to push the matter over the edge. It is possible to stipulate explicitly--and to teach--the requirements of good political judgment in precisely the same way that it is possible to define--and to teach--the canons of scientific inquiry.

THE STANDARDS OF POLITICAL JUDGEMENT

All of the social sciences endorse a system of standards of scientific inquiry. Learning to do social science is essentially learning to be guided by these norms in the process of investigation. The rules are understood at a number of levels. In textbooks and basic methods courses, they are rigid and categoric, almost catechismal. In the higher realms of the philosophy of science, they become vague and problematic. Professionals understand the distinctions between these levels, and that each has its place in the education of a social scientist. They know that eventually one comes to acknowledge these norms instinctively and is guided by them, without undue soul searching or metaphysical perturbation. They give coherence to the scholarly enterprise. They make science possible.

The rules of scientific procedure are themselves normative in character. They are "oughts" that follow from no verifiable "is." Whether they are necessary or not to any rational thinker cannot be finally confirmed or disconfirmed. What can be said instead is that they follow from the character of the scientific enterprise itself. They are required if one is to do what we call science.

The canons of scientific inquiry do not tell us what is true or false about the nature of the world. Rather they tell us what counts as a good argument and what does not in making statements about the nature of the world. They define an arena of discourse.

By the same token, I would argue, it is possible to stipulate certain criteria of good judgement for the policy sciences. It is possible to identify certain requirements that a reasonable political evaluation would have to meet. One can no more offer a proof for these norms than one can for the rules of scientific inquiry. Rather they are simply logically essential if we are going to engage in policy evaluation, as the rules of scientific procedure are essential if we are going to engage in scientific inquiry. They will not tell us what decisions to make any more than scientific norms will tell us what theories or findings are true. Rather they tell us what counts as a good reason for a policy decision and what counts as a mistake in policy reasoning.

There is nothing particularly mysterious about the norms of political judgement. Most are inherent in the conceptions of decision rationality that we do espouse, and in what we ordinarily take to be at issue in political debate and deliberation. In the first instance all that really has to be done is to make them explicit, though to fully explore the implications of such a theory of practical reasoning would be the work of a generation.

First there are standards that follow from the world view of scientific value relativism, and which must be acknowledged if we are to remain consistent with that primary philosophical commitment. Thus it is a mistake in political reasoning to argue that values can be derived from statements of fact, or that they can be proved true or false either through deductive inference or inductive generalization. However, there is nothing in the philosophy of positivist science that precludes the possibility of systems of moral or political rationality parallel to that of scientific rationality. It is unwarranted to claim that because values cannot be verified through scientific procedure no reasons can be given for concluding that one statement of individual preferences is more reasonable than another as a basis for public decision.

Second there are standards that follow from the rules of logical consistency and generality which, as MacRae has noted, are common to both scientific and normative discourse. It is true that the basic modes of rationality play a different role in political reasoning than they do in scientific thought, for in the one case the aim is a body of coherent knowledge, and in the other, a justifiable ground for public decision. We can accept the contention that the operations of logical consistency and experimental procedure cannot provide a final justification for political principles. But this does not mean that consistency with principles and argument about the accuracy or pertinence of factual assertions have no place as standards of political reasoning. There is a clear distinction between the positivist claim that we cannot prove principles and the requirement that our decisions not be arbitrary or our testimony false. These are not merely matters of preference. They are requirements that must be met if our political judgements are to be regarded as reasonable at all.

Thus when we justify a decision in the light of a standard, we are committing ourselves to apply the same standard to all future cases that are similar in relevant respects. Or else we are justly accused of not acting for a reason at all, but simply in light of the whim or opportunity of the moment. We purchase our principles on a line of credit extended against future decisions. If we decide in one case (against a regulatory policy let us say) on the ground that "that government governs best that governs least," we have established a presumption for future argument. Either we must sustain the principle or else we must plead that we have made a mistake in reasoning or changed our minds--that we acknowledge good reasons for departing from our earlier conception of appropriate grounds of evaluation.

The question of justifying decisions through the use of principles is as central to political reasoning as falsifiability is to scientific inquiry. Becoming aware of the standards we actually do use to judge the desirability or undesirability of public actions, considering the consequences that would follow if we did endorse them consistently, revising and perfecting these decision rules so that they account for relevant exceptions and distinctions, stating them to accommodate and order the considerations that are pertinent to choice--all these things are pretty much what moral clarification is all about. These are skills that can be nurtured through education and developed through practice, until they become as intuitive as the habit of the scientist to state propositions in hypothetical form.

Third there are requirements of good political judgement that follow from the formal logic of decision rationality.(13) If we are to judge rationally among alternatives in the light of standards, criteria of decision must be clear, interpretable, and hierarchically ranked. We cannot simply say, for example, that we favor both efficiency and equity, for no potential course of action may satisfy both criteria equally. To commend a particular option as the best policy to follow, we must compare a reasonably comprehensive agenda of alternatives. We can always make A the winner if we confine our analysis to A, B, and C, when X or Y may in fact have greater promise.(14)

Fourth, and finally, there are questions of evaluation that must be addressed in any exercise of political discourse, deliberation, and decision. To justify any policy recommendation, the course of action proposed must be shown to be an exercise of legitimate authority and in the public interest. It must be argued that it is equitable, that it is efficient in the use of resources and feasible, that there are reasonable grounds to expect that it might actually be put into effect, and that it will have the desired results. Such values are not merely matters of preference. They are in some sense obligatory standards of evaluation. These values are simply inherent in the activity of political discourse. They give it point and purpose.

To justify a policy recommendation we must give grounds for supposing that it is a legitimate exercise of public authority and in the public interest. Not all problems are public problems. A fundamental distinction must be drawn between those matters that are objects of public concern and those that are not. If we presumed that public authorities could do precisely as they wished, no problem of political evaluation would really arise. Public decisions could be made for any reason or for no reason at all.

A policy proposal must meet the tests of equity and justice. This does not require concurrence on an absolute maxim of justice. But as a minimum requirement of political plausibility, procedures must be shown to be impartial among contending claims and interests, and the distinctions drawn in law and policy must be relevant to some legitimate public end. Policies will either apply equally and universally, or they will apply differentially to specified individuals and groups. And when the latter is true, such distinctions cannot be made arbitrarily, but must be justified by reference to some appropriate public object or end.

It is easy enough to show that efficiency is a requisite value in political thought and judgement. Simple instrumental rationality requires that means be appropriate to ends, and it is always a legitimate criticism of a policy argument to point to measures that would more effectively and economically serve the purposes in view. However, in political discourse the value of efficiency has a more extended meaning than it does in economics. Efficiency implies feasibility, that measures will have the effect intended. Political argument entails assertions about causality, and models of presumed behavioral regularities. Such arguments must be necessarily conjectural and contingent, for relationships of cause and effect in human affairs cannot be confirmed or rejected absolutely. But that such conjectures must be made, as a warrant for establishing the plausibility of any statement about policy, seems necessary and inherent in the logic of political discourse itself.

Thus to justify a statement about desirable public purpose, to show why a proposed action should be regarded as good public policy, it is necessary to provide a coherent response to each of these questions of evaluation. We would regard a policy argument as irrational or at best unreasonable if it simply dismissed one of these values as irrelevant to the problem of public choice. One simply cannot say, "I don't care if it's blatantly illegal, manifestly unfair, and rides roughshod over established rights, it's still the most efficient way of getting the job done."

To be sure, ideas like the public interest, justice, and efficiency have no clear, uncontestable meaning. But neither do such fundamental constructs of scientific thought as validity, significance, and objectivity. Different scientific disciplines endorse different tests of warranted assertion, what is good enough to qualify as evidence, or to establish the fit between theory and fact. By the same token, different systems of political analysis may establish different criteria of legitimate authority, or of justice. Yet just as any scientific argument must account for the problem of experimental demonstration, so any political argument must account for the problem of the propriety of universal or differential treatment of cases.

There is no final justification for either the norms of scientific inquiry or for those of political evaluation. They cannot be deduced from axiological premises of reason, nor from any truth about the nature of the universe or essential human ends. They follow from the nature of the activity itself, from what we do when we engage in scientific inquiry or political discourse. There is no way of showing that a policy must be just, any more than it can be shown that a proposition must be verifiable. What can be said instead is that, just as there is nothing binding about the norms of scientific inquiry unless we are doing science, so there is nothing binding about the norms of political discourse unless we are engaged in making public decisions.

CONCLUSION

The object of a philosophy of political education is not to tell us what we ought to do but to provide a discipline for thought. The point is not to inform students about the essential ends of the state or the best methods of achieving them, but to commend a process that will lead to the discovery of clear, rigorous, and defensible statements on such matters. This is what political education should be expected to accomplish, and it is all that should be expected of it.

It is by no means apparent that the quest for a scientific understanding of society will automatically yield an adequate philosophy of political education. What in fact do we take to be the relationship between the scientific enterprise and our pedagogic purpose? Surely, it is not enough simply to teach the findings of social science inquiry. Nor can it be assumed that inculcating the habits of mind that are appropriate to scientific inquiry is all that is required in the preparation of citizens.

Less than a generation ago the aspirations of the policy sciences were great, and their spirit was almost smugly self-confident. We might solve the problems of the ghetto as other technologists had landed a man on the moon. We would fine-tune the economy to create lasting prosperity. Today the mood is more one of searching self-criticism. All the policy sciences are going through something of a fundamental epistemological crisis. Established knowledge is relentlessly controverted. Even the basic assumptions of the enterprise have been called into question. This would seem as good a time as any to re-examine the agenda.

Conventionally, we test the significance and merit of research and scholarship in the social science by its prospective contribution to a comprehensive, coherent science of society. However, it is by no means apparent that this is what is expected of us, or even that it is what we expect of ourselves. Perhaps it is time to re-examine the nature of our social function, what we in fact do, and why it matters. In the final analysis the significance of the policy sciences lies in what we teach. We might then very well ask, in testing the significance and importance of research and inquiry, how it bears on the process of political education. And we might also ask, in debating the fundamental theory of our fields, not only what is required to generate a systematic body of knowledge, but what we need to do to develop a coherent philosophy of political education.

NOTES

1. Bertrand de Jouvenal, Sovereignty (Chicago: University of Chicago Press, 1957), p. 8.

2. Arnold Brecht, Political Theory (Princeton: Princeton University Press, 1956), p. 7.

3. For various formulations of the classic ideal of decision rationality, see Charles E. Lindblom, The Policy-Making Process (Englewood Cliffs, NJ: Prentice-Hall, 1968), p. 13; Yehezekel Dror, Public Policy Reexamined (San Francisco: Chandler, 1968), pp. 129-149; Richard Zeckhauser and Elmer Schaefer, "Public Policy and Normative Economic Theory" in Raymond A. Bauer and Kenneth J. Gergen, Eds., The Study of Policy Formation (New York: Free Press, 1968), p. 29; Irving L. Janis and Leon Mann, Decision Making (New York: Free Press, 1977), p. 16.

4. Charles L. Schultze, The Politics and Economics of Public Spending (Washington: The Brookings Institution, 1968), p. 16.

5. On the pragmatic tradition in political science, see Bernard Crick, The American Science of Politics (Berkeley: University of California Press, 1959); Edward A. Purcell, Jr., The Crisis of Democratic Theory (Lexington: University of Kentucky Press, 1973); Albert Somit and Joseph Tanenhaus, The Development of Political Science (Boston: Allyn and Bacon, 1967).

6. Thomas L. Thorson, The Logic of Democracy (New York: Holt, Rinehart and Winston, 1962), p. 120.

7. See Max Weber, "Objectivity in the Social Sciences," in The Methodology of the Social Sciences, Edward A. Shils and Henry A. Finch, Eds., (Glencoe, IL: The Free Press, 1949); Charles Taylor, "Neutrality in Political Science," in Peter Laslett and W.G. Runciman, Eds., Philosophy, Politics and Society, Third Series (Oxford: Basil Blackwell, 1967), pp. 25-57; Charles Frankel, "The Autonomy of the Social Sciences" in Charles Frankel, Ed., Controversies and Decisions (New York: Russell Sage Foundation, 1976), pp. 16-37.

8. An interesting example of this approach is Benjamin Ward's "Ideal Worlds of Economics": The Liberal Economic World View; The Radical Economic World

View; The Conservative Economic World View (New York: Basic Books, 1979).

9. Peter Berger, A Rumor of Angels (New York: Doubleday, 1969), p. 50.

10. David Easton, The Political System (New York: Alfred A. Knopf, 1971).

11. Ibid, p. 231.

12. Duncan MacRae, Jr., The Social Function of Social Science (New Haven: Yale University Press, 1976), p. 93.

13. For an excellent statement of these requirements, see Brian Barry and Douglas W. Rae, "Political Evaluation" in Fred I. Greenstein and Nelson W. Polsby, Eds., Handbook of Political Science I (Reading, MA: Addison-Wesley, 1975), pp. 337-401.

14. Alan C. Enthoven, "Ten Practical Principles for Policy and Program Analysis," in Richard C. Zeckhauser, et al., Benefit Cost and Policy Analysis: 1974 (Chicago: Aldine, 1975), p. 463.